A HISTORY OF

MODERN CRITICISM

1750–1950

IN EIGHT VOLUMES

A HISTORY OF MODERN

Criticism: *1750–1950*

BY RENÉ WELLEK

VOLUME 8   French, Italian, and Spanish Criticism, 1900–1950

YALE UNIVERSITY PRESS
New Haven and London

Set in Baskerville types by Tseng Information Systems.
Printed in the United States of America.

Library of Congress Cataloging-in-Publication Data
(Revised for volume 8)

Wellek, René.
A history of modern criticism: 1750–1950.

ISBN 0-300-05451-3
Includes bibliographical references.
Contents: v. 1. The later eighteenth century — v. 2.
The romantic age — [etc.] — v. 8. French, Italian,
and Spanish criticism, 1900–1950.
PN86.W4   801'.95   55–5989

A catalogue record for this book is available from the
British Library.

The paper in this book meets the guidelines for
permanence and durability of the Committee on
Production Guidelines for Book Longevity of the
Council on Library Resources.

10 9 8 7 6 5 4 3 2 1

For Lowry Nelson, Jr., and Pier Pasinetti

CONTENTS

ACKNOWLEDGMENTS

I use the following articles of mine, sometimes expanded, cut, and changed.

French "Classical" Criticism: "French 'Classical' Criticism in the Twentieth Century," in *The Classical Line: Essays in Honor of Henri Peyre. Yale French Studies* 38 (1967): 47–71.

Albert Thibaudet: "Albert Thibaudet," in *Modern French Criticism from Proust and Valéry to Structuralism*, ed. J. K. Simon (1972), 85–107.

Charles Du Bos: "Poulet, Du Bos, and Identification," *Comparative Literature Studies* 10 (1973): 173–93.

Paul Valéry: "Paul Valéry (1871–1945)," in my book *Four Critics: Croce, Valéry, Lukács, Ingarden* (1981), 19–36.

Benedetto Croce: "Benedetto Croce, Literary Critic and Historian," *Comparative Literature* 5 (1953): 75–82. Also "Benedetto Croce (1866–1952)," in my *Four Critics*, 3–18.

Mario Praz: "Mario Praz: Memories and Literary Criticism," *English Miscellany* 30 (1984): 241–57.

PART I FRENCH CRITICISM
1900–1950

1 : FRENCH "CLASSICAL" CRITICISM
IN THE TWENTIETH CENTURY

IN MANY CONTEXTS, I have defended the view that the history of criticism is largely determined by individual critics who are good or great writers. One could argue that often the critic is a better writer than the author discussed, and that Oscar Wilde's paradoxes in *The Decay of Lying* are not so farfetched, when he exalts criticism as the "Fourth Estate," or simply a new genre after poetry, novel, and drama. France, however, is in some ways an exception. The literary situation there is closely centered on Paris, and for centuries a debate has been carried on between what we may call "classicism" and "romanticism." This debate petered out in the middle of the nineteenth century, and it would be difficult to find formal discussions of the contrast between classicism and romanticism in the second half of the century. One could describe French criticism toward the end of the nineteenth century as vaguely romantic, strongly influenced by relativism and by the acceptance of the view that classicism and romanticism coexist in France and are of equal, or at least comparable, importance. In the twentieth century, however, there has been a resurgence of a new version of classicism that quite definitely links up with the literary tradition of the age of Louis XIV. It is thus legitimate to trace a coherent and continuous group of critics who appeal to the great classics, particularly Racine, and to give an account of them. This classical group is coherent and polemical, whereas opposing or divergent opinions present neither a unified point of view nor a clearly combative position. Therefore, it is best in this instance to discuss critics individually.

Any attempt to write the history of French criticism in the twentieth century, a task not yet performed on a large scale, will necessitate distributing "en quelques enclos surmontés de pancartes indicatrices"—to use Henri Peyre's words in a similar context (*Hommes et oeuvres du vingtième siècle* [1938], 54)—the masses of writers and books with which we have to deal. We shall have to classify them according to the "isms" they represent or adhere to: classicism, symbolism, Bergsonism, Catholicism or Thomism, surrealism, Marxism, existentialism, structuralism. We could

3

think of others, such as Freudianism, or we might play the game of combining them in diverse permutations: Marxist existentialism, Catholic
Bergsonism or Bergsonian Catholicism, Catholic classicism, and so on.
We could speculate on which of these combinations, being utterly incompatible, do not occur or cannot occur, or we could trace the career of a
particular critic who has passed from one "pancarte" to another. But that
might seem merely an academic exercise that shirks the main task of a
critic of critics: to characterize individuals and assess their merits. Yet it
is an inevitable preparatory step for the historian who must bring about
some order; he must have a sequence of exposition more meaningful
than that supplied by chronology alone. Obviously, the enormous political changes—the First World War; the interwar years of short-lived peace
threatened by the tensions between France and defeated Germany; the
rise of Nazism; and the Second World War, with the occupation of Paris
and the emigration of many French intellectuals, not only Jews—must all
be kept in mind.

However we may fret about the appropriateness of some of the ready
labels, we cannot deny that there was a group of French critics in the
twentieth century who proclaimed themselves "classicists," consciously
appealed to classical antiquity, to the classical age of French literature,
and to the "eternal" classicism in Western civilization. In "The Term and
Concept of 'Classicism' in Literary History" (in *Discriminations* [1970],
55–89), I tried to show that the word "classicism" occurred first in the
classical-romantic debate in Italy in or just before 1818 and that it was
imported into France and French by Stendhal in *Racine et Shakespeare* in
1823. But it did not become an established term for many decades since
it was considered to be an ugly neologism. Sainte-Beuve and Taine got
along without it. The term became fairly widespread in literary studies
around 1890, precisely at the time when Jean Moréas propounded a new
"classical" movement in poetry. Moréas (the pseudonym of Iannis Papa-
diamantopoulos, 1856–1910) had shortly before promulgated the slogan
"symbolisme" and used the term "Ecole romane" for his little group in
1891.[1] But his most vocal follower, Charles Maurras, soon preferred the
terms "classical" and "classicism" and began to announce a classical revival.[2] What at first was only the polemical gimmick of a small côterie
became in the hands of Maurras a powerful ideological weapon in a movement that extended far beyond poetry and even literature.

It is difficult to speak of Charles Maurras (1868–1952) with equa-
nimity: his role as the leader of the Action française, his behavior during

1. See page 340 for this and subsequent notes.

the Second World War, and his condemnation to life imprisonment are too fresh in memory not to color one's attitude even toward those of his writings that are remote from the political struggle. Undoubtedly he drew the slogan "classicism" into a general ideological scheme in which monarchism, belief in the Church as an institution, and a concept of history, of France and its past, were all amalgamated into something like a coherent or at least compatible set of ideas. It was no accident that a pupil, Pierre Chardon, was able to compile a *Dictionnaire politique et critique* in five large volumes (1933), drawn entirely from Maurras's scattered writings, which mingles literary and political entries indiscriminately.

The antecedents of Maurras's creed can be quickly identified: as a good traditionalist he himself appealed to them. The royalist, papist, or simply conservative theory had been formulated during the Restoration by Joseph de Maistre, and Maurras himself often referred to the later political schemes of Auguste Comte. The enmity toward Rousseau traditionally begins with the *philosophes,* whom Maurras condemned as the instigators of the Revolution. The anti-romantic arguments of the debates of the 1820s and 1830s in literature could be easily restated. They had been codified by Désiré Nisard, who exalted the French seventeenth century over the eighteenth and characterized the romantics in terms of the Latin poets of the age of Decadence, and later by Ferdinand Brunetière, who combined a classicist creed with motifs derived from evolutionism. Brunetière, however, was far less rationalistically doctrinaire than Nisard. In 1883, in his article "Classiques et romantiques" Brunetière criticized Nisard for reducing the classical spirit to "order, clarity, measure, discretion and taste" and propounded a view that is essentially that of Henri Peyre's account in his *Qu'est-ce que le classicisme?* (1933). "That which properly constitutes a classic is the balance within it of all the qualities that contribute to the perfection of the work of art": imagination *and* reason, logic, sentiment, good sense, form *and* content in perfect balance (*Revue des deux mondes* 60 [1883]: 412–32; reprinted in *Etudes critiques sur l'histoire de la littérature française,* vol. 3 [1890], 291–326). Brunetière seems also to have been the first to reinterpret Racine not as a painter of courtly manners (as Taine saw him) or as a tender elegiac poet (Sainte-Beuve's view), but as a tragedian of the fatal passion of men and women: modern, classical, and Greek all at the same time.[3]

It seems obvious to conclude that Maurras picked up the thread of this classical tradition in criticism, pushed Brunetière's views to their extremes of intolerance, and assimilated them to his general ideology. But things did not happen that way. Maurras had a very low opinion of Brunetière. He lacked, Maurras argues, judgment and taste; he tried to make up for them by espousing the best principles he could find: those of the classical tradition. But these principles are of no use in judging modern poetry, for which one needs feeling, sensibility, and taste. Maurras censures Brunetière for praising the Parnassians and obtusely dismissing Baudelaire. Brunetière to his mind is a system maker who erects monstrous Arabian palaces of no earthly use (*L'Allée des philosophes*, 206ff).

Maurras derives his classicism from different sources: from Frédéric Mistral, Jean Moréas, and Anatole France, whom he met in 1889 and 1890 and never ceased to admire. Maurras, though from Provence himself, first discovered Mistral's poetry in Paris. He became convinced of the possibility of a Provençal Renaissance, linguistic and poetic. Provence provided him with the symbolic center of Latinity: the crossroads of the Greek, Latin, and French traditions. In Maurras's eyes Mistral was the commanding poet of the middle of the nineteenth century, the counterweight to Hugo, the true heir of Vergil and Dante (*Maîtres et témoins de ma vie d'esprit*). Maurras did not see the romanticism of the folklore and the medieval history in Mistral, but only the Vergilian charm and calm.

Maurras also had a lifelong admiration for Moréas's poetry. As late as 1950 Maurras stated that Moréas had "more talent than Régnier, Stuart Merrill, Francis Jammes, and Mallarmé together" (*Maîtres et témoins*, 269). In 1896 he proclaimed Moréas "the living symbol of national poetry" and announced the forthcoming tragedy *Iphigénie* as "the revenge for the disaster of *Hernani*" (Roudiez, 169). Its performance in Orange in 1903 was hailed as a triumph of the new classicism just as Moréas's *Stances* were a triumph for neoclassical poetry. Maurras, however, disapproved of the early poetry of Moréas. *Le Pélerin passionné* seemed to him a "disastrous blend of Baudelairism, Parnassism, and Verlainism" (*Maîtres et témoins*, 220). He could not have approved Moréas's delimitation of the tradition, which proclaimed the "Greco-Latin principle the fundamental principle of French letters" but included in it the troubadours and trouvères, Ronsard and his school, as well as Racine and La Fontaine. But Maurras must have agreed with the exclusion of romanticism and its Parnassian and symbolist descendants from the "Gallic chain."

His early admiration for Anatole France was equally important. Maurras agreed with Maurice Barrès that "Anatole France has preserved the French language," adding "the French genius, taste, and spirit" (*DPC*, 2:105). France endeared himself to Maurras also by his praise of Racine: Maurras endorsed the inflated thesis of Gabriel Des Hons, which tried to make France a disciple of Racine (*PV*, 100–112). The open political rift between Maurras and France, brought about by the Dreyfus case, seems never to have diminished Maurras's admiration for the writer.

Though Maurras rarely mentions him, a fourth immediate model for his criticism was Jules Barbey d'Aurevilly, who has Maurras's harsh polemical manners, shares his condemnation of the nineteenth-century faith in progress and liberalism, and also shares his tastes and distastes: contempt for Hugo and admiration for André Chénier, Alphonse de Lamartine, and Maurice de Guérin.

Here among these four writers are the elements of Maurras's literary theory and taste. It seems unjust to deny that he had a critical theory and a developed taste, which no doubt harmonized with his political convictions but chronologically and psychologically predated them or, at least, their conscious elaboration. Maurras was, all his life, well able to distinguish between poetry and politics, between professed ideology and the attitudes that enter a work of art. In 1928 in a debate about romanticism he said wisely: "Let the poet be Guelph or Ghibelline, Huguenot or Papist, internationalist or patriot; I deal only with the soul of the ideas mingled in his song, with their interior structure, with their secret economy" (Un Débat sur le Romantisme, 57). In his fullest statement of a theory of criticism, "Prologue d'un essai sur la critique" (1896), Maurras sharply distinguishes between genuine literary criticism and moralistic and religious criticism: "Such distinctions may anger muddled minds. I delight in them, and not, as some might reproach me for doing, in order to divide, to separate what is unified and connected, but in order to prevent anyone from making improper connections or from calling connected that which is held to be quite distinct." Literary criticism "consists in discerning and showing the good and the bad in works of the spirit" (OC, 3:17). Maurras even claims that politics do not influence his criticism but that it is the other way round: "Disgust with barbarity has led us to search for the principles of order in art first of all, and then in the rest of the city" (DPC, 1:310). It must be granted that Maurras knew the difference between art and politics, between the aesthetic value of certain works and their possibly pernicious influences on society. The condemnation of romantic literature is primarily social and political; the descent from Rousseau to Hugo and Zola is a line of revolutionaries and liberals, but it is also, in Maurras's eyes, a line of corrupters of taste, of bad writers, of rhetoricians, verbalists, and muckrakers.

Still, he has a clear image of the French poetic tradition that is not merely governed by social or political considerations. It begins with Malherbe, whom he admires in detail and with examples. He loves La Fontaine as the greatest French poet (DPC, 2:383), and he has an unbounded affection for Chénier, on whom Maurras wrote at greater length than on any other poet. In a late essay (1940), he distinguishes perceptively between the different strands of his art and tries to locate them by their derivation from the great writers of the seventeenth century: Corneille, Molière, La Fontaine, and Racine. Although Maurras makes much of Chénier's continuity with the great tradition, he attempts to bring out his individual difference when set against the whole context of the eighteenth century: the sensuality and sensualism, the static picture-making, the use of myth and science, the critical spirit that went beyond the rationalism of the Encyclopedists. Chénier is interpreted as "a polytheist, I mean an orthodox pagan, in whom there lives and burns, as a leading thought, the boldly proclaimed notion of natural hierarchies" (OC, 3:306). Maurras regrets that Chénier did not live to become the greatest poet of the nineteenth century, the French Goethe. Though the speculation is gratuitous, it does not diminish the interest of Maurras's sketch of Chénier's influence, through Sainte-Beuve, on Baudelaire, on the Parnassians, and on his fellow Greek, Moréas. Maurras admires Lamartine highly; "Le Lac" seems to him Horatian in composition. Lamartine is a generous, genuine poet who stands behind Mistral and Verlaine (3:324). Maurras detests Hugo and finds Alfred de Vigny cold and dry. Les Amants de Venise (1905), Maurras's satirical study of the romantic sensibility, the religion of passion, is written not only with psychological penetration and stylistic verve but also with some sympathy and understanding. Maurras seems to be right when he considers Antoine Adam's reexamination of the affair Musset–George Sand as a confirmation of his own diagnosis (PV, 244–63).

Maurras also singles out Gérard de Nerval among the French romantics as a rare spirit and writes admiringly of Maurice de Guérin. In his preface to a revised edition of Le Centaure and La Bacchante (1925) he defends poetic prose and well defines Guérin's polytheism as different from Chénier's: "A polytheism that never smiled, . . . a liturgical emotion for the great forces of nature conceived as the mothers or elder sisters of our weakness" (DPC, 5:400). Maurras praises Gautier on occasion, admires Baudelaire with some reservations, and gives the highest praise among the later nineteenth-century poets to Verlaine.

Neither Chénier's nor Lamartine's politics could have pleased Maurras. He saw the relation of Maurice de Guérin to Lamennais and Chateaubriand. Verlaine's life was not for Maurras a model. One should recognize that Maurras had a special poetic taste that he knew how to defend and for which he traced a genealogy. He fulfilled the task of a critic: the definition of taste, of the classics, the selection of the tradition. One cannot say that Maurras's taste is simply academic classicism or exclusive of many poets whom we might class as romantic. It ignores political allegiances;

it has a logic and feeling of its own; a sensual, erotic, mythic paganism seems at least one common denominator.

Maurras's classical creed was accepted and developed by his followers: the whole group that clustered around the Action française. But one must distinguish between three generations: his contemporaries Léon Daudet (1868–1942) and Pierre Lasserre (1867–1930); the generation of followers born in the eighties, of whom several of the most devoted were killed in the First World War; and a younger pair, Robert Brasillach and Thierry Maulnier, both born in 1909.

Léon Daudet, who joined the movement in 1904, cannot be taken seriously as a literary critic although he wrote on practically every literary figure, past and present, with gusto and force. His best-known book, if only because of its title, is *Le stupide dix-neuvième siècle* (1922), which contains, along with a general onslaught on progress, attacks on democracy, science, the Revolution, pacifism, and so on; only one chapter is devoted to literature: "L'Aberration romantique et ses conséquences." It says substantially what had been said before by Lasserre, the Baron Seillière, and the other anti-romantic polemicists of the early twentieth century, though often with more comical violence. One could laugh at Charles Leconte de Lisle being called "that frigid cretin" or George Sand being described as "a dryad with an ink-pot at her belt" (*Le stupide dix-neuvième siècle*, 113, 101) until one remembers that the ferocious contempt with which Daudet treated Jews and assorted foreigners had painful consequences in real life. *Ecrivains et artistes* (8 volumes, 1927–29), a collection of loose popular sketches of many writers, is often surprisingly appreciative of the most diverse types and kinds: Shakespeare and Rabelais, Dostoevsky and Baudelaire, Barbey d'Aurevilly and Molière. An amazing series of articles, "Les Faux Chefs-d'oeuvre" engages in snap judgments condemning, for example, Sienkiewicz's *Quo Vadis?* (in volume 2 of *Ecrivains et artistes*), Taine's *History of English Literature*, and Fromentin's *Dominique*. A late book, *Mes Idées esthétiques* (1939), is a freewheeling ramble through the history of art and literature, which has hardly anything to say on aesthetics or theory but conveys, in anecdotes, reminiscences, and asides, Daudet's inclusive taste and enjoyment as well as his fierce, predictable contempt for Hugo and Zola. Daudet even wrote an admiring little book on Goethe (*Goethe et la synthèse*, 1932), which couples him, as a universal spirit, with Mistral. Goethe is made out to be a Don Juan, a Casanova, deeply influenced by Choderlos de Laclos. Daudet imagines Goethe, aged about sixty, on an excursion with Christiane to a roadside *Gasthaus,* where he takes "from his pocket a collapsible gold cup, gift of a distant female admirer" (*Goethe et la synthèse*, 96). Such sentimental romanticism hardly fits the orthodoxy of the classical creed. *Le gros* Daudet had his loves and hatreds but lacked the critical spirit.

Lasserre started out with a pamphlet, *Maurras et la Renaissance classique* (1902). He had been to Germany and wrote a book, *La Morale de Nietzsche* (1902), in which Nietzsche is exalted as the crown witness against romanticism: romantic art is the expression of the slave mind and Rousseau its progenitor, while classicism (that of Goethe and the French) is the antidote to anarchy and decadence. Lasserre's main book, *Le Romantisme français* (1907), became the great arsenal of anti-romantic arguments, in which he closely analyzes ideas and texts and comes to grips with the main writers: Rousseau, Mme de Staël, Chateaubriand, Constant, Hugo, and Michelet. He ignores Stendhal, Mérimée, Balzac, and Sainte-Beuve; they did not fit the thesis completely. It is a simple and rigid theory: romanticism is "the total corruption of the higher parts of human nature," "the usurpation by sensibility and imagination of the right rule of intelligence and reason," "the decomposition of art because it is a decomposition of man" (*RF*, 70, xxiii, 320). The romantic worship of nature and progress led to pantheism and, when its vague optimism failed, to the new determinism and pessimism of the second half of the century. Lasserre concentrates his fire on Rousseau, Hugo, and Michelet, quoting effectively and often maliciously: Rousseau was a diseased, insincere charlatan, Hugo "a poet of rudimentary intelligence, a ridiculous philosopher, a worthless moralist," and Michelet "an entertainer who believes himself a prophet" (273, 371). In spite of the virulent tone of the book, it is a work of scholarship and was, after some difficulties, accepted by the Sorbonne as a thesis for the doctorate of letters.

The standards of objectivity, detachment, and impartiality that were required academically seemed to Lasserre merely signs of the corruption of the humanistic ideal: his pamphlet *La Doctrine officielle de l'université* (1912) voices dismay at the newly imported Germanic scientism and what many felt to be its false conception of neutrality and moral indifference. He calls Gustave Lanson (see this *History*, 4:71–74), most unjustly, "a public malefactor" (Frohock, 29); Lasserre wanted literary training to be an education in the humanistic tradition and not in scholarly research. The books *Mistral* (1919), quite in line with Maurras's views, and *Les Chapelles littéraires* (1921), a puzzled complaint about the cult of the "obscure" Claudel and the "vague" Péguy, as well as essays severely criticizing Bergson and Romain Rolland, remain within the framework of the doctrine. Slowly, however, Lasserre changed his mind about politics and religion. In the 1919 preface to a new edition of *Le Romantisme français* he at least recognizes, though he is unrepentant, the "simplicity of its perspectives"

(*RF,* x). In a retrospective book, *Mes Routes* (1924), he speaks nostalgically of his year in Germany, and in "Pour et contre le dix-neuvième siècle," he makes a sharp distinction: his early book was directed against romanticism and not against the whole nineteenth century. He has now come to value Ernest Renan, the liberal and the historical spirit (*Mes Routes,* 88). About the same time Lasserre criticized Maurras: he succeeded in showing how absurd Mme de Staël's ideas were about the superiority of the Protestant nations and literatures, but he did not and could not refute Renan and Taine (*Mise au point,* 54). Lasserre definitely became, if not a traitor to the cause, then a deserter. His three volumes on Renan— a project left uncompleted at his death—were planned as a pendant to Sainte-Beuve's *Port Royal.* It is not classicist criticism but solid intellectual history.

The younger generation of Maurrasians, born in the 1880s, was the most dogmatic. Two critics who contributed mainly to the *Revue critique des idées et des livres* (founded in 1908), Pierre Gilbert (Cardos) and Jean-Marc Bernard, were both killed in the First World War. They made a simple identification between literary doctrine and political ideology. Gilbert argues that "a certain social order is the condition of any literary culture" (*FC,* 1:488), while Bernard states bluntly: "for this new classicism to bloom, one condition is indispensable—the return of the King" (*Oeuvres,* 2:209). Still, each has his individual voice. Gilbert's anti-romantic attacks are hardly new: Bernardin de Saint-Pierre and Chateaubriand are easy targets for the moralist who disapproves of high-flown rhetoric in lovemaking. More curious is Gilbert's harsh criticism of *Madame Bovary* at a time when the book had achieved classical stature. Gilbert finds it contrived, devoid of sympathy, lacking in its much-vaunted objectivity: "Flaubert spreads I don't know what shade of desperate sadness across the colors of the French countryside, he lowers its sky to the point of crushing the earth and thereby makes the air quite unbreathable" (*FC,* 1:144). While accurate enough, this observation hardly justifies a negative aesthetic judgment. After all, Gilbert defined classicism as "the passion for personal analysis, psychological precision, moral realism." He admires Racine as a psychologist, minimizes, for instance, the political implications of *Bérénice,* and dismisses the new "savage" interpretation of Racine propounded by Masson-Forestier. Racine's tragedy is less action than passion. *Bérénice* is "the long embrace of two lovers who, even in their kisses, cannot dispense with making each other suffer." Only *Bajazet* is a deplorable exception among Racine's tragedies, a deviation into violence (1:518, 30–48; 2:30).

Gilbert's main literary hero is Stendhal: "To be Stendhalian . . . is a mode of being and of living in which Stendhal plays the role of accelerator." Gilbert effectively defends Stendhal's style: "He does not evoke, he provokes; it is an act with a view to pleasure; . . . writing serves to produce these sentiments and these emotions; it is not effect, but cause; it does not follow the pleasure, it precedes and begets it; he places expression and style above all else; an event does not truly touch him deeply until he has given it his own expression" (*FC*, 1:150, 154). This, Gilbert recognizes, may be true of any good artist, but with Stendhal it proves that criticism of his style is beside the point. Gilbert manages to reconcile such emphasis on expression with his anti-romanticism because for him romanticism is not individualism (the right kind of individualism defended by Stendhal); it lacks the moral realism, the psychological precision he admires. Romanticism gives the same dignity to all movements of the mind; it violates the hierarchy within the mind. Rousseau is the prime example: "a Nero who creates his own universe of pleasure," an egotist, not an individualist (1:348).

There is no quarter given to individualism in the writings of Jean-Marc Bernard. Romanticism is "a debauch of subjectivity" and the entire nineteenth century is "the tail-end of romanticism" (*Oeuvres*, 2:191, 197). Bernard has no use for sincerity, which is merely spontaneity, whereas poetry is composition, work. Bernard recognizes that the new classicism cannot simply return to the seventeenth century. It is rather "the adoption of a method of thinking and working capable of sustaining, directing, and universalizing our personality and our instincts" (2:210). It is the old ideal of universality, which with Bernard, in practice, is compatible with admiration for a good many different things. The series "Petits sentiers de la poésie française" sketches portraits of French poets from Charles d'Orléans to Parny and Chénier quite impartially, while another set of sketches sympathetically surveys Francis Jammes, Vielé-Griffin, Henri Régnier, and, surprisingly, the unanimistic writer Jules Romains. In Bernard as in Maurras, a frank enjoyment of sensuousness and sensuality softens the rigid ideology.

A surviving collaborator of the *Revue critique des idées et des livres*, Eugène Marsan (1882–1936), went very much his own way. A writer of elegant erotic fiction, he has been called "Maurras in lace" by Henri Clouard in his *Histoire de la littérature française*, (2 vols. [1947–49], 2:489). But his criticism, collected in *Instances* (1930), is mainly academic commentary— unfavorable (on romantic texts such as Hugo's preface to *Cromwell*), ironic (on Rousseau), and fervent (as in his eulogy of Moréas's *Stances*). Marsan finds formulas to reconcile classicism with symbolism. In 1928 he concluded that the age should be called one of "symbolist classicism," whereas

at other times he is content to speak of the eternal classicism, "art in its
state of perfection" (*Instances,* 329, 313, 127).

Marsan's defense of Moréas was directed against another Maurrasian,
Pierre Lièvre (1882–1939), who professed great admiration for Maurras's
criticism but broke away in favor of a rather indiscriminate eclecticism:
he wrote appreciative essays on Mme de Noailles, Jean Giraudoux, Valery
Larbaud, Pierre Hamp, and Paul Valéry. In a survey of the tendencies of
French literature between 1895 and 1920, Lièvre concludes that Anatole
France was the dominant figure and that his example holds out hope for
a revival of the traditional style of prose (*Esquisses critiques,* 3d ser., 29, 34).
In the essay on Maurras, Lièvre takes the position that Maurras without
the Action française would not lose anything distinct. Lièvre's criticism,
though fragmentary, is coherent. He endorses Maurras's dissection of
romantic sentiment and taste but sees a conflict between Maurras's taste
and his doctrine, which makes him praise works unworthy of his taste.
Moréas, Lièvre argues, is grossly overrated for doctrinal reasons; he is "a
pleasant vignettist, a clever balladeer, a tolerably literate imitator, nothing more" (*Esquisses critiques,* 2d ser., 171). A Maurrasian discovered that
the classical revival has not come to anything in poetry: "What good are
principles! However carefully we may elaborate them, there will always
be facts or people to whom we cannot apply them" (168). Lièvre learned
his lesson in intellectual humility.

One could not say about Henri Massis (1886–1956) that he ever
achieved intellectual humility, though he did submit to the discipline of
the Church. His best-known book, *Défense de l'Occident* (1927), is sweeping
in its warnings against anything non-Western; the Asiatic peril includes
German nationalism, Russian bolshevism, and Indian mysticism mixed
together in grandiose confusion. Massis had read Keyserling, Spengler,
and Berdyaev and shared their sense of apocalyptic doom, but he holds
out the quixotic hope of a Christianization of Asia: "Only Christ, placed
at the center of everything, can reconcile East and West" (*Défense de
l'Occident,* 269).

Oddly enough, Massis had started with a book of literary research,
Comment Zola composait ses romans (1906), a topic that could hardly recom-
mend the young man when he called on Anatole France, Jules Lemaître,
and Maurice Barrès; he wryly recalls these circumstances in *Evocations.*
But he earned his spurs with the right wing when he launched a violent attack against the Sorbonne, *L'Esprit de la Nouvelle Sorbonne* (1910–11,
under the pseudonym Agathon, in collaboration with Alfred de Tarde),
denouncing German scientism, sociology, bibliography, Durkheim, and
Lanson; he then became secretary of the Ligue pour la culture française

after being dramatically brought into its founding meeting (*Evocations,* 117ff.). The lectures of Bergson at the Collège de France, which at that time served as an anti-Sorbonne demonstration, helped Massis to liberate himself from the materialistic philosophy he had accepted early in his life and to prepare his return to Catholicism (84, 86, 88). His *Jugements* (2 volumes, 1923–24), followed by *Réflexions sur l'art du roman* (1927), books on Barrès (1909), Pascal (1924), and Proust (1937), are ideological criticism of considerable power. It is classicist only in the sense in which classicism means authoritarianism, a principle of order, an acceptance of tradition and the Church. A late book, *Les Idées restent* (1941), formulates it frankly: "Culture relies upon a dogmatism; it makes a choice, it establishes an order in products of the spirit, it supposes a tradition. . . . So it is with classicism. It is a point of view that permits one to judge. To be classic is to have a solid foundation on which to establish one's judgments" (64–65). Massis certainly exercises this right freely on Renan and Gide. In the essay on Gide in *Jugements* Massis protests against Gide's claim to be "the best representative of classicism." This is only "a voluntary and refined hypocrisy," a mask to disguise the meaning of his work, which is profoundly immoral and anarchistic (*Jugements,* 2:19). Massis substantially agreed with Maurras, though he had little of his interest in poetry. A book of reminiscences, *Maurras et notre temps* (1951, 1961), sides with Maurras on almost all issues and controversies of the time. In 1941 Massis had complained that Maurras lacked a theology, a consolation for death. The book of reminiscences makes much of Maurras's deathbed conversion and ends like a saint's legend (*Les Idées restent,* 42; *Maurras et notre temps* [1961], 425).

Maurras et notre temps contains also several rapturous pages on Robert Brasillach (1909–45), whom Massis mourned like a son after his execution as a collaborator. Brasillach had joined the Action française in 1930, and his criticism is colored by his admiration for Maurras, classicism, and soon also Fascism, Italian and German. His first book, *Présence de Virgile* (1931), is a pleasant evocation of the man and the mood of his work with few critical pretensions. His *Corneille* (1938) is little more than a biography, interspersed with descriptions of the plays and some critical remarks to bring Corneille up-to-date. Brasillach calls him blandly a "precursor of Fascism," speaks of Sertorius as "the chief of the anti-fascist brigade . . . escaped from the last novel of André Malraux," and even, in incredibly bad taste, compares Rodrigue and Chimène to "un couple sportif et brillant" (*Pierre Corneille,* 188, 384, 145–46).

But the collections *Portraits* (1935) and *Les Quatre Jeudis* (1943) are highly individual and, in taste and tone, far removed from the Master.

One essay praises him for his love of the concrete and of the soil of Provence, and interprets him as a "creator of myths," but other articles speak fervently of Colette, her sensual communication with the earth, of Claudel, of Giraudoux, and of Proust, whose *A la recherche du temps perdu* Brasillach wants to rechristen *A la recherche du bonheur perdu* (*Portraits*, 30, 67ff.). An essay on Malraux shows some detachment: the heroism of the characters (speaking of the early novels set in China) seems to him self-indulgent, used like a potent drug. It shows "a quite terrible complacency toward suffering and death" (224).

The pamphlet *Chénier* (1947), written in prison, starts as a literary essay disputing some of Maurras's views. Brasillach derives Chénier's poetry from the *Greek Anthology* and finds the rococo traits inferior. Chénier is most charming when he is incomplete, fragile, and romantic. But Brasillach read Chénier and wrote about him in prison as he saw a parallel between Chénier's antirevolutionary activities and the situation in which he found himself during the war. He wants to think of himself as the innocent victim of revolutionary fury. He quotes from "Iambes IX" (*Chénier*, 49):

> Allons, étouffe tes clameurs:
> Toi, Vertu, pleure si je meurs.

His close friend Thierry Maulnier (pseudonym of Jacques Talagrand, born 1909) established his reputation before the war with two books, *Nietzsche* (1925) and *Racine* (1936). The book on Nietzsche, written when Maulnier was an amazingly precocious schoolboy of sixteen, surprises by its fluency and the surety of its exposition of at least the main ideas of Nietzsche. Nietzsche's classicism is for Maulnier "the model of civilized heroism, the perfect union of inner richness and tragic simplicity, of lucidity and violence of the instincts" (*Nietzsche*, 167). This Nietzschean synthesis, or rather series of oxymorons, permeates the book on Racine. It is certainly not classicist in the usual sense: Maulnier expressly rejects Lemaître, who looked for realism, local color, and pure poetry in Racine. For Maulnier "classicism is not in the application of a learned technique. . . . Classicism is in happiness itself and in the infallibility of instinct. . . . A classicism is born of the atavistic conjuration between perfection and spontaneity" (*Racine*, 21). Maulnier rings constant changes on this theme: the absurdity of the supposed incompatibility of inspiration and technique, creative energy and intelligent order. He draws a sharp line between life and work: "There is nothing less literary than the private life of Racine, nothing less lived than his tragedies" (58). Maulnier has no use for stories about Racine's mistresses or the rumors concerning poisonings. Racine's tragedies are creations, not expressions. Maulnier makes Racine a kind of Nietzschean in love with fate. In ever new variations we are told that Racine unites instinct and intelligence, actuality and erudition, generality and real life. If we are dazzled by Maulnier's rhetoric, we also feel cheated by his dialectics: he has it always both ways. It is difficult to see why the book should have been praised by the historian of Racine criticism for having accomplished the synthesis of three centuries of criticism (Alvin A. Eustis, *Racine devant la critique française, 1839–1939* [1949], 230).

In spite of all the rhapsodies about classicism, Maulnier's taste is definitely Baroque, precious, even hermetic, as his later writings show. His *Introduction à la poésie française* (1939) is an anthology with a one-hundred-page introduction that attempts to rewrite the whole history of French poetry. The anthology (much of it composed of snippets) contains not a single line of verse from poets between Racine and Henri de Latouche. Chénier, for example, is not represented. It ends with Maurras and begins with Villon, but all the emphasis is on the Lyons Renaissance, on the Pléiade, and on the Baroque poets of the early seventeenth century. In the discussion Maulnier is content to remain baffled by the mystery of poetry, the ineffable magic of language, though he makes an effort to reject both Surrealism and absolute poetry by speaking of poetry as "superior reason" (*Introduction à la poésie française*, 24). He reflects on the peculiarities of the French tradition: its divorce from folklore and the great events of French history. The most popular French poets (Hugo, Béranger) are the worst. The heroes of French poetry are called Hector, Ajax, Prometheus, Phaedra, Antigone, Cleopatra. There are no French elves or demons. Maulnier, in contrast to the ideologists, has little use for theory and recognizes that terms such as "nature," "tradition," and "liberty" may mean quite different things in different historical contexts. The one doctrine he condemns is that of romanticism: it seems to him merely an exaltation of facility. Neoclassical poetry in the eighteenth century had become overfacile, and the romantics did not change matters. Maulnier is no admirer of the usual classical virtues: "the facile charms, the easy flow of oratory, the odious 'sublime' of sentiments, the clarity, the 'measure'" (40, 44, 69). He would instead restore the treasury of its profundities to French poetry: Scève, D'Aubigné, Garnier, whom he admires as a French Elizabethan. Maulnier deplores that the seventeenth century is usually identified with the age of Louis XIV and draws attention to another flowering around 1630 under Louis XIII. Malherbe and Maynard are, he asserts, as great as the classics. In an essay in *Langages* (1946), "Les Derniers Renaissants," he comments enthusiastically on the poets today called Baroque: Théophile, Jean de Sponde, Godeau, and others. Maulnier argues that the seventeenth century as a whole was more *précieux* than classical. The great classics lived in surprising solitude; being bourgeois, they led tame lives compared to the adventurers and outcasts of the preceding age (*Langages*, 30, 38–39). Maulnier actually admires only Racine in the age of Louis XIV, as "having fallen into the midst of his age like an inexplicable meteor, the bearer of a fire from another world" (*Introduction*, 94). Racine could not and did not have any heirs. The eighteenth and nineteenth centuries are the dark ages of French poetry, and Maulnier exempts only Nerval among the romantics. The essay "L'Enigme Hugo" puts the objections to his work in the strongest terms: verbalism, flaccidity, a metaphysics that to Maulnier seems "the mask of vulgarity, against a common mystic-magical background." He has no use for the "mythology of the gigantic and the abstract rhetoric" of the late poems, which were then beginning to be appreciated by the Surrealists (*Langages*, 205, 216). But Maulnier recognizes the impact of Hugo: of "le mythe Hugo," the hero of literature, which suffices to explain the riddle of his commanding position. French poetry was saved and revived by Baudelaire, Rimbaud, Mallarmé, Claudel, and Valéry. Maulnier knows that his revaluation of the whole history of French poetry would not have been possible without them. Maurras's *Reliquiae foci* is the last poem in the anthology. The symbolic title is a gesture by the anthologist, who has left behind the hearth of the Action française, which, in 1939, went through its worst ordeal and stood it badly.

All these writers were followers of Charles Maurras, however far they went beyond his ken. But there were other classicists among the French critics who were violently opposed to him and all his works and yet shared many of his literary doctrines. Among his exact contemporaries Julien Benda (1867–1956) is the most striking case. At first sight he seems totally opposed to Maurras, as a Jew and as an ardent Dreyfusard. Benda's most famous book, *La Trahison des clercs* (1927), is an attack on writers engaged in politics, a plea for intellectuals to detach themselves from the passions of the time. But, inconsistently, Benda himself was as "committed" as Maurras and as violently nationalistic as any of the integral nationalists. He was as much an enemy of romanticism as they and, like them, exalts the French classics as "a refuge against literature which is only used to touch our sensibility" (*Exercice d'un enterré vif*, 221). But philosophically Benda stands elsewhere. Whereas Maurras must be described as a positivist, a melancholy hedonist who returned to the Church, Benda is an extreme rationalist, a Spinozan who persecutes every kind of irrationalism with a fervor that oddly clashes with his cool creed. Bergson was the bête noire of his life. *Le Bergsonisme* (1912) is the most systematic dissection, but Benda's many books are all running polemics against the modern age, exalting the ideals of a rational science, clear reason, and classical, ordered art. *Belphégor* (1919) contains the most effective exposition of his views: the sharpest criticism of intuition, of the worship of the particular and unique, of the cult of the obscure and the vague, of the thirst for novelty at any price, of the indulgence in unrestrained emotion. Benda clearly distinguishes the "emotion of sympathy" from "aesthetic emotion." Masterpieces such as the fugues of Bach or the tales of Voltaire do not cause the heart to flutter (*Belphégor*, 55, 197). A late book by Benda, *La France byzantine* (1945), is possibly the most interesting from a purely literary point of view, because the usual diagnosis of contemporary ills is here expanded to include Mallarmé, Gide, Proust, Valéry, Alain, Giraudoux, Suarès, and the surrealists. Benda cites the worship of the dream and of the unconscious, the advocacy of *disponibilité,* Hegelian dialects, preciosity, obscurity, and so on to support his conclusion: France is decadent, has become the new Byzantium. The intellectualism of Valéry seems to him only a disguise for extreme aestheticism. Benda, surprisingly, judges the French romantics more leniently than his contemporaries do: he praises Lamartine, Musset, and Vigny. Chateaubriand is defended as a new, though different classic. The real decadence of French literature came in the 1890s with the influence of Bergson: Bergson opened the door to German irrationalism and initiated the destruction of reason. Benda exalts French classicism as the great counterforce, but deprived of its historicity and even nationality, it becomes something abstract, rational, and even scientific. Benda characteristically asserts that poetry is independent of the language in which it is expressed: "The architectural perfection of a tragedy by Racine, the truth of a page out of *Faust* exist exclusive of the languages in which they are embodied" (*La France byzantine*, 140, 170–71). By a peculiar dialectical reversal Benda comes close to his enemies, the Action française, in his hatreds and loves, but he lacks their saving grace: the concern for poetry that cannot be independent of the senses and feelings. Benda is an unpoetic mind whose elegant form conceals desiccated rationalism preached with the cold fury of an Old Testament prophet.

Classicism as a slogan was not the exclusive property of the Maurras group or even of the other anti-romantic polemicists such as Julien Benda. The *Nouvelle Revue Française* for a time used the term and concept. Gide, during an interview with Emile Henriot in 1921, declared: "Having founded the principal secret of classicism in modesty, I can now tell you that I consider myself today to be the best representative of classicism." This obviously was not meant to be a boast or irony, as Gide asserts, in the same context, that classicism tends toward *litotes*, understatement: "It's the art of expressing the most while saying the least. It's an art of reserve and modesty." The great classical artist endeavors not to have any individual mannerisms: "he strives toward banality" (*Oeuvres complètes* [1932ff.], 11:35, 39, 36). Gide disapproves of the merely laudatory use of the term and recognizes that neither Pascal nor Rabelais nor Villon, not to speak of Shakespeare or Dostoevsky or Dante, is classical in his sense. Since antiquity there were classics only in France, if one excepts Goethe. Classicism is a French invention; elsewhere it remained artificial, as the example of Alexander Pope well shows. Gide in 1909 had applauded Lasserre's book on romanticism; he professed to have always detested romanticism and artistic anarchy but he could not agree with the way romanticism was being read out of French literature, or with the resignation and sense of doom with which the Maurrasians looked into the future (6:7). Henri Clouard (another Maurrasian who had become an orthodox Catholic) in 1911 called Gide "a new Lasserre" (*Mercure de France*, 1 August 1911, p.226). But Gide, who wrote on Dostoevsky as if he were writing of himself and for a time professed Communism, clearly never was a classicist in any strict sense, however highly we may value his relations to antiquity or the French classics.

Nor can one call Jacques Rivière a classicist, though the well-known essay "Roman d'aventure" (1913) prophesies a new classicism. It begins by rejecting romanticism as "an inferior art, a sort of monstrosity in the history of literature." Praising Descartes as "the father of classicism," Rivière predicts a new classical work which, he knows, will not be like that of Descartes or even the works of the seventeenth century but rather would imitate "the scrupulosity of pure thought" characteristic of classical works (*Nouvelles études* [1947], 251, 253, 256, 258). In 1923 Rivière asserted that his prediction of an "adventure novel," a novel that advances through constantly new events, had been fulfilled by Proust's great novel cycle (quoted by Blanche A. Price in *The Ideal Reader: Selected Essays by Jacques Rivière* [1960], 74)—an odd interpretation given that in 1913 Rivière's thought surely was directed against the psychological and symbolic novel. When in 1919 Rivière returned from German captivity to assume the editorship of the *NRF*, he promised in his statement of purpose to "describe what seems to us to foreshadow a classical renaissance, not literal and purely imitative, as the disciples of Moréas and the writers of the *Revue Critique* understood and defined it before the war, but a deep, inner classicism"

(*NRF* 13 [June 1919]:8). But nothing of this sort happened, and neither Jean Paulhan nor Albert Thibaudet, Rivière's successors at the *NRF,* can even by a long stretch be described as classicists.

There is also a clear classicist strain in Paul Valéry. He prefers classicism to romanticism because of its set conventions, "its bizarre rules." Perfectly arbitrary metrical rules or theatrical unities seem to him valuable, as all art is "difficulty overcome." *Phèdre* is the model of perfection: "It resists all attempts to change it" (*Variété,* 5:196). Discipline, purity, form, restraint— the "dance in fetters"—are classicist motifs in Valéry's theory of poetry, but they are surely overlaid by the ideal of absolute poetry derived from Mallarmé. It cannot be called classical in any accepted sense.

The theme of classicism in twentieth-century French criticism could be pursued much further. It would, however, be extremely difficult and even impossible to distinguish between the impact of Maurrasian classicism and an independent recourse to the classical tradition. One can never-theless be reasonably sure that Gide, Rivière, and Valéry felt its presence and reacted to it.

Finally, it might be pertinent to reflect on some of the causes and re-sults of the French neoclassical movement. It is easy to take a political or sociological point of view and dismiss French classicist criticism as "re-actionary." There is no denying that it was, as a distinct trend, associated with the Action française and with the ideology of integral nationalism, which later assumed affinities with Fascism. But this says little about the actual literary criticism, which had roots in a remote past that cannot simply be labeled feudal or bourgeois.

At the risk of excessive simplification I suggest that classicism as a doc-trine and model preserved (or renewed) its appeal because it upholds a concept of beauty and art that is fast disintegrating. Whatever the con-quests of modern art and its appeal to other traditions in the past—the primitive, the archaic, the Byzantine, the Romanesque, Mannerism, the Baroque, and so on—there will always be the radiant example of Greek art of the fifth century, of Vergil, of the Italian Renaissance, of the age of Louis XIV, and of the great Germans, Goethe and Hölderlin. No doubt neoclassicism is and often was escapist and academic; in France it combined with xenophobia, a special parochialism that neither saw nor wanted to see what was happening in the rest of the world. But the neo-classical movement (which has disappeared in present times) provided also something worthy: a resistance against the abolition of art, which progressed during that time and continues today with frightening vio-lence as is evident in pop art or op art, concrete poetry, and electronic music. Neoclassicism saw both the danger for art of the confusion between art and life in Naturalism and the opposite danger—the dehumanization of art in the purism of absolute poetry, in the tendency toward the unorganic, in the divorce from the soil and the senses, in the "loss of center" diagnosed by many contemplators of the contemporary scene. Though perhaps representative of a narrow taste and a specific image of man and beauty, Phidias and Vergil, Raphael and Titian, Racine and Goethe will always provide a center of security, a point of stillness, an exemplification of what art is or at least one kind of art admired through the ages. No amount of skepticism, relativism, or experimentation can ignore or destroy this kind of beauty.

2 : RETROSPECT

ALAIN (1868–1951)

EMILE-AUGUSTE CHARTIER took the pen name Alain when he started to publish, rather late in life. He was an enormously successful teacher and lecturer and had a considerable reputation as a philosopher, particularly as a philosopher meditating on art. In his early years he wrote occasional philosophical and psychophysiological studies that were published in local newspapers and in journals outside Paris, and he took part in the 1904 Congress of Geneva, where he was apparently the only supporter of Bergson. Some of the contributions to different periodicals were collected in 1908–09 but attracted little attention. In 1920 he collected his contributions as *Les Propos d'Alain* in two volumes, but Alain did not become well known until *Propos de littérature* appeared in 1933 and a little book on Stendhal in 1935. Alain died in 1951 at the age of eighty-three, but his wide readership was established only posthumously, particularly with the four-volume Pléiade edition of his writings. He ranged over every topic one can possibly think of and wrote several monographs (the one on Stendhal, one on Dickens, and one on Balzac) as well as a whole aesthetics called *Système des beaux arts* (1920), which is devoted mainly to the so-called fine arts, but has also a chapter on poetry. His book on Stendhal begins in the strangest way: "An incredulous man is a rare man. It is not difficult not to believe in anything, but it is difficult never to be a dupe and at the same time believe in man and love man as he is." Because of this "total amity toward man," Stendhal seems to Alain without blindness and, in his time, the "only person of his species." Alain then develops this idea of Stendhal's love of man, a love moderated by insight into his weaknesses and even his evil traits.

En lisant Dickens (1945) is one of the most peculiar hymns to a writer I have ever read. Alain admires everything about Dickens in panegyrical terms—the atmosphere, the characters, even the plots—and he praises all the books one after another, culminating in a glorification of *Our Mutual Friend,* which seems to him the greatest masterwork of novelistic art. He admires the most extravagantly fanciful and melodramatic traits in Dickens and identifies sympathetically even with characters whom Dickens portrays as evil and malicious. Only once does Alain hesitate: his praise of *A Christmas Carol* is ambiguous, since he sees that it is an apology of peaceful, passive, philistine life. But this appeals to him, too, as he recognizes that Dickens wanted and at least tried to achieve such an idyllic life with wife and children around the hearth. Alain is only a little cooler toward the early Dickens, specifically toward *Pickwick Papers* and the bootblack Sam Weller, where he finds, oddly enough, a "form *à la* Voltaire" (*AD*, 835). Alain makes many often surprising statements. He believes, for instance, that the "emotion" of a story gives it existence, and that the "movement" of the story inspires the characters.

Alain's whole scheme is based on a historical scenario: man is first at a lower stage, a physical being near to or even identical with animals; he rises to a second degree when he invents society and becomes a member of a community; and, finally, there is the spiritual level (where *spiritual* is used in the broadest sense), encompassing not only religion but also all human endeavors in art, science, and literature. His book *Les Dieux* (1947) ends with an elaborate attempt at a new mythology. Man admires and glorifies heroes as gods. Alain identifies strongly with the hero worship of the Ancients, for instance, praising Caesar as a god. He then easily switches over to Christianity. Jesus Christ appears as a hero-god, the Virgin Mary is approved of for the cult surrounding her, and there is an elaborate defense of the concept of the Trinity. This mythology is obviously Greek and Christian, but in theory Alain hopes that it will be conceived of as universal, embracing every kind of nation, ending in a rather indiscriminate pantheism. To say it bluntly, Alain has his merits as a *vulgarisateur*, but hardly as an independent critic.

RÉMY DE GOURMONT (1858–1915)

Rémy de Gourmont was a novelist and critic of considerable reputation and influence. In England he affected Ezra Pound and T. S. Eliot in particular. In 1926 Pound published *The Natural Philosophy of Love*, his translation of Gourmont's *Physique de l'amour* (1903), while Eliot in *The Sacred Wood* (1920) praised Gourmont as "the perfect critic." Richard Aldington in 1928 compiled an extensive two-volume anthology propagating Gourmont, and in 1921 Aldous Huxley published *A Virgin Heart*, his translation of *Un Coeur virginal* (1907).

In France, Gourmont's fame reached its peak in 1902 with the publication of *Le Problème du style,* which received wide comment. An early book, *Le Latin mystique* (1892), studied medieval symbolism openly in support of the new French symbolism. Gourmont's association with the symbolists was close and personal. He was an assiduous frequenter of the salon of Mallarmé and knew and praised Villiers de L'Isle-Adam and Vielé-Griffin. Years later Gourmont wrote perceptive reminiscences of these early symbolist schools. Gourmont came from a prominent Norman landowning family and was for many years an official of the Bibliothèque Nationale. He was forced to retire in 1891 as he was afflicted with the skin disease lupus, and he spent the remainder of his life in almost complete isolation.

Gourmont founded the periodical *Mercure de France,* which for a long time he filled almost single-handedly. His many collections of essays are drawn from articles originally published in this review. Gourmont was, on the whole, a tolerant critic. In his early years he was a strong opponent of Naturalism; Zola was his main target. Gourmont's relationship with Gide was, however, most detrimental to his fame. In *Corydon* (1924) Gide attacked the theories of *Physique de l'amour,* and he continued to disapprove violently of Gourmont, at least in private. In a letter of Gide's, which possibly was never sent but is transcribed from his papers in the Bibliothèque Nationale, he spoke of Gourmont as "one of the spirits I detest most" (1902). There seems to be general agreement that Gide's antagonism speeded the decline of Gourmont's reputation after the outbreak of the First World War. We are told that he was in eclipse for years, though today there are numerous, mainly academic, monographs about him, referring mostly to his linguistic ideas. His philosophy cannot be taken seriously. It professes to be idealist, but idealism here means only a rejection of materialism. In effect, Gourmont is completely materialistic and even positivistic. Everything is explained by physiology. The "idealism" is only an odd echo of Schopenhauer, which Gourmont probably received secondhand from Théodule-Armand Ribot's *La Philosophie de Schopenhauer* (1874). Representation to Gourmont means actually subjectivism: "The world is my representation"—a complete misunderstanding of Schopenhauer. A quotation reveals Gourmont's merely verbal idealism: "The causes of idealism are rooted deeply in matter. Idealism means materialism; and, conversely, materialism means idealism" (Uitti, 71).

In practice, Gourmont is often an extreme art-for-art's-sake theorist. Every artist should have his personal imprint, which is determined by his physical makeup and his creative capacity. We find such aphorisms as "Art does not conclude; where there is conclusion, there is criticism" (Uitti, 93). Gourmont's theory of poetry is in many ways quite simple. It emphasizes the image. This theory was the source of Imagism as a literary movement, which for a while flourished in America. Poetry creates value and makes us see the world—"see" in the literal sense, *visual* seeing, not just realization. Gourmont is an enemy of abstract language and hence of much French poetry in the style of the eighteenth century. He admires much more the poets who are now called Baroque, the period of Ronsard and Malherbe. Gourmont shows great merit in editing and commenting on writers who were, in his time, almost forgotten, such as Théophile de Viau, a new edition of whom Gourmont introduced in 1907. He also discovered, though he surely was not the first, the poetry of Gérard de Nerval and produced a new edition of his work in 1905.

Gourmont admires few poets besides Hugo and Rimbaud, who also used metaphors primarily to make us understand the world. Ultimately Gourmont's reputation rests on his writings on the French language and on such perceptions as "the dissociation of ideas." *Le Problème du style* proclaims that "the real problem of style is a question of physiology" (9) and indulges in long-winded attacks on the then prominent textbook of stylistics, Antoine Albalat's *L'Art d'écrire*. Gourmont confronts Albalat, an old-fashioned stylist who recommended fluent and clear expository writing, with the theory that every style is individual and depends on diet, on whether one lives in the country or in Paris, on one's diversions, and on one's illnesses. Gourmont makes much of local differences and attempts something like a linguistic topography of France. Style is mainly defined in terms of its visual qualities, which are at the same time emotive; what is rejected is an abstract or sentimental style. Gourmont admits that there is an auditory memory as well as a visual one. He asserts that art is incompatible with moral or religious preoccupations. What matters is the sensibility of the writer. He argues that models are of little use, that imitation in that sense is useless and irrelevant, as is a style that is willful and artificial, such as the highly colored style of Hippolyte Taine. Gourmont discusses Homer's metaphors and the rarity of metaphor in *The Song of Roland*, which is brutally realistic, and notes that Chateaubriand and, later, Flaubert understood that the art of description is the art of seeing. But Gourmont actually modifies this emphasis on the visual by admitting that sensibility is to be understood as a general power of feeling, which develops diversely in every human being.

Le Problème du style continues with a sort of history of French style. Gourmont makes much of Fénelon's *Télémaque* and of Stendhal, and he constantly returns to attack Albalat and other writers who view style as independent of subject matter. Gourmont also greatly admires Buffon. The book roams over such related issues as plagiarism and illustration: Gourmont says, too sweepingly, that "one can never illustrate a novel" (*PS*, 150). He reverts always to the good maxim that matter and style are identical.

ANDRÉ GIDE (1869–1951)

ANDRÉ GIDE WROTE a large number of essays and reviews for the *Nouvelle Revue Française,* many of purely ephemeral interest, devoted to now completely forgotten writers or discussing political problems of the day, such as "Reflections on Germany" (1919) and "The Future of Europe" (1923). Some of the memoirs are of great interest to a historian of criticism, particularly the well-known piece on Mallarmé (1898) praising his "immortal serenity" and his convictions, which were intransigent and hardly affected by criticism. Gide's reminiscences of Oscar Wilde (1902) describe their encounters, first in 1891 and then in Paris after Wilde's condemnation and prison years. Gide thinks of Wilde mainly as a public figure, quoting him as saying that he put all of his genius into his life and only his talent into his work. Gide gives an account of the complete change that prison effected in Wilde and sympathizes with his plight, but without any signs of real indignation. In another group of essays Gide defends the classicism in French literature. Classicism is for Gide "the triumph of order and measure over inner romanticism" (*P,* 195). It requires, in his view, modesty, understatement, and reserve, and it seems to him a particularly French phenomenon. This concept has little to do with historical classicism of the age of Louis XIV or with the German discussions of the two styles of writing.

The essays show Gide's general literary taste. He is a critic in the old sense, judging and commenting in a leisurely way, without much theoretical awareness, unless we consider the advocacy of classicism a contribution of importance at that time. Among French writers Gide admires particularly Flaubert, Baudelaire, and Théophile Gautier. Asked to name his favorite French novels, he answers with, not surprisingly, Stendhal's *La Chartreuse de Parme* and, surprisingly, *Les Liaisons dangereuses* of Choderlos de Laclos. Though Gide also lists *La Princesse de Clèves* by the comtesse de La Fayette, he complains of its lack of reticence and mystery: it is a "dead end" (*P,* 147). There is nothing new in Gide's praise of Balzac and Flaubert. On occasion, particularly in public lectures, Gide engages in general reflections on literature—praising poetry, quoting Keats, dismissing the questions of influence and dependence as secondary considerations. "Great minds," he says, "never fear influences; on the contrary, they seek them with a sort of eagerness like the eagerness of being" (31).

Gide has no use for nationalism in literature, and he ranges widely. He obviously knows and admires the Russians, including Pushkin and Gogol. Gide's book on Dostoevsky (1923) consists mainly of lectures given in 1922, but it is based on earlier writings, particularly a long piece on the correspondence dating from 1908. His interest in Dostoevsky goes back, according to Gide himself, to his youth. Gide flatly rejects Melchior de Vogüé's account in *Le Roman russe* (1886). Vogüé, who introduced Dostoevsky to France, was completely indifferent to all of Dostoevsky's later writing except *Crime and Punishment* and totally ignored Dostoevsky's religion and doctrines, thus greatly distorting his image. Gide's first chapter is a skillful selection of excerpts from the French edition of Dostoevsky's correspondence (1908), retelling the life with great sympathy. Only the emphasis on Dostoevsky's epilepsy seems doubtful in the light of modern research. The second part of this section expounds Dostoevsky's views on Catholicism, summarizing his belief that Christ has been lost through the error of Catholicism. Gide compares Dostoevsky with Maurice Barrès, emphasizing their differences: although they appear similar in their worship of the soil and the nation, Dostoevsky appeals to universal humanity and always surmounts a narrow nationalism. Gide concludes by referring to Dostoevsky's praise of sacrifice. The joy beyond suffering is latent in all of Dostoevsky's work, argues Gide, "a joy that Nietzsche had rightly sensed and which I charge M. de Vogüé with having missed entirely" (*D*, 42).

The remainder of the book consists of the addresses Gide gave in 1922 at Jacques Copeau's School of Dramatic Art, which apparently were a considerable success. Gide himself noted in his journal on 22 April 1922 that "Dostoevsky is here often only a pretext to express my own ideas and I excuse myself beforehand if I have falsified the thought of Dostoevsky." On 4 August 1922 he wrote in the journal, "I present my own ethics under the cover of Dostoevsky." But this seems to be not at all true. Gide's objective and substantially accurate account of Dostoevsky's main ideas recognizes that they are never expressed abstractly but always through the medium of the character expressing them. Gide rightly characterizes Dostoevsky as humbly human, in contrast to the conceited Rousseau. He gave himself without stint in his work, says Gide: "He lost himself in each of the characters of his books and for this reason it is in them that he can be found again" (D, 48). Gide discusses sympathetically Dostoevsky's early writings, his condemnation and mock execution, and the years in a Siberian stockade. On the question of Jesus Christ, unlike Nietzsche, who was jealous of Christ to the point of madness, Dostoevsky "felt he was face-to-face with something superior not only to himself but to all of mankind, something divine" (74). Gide then makes much of the Russian setting of the novels, but suspends judgment on such questions as Dostoevsky's supposed confession to the rape of a girl. In Gide's new version of this story, Dostoevsky confesses to Turgenev—a most unlikely embellishment of an unsubstantiated suspicion based on Stavrogin's confession in the suppressed chapter of *The Possessed.*

Gide is mostly interested in Dostoevsky's psychology. For instance, he speaks as if Dostoevsky had established a law that a man who has suffered humiliation will in turn seek to inflict humiliation. Gide was one of the first to argue that Dostoevsky's characters are not graded by their goodness of heart, but by the degree of their pride. Pride in Dostoevsky leads inevitably to disaster. Gide compares Dostoevsky with Balzac, claiming extravagantly that in Dostoevsky's work two factors do not exist: the intellect and the will. In all of Dostoevsky there is not a single great man. The most perfect and most admired—Father Zosima—is a saint and not a hero. Gide perceives that Dostoevsky often attributes his most daring ideas to subordinate characters, as he was apparently not willing to proclaim them as his own, but rather tried to shield his radicalism from too much criticism. His characters often remain in a shell, their feelings, thoughts, and passions deeply encased in a pure, isolated state. Dostoevsky believed passionately in the discontinuity of man's psychic states and the simultaneity of contradictory states in man's soul and mind. In alluding to the whole problem of doubles, Gide refers to Stevenson's *Dr. Jekyll and Mr. Hyde.* The double nature of Dostoevsky's characters is substantiated by his view "that nearly all men are polygamists; I mean that, doubtless by way of satisfying the complexity of their natures, they are almost all capable of several attachments simultaneously" (D, 123). But Gide seems wrong in denying that jealousy plays an important role in Dostoevsky's work. Gide's own account of *The Eternal Husband,* in which he speaks of the doubtful hero's intense jealousy, refutes this.

Gide then proceeds to expound the ethics of Dostoevsky, which seem to him the essence of the Christian religion: "The individual triumphs by renunciation of his individuality. . . . He who surrenders it shall gain the fullness of life eternal" (D, 150). This doctrine seems to Gide the antithesis of the teaching of the Roman Catholic Church: "I know no author at once more Christian and less Catholic in spirit" (152). Gide, like Dostoevsky, has a low opinion of the intellect. The temptations and problems of the intellect are evil, perhaps even suggested by the Devil. Intellectual rebels such as Raskolnikov ultimately are bankrupt. *Notes from the Underground,* with its depreciation of thinking and paralysis of action, is rightly considered the keystone of Dostoevsky's whole work (160). Dostoevsky's heroes are all distrustful of the intellect, and are even poor in mind, like Myshkin. Gide notes Dostoevsky's affinities to Eastern religion and constantly contrasts him with Nietzsche, whom Gide sees as Dostoevsky's most important antagonist.

Gide is fascinated by the figure of Kirilov, who he thinks carries on his shoulders the entire plot of *The Possessed*—surely an overstatement, as Stavrogin is the book's center. Kirilov seems particularly Russian to Gide, for whom nationality is a presupposition of any universal statement. The book concludes with Gide's assertion that Dostoevsky viewed Russia as offering herself as a sacrifice, like Kirilov, for the salvation of Europe and the rest of humanity. Later, Gide saw no contradiction between his acceptance of Dostoevsky and his own new adherence to Communism, which was, however, short-lived. A visit to the Soviet Union, which he described in *Retour de l'U.R.S.S.* (1936), disillusioned him completely when he saw the chauvinism, the anti-Semitism, the xenophobia, and the inheritance of tsarism. But Dostoevsky remained for Gide a propounder of self-reliance, individuality, and freedom. No doubt Gide ignored many sides of Dostoevsky, but his lectures give a clear, straightforward, and sympathetic exposition of most of Dostoevsky's ideas. His emphasis is on the psychologies and types of men depicted in Dostoevsky's books, as well as the religious message, which at that time Gide still accepted.

JACQUES RIVIÈRE (1886–1925)

Rivière was born in Bordeaux in 1886. He was secretary of the *Nouvelle Revue Française,* founded by Gide in 1912, but as a soldier in the First World War he was captured and spent nearly four years in a Swiss internment camp. After his return he became the main editor of the *NRF,* a post he held until his premature death in 1925. Rivière's first collection of essays, *Etudes,* appeared in 1911 and established his fame. His reputation was not enhanced, however, by his book on his war experiences, *L'Allemande* (1918), which was interpreted as an apology for Germany because it described his favorable, or at least gentle, treatment in the prisoners' hospital. Rivière was raised as a Catholic, and in 1913 he became an ardent believer and regularly took communion, partly through the influence of Paul Claudel, with whom he engaged in an elaborate correspondence though they had met only briefly in 1907. Rivière has attracted interest not only for his religious development and his correspondence with Claudel and Gide, but also as the brother-in-law of Alain-Fournier. Rivière was also an early propagandist for Proust, whom he met in 1914 and reviewed favorably from the outset, at a time when Gide, who was then a reader with the publishing house of Gallimard, had rejected *Du côté de chez Swann* for publication.

Rivière's spiritual struggles, his attempt to understand his own being and feelings, led him to investigations into himself and his contemporaries that could be called psychoanalytical in an unorthodox sense. He wrote favorably on Freud, combining his philosophy with that of Proust: both were interested in the relation between life and suffering, desire and anguish. Several essays on Proust and Freud circle around the concept of the new psychological novel. "Marcel Proust et la tradition classique" (1920) is still somewhat reserved. Rivière complains about a certain intellectual heaviness in Proust's sensibility and treats the books as a study in feelings, a discourse on the passions, almost as a treatise on psychology. A later essay, "Marcel Proust et l'esprit positif" (1923), judges him mainly in terms of his "immense, tranquil and natural skepticism." There seems to Rivière a certain difficulty in Proust's character, a suspiciousness that made him a terrifying revealer of himself and others, an unmasker of hypocrisies, an enemy of illusions, particularly of love. Rivière's ideal is sincerity, which he considers, however, the exact opposite of life: we must choose between the two. Still later, in "Une Nouvelle Orientation de la psychologie," Rivière severely criticizes Proust's interpretation of Swann. Proust's identification with Swann reveals an inner deficiency. Proust denies or fails to recognize any deep contact between humans, which eliminates the dramatic element from life and from consciousness. Oddly enough, Rivière argues that Proust is "classical" in his offensive against the enormous psychological mask disengaged by romanticism. In spite of his many reservations about Proust, Rivière was highly effective in spreading his fame, especially through a special issue of the *NRF* in March 1923.

My emphasis here on Proust, however, has been somewhat misleading, as both *Etudes* and *Nouvelles études,* published posthumously in 1947, contain a wide range of essays: on Baudelaire, on painters such as Ingres, Cézanne, and Gauguin, on Claudel, on the composers Franck, Wagner, Debussy, and Mussorgsky. A curious piece in the earlier collection is devoted to Wagner's *Tristan und Isolde,* in which Rivière insists monotonously that Tristan experiences immense despair and a somber but triumphal entry into nothingness.

Etudes culminates in a long section devoted to André Gide, who is obviously the master Rivière admired almost without reservation and whom he imitated in style in a way that sometimes sounds like parody. First there is a long chapter on Gide's style which distinguishes between his first stage, represented by *Les Nourritures terrestres* (1897), and his second, represented by *L'Immoraliste* (1902). Rivière is anxious to emphasize that Gide is no abstract thinker, that in his work form and content fuse, and that his style is imbued by some kind of "interiorism." The early style is lush and rhetorical, the second is of calculated simplicity. Rivière shows how Gide's books are composed very differently from volume to volume. In the earliest, *Les Nourritures terrestres,* the continuity seems to be broken, and at every instance the book begins again. These early books are held together by a general tone and some emotional unity; they are designed according to inner movements. The section on style is followed by a section Rivière calls "the soul," which emphasizes Gide's immense love of restless movement and the apparently conflicting irony and detachment that become most prominent later. Rivière sees that in many ways *L'Immoraliste* is a self-portrait, though he does not press the relation. Isabelle, the heroine of the story, especially shows Gide's soul. The section concludes with a eulogy of Gide, who seems perfectly clear and optimistic in his praise of the world and the joy of life, reminding Rivière of Nietzsche.

Another long portion of *Etudes* is devoted to Paul Claudel, whom Rivière expounds in great detail: his doctrine and theology, his teaching about original sin and redemption, and his curious ideas about the soul of man after death. Rivière admires Claudel immensely and sees that his conversion to orthodox Catholicism was prepared as early as 1906–07.

The oddest essay is the one on Baudelaire (1910). I find it hard to recognize this Baudelaire, though Rivière quotes supportive lines from his poetry. Baudelaire is seen as somehow strangely harmless, even idyllic and pastoral, pitying the humble and lowly and celebrating a hidden paradise. There can be no greater contrast than that between the Baudelaire expounded by Erich Auerbach and that by Rivière. Only in a footnote does Rivière allude to the power of evil and Satanism, which he seems to dismiss simply as the bad taste of the time. Rivière interprets Baudelaire's poetry as full of love and hears in it the voice of an angel, a wise and desperate angel, which has no illusions but even in speaking of horrible and violent things is able to preserve an immense love of life. The essay, which is the first in *Etudes,* begins by evoking an image of Baudelaire walking along the street preoccupied with his debts and hoping to help pay them off by writing articles for money. Or perhaps, says Rivière, he is thinking

up some practical joke to play on the friend he is going to visit or working mentally on one of his poems, arranging words "that don't go well
together." Rivière admits that he might have known no more of Baudelaire than his fantasies: "But he had a soul. He carried it in the midst
of his life. It was present when suffering occurred, or pleasure. It was
ready to feel everything; not with dilettantism, but like a genuine poor
soul made for pain and trouble. The soul, this thing unknown in us, and
which spies on us in all our adventures! Back home, he would let it free.
It spoke wisely, it spoke of its ordeals without violence, without shouting.
It made its self-examination" (*E*, 10–11). This scene, which visualizes the
soul as distinct from the body, inhabiting it as an almost totally strange
entity, is Rivière's central theme. Man and work have nothing or little
to do with each other. But he did eventually modify this view and even
replaced it with an intense concern for biography.

This early volume hardly prepares us for Rivière's later writings, which
are more lucid and have abandoned the enthusiastic celebrational tonali-
ties and the attempts to imitate the authors discussed. A bold and striking
essay called "Reconnaissance à Dada" (1924) is not about Dadaist writings,
which are dismissed as not only unintelligible but also unreadable. Rivière
is, however, deeply impressed by the Dadaists' comfortable acceptance
of the idea of contradiction. He accepts the view that we shelter within
us several consciousnesses. Contradiction, according to the Dadaists, is
simply not possible: "The existence of the individual is sufficient reason
for everything that he expresses. A word, a gesture, possess their necessity, their explanation, their rightness, from the fact that they come from
myself: the one cannot conflict with the other" (*NE*, 201). The Dadaists
accept incoherence. They know that art is "trick" and "artifice" and thus
needs "suppression, combination, arrangement." They quite consciously
give up the creation of works of art. Rivière admires their boldness, their
"stroke of genius," as the Dadaists "leave art, go into an indefinable region of which it can only be said that the aesthetic quality ceases to exist
in it" (202). Tristan Tzara is quoted as saying that they write "beyond the
rules of Beauty and its dominion." The Dadaists escape from all values,
"whatever the category." They think it sufficient to do precisely everything that goes through one's mind. They worship paradox and do not
try to resolve it. "The immediate corollary of these principles," writes
Rivière, "is that language has no fixed or definite value" (203). It is not
a means for the Dadaists, but a "presence," and the question of syntax
is accompanied by a sort of mysticism. Rivière does not distinguish between Dadaists and surrealists, and he quotes André Breton, who accepts
a whole series of misunderstandings that inevitably show that a poem is

not absolutely solitary. Writing is a private act and not really necessary. It seems to the Dadaists an attempt "to deceive others, to tempt them into some mirage" (205). "Before the Dadaists we lived in reticence," claims Rivière. Somewhat surprisingly, Rivière brings in Flaubert and his main critic, Albert Thibaudet, who thought of him as a striking example of an author who "thinks by themes." Rivière agrees with Thibaudet's emphasis on Flaubert's statement "In *Salammbô* I wanted to give the impression of the color yellow. In *Madame Bovary* I wanted to produce something that would have the color of the moldiness in corners where there are wood lice." I wonder whether such petards of Flaubert can be taken seriously. Rivière wants something quintessential, something completely free from ordinary subjects. He singles out in particular Rimbaud, whom he calls the greatest French poet. Rivière admires Mallarmé for writing poems that are built out of groups of words. But Dada went further. It concluded in favor of "linguistic nothingness" (215). Rivière picks up a saying of Breton: "It is inadmissible that a man leave any trace of his passage upon the earth." Rivière wants to change all art: "We must give up subjectivism, effusion, pure creation" (216). But then he turns again and hopes for a rediscovery of the creative process, its power of transformation. The writer "will always remain an inventor, a deceiver, but he must neither appear to be one nor know that he is one." And he ends with optimistic praise of the writer: "The unreal world that it is his mission to bring to life must be born of his diligence in reproducing the real one, and the deceit of the artist must no longer be engendered by anything but the passion for truth" (217). This essay, which initially appears nihilistic and sympathetic to the abolition of art by the Dadaists, ends as a celebration of a new truth for art. It is another one of Rivière's strange ambiguities.

The title "Le Roman d'aventure" (1913) is somewhat of a misnomer as the essay discusses symbolism at length, and recommends indulgence in the pleasures of art. Rivière wants a new novel written according to classical principles, an "adventure novel," which he contrasts with symbolism: "The symbolist writer was in a state of memory; [the writer of tomorrow] will be in a state of adventure" (*NE*, 265). We might be baffled by the term "adventure novel." It is postulated simply as an enemy of the French psychological novel of such authors as Paul Bourget and Anatole France, and Rivière evokes the shades of such incongruous foreign writers of adventure novels as Dickens, Dostoevsky, Defoe, and Stevenson.

What strikes a reader most is the amazing, densely written system of metaphors that Rivière at first uses to describe symbolism, which he boldly identifies with subjectivism and relativism; it is absorption in the ego of the writer. Symbolism is declared to be dead; we can only admire it from a distance as a spectacle (*NE*, 245). "The symbolists," writes Rivière, "knew no other pleasures than those of tired people. They came at the end of a century in which people worked hard; they lived in an atmosphere of the end of a day. Not without reason was symbolism linked to idealistic philosophy." Rivière continues with his account of symbolism:

> The sensible world was reduced to a legendary tapestry decorated with nobly fantastic motives, which seemed to be stretched over the interior divisions of the brain. The people who lived in the middle of this dream naturally could taste only ideal pleasures. They closed themselves in with their spirit and amused themselves by fingering one by one all their trinkets, moving them about and then putting them back in order. Their present is nothing more than the end of a long past. They loved above all to remember; they spent their time poking about in their memory and, letting the cloudy sky lean against the window-panes, they wondered in silence, with a timid gaiety, at the little flames that had been rekindled. (246)

The essay goes on constantly in that vein and style, with no reference to any specific text or author or picture or piece of music. It is a fantasy with abstract concepts. The new literature that Rivière advocates, the adventure novel, breaks with all these moods and ideas; it breaks with romanticism, which he detests as not only out-of-fashion but as "truly an inferior art, a sort of monster in the history of literature" (*NE*, 251). Rivière sees the new literature as classical in the sense of getting away from any emotion, any feeling. He admires Descartes as the originator of this new attitude that asks for perfection, for completion. In a note he quotes the painter Poussin: "I have neglected nothing" (254n). To Rivière this is the essence of classicism, the sense of having arrived at some unity that is identified with truth. Without naming a single book or writer, Rivière develops this ideal of a new work that will be all-embracing and aim at "perfect clarity and differentiation" (259). This original insight into the nature of the world is menaced by the whole development of the modern mind, the decay of religion, and the loss of contact with primitive art. Suddenly Rivière produces the example of Brueghel the Elder and his painting *The Census of Bethlehem*. Rivière sees the same decay in music—in Wagner, who drowns all emotions in fluidity, and even in Debussy. The only composer who meets his demands is Johann Sebastian Bach, who has everything in its place with perfect clarity. Rivière sees that revolution in Stravinsky's *Le Sacre du printemps*. In painting he defends Cubism in theory, though he dislikes the actual products.

In the new novel that Rivière imagines, he would want the whole of reality presented in the greatest detail. He would not mind an enormously long novel. The very year of this essay, 1913, Proust submitted *Du côté de chez Swann* for publication. Rivière develops his conception of the characters in the new novel. They will be living beings: the reader will perceive the reason for everything a character does. The character will be grasped in his essence, but also in the most trivial behavior, his ways of drinking and eating. Rivière speaks of the "ignorance and naïveté" of the new novelist, but sees novelty in "the orientation toward the future, toward unknown things" (*NE*, 272). The new novel will "advance by shots [*coups*] of novelty" (273). Rivière reflects that this new adventure novel has two basic kinds: in one the adventure is the form of the work rather than its matter; the second type is the "psychological novel of adventure" (274). Literature here surpasses painting, which is immobile. A novel can put the point foremost and can also ask the simple question: Is he, the hero, good or bad? Or simply: What is he going to do? This new psychological novel, says Rivière, did not yet exist in France, but Dostoevsky had accomplished it, particularly in *The Raw Youth*.

The emotion of the new adventure novel is defined in direct opposition to poetic emotion. Rivière comments harshly on oratorical and sentimental poetry and stresses that "the emotion that we must demand of the adventure novel is, in contrast to poetic emotion, that of waiting for something, of not yet knowing everything, it is that of being brought as close as possible to the edge of that which does not yet exist" (*NE*, 277). Mixed in with the emotion that the adventure novel gives us there is always intelligence. Rivière does not praise the current psychological novel, particularly those of Bourget. It is all merely theory, a description of a pathological case. But he has some hopes for the collaboration with the detective novel, and he refers to Edgar Allan Poe as "the inventor of this sort of novel" (281n). At last he mentions a few titles that he seems to admire, adventure novels by Dickens and Dostoevsky, Defoe and Stevenson. He notes particularly Stevenson's story "The Ebb Tide" (1894). The names are all those of foreigners, but Rivière thinks that the moment has come when, like so many times before, French literature will "rejuvenate" itself through its borrowings, by drawing from the blood of the foreign novel (282). He ends by saying that he would require an exposition of the technique of the new novel of adventure, but he never published anything of this sort.

Most of the later writings in the *Nouvelles études* are reviews praising particularly the Russian ballet that had appeared in Paris, defending Marcel Proust against insensitive attacks, and reflecting briefly on such matters as Catholicism and nationalism. Rivière in his best pages certainly represents the culminating point of French metaphorical criticism.

It is a mistake to call it "impressionism." Rather it is an elaborate, often quite abstractly designed metaphor describing either the works he knows and accounts for or the works he would like to see written. The abstract schemes, as in the essay on the adventure novel, do not, however, survive close inspection.

RAMON FERNANDEZ (1894–1944)

One of the main trends of French literary criticism in the early twentieth century could be labeled "philosophic criticism," though it often became identified with a mystical conception of poetry and certainly thought of poetry as a way to religion. As far as I know, the earliest book in this tradition is Ramon Fernandez's *Messages* (1926). Fernandez has disappeared from sight, from histories and encyclopedias, largely it would seem because he was a collaborator during the German occupation. He was born in Caracas, Venezuela, in 1894 to Mexican parents and died on 3 August 1944, possibly by suicide, just before the Allies captured Paris. Fernandez was extremely well known in his time. *Messages* was translated into English by Montgomery Belgion in 1927, and T. S. Eliot printed it in *Criterion* and commented favorably on it. Perhaps through Eliot, or perhaps directly, Wallace Stevens also became interested in Fernandez, and Stevens's poem "The Idea of Order at Key West" culminates in an address to "R. Fernandez." In a letter to Bernard Heringman of 1 September 1953, however, Stevens says: "Ramon Fernandez was not intended to be anyone at all. I chose two everyday Spanish names. I knew of Ramon Fernandez, the critic, and had read some of his criticisms but did not have him in mind" (*Letters of Wallace Stevens*, ed. Holly Stevens [1966], 798).

Messages begins with an essay on philosophic criticism which tries to supplement Albert Thibaudet's distinction of three kinds of criticism— academic criticism, criticism by artists, and spoken criticism—by adding philosophic criticism. Fernandez thinks that Thibaudet's scheme is quite insufficient and that it ignores the "spiritual dynamism" of the time. He explains his conception of poetry as an "imaginative ontology" and asserts that "the fundamental problem of aesthetics is no other than the metaphysical problem of being, but transposed to the plane of the imagination" (*M,* 7). Fernandez defends an irrationalist philosophy that presents an artistic object as "an independent complex of which the organic unity and cohesion result from a synthesis ensuring it a life of its own" (12). He alludes to Eliot's "objective correlative" and looks for a philosophical substructure of the work in the body of ideas that supply an extension of the essential character of a work, by relating them to the problems of general philosophy that may be implied in them. Fernandez is obviously very much under the influence of Bergson, objecting to anything that could be called abstract art, but also appealing to *Erlebnis,* to human experience. He thus rejects both pure art, in the sense of hedonism, and mimetic art, which is merely descriptive of external reality. He also rejects intention: "Soon a confusion fatal to common sense has occurred between the work *as it is created* and the work *as it is explained,* that is to say, imagined and willed by the author" (24). A sharp distinction is drawn between the work of art and commentary, even by the author himself, who is not obliged to explain his own work. Some of the later essays in the book make much of this contrast between intention and performance, in Balzac and Stendhal in particular. Fernandez thinks that he gets rid once and for all of the whole problem of cause and effect, the whole question of the biography of the poet. A work of art is conceived of as resting on intuition, in the sense, I suppose, of Bergson. The poet is a creator who need not merely reproduce reality. Fernandez attacks impressionism, which he interprets as largely an attempt to minimize man's creativity and reduce him to a passive receptivity. He considers Proust's novel an example of such art, which falls fatally into sensation. In a later book, entitled *Proust* (1943), Fernandez is harshly critical of Proust for his passivity, which is also, of course, moral. Proust, along with much modern art, is criticized for egoism and even solipsism. Deliverance from self is to Fernandez the best way toward truth. The creative share is decisive in its affirmation of existence, which must not, however, be affirmed abstractly, but in movement and change.

The rest of *Messages* gives perceptive examples of the method, branching out into new subjects such as the distinction between plot in a novel and *récit* (tale) in a novella, particularly in Balzac. Fernandez more or less agrees with what he did not know at the time, that is, the Russian Formalists' definition of *recital* as "a presentation of events which have taken place and of which the reproduction is regulated by the narrator in conformity with the laws of exposition and persuasion" (*M,* 63). Fernandez even alludes to Sterne and Gogol and clearly describes the difference between a novel and a *Novelle* (in the German sense) with this term *recital* (*récit*), which "tends to the substitution of an order of conceptual exposition for the order of living production, and of rational proofs for aesthetic proofs" (65). Fernandez emphasizes Balzac's distinction between these two types of narration, which then is also illustrated by how differently characters are conceived in recitals in contrast to those in novels.

Fernandez in many ways anticipates the later view of Balzac as a nonrealistic writer: Balzac's characters are "not conceived in order to live, but in order to serve as pawns in a maneuver leading to a tactical result" (84).

The essay on Stendhal, "L'Autobiographie et le roman," shows clearly how false it is to identify the ego known positively in the works with the person whom we may reconstruct from autobiographical writings. The literary work of art is conceived as "a synthesis obedient to specific laws of combination and development, absolutely distinct and different from the synthesis of our *human interests*" (*M,* 101). Again Fernandez alludes, in obvious agreement, to T. S. Eliot's famous article in which the mind of a poet is compared to a "shred of platinum" (102). The artist should try to eliminate all elements of the ego that may have remained in his writings as survivals from his life experiences. In fiction, all personal significance becomes "simply the concrete material, the human stuff, so to speak, of creation" (113). Autobiography—and, of course, biography of an imaginary being—is composed, Fernandez admits, of "living elements borrowed from the nature and experience of the author," but they become a work of art only when superseded by a fictional distancing (113). Fernandez cites examples from Stendhal's autobiographical book *Vie de Henri Brulard* (1890), where Stendhal is compelled to isolate the real residue of his recollections and to purify them of any imaginative construction. Stendhal recognizes the gulf between an autobiography and a real work of art. Emotion is not expressed but only embodied in an "objective correlative," again borrowing the term from Eliot. Studying a work of art independently of biography, "irreducible to psychologism," we discover the underlying conception of life, even though it may not be expressed at all, or perhaps could not be, in a work of art. We discover "the inclinations and postulates of the mind" (136).

The article on the art of Conrad is surprisingly unfavorable about Conrad's "elaborated impressionism," which is interpreted as lack of thought or intellect. Fernandez comments on the "opacity" of Conrad's characters and scenes, which "is never completely dissipated" (*M,* 148). He makes the usual comments on Conrad's underlying attitude, according to which man is "only a feeble gleam in the storm, but this gleam resists and this gleam is all" (151). Conrad is here made to sound like Bertrand Russell.

Also somewhat surprising is the essay "Le Message de Meredith." It was written when Meredith was at the height of his fame; I myself wrote an article in Czech examining the novels with great sympathy ("George Meredith," *Listy pro umění a kritiku* 3 [1935], 178–84). Meredith provides a contrast to Proust. According to Fernandez, Meredith's characters are alive, they develop, whereas those of Proust are composed "with recollections even as our grandmothers covered cushions with strips of hangings" (*M,* 159). Fernandez admires extravagantly Meredith's optimism and considers him a poet who "thinks directly with images" (171). A "sacred sense of life" never deserts him (175). Fernandez prefers Meredith to Stendhal, who seems to him only a "clever player." His psychology appears to Fernandez "schematic and superficial" when compared with Meredith's (179). Meredith, says Fernandez, "beheaded romanticism" (190). Fernandez ends resoundingly by comparing Meredith with Goethe as a writer who "deserves that one should learn a foreign language merely in order to read him" (190).

While Fernandez of course admires Proust, the essay entitled "La Garantie des sentiments et les intermittences du coeur" builds on the unfavorable remarks in the Meredith article. According to Fernandez, the work of Proust "does not erect a hierarchy of values, and it does not manifest, from its opening to its conclusion, any spiritual progress" (*M,* 194). Proust's attempts to arrive at a spiritual life fail in comparison with Cardinal Newman's *Grammar of Assent* (1870), to which Fernandez devotes a separate essay. In an interesting note on Proust's relationship to Bergson, Fernandez rightly observes that Proust is often "clearly anti-Bergsonian" and that he "tends to be oriented toward a *spatialization* of time and memory" (210 n. 8). Fernandez has a low opinion of Proust's constructive powers, remarking that "he sews recollections together and leaves the seams showing" (219).

The essay on Jacques Maritain is essentially a rejection of Maritain's Thomism, which Fernandez thinks is just an apology for intelligence in the sense of reason. Maritain, he writes, gives no arguments and his book *L'Art et scolastique* is only "a profession of faith" (*M,* 274).

Finally, three shorter essays are grouped under the collective title "Notes sur trois aspects de la pensée moderne." The first is devoted to Freud, whom Fernandez considers quite insufficient in his defense of normality and his explanation of man by his past. The second piece severely criticizes Walter Pater for his aestheticism and ridicules the famous passage on "The House Beautiful" as "the sentimental projection of a synthesis of all human powers elaborated and sublimated by culture" (*M,* 294). The last of the "Notes" is devoted to the classicism of T. S. Eliot, which Fernandez considers unoriginal: "Nothing appears to distinguish Eliot's thought from that of Lasserre and of Benda" (297). He sees Eliot's affinity with Bergson's finest pages in his *Introduction à la métaphysique,* which seems to Fernandez the best formulation of the new classicism. The article was written before the appearance of *The Waste Land,* and Fernandez adds a note calling Eliot's latest poem "very remarkable," but reproaching it "perhaps with having too great an autonomy of the aesthetic synthesis" (304 n. 9).

The essay on Eliot concludes the original version of *Messages*—which has not been greatly modified in the new 1981 edition by the addition of several articles, which were collected from Fernandez's contributions to the *Nouvelle Revue Française* during the short time he completely moved into political writing. From our point of view, the most interesting of these additional essays is a piece on Thomas Hardy (1928) whom Fernandez greatly admires but, oddly enough, considers some kind of superior Zola, mainly on the basis of *Jude the Obscure*. There are some interesting reflections on space and time in Hardy's novels, though I find it difficult to accept the view that Hardy's pessimism is determined by his technique. "The more tragic the scene, visually tragic, and the more impressive it is," argues Fernandez, "the more it accumulates duration in the present" (*Messages* [1981], 184). According to Fernandez, Hardy's novels represent "the conflict between modern thought and ancient sensibility" (184). "Modern thought" means, I suppose, Schopenhauer, while "ancient sensibility" means the folklore that Hardy draws on so importantly in his description of the life of English peasant farmers. Hardy seeks to "justify his thought by the representation of a way of life and a collection of circumstances that remain exterior to that thought in so far as it pretends to conceive and formulate a law of man" (188). As always, Fernandez tries to construe a conflict between intention and performance.

Another essay of interest is "Poésie et biographie" (1929). It defends biography, though Fernandez would like to keep a writer's biography separate from his work, as he argues in his articles on Stendhal and Balzac. Still, he says, every work "clearly expresses a certain 'response' to life" (*M*, 210), which as such cannot be generalized and is only valid for those who are by their personal adventures led to invent such responses. An odd essay is devoted to Maupassant (1942), whom Fernandez defends against those who dismiss him as a second-rate writer; he particularly admires, I think rightly, the novel *Bel-Ami* at a time when Maupassant was completely under a cloud. The last essay in the volume, dating from June 1943, is devoted to Maurice Barrès, who seems to Fernandez "the last great writer of the nineteenth century alongside Anatole France" (306). Fernandez admires concreteness and has little use for the theories that remind one of *Blut und Boden*.

It seems unjust to ignore a man who has had such influence, in English as well as in French, and who so clearly represented the aim of the new

criticism in France—to reject impressionism and turn instead to a definition of the philosophical implications of literature.

BENJAMIN CRÉMIEUX (1888–1944)

Benjamin Crémieux was born in Arbonne in 1888. He took part in the
First World War and was involved in Allied propaganda in Italy. In 1919
he became chief of the Italian bureau of the French Ministry of Foreign Affairs. Crémieux collected some of his contributions to the *Nouvelle
Revue Française* under the title *Vingtième siècle* (1924). The most important piece in the volume is an excellent essay on Marcel Proust, which
was written, one must not forget, during Proust's lifetime and thus is one
of the first perceptive general views of Proust, emphasizing his psychology and commenting on his picture of French society. Crémieux is very
good in defending Proust against the then usual charges of his lack of
composition and even disorder. He argues that Proust is well organized
and that his series has a central systematic preoccupation with forgetting
and remembering, and particularly, of course, with involuntary memory. Crémieux also stresses that Proust is concerned with the continuity
of our selves and that he thinks memory allows us to touch the real, the
durable. Thus memory is interpreted as a transcendental, almost mystical, function of the mind. Crémieux reflects that Proust has a dynamic
style which at the same time, surprisingly, is not at all oratorical. He sees
Proust as breaking with the romantic tradition and opening the way to a
"new classicism" (94). He attempts to define Proust's limits by saying that
"God is absent in Proust's work, but he brings the divine to earth" (96).
Proust expounds a wisdom that has "a simple morality of abstention." It
is, finally, a Stoic or even Christian abstention. Crémieux ends, somewhat
too simplistically, by saying that in this "'earthly comedy' . . . love represents Hell, the 'world' Purgatory, and art is Paradise" (98).

In 1928 Crémieux received his doctorate of letters at the Sorbonne
with his thesis *Essai sur l'évolution littéraire de l'Italie de 1870 à nos jours* (also
published in 1928). In the same year he published a smaller, more popular version of his Italian studies, called *Panorama de la littérature italienne
contemporaine*, which is phrased much more openly and even bluntly. It
begins by saying that the fall of Rome in September 1870 is a great literary date because it marks the end of the "national messianism" which
for centuries had haunted the best Italians. "Unity was achieved," writes
Crémieux, "a new era began. . . . What has [literature] learned to do since
that great day?" (11).

Crémieux thinks that this culmination of the process of unification posed completely new problems for Italians. Italian literature, he asserts somewhat surprisingly, is really two literatures. One is the spontaneous secular literature of the peninsula, which grew up locally, largely around a little capital, a literature that is sometimes in dialect and that incarnates the spirit of every single province and thus reflects the Italian nation and its basic feelings most closely. It is skeptical, prudent, resigned, and pacific to the extreme of weakness or softness. The other literature is the literature of an ideal, abstract Italy that lives in opposition to the mediocrity and servitude of daily life, in opposition also to the scattering of local talents. It always seeks inspiration in memories of an ancient Italy unified by Rome and finds its raison d'être in the hope for a political and moral regeneration of the whole peninsula. It cultivates a classicism that is sometimes cold but also often animated by patriotic fervor and by indignation at the conditions of contemporary Italy. It is the grand Italian literature, a collection of works of civic, national, and religious inspiration. It has a utilitarian, moralizing quality that contrasts with the more natural Italian spirit, which is anarchical and an enemy of constraint. Crémieux argues that the greatest Italian writers are in a permanent opposition to the spontaneous genius of the nation. The great men of Italian literature are not representative men. They are heroes and behave in contrast to the people. They present an exception and not the rule. They are in contradiction and not in accord with the race to which they belong. Vincenzo Monti is more "Italian" than Dante and Leopardi, just as Boileau is more "French" than Pascal or Descartes. Nowhere is the divorce between the heroes and the masses so manifest as in Italy. All the great writers go against the current of the Italian people. Dante, the Petrarch of the political poems, Machiavelli, Parini, Alfieri, Foscolo, Leopardi, even Manzoni and Carducci, are finally all writers of combat. They are great, isolated men, often castigating without pity their compatriots.

These two literatures are opposed not only in matter and inspiration, but also in essence. The regional literature shapes its forms on current life. It reflects places and epochs. Its language is borrowed from spoken language and reflects the social order in its incessant evolution. In short, it is a "modern" literature in the sense the word is used by romantic critics. The national literature, on the contrary, is all classical, one could say mythical. It borrows from antiquity the myth of a unified Italy. It lives by the myth of an Italian language that is common to the whole of the peninsula, an ancient language conceived as incorruptible, distinct from oral language, even sometimes, one may say, an allegorical language, a language of lyrical meditation, of synthesis and explication, which plunges into the heart of reality, a language so extreme in its reserve, so absorbed by itself, that it is often difficult for foreigners to have access to it. The classicism of the great national Italian literature does not render it universal. Rather, by holding to a strict nationalism, it is one of the most closed literatures and therefore one of the most untranslatable, whereas the other, the regional and popular literature, easily crosses frontiers. All literary works exported successfully since the fourteenth century reflect the easy and spontaneous genius of Italy, as with the popular tales and the *commedia dell'arte,* often under a more stylized form as in Ariosto and Goldoni. Sometimes writings draw on European inspiration, which is then elaborated in the Italian manner; even classical perfection is embellished and purified, as in the *Canzoniere* of Petrarch or in the *Orlando furioso* of Ariosto, which encompasses Carolingian and Arthurian romance. Crémieux cites also Marino's huge poem *Adone,* which condenses preciosity, the poems of Leopardi, which concentrate a Roman pessimism, the novels of D'Annunzio, a mixture of Nietzsche and Tolstoy, and the dramas of Pirandello, which are powerful echoes of contemporary relativism.

Though these Italian writers draw on the European background, what is absorbed is usually only a part of their work and not always the most important part. Their works are often misunderstood in Europe. For instance, Petrarch and D'Annunzio are only selectively understood: the love sonnets of Petrarch, D'Annunzio's novels and dramas of blood lust and death. Outside of Italy Petrarch has come to represent insincerity, empty and purely formal art. Ariosto is considered simply a burlesque writer, and Boccaccio a pornographer. Machiavelli is disfigured as a political theorist. Of D'Annunzio it is the least authentic part, the most declamatory, that triumphs abroad. As to Leopardi, who in Italy is rightly considered the great classical poet of the nineteenth century, he is dismissed abroad as a wild romantic. Italian literature is constantly presented to foreigners with a strange distortion. Its greatest works, its essential classics, are rejected in favor of the most cheerful, the most modern writers; since the sixteenth century attention has been paid mainly to rhetoricians and to clowns.

The attitude of the Italians toward their heroic works, which are obscure and abrupt, is not very different. The great national works might inspire during a period of crisis, might lift people up, but in normal times the less rigorous and lightest works are always preferred. Crémieux tries to answer the question he hears in Italy: Why is Italian literature not popular in Italy? Among the principal reasons, he argues, is that Italian literature is not a mirror of society, like French or English literature, but a literature of models, and a literature of isolated authors rather than of schools. The individualism of literary production in Italy is both its greatness and its weakness. There is no influence of courts or salons, which is of first importance in French literature. The literary schools in Italy, such as Petrarchism or the *précieux* or general academism, have not created any vital works. All the great Italian writers are marked by reaction against the literary schools of their time. There is no evolution of a genre as one finds in France—for example, the evolution of tragedy from Alexandre Hardy to Racine. In Italy one finds nothing comparable to the writers in the *pléiades* of romanticism and symbolism.

The one apparent exception—the continuity that stretches from the earliest Venetian chronicles to Ariosto by way of Boccaccio and Pulci—does not contradict such a view but, on the contrary, confirms it, for the very reason that it is in the domain of popular literature. From the day that Ariosto formed this centuries-old chivalric matter into a classical shape, it has evolved no more and has fallen silent. The great writers of Italy appear like meteors. They create an artistic universe and forge their own language, then disappear, leaving behind no disciples who might continue in their vein. Only bad imitators persist. Crémieux thinks that Italian literature probably has more geniuses and talents of the first order than any other literature, but that Italy offers a literary climate inhospitable to the development of secondary talents. Without a radiating center like Paris and social strata capable of supporting a vast and ordered literature, critical judgments in Italy are completely anarchical and partisan. All the great authors were engaged in literary battles, fending off a mob of enemies. Manzoni, a Lombard gentleman, and D'Annunzio, a cosmopolitan aesthete, are the exceptions. In Italy it is considered a show of strength to call oneself *maleducato*. There is in literary circles something like a snobbery of crudeness. Italian writers of the nineteenth century often came from the countryside. They were peasants by origin, in contrast to the French urban bourgeoisie. More recently, another contrast is striking: in France, few writers have attended university, whereas in Italy many noted writers are professors. Even those like D'Annunzio and Papini, who are not university trained, can in a sense be called autodidacts in that they try to compete in erudition with the professors. In Italy, antiquity is not exclusively the "bread of the professors." The taste for antiquity blends with the classicism of national pride in the Roman heritage.

In the later chapters of *Panorama de la littérature italienne contemporaine* Crémieux surveys Italian literature between 1870 and 1920, proceeding by fairly conventional methods and giving rather standard opinions on individual authors, sometimes surprisingly harsh. He criticizes both Manzoni and Carducci, whom he sees as the main figures of Italian literature of the later nineteenth century, for bombastic rhetoric and conventional Catholic piety. Crémieux's loves are Verga and Pirandello. He admires D'Annunzio as a virtuoso, but shows distaste for his boastful nationalism and his exploits during the war. In his thesis, Crémieux formulates his view of Italian literature forcefully and concisely. "Italian literature," he says, "of all European literatures is the one least subject to any creative currents and is richest in contradictions and sudden surprising changes" (*Essai sur l'évolution littéraire de l'Italie,* 312).

Crémieux's last book was called *Inquiétude et reconstruction: Essai sur la littérature d'après guerre* (1931). This is an ambitious attempt to characterize French and occasionally Italian literature since the end of the First World War. The book formulates the idea of a pendulum swinging from side to side that also regulates literature. Every epoch has a different hierarchy of genres and a different grasp of the world and man and different myths. Crémieux is obviously a strong defender of tradition and of humanism, and he condemns or is shocked by what he considers the nihilism of the new times—the view that nothing lasts and possibly nothing exists. He speaks of a "universal mobilism," of a breakdown of standards; relativism seems to him the dominant novelty, which was first sharply formulated by Dadaism. Crémieux argues that irrationalism has triumphed. The influence of Gide and Bergson dominates. Bergson teaches us to go beyond intelligence and to experience the *élan vital.* Gide teaches us to break all chains, as did Nietzsche. Freud becomes the defender of the libido, which he sets in the unconscious. Proust and Pirandello show the utterly continuous variations of the human person. Proust asks whether the coherence of the human "I" is assured by the phenomenon of involuntary memory. Gide has taught us permanent *disponibilité* and has depicted acts for which he cannot find a cause and which thus remain purely gratuitous. Dostoevsky has become important in telling us that sentiments have a double face, are ambivalent and dissociate the personality. Crémieux thinks that in 1930 some kind of stabilization came about. He distinguishes among three main kinds of literature: a literature of effusion, a second literature of aestheticism and play, and a third of inexhaustible analysis of a superabundance of images and ideologies. And everywhere they go in search of sincerity.

Crémieux proceeds to speak of a crisis of universalism. He sees community among people breaking down and ideological frontiers hardening. The Communists exclude the bourgeoisie from the proletarian paradise; the Fascists reject the liberals. The bourgeois person, however, affirms himself as a bourgeois and spreads his culture to people who actually detest it. Much is made of the contrast of generations. Crémieux argues that people born between 1892 and 1898, who experienced the First World War, are very different from those born later. He speaks of a crisis of the idea of individual liberty and quotes at length Jules Romains on Unanimism, which assumes a psychic continuity among men. But Crémieux thinks that this is not a general condition. There is plenty of solitude, for example, Proust and Malraux. Crémieux describes the theory of surrealism; he feels it was anticipated and more clearly formulated by Dadaism, which denies progress and any possibility of social improvement and at the same time hates conservatism and proclaims revolution. "War at any price" is its slogan. This absolute negation by Dadaism and surrealism is, however, in literature clearly opposed or refuted by what Crémieux calls "literature of evasion," for which Rimbaud is the great model—Rimbaud interpreted as a totally free adventurer. The literature of evasion is represented by the enormous travel literature of the time. This evasion is also shown in the great interest in childhood and children and in attempts to return to the primitive. Crémieux then takes up what he considers the "breakdown of the self." He thinks that the cult of sincerity has not succeeded, but has brought about a breakdown or dissociation of personality. Crémieux considers inner monologue and all of psychoanalysis to be attempts to answer the question "Who am I?" and to probe the individual. He speaks of an "integral psychologism." In the end, Crémieux argues that Europe is becoming one and that a new humanism and what he calls "totalism" is emerging. Crémieux was obviously influenced by Spengler's *Decline of the West* and the books of Keyserling, and he holds out an extremely optimistic view of the near future.

This optimism must have been shattered by the rise of Nazism. Crémieux published nothing more, at least in book form. As an official at the Ministry of National Education Crémieux often had been sent abroad, even as far as South America. But after the German invasion of France, though he was in Geneva in March 1941, he refused an offer of asylum and reentered France. He apparently followed his son into the Resistance and aided him in undermining the police and the Vichy administration. Crémieux was arrested in April 1943, tortured, and then transported to various camps in France. He was finally deported to Germany and died in Buchenwald in April 1944, a few days before the liberation by British forces (Eustis, 74).

ALBERT THIBAUDET (1874–1936)

In the 1920s and early 1930s Albert Thibaudet seems to have assumed a position similar to that of Sainte-Beuve in the fifties and sixties of the nineteenth century. His regular articles in the *Nouvelle Revue Française*, his books on Maurras, Barrès, Flaubert, Bergsonism, and Valéry, and particularly the 1926 expanded version of *La Poésie de Stéphane Mallarmé*, which had gone almost unnoticed in its original 1912 edition, established a great reputation. After his death the *Histoire de la littérature française de 1789 à nos jours* attracted much respectful attention, and his *Réflexions*, collections of his articles from the *NRF*, kept his memory bright right up to the Second World War. The comparison with Sainte-Beuve seems not inappropriate if one thinks of the range of Thibaudet's work and of the unmistakable similarity of temperament, the tone of detachment, fair-minded justice, and toleration extended to the most diverse kinds of writing. Thibaudet, in frequent asides, speaks himself of his "literary pantheism," his "pluralism," his "multilateralism," his "anti-cyclopism" (*Cluny*, 30; *RL2*, 137, 16, 172)—meaning his disapproval of a one-eyed view of the world—and one can speak of Thibaudet's frank Epicurean-ism and skepticism as one can speak of Sainte-Beuve's. It is not by chance that Montaigne was a revered model for both. (Thibaudet had been pre-paring a book on Montaigne for many years which, though incomplete, was published posthumously in 1963.)

A stillness has, however, settled around Thibaudet. A number of the *NRF* was devoted to his memory and there are two books on him, one by an American admirer, Alfred Glauser, the other by an Australian scholar. There is a brilliant article by Leo Spitzer, "Patterns of Thought in the Style of Albert Thibaudet," which, oddly enough, remained unknown to the two writers of the books on Thibaudet. While the silence of the French since the war is ominous, the almost total disappearance of Thibaudet from the horizon can, in part, be accounted for easily enough. Much of his writing for the *NRF* concerns ephemeral publications of the time. Some of his main topics, Maurras, Barrès, Amiel, do not today excite much critical interest. Many of his writings are studded with allusions to people, books, and characters in books that today need commentary almost as much as Dante's allusions in the *Divine Comedy* or Pope's in the *Dunciad*. Some of his stylistic mannerisms may seem tiresome: the *calembours* and obvious rhetorical figures and particularly the extraordinarily luxuriant undergrowth of his metaphors. Many of these are pleasant and witty but others seem merely fanciful and ultimately pointless. Spitzer and Glauser describe and analyze them admiringly as examples of "creative" criticism.

But there is little illumination in comparing Hugo's work with a triumphal arch or the Iberian peninsula, Lamartine's with the Greek archipelagos, or Chateaubriand's prose with the contours of the Gulf of Naples. We may smile at hearing Sainte-Beuve compared, punningly, with the meandering river Doubs, but what is achieved in comparing Amiel's journal with Lake Geneva, Gide's with the Arve, and Valéry's with the Rhône? (*FL*, 137–38, 134, 46; *HLF*, 155–56, 151, 53; also "André Gide," *Revue de Paris* 34, pt. 4 [1927]: 757).

One could also argue that much of what Thibaudet wrote has been superseded. The book on Mallarmé is overshadowed by the massive efforts of the past decades, from Kurt Wais's stout volume to Jean-Pierre Richard's *Univers imaginaire de Stéphane Mallarmé*. The little book on Valéry is outdated simply because Valéry wrote so much after its publication. Thibaudet shares the fate of many pioneers.

Still, all this cannot be decisive. A critic is not forgotten because of the exuberances of his style or even the inevitable obsoleteness of some of his themes and concerns. He is neglected or condemned because of the perversities of his theories, the obtuseness of his taste, the mistakes of his rankings, the narrowness of his information, the falsity of his outlook. And here Thibaudet cannot be found wanting. His near oblivion seems simply mistaken. Thibaudet needs rehabilitation by a restatement of his principles and ideas, which, in substance, are sane and true.

Thibaudet holds a sound and flexible theory of criticism. Contrary to frequent assertions that he was an "impressionist"—or as he quotes Julien Benda speaking of himself, "un debussyiste intellectuel" (*FL*, 464; *HLF*, 528)—Thibaudet upholds an intellectual ideal of criticism. It should, he repeats over and over again, translate what is conceived in poetic terms into intellectual terms. Criticism, he says, can be understood as "a kind of comparative philology which establishes the roots and changes common to the two languages and techniques" of poetry and philosophy (*PV*, 135). Criticism changes the concrete into the abstract, obeying "the inevitable necessity of its vocation: like Faguet, to hold up the poet somewhere in the woods, and ask him for his 'ideas'" (153). Thibaudet chides André Barre, the author of a thesis on symbolism, for abdicating his task. He quotes him as saying that Verlaine's poetry is music—"it can be felt but cannot be analyzed." "Excuse me," Thibaudet interrupts, "but this is your job as a critic. What you feel strongly you must analyze profoundly" (*RL*, 16). All poetry, Thibaudet insists, is finally intelligible; even Mallarmé's and Valéry's always makes sense. He attempts to understand them, to read their poems as he would read any other poems. Valéry's *La Jeune Parque* has its logic, "which criticism and its technique are allowed to put

into the form of an argument" (*PV*, 126). Still, while insisting on this task
of analysis and translation, Thibaudet knows its perils. He is afraid "to
substitute for the profound clarity of an image the semi-obscurity or the
shadow of an idea" (160). Art and thought, literature and philosophy, are
and will remain distinct.

Analysis, close reading, interpretation, and translation into intellectual terms are, however, only some of the procedures of criticism. It requires two others: pure criticism and historical criticism. Pure criticism
is Thibaudet's term for what we would call theory of literature: "Not a
study of works but of essences: of genius, of genre, of the Book" (*PC*,
139). A theory of genres is the main problem of this higher criticism. It
is the problem of universals, the problem of the Platonic ideas which, he
decides, must now be seen rather in the Kantian terms of a regulative
idea. Genres are obviously nothing fixed or stable: "To create in a genre,
means to add to a genre: to change its form, to surpass it. . . . The genre
is behind the artist; it is not in front of him" (188).

In practice, Thibaudet's concern was mainly with the novel as a genre.
The drama is mostly used only as a contrast. He wanted to write a book
that would culminate in a metaphysics of the novel, for which he devised
an ingenious classification by themes based on empirical psychology. He
would begin with the novels of pleasure and pain and then consider types
of novels according to the psychological motives they use: the impressionism of sensation, the world of sentiments and passions, the problem
of conscience (here also of analysis), the problem of memory (the autobiographical novel and the diverse *recherches du temps perdu*), the play of
association of ideas and the imagination (Giraudoux), the world of intelligence and of genius (the intellectual novel), chapters on the will and on
free will (the novel of destiny and the novel of action), then the moral
problems, with the rich world of *romans à thèse*. Only part of this project
is carried out in the essays collected in *Réflexions sur le roman*, which study
also, with great subtlety and perception, the technique of the novel, the
role of the narrator, the use of tenses, the sense of time. Thibaudet always
takes an undogmatic view of different theories. Thus he considers the
objective novel, with the narrator absent or concealed (Flaubert, Maupassant) as aesthetically superior to the older type, but he warns sensibly
that "the essential thing is not to have one or the other theory but to
have genius, with either one or the other" (*RR*, 24). He contrasts the well-
composed French novel with the loose works of Tolstoy and the English
novelists, recognizing that these are simply two different aesthetic ideals,
which he explains in terms of their different feeling for time.

Thibaudet has read and studied Bergson and constantly uses his concepts. *Durée* is a key word in his writings. It is used in many different contexts, which allow considerable freedom and ambiguity. It is the individual's sense of time; it is the time of a work of art; it is the stream of history; it is the survival of the past in the present. Thibaudet believes that no two people live the same kind of time and suggests that a more advanced psychology would find the formula for each person's time, an idea that must have been the starting point for the speculations of Georges Poulet. Thibaudet merely indicates that every man puts a different accent on his present, past, and future, and he gives examples that seem also to make historical distinctions. Chateaubriand and Bossuet lived in the past, Stendhal in the present, and Nietzsche and Mallarmé in the future.

But usually Thibaudet employs the concept of *durée* for the sense of time implied in a novel. He contrasts, on this point, the French novel and the English novel. The French novel tends to imitate French tragedy, to eliminate or at least to foreshorten time, whereas in the English novel (and in the French exception, Stendhal's *La Chartreuse de Parme*) there is a seemingly perfect isochrony between the unfolding of the novel and the normal unfolding of life. "The time of the English novel," he asserts, "does not undo or destroy, it constructs" (*RR*, 95–96). Thus the English are supposedly incapable of writing short stories, while Americans have succeeded in that form. One wonders about the truth of such generalizations on national characteristics. Thibaudet's own example—the contrast between a novel by Bourget constructed in theatrical terms and novels such as *The Mill on the Floss* (his particular favorite among the highly admired novels of George Eliot) and *Anna Karenina*—recognizes that the majority of great European novels are not "rhetorical or dramatic compositions, but life creating itself through a series of episodes" (184). Thibaudet himself ends the essay by speaking of the new French roman-fleuve, of *Jean Christophe*, and of *Les Thibaults*. He hints at art here dissolving into life: "At the theoretical limit of the novel is a pure scheme of life just as at the limit of the theater there is a pure scheme of movement" (*GF*, 89).

Thibaudet also tries another classification of the novel, allowing him to rank novels according to their artistic value, which at the same time is an approach to the true sense of life. He draws distinctions between hazard, chance, and destiny shaping a novel, with novels of hazard ranked as the lowest kind, novels of chance such as those by Dumas and Dickens second, and those of destiny ranked highest. In *Wilhelm Meister* and *Madame Bovary* "the events are modeled on the feelings, the external modeled on the internal, the line of chance modeled on the line of destiny" (*RL*, 239).

The other kind of criticism is historical criticism, which must be nourished by a knowledge of literary history without which no critic can become part of literary history. The main task of historical criticism is to "establish sequences of writers, to compose families of the mind, to make out the diverse groups situating and balancing each other in a literature. A work can be classified in a series, considered within a literary order, in a family, with its antecedents and descendants" (*PV*, 1). The echoes of Sainte-Beuve's article on Chateaubriand and of Ferdinand Brunetière's defense of the order of literature are obvious, but we must not identify Thibaudet's outlook with either Sainte-Beuve's or Brunetière's on this point. Thibaudet is not interested in the psychological typology that Sainte-Beuve demanded, nor does he approve of Brunetière's evolutionary theories. Rather he conceives of the past of literature in two complementary ways: either as geography or as genealogy.

The critic contemplates the map of literature, which Thibaudet assumes to be something seen, something out there somehow. He has a rather surprising attitude toward the rankings and situations of a past time. For instance, he would not want to assign Benjamin Constant a higher place than Mme de Staël though he recognizes that *Adolphe* is a better book than any of hers. One must, he says, "preserve in literature the character of an order, respect the places attained, refuse to abandon literature without ranks to the anarchy of personal tastes" (*FL*, 50; *HLF*, 56). Thus Thibaudet disapproves of Léon Daudet's indignation at the overpowering conceit of Hugo: "*Le Satyre* is there as Versailles is there. Cheops probably lacked humility. But with a grain of humility he would not have built his pyramid" (*RC*, 124). Hugo is looked on as a fact of nature, like a mountain that we have to climb.

Criticism becomes literary geography not only in this metaphorical sense but also literally, as Thibaudet has a strong sense of the locality from which French writers came or where they lived and wrote. There is "un massif breton" in French literature consisting of Chateaubriand, Lamennais, and Renan. There are two Burgundys, one northern and one southern. Northern Burgundy produced "the powerful, eloquent and virile Saint-Bernard group, the Bossuets and Rudes," while the southern part is the country of Lamartine, Quinet, Prud'hon, and Greuze, whose temperaments are more feminine (*Cluny*, 10). Thibaudet's belief in the stability of regional characteristics goes so far that he explains Renan's skepticism by his maternal ancestors from Bordeaux, the country of Montaigne. In drawing a parallel between the art of Lamartine and that of Prud'hon he thinks it worthwhile to tell us that Lamartine's ancestors came from Cluny, Prud'hon's birthplace. Constant, who wrote the first novel of the battle of the sexes, is mysteriously linked with his compatriot from Lausanne, the general Jomini. One sometimes does not know whether this is merely fancy, wit, and display of farfetched information or whether it has to be taken seriously as a kind of *Blut und Boden* theory. Certainly the fact that Montaigne, Proust, and Bergson— all greatly admired authors—were half-Jewish seems to Thibaudet very important. All three exemplify the mobility, the restlessness of Israel— the tents which Bossuet took to be the symbol of the chosen people as opposed to the house on the Roman rock.

On occasion Thibaudet recognizes the tenuousness of such ideas. The sunny south, the succession Greece-Rome-Provence is "un mythe oratoire" (*RL*, 118). Neither can one say that southerners are frivolous; rather, the "Marseillaise" strikes him as sad. Thibaudet is not duped by such a notion as "French and German truths," which may be "a principle either of tolerance or of fanaticism" (*RL2*, 285). Though Thibaudet served in the First World War at the front and admired Barrès and Maurras extravagantly, he always tries to preserve a sense of equity toward the Germans. He defends, for instance, their classical scholarship and corrects obvious misinterpretations of Kant and German philosophy. Still, the "explanation of man by the earth, . . . the realism of a gardener" (286) appeals to him strongly. He dislikes an abstract rationalism such as that of Julien Benda, who, he complains, has a positive hatred for the peasant. Thibaudet self-consciously played the role of a provincial with deep roots in his native Burgundy.

Thibaudet's spatial and racial view of the history of literature (which may remind one of the Austrian Josef Nadler's parallel effort to write a history of German literature according to regions and tribes) is outweighed in practice by his sense of time and flux, by his Bergsonism. But Thibaudet is misunderstood if he is interpreted as a worshiper of an irrational Bergsonian flux. He always holds firmly to a space-time scheme of history. Bergsonism equals for him historicism. He expressly endorsed an identification of the two but refused to consider historicism merely as relativism, suspension of judgment, anticriticism.

Rather, Thibaudet recognizes the necessity of judgment in regard to the past and of a criticism of defense and prosecution for the present. He is by no means averse to making judgments himself: sometimes superlative praise or strong disparagement. To call Hugo "the greatest phenomenon in French literature" may be considered an objective statement, but to call his poem *Le Satyre* "the greatest of personal lyrics" and to speak of his love letters "as the most beautiful . . . in the world" seems extravagant (*FL*, 155, 134, 255; *HLF*, 176, 151, 253). Lamartine represents to Thibaudet "the high point of Christian poetry" (*FL*, 114; *HLF*, 128). Giraudoux's *Suzanne et le Pacifique* is "one of the most beautiful books ever written" (*RR*, 147; cf. 149). But he also says that Béranger is a bad, unreadable poet, that Quinet writes fourth-rate prose, and that Catulle Mendès's poetry is "a museum of specimens from the whole production of the Parnasse, where everything soon dissolves into refuse and rubbish" (*Revue de Paris* 40, pt. 4 [1933]: 119; quoted by Glauser, 274). A wickedly witty article condemns Henry Bordeaux as a facile and feeble writer. Throughout the *History* there is a constant ranking, grouping, and weighing. Implicitly, the way Thibaudet exalts Mallarmé and Valéry and draws the line of descent of French poetry through them is an act of judgment which merely by silence implies a refusal to acknowledge the claims of rival traditions and tastes.

Thibaudet says rightly, "There is no criticism without a criticism of criticism" (*PC*, 16). Many articles, chapters in the *History*, and the short, somewhat rambling *Physiologie de la critique* (1930) provide a fairly complete survey of the history of French criticism: unsystematic, often disproportionate, and on occasion unjust (as I think in the case of Hennequin and Zola), but far superior to anything that had been produced in France before. Thibaudet admires Sainte-Beuve, but criticizes Taine as a "methodical orator" with a "pseudoscientific imagination" (*RR*, 206, 200). His opposition to Brunetière and Faguet is pronounced, as they must seem to him doctrinaire, and he keeps up a running polemic against the *certitudiens* of his time: Maurras, Lasserre, Massis, and the very different Benda. Thibaudet admired Maurras excessively and devoted a whole book to his ideas, which he constantly sees, however, as a counterweight to his own preferences. The idea of rigidity, hardness, "muscle, vigor, density" (*Trente ans de vie française*, 1:67), permeates his discussion. Thibaudet cannot believe in the possibility of a return to classicism. Though he knew Greece and the Greeks and though he values classical tradition and training highly, he doubts that it is a panacea. The greatest French writers are not so deeply dependent on the classics as is often assumed. It may be true of Ronsard, Racine, and Chénier but not of Descartes, Corneille, and Pascal.

Thibaudet always tries to preserve a proper balance of judgment and taste: "It is a mark of intellectual cowardice to claim to understand everything while judging nothing, to let one's taste fall asleep and disappear, but one must also guard against launching, too indiscreetly and armed with an infallible blue pencil, an attack on authors" (*RL*, 136–37). Intelligence (meaning understanding) and judgment also must be kept in proper proportions: "A criticism of a Spinozistic kind, by which everything is understood as natural and necessary, would never judge, while a criticism which prides itself on pronouncing verdicts will play in the world of great works and great men the role of a comic Dandin [in Molière's *George Dandin*]. Criticism cannot but temper intelligence with judgment without going to the extreme of either one or the other" (*Intérieurs*, 132). Ultimately the critic will have to recognize the immense variety of literature, which should be treated as having two focuses of interest not exclusive of each other. The unique, the individual, the differences among works is one leading theme; the other is a "certain social sense of the Republic of Letters," "a sense of resemblances and affinities" (*RC*, 244), a grand net of comparisons. Criticism must attend both to the work and to its setting in history and society.

Much of Thibaudet's most original and—in its time and place—most meritorious work was an analysis of style in the widest sense, which went beyond the mechanical scholastic classifications usual in academic work and beyond the impressionism of the daily critics. His pages on Flaubert's use of "le style indirect libre"—which led to a curious exchange of letters with Marcel Proust (*GF*, 229 ff.; *RC*, 72–81; for Thibaudet's letter to Proust, see *RC*, 82–97; for Proust's "A propos du style de Flaubert," see ibid., appendix, 249–63)—and his analysis of Mallarmé's metaphors (*PSM*, 106–07), are highlights of Thibaudet's criticism. The concentration on the work itself is, in such contexts, completely free of biographical or social considerations. Thibaudet criticizes Lemaître's book on Chateaubriand for neglecting such a study of style. It seems to him as unreasonable as if a book on Rubens were to give less space to his manner of painting than to his embassies and two wives. The most appropriate method for a book on Chateaubriand (and, we must assume, on any writer) would consist in seeing his person and life purely as a function of his work. Thibaudet's own book on Mallarmé observes this principle. He refers to the man only when he refers to the author. Thibaudet's *La Vie de Maurice Barrès*, in spite of its title, has little or nothing to say of his life. We are even told that Barrès took offense at Thibaudet for not calling on him for biographical information (Davies, 68n). Nor did the usual psychological approaches to literature appeal to Thibaudet. He ridiculed some clumsy psychoanalytical studies as mere versions of the old method of allegorizing a text, and he was also wary of those who offer the "uncertainties" of scientific psychology as a solution to critical problems. Thibaudet does not believe in determinism: "In literature almost nothing happens which one could legitimately foresee" (*RL*, 184).

Still, this refusal to accept a biographical explanation of literature should not obscure the fact that Thibaudet actually wrote several intellectual biographies. The book on Flaubert—probably his best, and certainly his best-organized book—is based on a biographical outline that closely relates the work to the man, so closely indeed that the apocryphal saying "Madame Bovary c'est moi" is taken as the key to the interpretation of the novel. (The saying cannot be traced farther back than to René Descharmes's *Flaubert avant 1857* [1909], where it is reported on distant hearsay. It seems highly improbable that Flaubert could have said it, considering the many contemporary pronouncements of his detachment from and even distaste for the woman.) Thibaudet's intense, sympathetic interest in Amiel is mainly concerned with his psychic and moral life. The fine sketch of Fromentin in *Intérieurs* is set in a biographical frame, as is the inferior late book on Stendhal. The unfinished volume on Montaigne devotes many pages to his biography and psychology. In the *History* a chapter sketching Hugo's life in inflated heroic terms is a curious example of Thibaudet's stylistic mimicry. He often (though not always) writes about an author under the discernible influence of his style.

Thibaudet was always wary of any social determinism. He rejected Taine's triad—*milieu, race,* and *moment*—as well as his *faculté maîtresse.* They seem to him all "logical and ideological substitutes for life" (*RC,* 186; *PC,* 220). Many times he shows his distrust of historical, political, and social explanations. He rejects, for instance, the obvious idea that the decline of Ronsard's reputation in the seventeenth century was due to the order established during the reign of Louis XIV. He ascribes it rather to "the internal life of French poetry," to the rise of "prosaic poetry," which he refuses—somewhat obtusely—to relate to any social causes (*RC,* 22). He admits, quite generally, a coincidence of political and literary breaks but rejects an explanation by the action of politics on literature. It is explained rather "by the undercurrents they have in common, by a profound social trend in which they both partake and which they express in often quite discordant voices" (Davies, 182).

Neither does Thibaudet believe in the idea of literature as an imitation of life. Art is creation; man is *homo faber.* "Poetic creation does not hold up a mirror to the universe, but adds to the existence of the universe" (*PV,* 92). Thibaudet rejects Naturalism brusquely: "Talking of nothing but 'life,' it can picture only what in life anticipates death" (*RL,* 155). Thibaudet tells the story of a clown who won applause at a country fair by imitating the squealing of a pig. Next time a peasant substituted for the clown but was hissed by the crowd. He then uncovered a live pig he had concealed under his coat and which he had pulled by the ears to make it squeal. Still, the crowd rightly preferred the performance of the clown: "The truth of art is not the truth of nature. The clown had to convey better than the pig the illusion of a pig" (148). In the book on Mallarmé, Thibaudet ridicules those who criticized the poet for ignoring life. Life apparently meant "to some anarchist bombs, to others the purchase of some sociological books, to many more a salable novel or story, to certain others an administrative post and to the rest the forest of Fontainebleau" (*PSM*, 445).

Again it would falsify Thibaudet's position if he were seen simply as a formalist, a defender of art for art's sake, of pure poetry and the ivory tower. Actually, he sees literature constantly in relation to society, studies it as an index of society and as a social institution. Thibaudet was greatly interested in the social standing of the writer in France, in such institutions as the French Academy and the Goncourt Academy, the press and the publishing business. In a long paper, "Le Liseur des romans," he traces a history of the novel from the point of view of the habitual reader of novels, and in *Physiologie de la critique* he reflects on the different kinds of criticism in social terms: spoken, spontaneous criticism, the criticism of journalists, that of professors, and that of creative writers. Thibaudet would like to study the effects of reading, the influence of criticism on taste, and, like any reviewer of novels, he cannot avoid the questions: Is it true to life? Is it true to what we conceive to be the nature of man? In the case of the novel Thibaudet seems even to assume a scale of approximation in the rendering of life. But he never accepts determinism and hardly, so far as I know, alludes to Marxism.

Thibaudet's concept of literary history is also social; he considers it a particular trait of French literature to be "eminently social and sociable" (*RL*, 137). The plan of his *History of French Literature* is based on a sequence of generations. This has been hailed as a great discovery, but it is nothing new in literary historiography; as early as 1812 Friedrich Schlegel based his sketch of the history of German literature on a carefully devised sequence of generations, and since then the scheme has been worked out systematically for the nineteenth century in Germany. Thibaudet himself reviewed a well-informed book, *Les Générations sociales* (1920) by François Mentré, on the problem: he thought it rather demonstrated the difficulties of the concept. He is not taken in by any mysterious mysticism of numbers and recognizes the main obstacle to any clear definition of a generation in history: the absence of a marked beginning and end, the continuity of life, the imperceptibility of its changes. He sees also that the breaks are not the same in different countries. Still, he is impressed by the apparent regularities quoted by Mentré from Otto Lorenz: 1618, the beginning of the Thirty Years War; 1715, the death of Louis XIV; 1815, the fall of Napoleon; 1914, the outbreak of world war—thirty or so years later the series 1548, 1648, 1748, 1848 marked important historical events. But Thibaudet questions whether one can speak of "laws" and sees that there may be as deep divisions within a generation as there are between the generations themselves: each has its Right and its Left and even its extreme Left (*RL*, 120ff.).

In practice, in the *History* a generation is conceived as a group of people who at about the age of twenty undergo the impact of a great historical event. Thus the generation with which Thibaudet's *History* begins consists of those who were about twenty in 1789: Napoleon—whom Thibaudet values highly also as a writer—Chateaubriand, and Mme de Staël. The next generation is the one aged twenty in 1820: the youth of Musset's *Confession* who first formulated in France the concept of generation, Hugo, and the other writers born around 1800. Similarly, there are the generations of 1850, 1885, and finally that of 1914. Examining the series soberly it seems obvious that only the dates 1789, 1848, and 1914 constitute real turning points in French (and European) history, whereas 1820 and 1885 are chosen rather arbitrarily for literary reasons: 1820 as the approximate beginning of French romanticism; 1885 as the date of the emergence of symbolism as a slogan. The series, we may conclude disappointedly, coincides with the divisions pre-romanticism, romanticism, realism, and symbolism, and is an old rough-and-ready scheme.

Thibaudet, however, somewhat obviates this objection by introducing the concept of a half-generation, which allows for subdivisions in 1802, the return of the émigrés; 1832, the assumption of conspicuous positions by professors and publicists such as Cousin, Villemain, and Guizot; and 1871, the year of the Commune. The second of these seems arbitrary and hardly significant enough. Thibaudet himself suggested, on another occasion, that the thirty-three years of a generation might well be divided into groups of eleven ("Générations et expositions," *Nouvelles Littéraires*, 10 Oct. 1931; quoted by Davies, 177). Like every writer who makes much of the birth years of his subjects, Thibaudet runs into trouble with authors who began to publish late or who remained unknown in their time but greatly affected a younger group. Stendhal, born in 1783, appears in the *History* with the generation of the twenties, since his first novel, *Armance*, appeared in 1826; while Mallarmé and Verlaine, born in 1842 and 1844 respectively, appear with the 1885 generation, and Proust, born in 1871, with that of the First World War, as the first volume of *A la recherche du temps perdu* appeared in 1914. Such deviations give away the whole principle and show that one cannot distinguish biologically a series of people born in 1800–1833–1866, from one born in 1801–1834–1867, and so on. The only workable concept of a generation is a historical one, but this is hardly news. Thibaudet's *History* shows again that the historian has to struggle with the inescapable fact that he writes, so to say, in single file, one thing after another, though history is a process in which many things happen simultaneously. The literary historian must make compromises between chronology and groupings by genres or other affinities and cut through chronology to accommodate a long-active figure such as Hugo. The idea of generations is only an organizational device.

In spite of such schematic divisions Thibaudet has a strong sense of continuity, of flow, of imperceptible transitions, implied in his Bergsonism. On occasion he falls back on the concept of inexplicable genius, of sudden mutation, of "an accident of duration," for instance, when he reflects on the emergence of Rabelais and Montaigne (*RL*, 306). Often he labors, almost obsessively, the idea of doubles, contrasts, alternations either in sequence or in one single or approximately single time. Thibaudet picks these contrasts from almost anywhere. Some are metaphors as old as the succession of a golden age by a silver age, which seems to him a "law of nature" (*RC*, 46). Another is the rhythmic alternation of ages of feeling and intelligence, which is only a version of the old double: romanticism-classicism. Thibaudet uses it expressly or assimilates it to a contrast between a stable order and a Heraclitean or Bergsonian flux. Romanticism is defined as the enemy of "the old Aryan root, the fundamental square root of duration, stability, being, which is there, like a metallic flow, in the plenitude of that word 'state'" (*RL*, 36). In discussing some recent novels Thibaudet produces the distinction between a "really living work of art which is created as nature creates" and an "artificial, manufactured work of art as *homo faber* makes it." He confesses, obviously contradicting his usual vitalism, that he leans toward the second (*RL2*, 148). In the book on Mallarmé, Thibaudet develops another distinction at some length. Older poetry analyzes and describes human feelings, whereas the new poetry suggests and creates feelings. The writers of the seventeenth century were "experts of the human heart." With the new symbolists, "poetry has become the human heart itself" (*PSM*, 119). This seems an unnecessarily mystifying way of expressing an idea similar to that of the Nietzschean double of Apollonian and Dionysiac art. It is related to another fundamental dichotomy in Thibaudet's critical vocabulary: that of symbol and allegory.

Thibaudet knows that the distinction between symbol and allegory is of recent origin, and he quotes Kant's *Critique of Judgment* on the symbol. But he elaborates it rather in terms derived from Goethe and Carlyle. It is the contrast between mechanism and life: "Allegory presents itself to us in the form of a clear, precise, detailed intention while the symbol comes in the form of a free creation where idea and image are indiscernibly fused." He admits that all art has a tendency toward the symbolic, but insists that there is a difference: "The symbolic meaning of a work is the purer the more distant it seems from allegorical symmetry, the more it implies suggestion rather than expression." Besides, "the symbolic meaning of a work is the higher if the matter of the work, in its definition and concept, seems to carry less possibility of symbolization; the higher, then, if the symbol springs more directly from the particular, from the devices peculiar to an art, without the intervention of an intellectual generalization" (*RR*, 30–31). This contrast of symbol and allegory permeates the books on Mallarmé and Flaubert and also organizes much of Thibaudet's thought on the history of the novel from the *Roman de la rose* to his admired Giraudoux and Proust. Another related concept is type. Faust, Don Quixote, and Don Juan are symbols or types of humanity. Somewhat desperately Thibaudet tries to make out of Madame Bovary a type that would be more than a social type. The creation of types is always high praise for a writer: Bel-Ami is a type, as are Candide and Pangloss and even Ubu Roi. Tom and Maggie Tulliver in *The Mill on the Floss* seem to him "the two types of the English soul" (*RL*, 227, 253, 277, 107; *RR*, 33).

Thibaudet pursues these dualisms even further. Each genre has two styles: one "sharp," the other "flat"; one Doric, the other Ionic; one masculine, the other feminine. He contrasts Descartes and Pascal, Corneille and Racine, Bossuet and Fénelon, Voltaire and Rousseau, Lamartine and Hugo, and Balzac and George Sand in these terms. Amusingly, as a couple Chateaubriand and Mme de Staël show the same contrast, but with the literary and the real sex more or less inverted. There is only one exception. Molière remains alone in control of the realm of comedy.

This dualism seems to Thibaudet a feature peculiar to French literature, distinguished from the other great literatures of the West, which are dominated by single figures: Dante, Cervantes, Shakespeare, and Goethe. Thibaudet constantly refuses to choose between the two contrasting series in French literature. He is for both Voltaire and Rousseau: "I have the feeling of inhabiting a literature that lives under the law of the many or the pair" (*RL2*, 138). He disapproves of attempts to find the representative French author. He agrees with Charles Du Bos that Montaigne comes nearest to this idea, but in spite of great admiration, he feels that Montaigne is lacking in the exceptional and the heroic. Descartes, Corneille, and Pascal furnish the rational and the tragic: they break with average human nature. Thibaudet always returns to this conviction: "A nation is what cannot be contained in a single formula or permit a single point of perfection" (*GF*, 264). Thus Désiré Nisard, with his frozen ideal of the French spirit, and Brunetière, with his fixed concept of tradition, falsify and petrify history: "We need the Maurrases and we need the

Amiels, as we need the Barrèses and the Montaignes" (*RL*, 223). This universal tolerance, however, does not, Thibaudet insists, mean conciliation, a leveling of differences, a suppression of contradictions and conflicts that would only achieve a diminution of life: "In a world in agreement with itself individuals would become a scandal, an infirmity of being. God has done well in choosing a world of individuals" (*RC*, 190). Contrasting *Anna Karenina* with Turgenev's *Smoke*, he says characteristically: "In refusing to prefer one to the other, I do not surrender my judgment: there is something more beautiful than one or the other and that is one *and* the other, their opposition, and, hence, their harmony" (*RR*, 19). It is the same idea he expresses elsewhere even more strikingly: "In my impenitent bilateralism I refuse to choose, I do not abstain out of weakness, but with the firm decision not to decide" (*RL2*, 59). It is not an ideal of synthesis, of universal amalgation. It is rather the expression of the essence of historicism, which recognizes all the fantastic variety of the world and enjoys it in its conflicts and contradictions. Thibaudet successfully combines the two sides of historicism: a strong sense of individuality, particularity, uniqueness, with a constant feeling for the large historical processes in time. It is a view of literature and the world that is still immensely fruitful for its understanding, however much it may run counter to the fanaticisms, the limited preoccupations, and the possibly profounder metaphysics of our time.

4 : MARCEL PROUST (1871–1922)

PROUST, unquestionably the greatest French novelist of this century, was also a superb critic. His criticism attracted wide attention only in 1954, long after his death, with the publication of *Contre Sainte-Beuve*, a series of essays written in 1909. A collection of scattered articles from Proust's early days, *Chroniques*, had caused no stir when it was published in 1927. The Pléiade edition of *Contre Sainte-Beuve*, published in 1971, reprinted not only the 1954 collection but all the miscellaneous critical writings and fragments from notebooks and from Proust's voluminous correspondence. Two good books, Walter A. Strauss's *Proust and Literature* (1957) and René de Chantal's *Marcel Proust: Critique littéraire* (2 vols., 1967), both predating the Pléiade edition, assembled almost all of Proust's literary opinions so fully that there is no need to survey them here in detail. Proust speaks well in praise of the French classics and of the seventeenth century in general. The diarist Saint-Simon is obviously his favorite author and even model for some parts of his novel. Oddly, Proust is completely silent about the eighteenth century except for a few allusions to Voltaire. He praises two romantic writers: Chateaubriand and Nerval. In a late note he said, "Senancour, c'est moi" (see Philip Kolb, ed., *Textes retrouvés* [1968]; reprinted in *CSB*, 568–69). Proust was an avid reader of Balzac and was rather cool to Stendhal. He admired Vigny, Hugo, and Leconte de Lisle somewhat from afar. Baudelaire is for him "the greatest poet of the nineteenth century" (*OAL*, 9), and Flaubert appears as the great innovator and stylist in the art of the novel. Proust did not care for the Naturalists, the Goncourts and Zola, or for the symbolists (though it has been argued that he was a symbolist himself, first, I believe, in Valery Larbaud's preface to Emeric Fiser, *L'Estétique de Marcel Proust* [1933], 11). In the little article "Contre l'obscurité" written for the *Revue blanche* (15 July 1896; reprinted in *Chroniques* [1927] and in *CSB*, 390–95), Proust condemns symbolism as lacking life and depth (*CSB*, 394). He also composed a pastiche of Henri de Régnier, a mock-solemn description of a head cold. He has little that is strictly critical to say about his contemporaries: he indulged in gross flattery of some of his friends—Robert de Montesquiou and Anna de Noailles—and expressed distaste for Charles Péguy and Romain Rolland.

Almost all of Proust's criticism concerns French literature. There are, however, some pronouncements that show his interest in the novels of Goethe, Tolstoy, Dostoevsky, George Eliot, and Hardy. For a time Proust was attracted to Ruskin and translated (with help, as his English was deficient) *The Bible of Amiens* (1904) and *Sesame and Lilies* (1906). One could go on listing his opinions, but it is important to take into account their context. When Proust writes a letter he tries to please the recipient, or when he puts a literary judgment into the mouth of a fictional figure in the great novel series, it must be considered strictly as that of the fictional figure. The views of Mme de Villeparisis, or Bloch, or Bergotte characterize the speakers and cannot be taken necessarily as Proust's own. Proust sees the boy Marcel's enthusiasms for Théophile Gautier and George Sand with the hindsight of a matured taste and reconstructs his enthusiasms in his memory.

Proust is, however, not merely selecting and ranking authors and books. He expounds a very individual aesthetic. He discusses the role of the reader, asserts strongly the distinction between the writer as creator and the writer as private person, and analyzes style and grammatical devices in fiction. Even his casual pronouncements on individual authors often imply a theory of criticism as identification and a conception of a literary personality characterized by typical phrases, as Marcel explains to Albertine using Barbey d'Aurevilly as an example (see *RTP*, 3:382).

The aesthetics of Proust presents a problem to anybody who wishes to locate it in a history of aesthetics or to query its truth-value and applicability outside of Proust's personal experience. The fullest exposition is in *Le Temps retrouvé* as the narrator waits in the library of the duc de Guermantes. It serves as a justification of the whole enterprise of *A la recherche du temps perdu,* just about finished. It ties the beginning and the end of the series together. It is based on highly personal experiences: the *madeleine* dipped in tea, the steeples of Martinville, the uneven paving stones in Venice and in front of the Hôtel de Guermantes. They are not merely sensations, like déjà vu, which remind him of the past, but are conceived as returning him literally to the past, taking him out of time, giving him access to the essence of things and thus restoring a lost paradise. Proust insists on the involuntariness of this moment of restitution. It must simply happen. It cannot be evoked by an effort. It is not an emotional or intellectual device: it makes us see true reality, the essence of what is subjective and incommunicable. It is in the final analysis a mystical insight not transferable to any other human being except in the negations implied: the rejection of realist and didactic "engaged" art and of anything contrived by the intellect. Genuine art is always welling up from the unconscious.

It is, however, difficult to reconcile this basic view, which organized the whole great series, with Proust's admiration of much formal classical art obviously contrived by the intellect. The enormous stretches of conversations, discussions, and descriptions in his own great novel series cannot be accounted for by unconscious creation. One sees why Proust searches for precursors of his own almost mystical experience in memories, particularly of childhood, which he finds in Chateaubriand, Nerval, and Baudelaire.

Much has been written about the supposed Bergsonism of Proust's conception of memory, but there is little evidence that Proust was deeply marked by Bergson's thinking. They knew each other socially (Proust's cousin on his mother's side, Louise Neuberger, married Bergson in 1892 and asked the young Proust to serve as witness at the wedding), but Proust was never a student of Bergson, as is often erroneously asserted. We know of exchanges of compliments. In a letter, Bergson said of the first two volumes of *A la recherche du temps perdu* that "rarely has introspection been pushed further," calling the work "a direct and steady vision of interior reality" (30 September 1920; Henri Bergson, *Mélanges* [1972], 1326), and in an inscribed copy of *Sodome et Gomorrhe* (1922) Proust calls Bergson "the first great metaphysician since Leibniz (and greater)" but protests that "without rhyme or reason one speaks of my novels as Bergsonian" (see Jean Gritton, *La Vocation de Bergson* [1960], 40n). In 1920 Bergson and Proust served on a committee for the Prix Blumenthal, which awarded the prize to Proust's friend Jacques Rivière. In Proust's fiction his only direct reference to Bergson is in *Sodome et Gomorrhe,* in a conversation reported by the "Norwegian philosopher" (who seems to have been suggested by the Swedish philosopher Algot Ruhe; see Painter, 2:324–25) between Bergson and Emile Boutroux on the effect of sleeping drugs (*ARTP,* 1:934–35; *RTP,* 2:1016–18).

In spite of these friendly contacts, Proust always jealously denied any indebtedness to Bergson. In an interview given at the time of the publication of *Du côté de chez Swann* (1913), while emphasizing that his work is "dominated by the distinction between involuntary and voluntary memory," Proust even asserted that "this distinction not only does not occur in the philosophy of Henri Bergson but is even rejected by it" (*CSB,* 558). I can find no evidence for such an assertion, though I grant that the distinction may antedate Bergson's. A letter (*Correspondance inédite, 1903–14* [1948], 205) from 1910 indicates that Proust had not read *L'Evolution créatrice* (1907), but other evidence suggests that he had read in *Matière et mémoire* (1896) and in *L'Energie spirituelle* (1919). He regrets having to contradict "an admirable philosopher, the great Bergson," but Proust cannot believe that the soul survives the death of the body (see Megay, 22). In a late letter (June 1922), Proust denies any direct suggestion from Bergson for his attempt "to make appear to consciousness unconscious phenomena that had been completely forgotten and were sometimes located far in the past" (*Choix des lettres* [1965], 22).

Still, in spite of Proust's defensive rejection of any affinity with Bergson one must recognize the undeniable, very general resemblances between the two, simply in the preoccupation with time and memory, the distinction between the deep and the superficial self, the general depreciation of intellect, and the exaltation of art as a renewed vision of the world in its particularity. But what is central to Proust's view of the world and of art is utterly different and even contrary to Bergson's outlook. *Durée*, evolution, *élan vital* are all concepts of forward movement, of a cosmic optimism, of a joyous, almost physical expansiveness, whereas Proust seeks to escape from time, to make time come to a stop, to seize the privileged moments that would allow him to recapture the lost paradise. Proust's time is discontinuous and destructive. If we have to think of historical antecedents for Proust we must rather consider Neoplatonism, a realm of essences or, empirically phrased, a realm of signs that the writer has not only to decipher but to appropriate, even incorporate in his ego. Albert Thibaudet seems to me completely mistaken when he speaks of Proust's "ultra-bergsonism" (*Réflexions sur la littérature*, 1938). Bergson knew better. He wrote to Henri Massis that "the essence of Proust's thought is to turn his back on 'durée and the élan vital'" (Massis, *D'André Gide à Marcel Proust* [1948], 381 n. 80). If art is inspiration, even instinct, an act of identification with moments in the past, an escape from time that cannot be contrived by the intellect, then the writer is a man of intuition who reveals his deep self and not a reasoner who composes and plans a book. In *Contre Sainte-Beuve* Proust puts the contrast very strongly: "A book is the product of a different self we manifest in our habits." A writer's work is "the secretion of one's innermost life, written in solitude and for oneself alone" (*OAL*, 104). There is "a gulf that separates the writer from the man of the world," as "the writer's true self is manifested in his books alone" (106). Proust goes so far as to say that "any man who shares his skin with a man of genius has very little in common with the other inmate" (126). It seems to him "absurd to judge the poet by the man," and "as for the man himself, he is just a man and may perfectly well be unaware of the intentions of the poet who lives in him" (127). This sharp contrast between writer and man allows Proust to castigate Sainte-Beuve for his concern with biography, for his curiosity about a poet's religion, attitude toward nature and women, economic status, and so on. Proust particularly resents Sainte-Beuve's reliance on his own personal impressions or those reported by friends. Sainte-Beuve, Proust asserts, obviously does not understand that "there is something special about creative writing" (103), that "the poet's soul is a world apart, shuttered and sealed against all traffic with the outer world" (106).

It is tempting to consider these assertions about the gulf between the poet and the man as Proust's preemptive defense against the intruders who since have ferreted out details about his sex life and criticized his social snobbery. One should recognize, however, that Proust felt strongly the break he himself had made with his past as "man of the world" to become the writer who struggled in solitude with his deep self. His criticism of Sainte-Beuve is a justified protest against Sainte-Beuve's reliance on personal impressions. Stendhal appeared to Sainte-Beuve and his friends as an amiable, even witty man of the world, and Sainte-Beuve's low estimate of Stendhal's novels is colored by this image of the man. One can, however, plead mitigating circumstances for Sainte-Beuve's treatment of Stendhal. It is not true that Sainte-Beuve was unaware of the distinction between man and work. He grants expressly the possibility that "a man may leave finished works, monuments little understood by his contemporaries," who during his lifetime may have considered him merely a "distinguished eccentric" (*Nouveaux lundis* [1863–70], 3:110–11). However badly Sainte-Beuve underrated Stendhal, one cannot say that he did not discuss the novels on their own ground apart from the person of their author. Julien in *Le Rouge et le noir* appears to him an odious little monster, Fabrice shallow and vulgar, and *La Chartreuse de Parme* "a witty Italian masquerade."

Proust is entirely right in chiding Sainte-Beuve for underrating Baudelaire. Sainte-Beuve's attitude is that of a patronizing master to a naughty pupil. When the storm over *Les Fleurs du mal* broke, Sainte-Beuve wrote a public letter (February 1860) making excuses for not coming to Baudelaire's defense. Sainte-Beuve was, after all, the author of *Port-Royal*, a professor at the Ecole Normale, and a contributor to the *Moniteur*, the official organ of the government (see this *History*, 3:68). One might accuse Sainte-Beuve of a lack of civic courage rather than of a lack of critical perception. Sainte-Beuve praised *Poèmes en prose* and *Les Paradis artificiels* highly and was, possibly quite honestly, cautious about *Les Fleurs du mal* because of the censored poems. As a senator he could not appear to be a defender of immorality and homosexuality. It seems more a human than

a critical failing. In Proust's essays he assigned to himself and to Sainte-
Beuve positions that they did not actually hold. Proust, while asserting
in *Contre Sainte-Beuve* the gulf between poet and man, could not and did
not leave it gaping in his fiction. The whole great series is after all concerned with the lives of recognizable people and with a specific society
in a specific time. Inevitably it bridges the gulf, as the narrator Marcel is
only a slightly disguised Marcel Proust. Sainte-Beuve, although he made
theoretical pronouncements on the unity of life and work, saying "as the
tree so the fruit" (*Nouveaux lundis*, 3:13; cf. this *History*, 3:35, 282), and
had an avid interest in gossip and anecdotes, also studied the history of
thought, of religion and society, as well as literary history such as the history of genres and the classical tradition. Proust's essays in *Contre Sainte-
Beuve* score many points against Sainte-Beuve and display Proust's own
judgments on criticism and literary history. Proust is simply against the
concept of literary history as a process in time. He states that "in art there
is no such thing as an originator, a precursor (at any rate in the scientific
sense of the words): everything being comprised in the individual, every
man takes up the continuous attempt of art or of literature on his own
account, and for him the works of his predecessors are not, as they are for
the scientist, a fund of truth which those who come after may profit by. A
present-day writer of genius has it all on his hands. He is not much further forward than Homer" (*OAL*, 97). There is no progress in literature,
and every poet stands alone. Proust chides Sainte-Beuve for thinking of
literature as "a contemporary affair, and assessable by the standing of the
author. . . . So he differs from Emerson, who said one must hitch one's
wagon to a star. He tried to hitch his wagon to what was nearest at hand,
to politics, and to great social movements" (113). Proust, also in other
contexts, always showed an aversion to "engaged" literature, to literature
serving a temporary purpose. Only during the First World War did he
recognize that a writer might have overriding concerns, such as the war
and the future of his country.

The aesthetics of Proust in his preoccupation with memory and escape
from the bondage of time is so subjective, so subservient to the organiz-
ing principle of his great fictional series, that it can hardly function as a
measuring rod for concrete literary criticism. Proust's sympathies range
from such fact-bound, unmystical authors as Saint-Simon to a few poets,
particularly Baudelaire, in whom he could find anticipations of his own
nostalgia for the past. But irrationalistic aesthetics harmonized well with
Proust's theory of criticism, which amounts to a demand for identification
with the work criticized. Proust reflects on reading in an essay prefixed
to his translation of Ruskin's *Sesame and Lilies*, on the reading of a boy

who naïvely identifies with the hero of a tale such as Gautier's *Le Capitaine Fracasse*. But this is only a first stage. Reading should teach us to see: "Reading is the threshold of spiritual life; it can introduce us to it; it does not constitute it" (*CSB*, 178). Too much reading may even prevent us from descending into the deep regions of the self where the true life of the mind begins. Nor can the true life of the mind be found in erudition. Proust digresses on the illusion of finding true creativity in a trip to a Dutch convent to consult documents, though he admires erudition: Victor Hugo quoting Tacitus by heart, Schopenhauer collecting sayings on death from all over. Reading and knowledge produce the "good manners" of the mind. The romantics read the classics. Proust praises the appeal of old vocabulary and phrasing in Saint-Simon and Racine and concludes by evoking the two columns facing the lagoon on the Piazza San Marco, which continue "to delay their days of the twelfth century amid the crowds of today, in this public place where their distant smile still glows distractedly not far away" (194). The main argument of the preface directed against Ruskin, that reading should not play the preponderant part in life, is forgotten. Nearer to his own concerns, Proust concludes in *Le Temps retrouvé* (*RTP*, 3:949; *ARTP*, 3:911) that "every reader is the reader of his own self. The writer's work is merely a kind of optical instrument which he offers to the reader to enable him to discern what, without his book, he would perhaps never have perceived in himself." The function of literature thus seems to be limited to a lesson in training our own introspection.

Still, Proust is by no means unaware of the problems of criticism, which after all he practiced for many years in many forms: simply as a reviewer and also in his *Pastiches*, which are a form of criticism. They display not only his gift for mimicry and parody but also an intimate understanding, which could not have been merely instinctive, of the stylistic and thematic peculiarities of the authors imitated. In the preface to his translation of Ruskin's *Bible of Amiens* Proust formulates the aim of criticism as "helping the reader to feel the impact of an artist's unique characteristics," and even further, to reconstruct "the peculiar life of the spirit which belongs to every writer who is obsessed by his own special view of reality" (*Bible*, 10). Observing that this view of the world is expressed in the totality of the work, Proust defends his quoting of many passages from Ruskin's other works (and his references show that he at least dipped into many volumes of the Cook-Wedderburn collected edition): "To read only one book of an author, is like having only one meeting with that author. In talking once with a person, we may discern a special trait. But only on repetition under varied circumstances can one recognize the characteristic and essential" (9; similarly in "Journées de pèlerinage" in *CSB*, 75n). Proust ignores the possibility that an author might leave only one book, such as *La Princesse de Clèves,* which could still be accurately characterized. In practice, Proust is always searching for the individual voice, "the moral physiognomy" (*Bible,* 9) of an author which he feels in his rhythm and style. It is for him the first task of criticism. All writings about "the Man, the Writer, the Prophet, the Artist, the Impact of his actions, the Errors of his Doctrine . . . are beside the point for an understanding of the work, for the exact perception of a shade of meaning, however slight it may seem." He can conceive of a criticism that would go further. It would try

> to reconstitute the singular spiritual life of a writer haunted by special realities, his inspiration being the measure in which he beheld these realities, his talent the measure in which he was able to recreate them in his work, and, finally, his morality the instinct which, making him consider them under an aspect of eternity (however particular these realities may seem to us), has led him to sacrifice to the desire to comprehend them and to the necessity of reproducing them, in order to assure a durable and clear vision, all his pleasures, all his duties and even his very life—which has no reason for existence except as the only means of establishing contact with these realities, no value other than that which an instrument indispensable for his experiments might have for a physician. (11; not in *CSB*)

In theory, Proust's criticism demands that the critic recapture the vision of his hero. For instance, in an interview in *Le Temps* on the eve of the publication of *Du côté de chez Swann,* Proust stated that "style is in no way an embellishment, as certain persons seem to think. It is not even a matter of technique. It is—analogous to the way painters use color—a quality of vision, the revelation of a special universe which each one of us sees, which others do not see. The pleasure that an artist offers us is to acquaint us with more than one universe" (Dreyfus, 292). Elsewhere he writes: "Alternatively, we can say, style is for the writer as for the painter a question not of technique but of vision" (*ARTP,* 3:896). The aim of criticism is to "reconstruct the peculiar life of the spirit that belongs to every writer who is obsessed by his own special view of reality" (*PM,* 108–09). But in practice Proust does not attempt to reconstruct the vision of an author, rather he engages in an often old-fashioned method of criticism. He is quite an anthologist of single passages, confidently ranking lines and authors in ways that sometimes seem totally obscure or arbitrary. The whole essay on Baudelaire and Sainte-Beuve is such an anthology, which ranks passages first of all by calling them simply "beautiful" or "lovely" and with such sweeping statements as "The language of Baudelaire is one hundred times more powerful than Hugo's." Occasionally Proust remarks on an author's psychology, for instance, on Baudelaire's cruelty or on Balzac, whom Proust in many ways greatly admires but constantly characterizes as crude and slapdash. Rarely does Proust try to go further by providing stylistic and grammatical commentary and analysis.

The most famous of Proust's essays is that on Flaubert's style, which makes much of his use of French tenses. According to Proust, Flaubert has a particular grammatical beauty: "All portions of reality are converted in Flaubert into a homogeneous substance with vast surfaces which has a monotonous glitter. No impurity has remained in it, the surfaces have become reflecting areas" (*CSB,* 207). He calls Flaubert's grammatical use of tenses a revolution in French writing, comparable to Kant's revolution in philosophy (Strauss, 109). The imperfect is welcomed as a newcomer to literature, which Flaubert exploits in a novel way. Proust also says, extravagantly, that in Flaubert the conjunction "and" is never assigned the part in grammar to which it should belong but instead "marks a pause in the beat of the rhythm and acts as a means of dividing a picture into its parts" (*PM,* 134n). He sometimes complains about ugly, heavy adverbs in Flaubert and comments on the role of blanks and pauses. Proust is concerned at times with characters that he knows must have some universal import. He emphasizes that another law of life is to realize the universal or the eternal but to realize it only in individuals. He is particularly interested in the repetition of phrases, or what he calls *phrase-type,* in various authors. Proust is also interested in the use of tempo or time in certain authors, such as Flaubert, who conveys an impression of time and tempo in his metaphors. Sometimes Proust indulges in comparisons with music and painting that often seem farfetched or totally unprovable.

Surprisingly, the only two critical essays by Proust are the one on Baudelaire and the one on Flaubert's style. Everything else is a critique of Sainte-Beuve, and there are, of course, occasional remarks on living authors. He greatly flatters the countess de Noailles and his friend Montesquiou, and he has friendly words about Maeterlinck. But the primary interest of Proust's criticism is in his violent rejection of the identity of author and work, partially formulated in the essay on Sainte-Beuve and expanded in the remarks on Flaubert. A study of the early *Pastiches* would show that Proust had a considerable sense of the peculiarities of his contemporaries and their styles, and some of his parodies show a great gift for mimicry. But the essence of Proust's criticism is in the essays on Baudelaire and Flaubert and, of course, in the aesthetics that justifies the whole enterprise.

I have perhaps too strongly emphasized the contrast between Proust and Bergson and not quite clearly acknowledged the many general similarities. Both considered the writer to have a direct vision of nature: "He attempts to lift the veil from the habits, necessities of social life and language by making us face reality immediately." But Bergson is quite aware that the writer speaks of himself. Proust, like Bergson, emphasizes the individual and dismisses rationalization and argumentation in literature as inferior. Rather Proust examines the relation that art has to the sensations and memories that surround us, and he stresses the distinction between voluntary and involuntary memory. Bergson knows it too, and it was actually known to older, mainly German, psychologists, but in Proust it becomes a central concept in his aesthetics. The voluntary memory is common to all men, but the involuntary memory establishes for Proust the essence of a higher reality. He assumes that these essences are out of time and that by their impact on us without any presentiment we get in touch with the pure essence of reality. In experiencing these involuntary interventions of memory we establish contact with a life beyond evanescent daily life.

Unlike Bergson, Proust experiences a discontinuity in the stream of time. Proust wants to get out of time, but accepts that this can be done only through an act of grace beyond the control of the individual. His final decision is really in favor of a mystical view reminiscent of Neoplatonism, and its emphasis on passivity in waiting for an act of grace is reminiscent of the whole seventeenth-century movement called Quietism, as in such a writer as Fénelon, whom Proust read assiduously. Only in the last section of *Le Temps retrouvé,* published in 1926, is this notion expounded clearly, and therefore all commentaries published before 1926 are irrelevant. They do not see that the whole great series is based on a vision requiring a return to the starting point and that even in the very first pages of *Du côté de chez Swann* the promise of this return to a blessedness and even paradise is implied—though in Proust, one must never forget, there is a deep feeling for the evil and decay of the world, a pessimistic attitude that strikingly contrasts with the buoyant optimism of Bergson, who only rarely voices misgivings about the future of mankind. It is always difficult to discuss the great series without constantly having in mind that it is fiction, that many passages of philosophical or aesthetic interest are put into the mouths of characters whose views Proust cannot share. He sometimes distorts or parodies ideas quite explicitly. But in the very last chapter, "The Princess de Guermantes Receives," the author drops the pretense that the narrator is a fictional figure. And there are even passages where the concepts of time and aging and death are pronounced as statements that not only are accepted by the narrator but are simply expounded as if in a treatise outside of any fictional situation, which is after all quite minimal. The narrator is left stranded in the library waiting to be received by the princess de Guermantes, whose lowly origin is for the narrator a symbol of the wheel of fortune and the return to the past. The narrator wonders at the power of complete reconstruction possessed by time and marvels that "great tidal waves bring up from the depths of the ages the same sorrows, the same types of bravery," creating repetitions that seem to him precisely to demonstrate the irreality of time and the reality of a world outside of time. This extremely individual aesthetics, mystical at its core, is inapplicable outside of the mind of Proust and of little value for a history of criticism, however greatly we admire the introspection, the social picture, and the whole grandiose vision of this panorama of early-twentieth-century Paris, which everywhere reaches out into the persistent preoccupations of man throughout time.

5 : THE CATHOLIC RENAISSANCE

CHARLES DU BOS (1882–1939)

CHARLES DU BOS WAS A DIARIST, a preacher to himself, an *introspectif* in the tradition of Joubert, Emerson, and Amiel. His long struggle to find a haven in the Roman Catholic Church is fully documented in the nine volumes of his published *Journal*. The *Journal* also contains many reflections on literature, which Du Bos naturally used as a quarry for his published writings. If we wish to study Du Bos as a *literary* critic within a history of criticism, we should, however, look first at his books on Byron and Goethe, and at the seven volumes of his collected essays, *Approximations*. A critic should be judged by his formal pronouncements, not by the private jottings in his diary, which, in the case of Du Bos, are often self-depreciatory or at least self-critical.

Du Bos differs from his immediate French contemporaries in his strong affiliations with the English tradition (his mother was English, and in his diary he often slips into English in the middle of a sentence) and also in his considerable knowledge of German developments. His criticism has been described at great length by Charles Dédéyan under the appropriate title *Le Cosmopolitisme littéraire de Charles Du Bos* (5 vols., 1967).

Du Bos knew and admired Walter Pater in particular, and he was close to John Middleton Murry, whose book *Keats and Shakespeare* (1925) made a deep impression on him. Du Bos, like many of his time, adhered, at least in his early years, to the philosophy of Bergson. This philosophical orientation—intuitionist, irrationalistic—was strengthened by his acquaintance, acquired during a year in Germany (1904–05), with the *Lebensphilosophie* of Wilhelm Dilthey and Georg Simmel and by a fascination with Nietzsche. Du Bos had a wide knowledge of English poetry since the romantics, and he knew not only Goethe but also more recent German poetry, particularly Stefan George and Hugo von Hofmannsthal. His taste is definitely Edwardian in his predilection for the English aesthetic movement, for Shelley and Keats, and sometimes for writers such as Charles Morgan who we might feel have rightly fallen into oblivion.

But one cannot say that Du Bos had no critical standards, no likes or dislikes. He was a psychological, biographical, and often moralistic critic with definite standards of judgment and a well-defined point of view. He used all the procedures—expository, historical, evocative, and meta-phorical—that were available to him and other critics of his time. He had in particular one implied or openly expressed standard of judgment: "spirituality." It was at first a concern for the soul—in the sense of *Gemüt*, sensibility, delicacy—for the "chamber music of the heart," and often for what he called a "profane mysticism." Later it became more and more a concern for the immortal Christian soul, here on earth but preparing for the life to come. While Du Bos had, no doubt, very broad sympa-thies, it seems quite unwarranted to speak of his "renunciation of any personal life," of his complete passivity, submission to others, even empti-ness, and to construe a myth of identification which assumes an exchange of selves, as Georges Poulet does in *La Conscience critique* (1971). There is no evidence for a complete substitution of egos, nor can there be any.

Actually, Du Bos's two longest books, *Byron ou le besoin de la fatalité* (1929) and *Goethe* (1949, assembled from the essays in volumes 5, 6, and 7 of *Approximations*), are psychological biographies that show a considerable detachment from their subjects. The book on Byron develops the theory that he never escaped the predestinarianism inculcated by his Scottish up-bringing. Du Bos treats Byron as an "animal of the higher species" (*Byron*, 20), as a man who has committed the sin of pride and thus destroyed others and himself. Du Bos weaves a finespun web of psychological ex-planations for Byron's behavior toward his wife, which Du Bos defends fervently as "irreproachable," and for Byron's incest with Augusta, his half-sister (Du Bos's "Le Bonheur dans le crime" [207]), which induced remorse without repentance. One wonders at Du Bos's confidence in de-ciding when, how, and why women loved Byron or Byron loved them, or did not love them, "sincerely." The interest of this book is hardly lit-erary at all. It concerns the man and the Byronic hero. It treats much bad verse very solemnly and ignores, as Du Bos himself admits, the other side of Byron: his gaiety, his humor and satire. Despite all the warmly sympathetic, though strenuous and often turgid, analyses of Byron's feel-ings and those of his entourage, Du Bos always holds a final judgment in abeyance: "The absence of any interior life and at all events of any spirituality" in Byron (*Extraits d'un journal*, 149: 30 July 1923).

Du Bos applies the same standard to Goethe, and he too is found want-ing. These essays too are primarily a character study and moral biog-raphy. Du Bos depicts Goethe—in obvious contrast to himself—as "the anti-introspective genius" (*A*, 5:278). Du Bos makes much of Goethe's stu-dious avoidance of pain, again in contrast to his own "physical suffering,"

which in a later essay ("De la souffrance physique" [1937], in *Ap*, 1479–
95) he celebrated as a unique experience opening the doors of salvation.
Goethe lacks any sense of transcendence, lacks "soul"; even the word *Seele*
is rare in Goethe (*A*, 5:278). Goethe is an extrovert, all eye or all activity.
One essay, "Goethe before Goethe," examines Goethe's life as a student
in Leipzig in a strongly moralizing, disapproving tone. Another describes
Goethe's religious crisis after his return to Frankfurt from Leipzig and
interprets Goethe's leaving Frankfurt, when his Pietist friend Suzanne
von Klettenberg was dying, as "an incomparable symbol of life that does
not believe in death and of flight" (7:197). This "creative flight" is repeated in Goethe's relationship with Lili Schönemann, which is described
in another essay. It includes translations from Goethe's contemporaneous
letters to Auguste von Stolberg as well as a contrast between the hesitant
Goethe and the resolute Robert Browning, who rescued Elizabeth Bar-
rett, and an approving account of von Stolberg's late attempt to convert
Goethe to religion. Only once, according to Du Bos, did Goethe not flee
from love, and then it was too late. Du Bos interprets *Die Marienbader
Elegie* as reflecting Goethe's most passionate love, as a "nocturnal cry"
composed involuntarily, even against his will (6:140, 146–47). Du Bos
overlooks, however, the intricate formal complexity of the poem and
Goethe's own account of composing it in the coach leaving Marienbad.

The first ten years at Weimar—the topic of another essay—which Du
Bos acknowledges were the least productive in Goethe's career as a writer,
are called "the most fertile in works of humanity" (*A*, 6:77). Goethe's support of the grievances of the weavers of Apolda is singled out as such a
work of humanity: a man is always to be considered as higher than his
work. Du Bos admires Goethe's striving for perfection, his self-education,
but always voices the reservation, "We are on the plane of the *vital*" (6:85).
Goethe has not reached the spiritual: he represents "the triumph of the
purely human" (5:203). Though Du Bos translates many poetic texts,
he pays little critical attention to them except in one essay that discusses
Goethe's "orphic poetry." As a category or even a genre, orphic is construed to include in England "The Phoenix and the Turtle" and "Kubla
Khan" and in France some of the poems of Nerval. Orphic is contrasted
with hermetic poetry, of which Mallarmé serves as example, and with
mystical poetry, which presupposes faith (5:233–34). Du Bos translates
and expounds "Urworte" but cannot establish any link with Coleridge
or Nerval and concludes only that Goethe used symbols and believed in
a kind of panpsychism. Du Bos draws heavily on German criticism: on
Dilthey's *Erlebnis und die Dichtung* and on the books by Gundolf and Simmel. *Erlebnis*, the meaning of Goethe's experience, is the central concept.

Goethe's figure (*Gestalt*) and the type of life he led rather than his work are Du Bos's preoccupation.

One could argue that Du Bos's engagement with such alien and over-powering figures as Byron and Goethe is exceptional and that the new interest in Du Bos as a precursor of the Geneva School of critics of con-sciousness is mainly due to admiration for his essay "Sur le milieu inté-rieur dans Flaubert" (*Ap*, 165–82). In *La Conscience critique* Poulet praised Du Bos as his nearest precursor, and two critics close to Poulet make great claims for the essay on Flaubert. Jean Rousset in *Forme et significa-tion* calls it "one of the charters of modern criticism in France" (xvii). J.-P. Richard speaks of "several classic pages, pages from which, moreover, the whole of 'modern' Flaubert criticism has developed" ("La Méthode critique de Charles Du Bos," *Modern Language Review* 62 [1974]: 424). It may be worthwhile to analyze the essay closely.

The term "milieu intérieur" comes, as Du Bos tells us, from Claude Bernard's *Introduction à l'étude de la médicine expérimentale* (1863), the book Zola used (or misused) to apply to his *Roman expérimental* (1880). It is a deterministic expression, which Du Bos uses quite loosely for something that could be called the inner landscape or simply the psychology of Flau-bert. Du Bos, as a Bergsonian, always disapproved of determinism and causal reductionism (cf. *Ap*, 255). No causal, genetic, or historical expla-nations are offered. Rather Flaubert is characterized by quotations from his letters, his self-descriptions and self-interrogations. Du Bos starts by quoting one of Flaubert's early letters (15 August 1846): "I am a man of fogs and it is by dint of patience and study that I have rid myself of all the superfluous fat that weighed down my muscles" (*Ap*, 166). To begin with, Du Bos seizes on the second metaphor, developing it to make a point of Flaubert's inner environment as a "huge mass," only "semi-conscious, as if it were asleep": "A closer look reveals thousands of infinitesimal move-ments, all of which react on the whole compact mass: it is a stretched-out animal, on which can be observed the blind agitations of all the smaller animal cells that compose it" (166). After this purely fanciful arabesque, Du Bos returns to the first metaphor of fog, to Flaubert's "Nordic" tem-perament. Flaubert, Du Bos says, is akin to Jean Paul and to the Danish novelist Jens Peter Jacobsen (1847–85), author of *Niels Lyhne* and *Fru Marie Grubbe,* apparently only because all three indulged in *rêverie*.

In the next paragraph Du Bos returns to the metaphor of a huge mass. Mass suggests inertness, stupor: "Flaubert's stupor is of extraordinary in-tensity. In general, one might say that in him all so-called negative states reached the highest pitch of intensity. He starts, if one can say so, with the positivity of the negative. The sheer weight of sensation, and the en-

suing immersion in matter, seem to be the recurring characteristics of
Flaubert's world." Du Bos draws a parallel between Flaubert and Ingres,
who created a similar Turkish-bath atmosphere. Madame Renaud in the
first *L'Education sentimentale* (1845) reminds Du Bos of Ingres's portraits
of bourgeoises: "A voluptuous torpor, a concentration of all the senses
reduces the woman primarily to the status of a thing." Matter, torpor,
stupor suggest then the last page of *La Tentation de Saint-Antoine* (1874)
and Flaubert's ambition, expressed in a letter (16 June 1852), "to give an
almost material feeling of the thing he creates." Suddenly Du Bos drops
the bulk and matter development and uses a passage from Flaubert's early
story *Novembre* (1843), in which the lover of a prostitute describes the
effect of her perfume—"I feel my heart weaker and softer than a peach
as it melts on the tongue" (*Oeuvres de jeunesse inédites*, vol. 2 [1910], 199).
This allows him to speak of Flaubert's heart as "all pulp, without a core,
without resistance—an overpowering languor that borders on fainting,"
which is followed by an allusion to Flaubert's epileptic fits or fainting. But
Du Bos has nothing further to say about this improbable conclusion based
on a conventional erotic scene written by a nineteen-year-old. Rather,
he says that Flaubert was fascinated by the spectacle of human stupidity
and that there is an element of coarse, dark vulgarity in him. Flaubert
lacks proportion, indulges in excesses—this contradiction of the earlier
characterization as inert apparently does not disturb Du Bos.

Du Bos interrupts all these observations with an attempt to describe
Flaubert's style. Words in Flaubert are in the right place, every word reveals its full power: "It overflows, however, into the neighboring space, if
only by the stubbornness with which it occupies its hard-earned space."
This vague circumlocution (how can a word overflow?) for Du Bos's sense
of the close texture of Flaubert's style is then restated in pejorative terms.
Flaubert's style knows no *legato:* "I know of no other great writer in whose
style there is as little air as in Flaubert's." I find it difficult to associate air
or lack of air with any concrete feature of Flaubert's style.

Du Bos returns then to the theme of effort: Flaubert did not have "the
small change of talent." He is an example of self-creation. He wanted
the monotony of a long and difficult task; he wanted hard, harsh work.
Art became a religion for him. Du Bos quotes one letter describing Flaubert's ecstasy at seeing the naked wall of the Propylaea at the entrance
to the Acropolis and another letter that speaks of Flaubert's ambition to
serve Life, Truth, and Beauty together "without ever sacrificing one to
the other." At this point, Du Bos for the first time comments on Flaubert's
books critically. In *Salammbô* (1862) a concern for truth is minor. *Madame*

Bovary (1857) is the classical novel. *L'Education sentimentale* is, however, Flaubert's masterpiece: "There is nothing to hold on to, everything oozes. One may experience the flow of time itself while watching the unfolding of this frieze, in which the figures seem to be sinking into the stone rather than to stand out from it, and over which hangs a sort of secret whitish haze." The book "renders at first a dry wooden sound, without timbre or accent," as life has been entirely transmuted into "truth." Life, however, is still present, "but it has been preserved and absorbed for so long that it may seem buried among its own ashes. But then, at times, an unforgettable phrase, like a glowing ember, will reach us with muted warmth, like the glow of a dying fire cast upon a looker-on."

One may admire this stream of metaphors, a freewheeling meditation shifting from topic to topic, changing its focus rapidly and abruptly, as an example of "creative" criticism. But if one upholds an ideal of reasoned characterization, one might conclude that the essay says little that has not been said before about Flaubert's dreamy youth, his struggle against his own romanticism, his painful labors of composition, the religion of art, and the hard texture of his language. We might agree with the final paragraph of critical judgments: Du Bos's preference for *L'Education sentimentale*. But the last lines of the essay quoted above, considered by J.-P. Richard "the peak of all poetic criticism," suggest only the flow of time and the subdued tone. The images of the figures on the frieze that do not stand out and the embers say merely that the characters do not come to life except in a few memorable phrases. Du Bos also shows distaste for Flaubert's sensuality, materiality, and vulgarity. Du Bos misses the spirituality that he looks for everywhere.

Du Bos's article on Flaubert is an extreme case. Others are usually more coherent and often more traditional in their methods. "Méditation sur la vie de Baudelaire" (*Ap*, 183–238) is an attempt to make Baudelaire a "poeta christianissimus" because of his strong sense of sin. Du Bos labels him a Gnostic, a Valentinian who believed that no filth, no depravity can affect the soul (232). The essays on Proust were important in their time as early panegyrical appreciations, though they were mainly expository. One written after Proust's death, "Points de repère," celebrates his profundity. Du Bos says little more, however, than that Proust was good with the surface of men and society as well as with psychological depths and that he was agile in moving from one to the other. Proust created "a three-dimensional world" but looked down as from an observatory on the inexhaustible flow of life (435).

His friendship with André Gide was crucial in Du Bos's life. *Le Dialogue avec André Gide* (1929) contains good literary criticism that inevitably led to an ethical conflict, to Du Bos's assertion of Christian spirituality against what he came to stigmatize as Gide's hedonism and Satanism.

Among Du Bos's essays on German topics, the one on Stefan George seems the best. The emphasis on George's aspiration to being as against becoming, the evocation of his tone and attitude of dignity, of "monumental intimacy" (*Ap*, 879), is right and finely phrased. Du Bos only hints at his reservations about the cult of secrecy, the pretensions to prophecy. Compared to the George essay, the two essays on Hofmannsthal take the poet's mysticism far too seriously. In the second essay Du Bos expresses his feeling that the death of Hofmannsthal is the end of a world of delicacy, honor, lordly courtesy, and infinite tact. Du Bos defends Hofmannsthal against the charge of aestheticism and praises his Austrian conservatism as a defense of the sense of quality against the dictatorship of vulgarity (938–62). The essay on Thomas Mann, a speech made in his presence in 1926, is marred by its official urbanity and heavy flattery. It is difficult now to relish the old cliché about the German attraction to death or the labored passage in which Du Bos expresses his wish to join the spiritual family of Tonio Kröger, sharing "his longing for the blond and blue-eyed, the happy, amiable, and ordinary" (666).

The essays on English authors are, considering Du Bos's lifelong preoccupation with them, disappointingly thin, at least in *Approximations*. Except for the book on Byron, most of Du Bos's plans to write about his favorites—Shelley, Wordsworth, Keats, Pater, and Browning—remained only plans or fragments. The short essay on Shelley in *Approximations* is a sentimental meditation on his death. In another essay, on André Maurois's *Ariel*, Du Bos gently hints that Maurois has not grasped Shelley's soul, the "region of his ecstasy" (*Ap*, 335–40, 447). The piece on Browning is only a report on an old French book by Joseph Milsand (363–71). The essay on *Marius the Epicurean*, however, is a substantial, careful delineation of the stages of Marius's moral and spiritual development with a strong personal engagement. Du Bos speaks of a debt of twenty-five years' duration: he is "bearing witness to what he loves" (745–46). The essay on Thomas Hardy makes much of his monotony and the architectural quality of his work. His tragic view of life seems to Du Bos ultimately "tonic, salubrious, charged with salt," even though Hardy said: "For Life I had never cared greatly" (856). Later Du Bos's interest shifted to definitely religious writers: he admires Coventry Patmore's unctuous celebration of marriage, and in the essay on Charles Morgan's *Fountain* (1932) he goes into raptures at its contrived modern Platonism.

The passages in the *Journal* on English authors are often more elaborate: one can piece together Du Bos's views on Wordsworth, Keats, Henry James, Browning, George Eliot, and others, though they seem rarely to go beyond detached perceptions and metaphorical flourishes. Keats was important to Du Bos as an example of spiritual growth. The letter on life as "a Vale of Soul-making" is quoted frequently, but Du Bos's attempt to characterize Keats's poetry consists of little more than circumlocutions for plenitude, succulence, and so forth. A long *Journal* entry culminates in the fanciful metaphorical description of Keats's poetry as "the caress of a star by a fruit" (*J*, 1:205). The remarks on Henry James, some of them in the debate with Gide, who had condemned James for intellectualism, are ingeniously phrased defenses of his "labyrinthine genius" and of his art as running like telephone poles along a railroad track "parallel to life." Again, however, Du Bos misses "a spiritual, religious, and metaphysical content untouched by all the inner moral dramas," complaining of James's "whole tremendous moral power belonging to a world of standards, of taste, always *in fine* of art" (1:266; in English).

Du Bos's comments on Russian writers are comprehensibly rarer. The essay on Tolstoy in *Approximations* is largely descriptive and expository, though Du Bos remarks on Tolstoy's tempo, which seems to him *accelerando* in contrast to Proust's *ritardando*, and embraces Percy Lubbock's schematic view (in *The Craft of Fiction*, 1921) that the subject of *War and Peace* is the ages of man (*Ap*, 779, 823). The scattered remarks on Chekhov in the *Journal* are far subtler. They define well his desperate gentleness, his intellectual honesty, his modesty and decency. Du Bos planned a book on Chekhov, in which he wanted "to show what man can attain without religion, and more subtly still, without any form of heroics" (*J*, 2:105). One could continue in this vein, as Du Bos comments on almost every writer of the preceding hundred years. He has only one blind spot: he has no use for the eighteenth century or for French classicism.

Du Bos wrote mainly appreciations using traditional methods, translating, paraphrasing, commenting, judging, and often indulging in metaphorical fancies that lack any definite, even symbolic, coherence. Du Bos believes in intuition, in Bergson's sense, as "the kind of intellectual sympathy by which one places oneself within an object in order to coincide with what is unique in it and consequently inexpressible" (*An Introduction to Metaphysics*, trans. T. E. Hulme [1949], 23–24). But this view leads to Bergson's logical conclusion that metaphysics (that is, the science of intuition) dispenses with symbols. Du Bos, like many of his contemporaries, is thus deprived of a symbolist or mythic world-view: he can only feel into this inner flux, which Bergson tells him cannot be represented by images. Still, Du Bos cannot be content with saying—as he does say many times—that something is inexpressible, ineffable, incommunicable, indefinable, and so forth (see the chapter "L'Ineffable et les images," in Martens, 66ff.) He has to have recourse to images, and as he has no system, no firm network, he can indulge in farfetched and irresponsible analogies. Du Bos is particularly profuse in his comparisons between the arts which cannot in any way be controlled. Thus *Marius the Epicurean* reminds him of the adagio of the Fifth Brandenburg Concerto and the first movement of Beethoven's Fourteenth Quartet (*Ap*, 746). He sees a similarity between a sentence in *Le Rouge et le noir* and the *Antiope* of Correggio. Another phrase in Stendhal's novel evokes certain figures of Boucher and yet another reminds him of *Die Zauberflöte* (270–71). Du Bos sees an affinity between Hofmannsthal's "Ballade des äusseren Lebens" and a picture by Bellini, and a similarity between *Der Tod des Tizian* and Dossi's *Circe* and also the initial phrase of Beethoven's Violin Concerto (7, 8, 723). At the conclusion of the essay on Pater, Du Bos develops a grand metaphor: "The spirit of Pater resembles one of those cathedrals which one enters at nightfall. . . . *Marius the Epicurean* remains the great office which he celebrated, in a voice without reproach, whose every inflection penetrates to the heart of those who have withdrawn further within, and which seems always to summon the apparition, on the altar, of the Holy Sacrament which it does not dare to raise up there itself" (769).

But Du Bos did dare to put the sacrament on the altar later in his life. His last book, *What Is Literature?* (1940), a series of lectures in English given at Notre Dame University in Indiana, defines literature as "Life becoming conscious of itself when, in the soul of a man of genius, it joins its plenitude of expression." To the question What is Life? Du Bos now answers: Life is Christ. "Catholics," he asserts, "are singularly favored; we know that we are here below, as Saint Paul says, to retrieve the time, to redeem it." Literature is the meeting ground of souls. "Soul" is now not merely mind or *Gemüt* but the substantial immortal soul opposed to intellect and feeling. An aesthetic Platonism is proclaimed: "Beauty exists even if it is not yet perceived." Beauty *is*, it is a thing, it is the body of essence, it is an attribute of God. Literature is, by being Word, related to the Mystery of Incarnation, and through it, to the Word itself, to the Second Person of the Trinity. The attack on the Word, on literature, is sheer ingratitude. Du Bos closes by saying: "May God grant to this world a truly Catholic literature" (*What Is Literature?* 5, 13, 14, 25, 79, 91, 101, 108, 124).

Du Bos must be viewed as part of the Catholic Renaissance in France, in the company of Charles Péguy, Jacques Rivière, Paul Claudel (whom he called "the greatest genius of the Word"), and later the Abbé Bremond,

Etienne Gilson, and Jacques Maritain. The early Bergsonism is not incompatible with this final commitment, for we know of Bergson's own
late rapprochement with the Church and of the interpretation of Bergson by some of his Catholic followers such as Jacques Chevalier. Strictly
as a literary critic, Du Bos remains well in the tradition of nineteenth-
century metaphorical criticism. It can be called "creative" if this merely
means that the critic tries by metaphors and associations to characterize
his author, to evoke the exact impression or the general mood his work
conveys. It is a hazardous method if one clings to a rational concept of
criticism. Du Bos and many others constantly lose contact with the text.
The work of art often dissolves into a network of ingenious metaphors
and arbitrary associations. In the case of Du Bos, they are at least an-
chored in an implied mental scheme, with levels from the external and
sensual to the innermost sanctum of the Christian soul, what Du Bos calls
the God in him or "Le Moi de Deus." His creed supplies him not only
points of reference but also critical standards.

JACQUES MARITAIN (1882–1973)
AND HENRI BREMOND (1855–1933)

The role of Catholic intellectuals grew markedly during the reign of De
Gaulle, who tried to play down the influence of Socialism and Communism on French intellectuals. Among intellectuals he favored people like
Jacques Maritain and his wife Raïssa, who had written at length on poetry.
Maritain expounded the Thomist view of art best in his earliest book, *Art
et scolastique* (1920), and he elaborated his views on poetry in *Frontières de
la poésie* (1935). Maritain's *Situation de la poésie* (1938) reproduces an address to the Second International Congress of Aesthetics, held in Paris
in 1937. "Sens et non-sens en poésie" argues that the poetic sense must
not be confused with the poem itself. Maritain also strongly defends the
view that poetry is formally required to have a logical sense. The sense of
the poem cannot be separated from its form. Poems are signs which have
objects, and the objects are carriers of images. He devotes a whole page
to the argument that poetry therefore cannot be translated. Translation
makes the poem evaporate. But then Maritain seems to retract this view
by saying that poetry is not a material object but refers to the universality
of beauty and being. The image is, for him, "a magic form of the principle
of identity" (*SP*, 18)—a statement he derives from an article by Pierre
Guéguen.
    Maritain admits that the relation between poetic sense and objective
sense is obscure. He seems to undermine his emphasis on logic by ap-

pealing to poets like Lautréamont and Rimbaud. He quotes Rimbaud
saying that the poet is "a thief of fire" (*SP*, 23) and constantly repeats
the notion that obscurity is "the soul of poetry" (25). The poet tries to
grasp the unfathomable, unsoundable mystery of things, an effort which,
however, Maritain thinks has to fail in the end. It is for him the justification of the poetry of Claudel and the "non-sense" of Mallarmé. Mallarmé
was strongly aware of this magic. For him, poetry is "spoken music," the
opposite of the "musical poetry" of Verlaine (31). Maritain uses Mallarmé as the example of a complete retirement into mystery and "non-
sense." There is, however, also a tradition of clarity in literature. Maritain
lists Homer, Vergil, Dante, Shakespeare, Racine, Goethe, Pushkin, and
Baudelaire as masters who have achieved a clarity that is absent in the
other type of poetry, which reaches for deep obscurity. This other poetry
is not, however, simply mysticism of the kind Henri Bremond expounds.
It is a "particular essence," it touches the "uncreated Abyss, the God-
Saviour," known only obscurely as present and united with the soul of the
poet who contemplates this abyss (38). A mystical union gives the poet
perfect joy in the adequation of the created form and the creative inspiration. Maritain constantly tries to distinguish between the experience of
mystics like Suso, Jan van Ruysbroeck, Teresa of Avila, and John of the
Cross and that of poetry. Poetry tries to achieve something individual, to
give something to the poet, which Maritain identifies finally with purgation, with catharsis. Poetry, then, is free and self-sufficient and inevitably
brings together a sense and at the same time a logical "non-sense."

Another address, "Magie, poésie, et mystique," appeals to Albert
Béguin for an aesthetic of symbolism and surrealism. The first form,
magic power, is exemplified by Rimbaud, who finally escaped the temptation of mystical creation by renouncing poetry itself (*SP*, 52). Here
Maritain is not sure whether the poet seeks God or the Devil, whether
the poet's sorcery or witchcraft is not also evil. He quotes at length
Edgar Allan Poe's story "The Power of Words" and recognizes that his
mythology is pantheistic. He also quotes passages from Béguin's *L'Ame
romantique et le rêve*, like that by Karl Philipp Moritz, who asks us to re-
join the essential unity of the universe, and that by G. H. von Schubert,
who finds this pantheistic view filled with enthusiasm. But the recurrent
theme is that poetry is not mysticism: "Whatever value one ascribes to the
act of poetry, it remains an act subject to the necessity of form" (69–70).
The address ends with the word, which is silence—*Silentium tibi laus*—the
highest praise that man and poet can offer God (70).

The next lecture is called "De la connaissance poétique." Maritain
sketches in bold terms a history of the ripening of consciousness in the

Middle Ages and the Renaissance, to Racine and La Fontaine. After them he sees a complete decay, but "in the middle of this general disaster something was gained which could not be lost: poetry became aware of itself as art" (*SP*, 86). The question What is art? then became the "thorn in the side" of the eighteenth century, a question to which classicism responded but poorly. Romanticism, however, went further in deepening the perception of art, and a moment arrived in the nineteenth century when "poetry began to become aware of itself *as poetry*" (87). Baudelaire seems to Maritain a crucial figure in this evolution. The importance of poetry's becoming aware of itself as poetry is "immense" for Baudelaire. He is more clearly aware of the problem of poetry, and it is his mystical knowledge of poetry that gives his verse such astonishing magical power. Baudelaire is important for taking the poem as an independent entity, for understanding the essence of the poetic state. Maritain then praises Henri Michaux's poetry, which leads to complete negativity and makes everything in poetry reducible to language (93). Maritain, quoting Nietzsche ("Aber ich will kein Mensch sein" [94]), tries to quit the human race. Maritain thinks all this is not really anti-Aristotelian. Quoting Rimbaud, he says that poetry tries to "vindicate the absolute life." It wants to be everything and to give everything, to achieve miracle. Poetry "is in charge of humanity" (108).

One sees how these early writings of Maritain can be interpreted as Thomist, as strongly orthodox. Maritain naturally rejects the views of Henri Bremond, which seem to him nonsense. A great stir was caused in 1925 by a lecture given by Bremond, the well-known author of the *Histoire littéraire du sentiment religieux en France* (6 vols., 1916–33). This history was not only psychologically penetrating, it uncovered for a new French public the existence of an enormous body of religious literature that had been totally neglected, overshadowed by the reputation and success of French classicism. Bremond was at the time a prominent figure and a member of the French Academy, and thus his lecture there on "pure poetry" excited a great deal of attention. It was published in 1926 along with a series of comments, or *Elucidations,* motivated by the response to the lecture and an essay, "Un débat sur la poésie," by Robert De Souza, who represented a point of view that Bremond found particularly congenial.

Bremond's thesis is quite simple. He defines poetry mainly by rejecting what he considers false views and concludes that poetry is simply "prayer." He begins by rejecting the view that poetry is merely beautiful sounds or rhythms. Its essence is behind the words, though words are the indispensable means of the poet. He ends by quoting Walter Pater to the effect that all the arts aspire to become music. "No," replies Bremond, "they all aspire, but by those mediating charms that are proper to each—words, notes, colors, lines—they all aspire to become prayer" (*La Poésie pure*, 27). This thesis is bolstered by an appeal to the tradition of pure poetry. Bremond cites not only Poe, Baudelaire, Mallarmé, and Valéry, but also Wordsworth and Keats, and even Shakespeare and Burns.

The phrase "pure poetry" was used in the eighteenth century by Joseph Warton in his *Essay on the Genius and Writings of Pope* (2 vols., 1756, 1782), where it refers to the poetry of Shakespeare rather than to what Warton considered the rhymed or metered prose of the satires of Horace, Boileau, and Pope. The term "pure poetry" was not used generally again until it was revived by Bremond, who made it fashionable as well as the occasion of a long-winded and repetitious debate. In practice, "pure poetry" could refer to very different works. For instance, as editor of *An Anthology of Pure Poetry* (1924), the Irish novelist George Moore wrote that pure poetry is poetry free from thought, ideas, morality, and propaganda. It is free from personal emotion, a poetry of things and not of feelings. Moore thus admires Gautier's purely descriptive poem "La Tulipe." In Valéry one gets a totally opposite point of view: pure poetry is "absolute" poetry, Platonic or Neoplatonic, transcendental, austere. Bremond protested strongly against Valéry's conception. His own pure poetry was based on personal feeling, on a sincere religious emotion. Much of that whole debate, which lasted several years in France, seems merely about terminology.

Maritain had apparently such a strong reputation as a Thomist—which he confirmed during his years at Columbia University, New York University, and Princeton University between 1940 and 1944—that De Gaulle nominated him French ambassador to the Vatican, where he was active from 1945 to 1948. He returned to Princeton in 1948 as professor of philosophy. In the spring of 1952 Maritain was invited to deliver the initial series of the A. W. Mellon Lectures in Fine Arts at the National Gallery of Art in Washington, D.C. These lectures were published by the Bollingen Foundation in 1953 as *Creative Intuition in Art and Poetry*, a sumptuous volume that contained a well-chosen set of black-and-white illustrations. The book has been somewhat neglected, certainly by French commentators, though it deserves attention for its well-organized, acutely argued positions. It contains, besides the main argument, often interesting digressions, such as a long account of Dante's *Divine Comedy*, and descriptions of the situation of most contemporary French poetry, mainly surrealist, a term Maritain uses in a wide sense to include everybody of any renown from Guillaume Apollinaire to Paul Eluard and Philippe Soupault.

The lectures begin with standard topics such as the concept of imitation and poetry as representative of man at a certain time and of things at that time. Maritain is enthusiastic about the art of the cavemen who painted on walls accurately and in correct proportions the deer and bison they wanted to kill: they seem to him "the prime achievements of human art and poetic imagination" (*CI*, 34). This chapter, like the others in the book, is followed by a section titled "Texts without Comment"—extracts from relevant books on the subject, in this case in particular quotations from the Indian aesthetician Ananda K. Coomaraswamy. The second chapter, "Art as a Virtue of the Practical Intellect," allows Maritain to discuss modern and ancient architecture and other utilitarian aspects of the arts, which in his view, however, are always transcended by the search for beauty or some kind of transcendental feeling. Thus the Brooklyn Bridge "was able to stir the deepest emotions of Hart Crane," and the entire "chaos of bridges and skyways, desolated chimneys, gloomy factories, queer industrial masts and spars, infernal and stinking machinery which surrounds New York is one of the most moving—and beautiful—spectacles in the world" (61).

The third lecture, "The Preconscious Life of the Intellect," is concerned largely with the concept of myth and mythology, and with the collective subconscious of man, as drawn by Maritain largely from Carl Gustav Jung. Maritain believes in a subconscious life that wells from below and is not inspired from above, though he discusses later with great earnestness and obvious acceptance that kind of inspiration. In this third lecture the subconscious is a collective myth or mythology, and not anything like personal experience, which, however, Maritain constantly pays attention to in later discussions on the share of the self in poetic intuition. Maritain quotes modern American poets like Allen Tate and John Crowe Ransom, arriving at an idea of poetic knowledge which he at first thinks is fully expressed only in the work—for instance, in *Moby Dick*. But he argues of course that knowledge in *Moby Dick* is not only the obvious information on whales or even on astronomy, but a poetic knowledge that is saturated with emotion. Because he preserves, in spite of all his mysticism, a residue of Thomist rationalism, Maritain worries how one can imagine emotion to be raised to the level of the intellect. He considers poetic intuition both emotional and cognitive. Maritain thinks of his philosophy as non-dialectical, even anti-dialectical: one can hold two divergent and even contradictory attitudes. Poetic intuition is "filled with the subjectivity of the poet as well as with the thing grasped" (*CI*, 127). It is often difficult to understand the way Maritain uses these terms. "Poetic knowledge" becomes "poetic intuition," which is "creative" and reaches into the depths of the human soul. He speaks also of a "self-centered ego," and at one point criticizes in a note T. S. Eliot's essay "Tradition and the Individual Talent" for having "missed the distinction between creative Self and self-centered ego" (143n). A baffling succession of identifications leads finally to a glorification of poetry as silence, in the sense of Mallarmé, or nothingness, which Maritain feels is behind Mallarmé's idea of poetry.

A special chapter is devoted to poetry and beauty. Maritain rehearses the Platonic or Neoplatonic concept of beauty, but then argues that modern man has abandoned the concept of beauty and often finds beauty in ugly or distorted images. In practice, Maritain defends French surrealism, and he quotes all kinds of modern poetry that he admits to be obscure, incoherent sequences of images. One interesting digression is an attack on "the shibboleth of sincerity" (*CI*, 193), which he ascribes to romanticism and its supposed originator, Jean-Jacques Rousseau, who is a constant target of his disparaging remarks. What Maritain admires is the opposite tradition, that of personal confession, the kind of tradition that Rimbaud claimed for himself in the famous letter where he wants the poet to become a "seer," a state of mind that can be reached only by "a complete, persistent, and reasoned *disturbance* of *all the senses*" (203). Maritain finds this visionary concept in a whole tradition of French poetry beginning with Lautréamont's *Chants de Maldoror* and culminating in Rimbaud. Even the surrealists fit into this scheme, André Breton in particular.

Maritain in these lectures moves constantly nearer and nearer to a mystical idea of poetry. He quotes a well-known poem by Archibald MacLeish that ends with the lines "A poem should not mean / But be" (*CI*, 260). Maritain is not content with this concept of being. He thinks there are at least two kinds of obscurity in modern poetry. One can be explained, for instance, in the poetry of Mallarmé, Valéry, or Eliot. This is "difficult" or "hermetic" poetry, but it is not the second, real kind of poetry, which in Maritain's conception reaches the inmost self, the deepest recesses of our mind. Maritain then discusses magic in poetry, but rejects the ordinary sense of magic, which is wrongly applied to poetry. In moving toward a mystical concept of poetry Maritain elaborates what he calls the "internalization of music." Poetic intuition is "the beginning of a wordless musical stir" (300). The attempt to make poetry musical is either a very trite idea, which is of course easily illustrated by meters and stanzaic forms, rhythms, and so forth, or, as in Maritain, a new metaphor for something we can only vaguely comprehend, where the poetic intuition is transmitted by the poem. It is an irrational inquiry not easily comprehensible: the intuition is there before the poem, it precedes the poem. Maritain uses this idea of the "internalization of music" to defend French classical poetry, Racine in particular. There is a "music of words" in classical French poetry, as with Racine, or possibly, surprisingly, in William Blake. Maritain devotes another digression to criticism, which is obviously seen as the concern of poets alone. Criticism is a special gift of dealing with a figment of the mind. Maritain does not believe that there is a true critic who is not a potential poet: "The critic is a poet, and has the gifts of a poet, at least virtually" (324). Du Bos, for example, was a critic and not a poet but is declared by Maritain to have been one potentially.

The final chapter develops the idea of poetic sense as an "inner melody" that can become action and theme and allow a "harmonic expansion." Maritain presents here a cautious theory of genres. He is convinced that lyric poetry is the basic poetry, and that the other genres are derivative of the lyric. But "action" is the main element in the epic, and finally there is what he calls "theme" as the basic concern of the modern novel. He proclaims that "the poetic sense or inner melody, the action and the theme, the number or harmonic structure, are the three epiphanies of poetic intuition or creative emotion passing into the work" (*CI*, 369). Maritain digresses to discuss chance in poetry, the interference of some external event. He also sees chance as playing a great role in the accomplishment of a period of classic style. It seems to Maritain mere luck, mere contingence, that there was a great poet like Racine, whose absence would have completely altered the history of French poetry. Maritain sums up by saying that poetry "is the free creativity of the spirit, and the intuitive knowledge through emotion, which transcend and permeate all arts, inasmuch as they tend toward beauty as an end beyond the end" (393). He reflects on three different kinds of poetic sensibility: lyric sensibility, histrionic sensibility, and introspective sensibility—another triad in his concern for classification. At the end, Maritain makes rather strange pronouncements such as his claim that writers like Ronsard, Hugo, Byron, and Goethe have "little or no magic," while he identifies Racine, Dante, Keats, Coleridge, Pushkin, Baudelaire, Hölderlin, and Rimbaud as "magical poets." Creative intuition is then called "the only supreme gift that a poet, in any art whatsoever, ought to seek," and he concludes with an appeal: that "what Pascal felt about another kind of grace . . . holds true for [poets] also: 'Take comfort, thou wouldst not be seeking me, hadst thou not found me'" (405).

An outsider who is suspicious of vague and mystical concepts must feel some disappointment with this rich book, must feel dissatisfied finally with the (to my mind) inappropriate appeal to a passage from Pascal on the grace of God, grace in the sense of giving man his absolution from sin. It seems forced and remote in its application. It is a pity that such a book, filled with fine reflections on poetry, on inspiration, and on different genres and figures in literary history, ends with a somewhat empty gesture toward a religious metaphysics.

PAUL CLAUDEL (1868–1955)

Paul Claudel is often considered the greatest French poet of the twentieth century, and most certainly he was a prominent and vocal figure in the whole French Catholic Renaissance of the early part of the century. He spent his entire adult life in the diplomatic service, for instance, as French consul in Prague in 1910–11, as ambassador to Japan for a number of years, and as ambassador to the United States. His extremely miscellaneous writings cover all possible subjects, like politics, sociology, and religion, as well as general meditations on such topics as national characteristics. He had a wide acquaintance not only with literature but also with music and painting. His attacks on Richard Wagner are most conspicuous and often quoted. Claudel apparently admired Wagner's music, but he ridicules the story of *Der Ring des Nibelungen* and in other contexts expresses boredom with *Die Meistersinger* and approval of the stories of *Tannhäuser* and *Parsifal*, though by his own admission he never attended a performance of *Parsifal*. He thought of Wagner as being touched deeply by religion and Catholic asceticism, but having abandoned this feeling after *Tannhäuser* to plunge into what Claudel perceived as the ridiculous Germanic story of the *Ring*. Claudel violently disliked Teutonism, and in one piece written in 1927 he claims that in listening to Erda "we cannot suppress a smile and a yawn." The poetry of Wagner "is like the Rhine that flows between old 'burgs,' castles that have been dismantled or, which is sadder still, restored in the taste of Kaiser Wilhelm" (*Oeuvres en prose*, 63).

But it would be a complete error to think of Claudel as mainly a polemicist and satirist. He was a serious, deeply religious man who gives a moving description of his conversion, which occurred at a specific pillar in Notre Dame where he heard, as in a voice from above: "There is a God." It was another four years before, in another apparently sudden flash of recognition on looking into the Protestant Bible, he came upon the quotation "And Christ said, I am the Son of God." Thus he accepted the mystery of the Trinity (1008–14). As a poet, Claudel drew heavily on the Bible and even composed mysteries in the medieval sense. But even this does not touch his prolific output of journalism and often quite remarkable literary criticism. It is framed by his strongly religious faith, which shows in his disparaging remarks on figures like Luther and Kant, but he discusses the whole history of French literature often rationally and sensibly, not only from an ideological point of view. Claudel admired Rimbaud as a kind of divine child, a "mystic in the savage state" (514). He accepts the stories of the newborn child breaking into praise of God and believes that *Une Saison en enfer* is literal truth comparable to Dante's descent into Hell. "Arthur Rimbaud," says Claudel, "is not a poet, not even a man of letters. He is a *prophet* on whom the spirit has descended, not as on David, but as on Saul" (522). He sees a sixteen-year-old boy as having found eternity. Claudel accepts Rimbaud's sister's account of his deathbed confession and rejects with indignation the stories of "an English bluestocking [Enid Starkie, author of a critical book on Rimbaud] who asserts without any proof that he traded in slaves during his years in Ethiopia" (527).

His admiration for Rimbaud reflects on the other symbolists, particularly Mallarmé, whom Claudel visited and highly admired. But Mallarmé appears to him as a man who, while attached to the French classical tradition, spoke "humbly and joyously of his own absence," which is also "the eternal presence of another, namely the Creator" (512). Mallarmé is only on the way to God, asserts Claudel. He is corrupted by gloomy romantic pessimism. As a student, Claudel saw Verlaine on the street near the Sorbonne and at that time did not mind the blasphemy in his poetry, which Claudel sensed as having deep religious roots. But his greatest admiration is for Baudelaire, whom Claudel reads as a confessed sinner doing lifelong penance and thinking of himself as a fallen man beyond redemption. Claudel accepts the accounts of Baudelaire's deathbed conversion. He sees Baudelaire as yearning for a paradise, for a golden island of his youth, and dismisses his gloomy framing of such visions. Claudel and his follower Rivière make a striking contrast to Erich Auerbach's view of Baudelaire (see this *History*, 7:127–29).

Claudel remembers seeing as a child the enormous procession of Victor Hugo's funeral. In his later pronouncements on Hugo, Claudel usually speaks of him as a windbag, but imitates his style and his metaphors with striking artistry. Claudel is a great admirer of the French classical tradition and detests romanticism in general, though he makes exceptions for Senancour, Vigny, and Lamartine, all poets who are bitter pessimists, whereas Musset seems to him the lowest of the low.

Claudel rarely goes beyond the confines of French literature, though at a certain point of his life he learned a good deal of Chinese and wrote extensively on Chinese writings. He also knew something about Japanese literature as a result of his diplomatic service. There are also some isolated accounts of writers in other languages: for instance, an interesting three pages on Kafka's *The Trial,* of which Claudel saw only the very free adaptation for the stage by Jean-Louis Barrault. Claudel considers Goethe one of the "three evil geniuses of Germany," along with Luther and Kant, but also praises him as a wonderful naturalist (877).

Claudel, by all accounts, was what is usually called a violent reactionary, an anti-Semite. Let me end by quoting W. H. Auden's "In Memory of W. B. Yeats" (1929):

> [Time] will pardon Paul Claudel,
> Pardons him for writing well.

6 : DADA AND SURREALISM

THE ROMANIAN Tristan Tzara (1892–1963) settled in Zurich just before the First World War, possibly fleeing from the Romanian political atmosphere. He made his living there by founding a cabaret called the Voltaire, located in the basement of an old restaurant in the Spiegelgasse, where he performed as a master of ceremonies. He gave his group the name Dada, meaning "hobbyhorse," a term that apparently existed long before he adopted it. As Tzara at that time knew very little German or French, he started the cabaret with completely meaningless recitations of series of repeating vowels with music, and later produced little sketches or dramas, mainly in French, which have been called "Dada manifestos." The first major work is Tzara's *La Première Aventure céleste de M. Antipyrine,* which was performed on 14 July 1916. Tzara recruited some followers, particularly the German Hugo Ball, who defined the activity of the cabaret as being "to remind the world that there are independent men beyond war and nationalism." We must not forget that these sketches were written during the height of the First World War. The actual poetry, if it can be called that, composed by Tzara is either almost meaningless repetition, like "rendre prendre entre," or shocking and vulgar sensationalism, like "oiseaux enceints qui font caca sur le bourgeois." All the later manifestos amount to a complete rejection of conventional writing, with the aim of mystifying and irritating his audience. Tzara's *Second Dada Manifesto,* which was read in Zurich in March 1918, asserts that "beauty is dead" and that the Dadaists "engage in a great destructive work, sweep out, mop up," culminating in the statement that "life is a bad farce, without aim." The manifestos, with such proclamations as "Je suis idiot, je suis farceur," apparently drew the attention of writers in Paris, and of the surrealists in particular.

The question of terminology is troublesome. André Breton (1896–1966), who wrote the official manifestos of the surrealist group, was obviously its most erudite member. He knew, for instance, that Thomas Carlyle uses the term "natural supernaturalism" in *Sartor Resartus* (1833–

34) and that Heinrich Heine, in a passage later to be quoted by Baudelaire, proclaims himself to be a "supernaturalist in art" in contrast to his
"naturalism in religion" (see this *History*, 3:107). But the terminologies
are problematic. There are anticipations in terms like "supernaturalism"
in Heine, but the specific new meaning of "surrealism" referring to a
group of writers occurs only after Tzara's arrival in Paris in January 1920,
and then plays a central role in the first *Manifeste du surréalisme*, written
by Breton in 1924. Actually, Breton uses it quite vaguely to refer to all
writers whom he considers "modern," meaning opposed to the current
Naturalism, the kind of novels written in France in the early twentieth
century. Breton's first manifesto rambles all over the intellectual landscape, appealing to writers who never used the term, even in the distant
past, defining it often in a broad general way as anything that deviates
from ordinary realism, and quoting, for instance, a 1918 pronouncement
by Pierre Reverdy: "The image is the pure creation of the mind." Breton
says, "Soupault and I baptized the new mode of expression with the name
of surrealism," producing later in the manifesto a long list of adherents,
of whom only Aragon and Eluard are known today, and claiming that
practically every writer was a surrealist, even Dante and Edward Young
in his *Night Thoughts*. Breton calls Swift a "surrealist in malice" and the
marquis de Sade a "surrealist in sadism," and amuses himself with such
jokes as calling Hugo "a surrealist when he isn't stupid," Poe a "surrealist
in adventure," and Baudelaire a "surrealist in morality."

Tzara arrived in Paris immediately after the war and joined the surrealist group—with which, however, he quarreled soon afterward. Breton in
1923 sabotaged the staging of Tzara's play *Le Coeur agacé* at the Théâtre
Michel in Paris and provoked a furious fistfight. Breton leaped on stage
and began to attack the actors, who were unable to fight back because
they were encased in cardboard boxes. This marked the end of the Dada
movement. Breton called Tzara a fraud, though later they were reconciled and in his *Second manifeste* (1930) Breton apologized to Tzara and
praised his work.

His second manifesto contains Breton's often quoted description of the
simplest surrealist act: "Going out in the street, revolver in hand, and
shooting at random as much as you wish into the crowd." This glorification of mayhem should not, however, obscure the fact that Breton in
particular often presented solid arguments in his manifestos in perfectly
clear language, in which he advocated complete rejection of the past and
appealed to two aspects of composition—automatic writing and dreaming. Breton was reasonable enough to argue that there is a gulf between
an actual dream and its verbal formulation, and that even supposedly

subconscious writing requires organization, sitting down at a table, dipping the pen in ink, and writing with some aim or intention. Breton's own writing became more and more political, finally ending in declarations of adherence to Communism. We must not forget that Breton's strongest Communist declarations came at the time of the Popular Front in 1934 and 1935, and that he himself never joined the party. More and more he saw the aim of literature as an attack on the bourgeoisie, a depiction of the horrors of poverty, and a final glimmer of hope for the liberation of the proletariat. What strikes one today is that despite the extreme violence of the proclamations of "activism," as they called it, in practice neither the Dadaists nor the surrealists were ever able to free themselves from the milieu of Paris bohemianism. It seems unnecessary in a history of criticism to try to follow the turns of their arguments, the conflicts between individuals, or the quarrels between magazines and editors. The enormous publicity they generated is not warranted by any new critical ideas. Vladimir Mayakovsky's Russian Futurist exhortation to "throw Pushkin and his cohorts overboard" sums up what Dada and the surrealists had to say about their own past's literature. Both Dada and surrealism will appear in retrospect as movements overblown by publicity. They were ultimately nihilistic and barren.

7 : THE GENEVA SCHOOL

MARCEL RAYMOND (1897–1981)

MARCEL RAYMOND is generally considered the head of the so-called Geneva School. He seems to be the most authoritative voice for the view of literary history that includes literary criticism as a branch of general philosophy or cultural anthropology. Literature is constantly used as a document for the development and later for the essence of an author.

Raymond is the only proper Genevan in the group. Born in 1897, the son of a Protestant pastor, Raymond thus differs from his closest disciple and friend, Albert Béguin, who in 1940 converted to Catholicism. Raymond wrote widely on his own life, most impressively in a book called *Le Sel et la cendre* (1970), which contains much earlier writing and reflects on his work self-critically. The book is strictly autobiographical, frank, beautifully written, and based on extensive documentation, drawing on diaries and letters. Raymond was, early on, astonishingly introspective and observed his personal development and struggles with great analytical skill. What is surprising is how long it took him to publish a book. The autobiography shows that even as a child he had strong literary interests which led him to steep himself in French poetry at an early age, with some excursions into English and German literature. Apparently Coleridge's "The Ancient Mariner" was for him a revelation of imaginative poetry. Raymond went through the usual Genevan schools and was unwilling at first to pursue further academic studies in literature. When he arrived in Paris, however, he was converted to what seems a fairly conventional study of the history of French literature under the tutelage of Abel Lefranc, the great specialist on Rabelais. In 1927 Raymond composed an elaborate thesis, *L'Influence de Ronsard sur la poésie française (1550–1585)*. It was a straightforward study of sources and influences, but despite its shortcomings it allowed Raymond to read French poetry of the late sixteenth century and to acquire a taste for what he first called "baroque" and, later, "mannerist" poetry in France. This shaped his whole concep-

tion of the history of French poetry and made him the defender of a
French anti-classicist tradition.

After completing his thesis, Raymond was somewhat at loose ends.
In 1926 he had married and accepted a position as a French *lecteur* at
the University of Leipzig, where he stayed for four years. The experience in Leipzig was extremely important, at least as Raymond describes
it, for it revealed to him the existence of *Geistesgeschichte*. He heard a
good deal about Dilthey, and he comments at length on his reading of
Gundolf, whose *Shakespeare und der deutsche Geist* (1912) he admired enormously. In Leipzig Raymond also attended lectures by the biologist Hans
Driesch, who taught him about organicism, and visited Edmund Husserl,
from whom he acquired the foundation of an existential phenomenology.
Poetry, Raymond asserts, is metaphysics (*Le Sel et la cendre*, 85).

Raymond returned to Switzerland in 1930 to become professor of
French literature at the University of Basel. There he wrote his book
De Baudelaire au surréalisme (1930), which was his first publication besides
the thesis on Ronsard. It shows a complete shift of interest away from
old-fashioned literary history toward criticism. The book was a great success and apparently made a profound impression on his contemporaries,
completely changing the accepted idea of the history of French poetry.
I personally cannot believe that Raymond's conception is so new, if one
thinks of Thibaudet, but it is apparently a version of what today is more or
less accepted as the standard. Raymond emphasizes the fact that French
poetry has two main traditions, which are incompatible. The first of these
traditions holds that poetry reproduces the things of this world, that it
makes us feel the existence of the world as it is. It is what Raymond calls
"realism," in the sense that poetry restores the concrete reality of the
world, not literally describing what is out there but seizing the essence
of things in their concrete individuality. This is not by any means only
individual, however, but becomes collective in its impact and originates in
myth and symbol. The influence of Bergson seems predominant. According to the second tradition, poetry achieves or tries to achieve an absolute
world, the metaphysical, transcendental world that gives insight not only
into the present condition of man but also into his future and even into
his life after death. Raymond recognizes that both traditions struggle with
the problem of language, with the paradox that they must either present
things or the cosmos or simply the world in terms of language or suggest the super-rational world through language that can never reach the
absolute and thus condemns the poet, finally, to silence. Mallarmé is, of
course, the great example for this vision, offering an "orphic" explanation

of the earth—*orphic* being a term for the primeval or mystical, probably suggested by Goethe's poem "Urworte orphisch"—whereas poets such as the romantics want to identify with nature and even to be absorbed by it. There the distinction between the mind and the cosmos is abolished, subject and object identified.

All of Raymond's later writing elaborates these ideas, with some slight modifications. I feel that in his latest writings, as late as 1970, Raymond becomes definitely mystical. The death of his wife played a central role: poetry becomes some kind of assurance that he will meet her again in an afterlife. Raymond is sufficiently self-critical to see that the "critics of consciousness" are really uninterested in the notion of the work and even in that of the author. Still, the work has its formal side, which declares itself, imposes itself on the critic as an object. On many pages Raymond seems to paraphrase or even reproduce Leo Spitzer and the method of the circle of understanding. We start with details, even of the stylistic sort, and arrive at the conception of the whole, which is then confirmed or corrected by a new return to detail. Raymond has considerable interest in stylistics and often comments on formal characteristics such as, in particular, syntax. In his studies of the French tradition Raymond became more and more concerned with the German history of art and the program formulated by Oskar Walzel of the "mutual elucidation of the arts" (*wechselseitige Erhellung der Künste*). He was deeply impressed by Heinrich Wölfflin's *Kunstgeschichtliche Grundbegriffe*, which he translated with his wife in 1952. Raymond applies Wölfflin's categories very cautiously, however, and gives a skeptical account of the attempts to transfer Wölfflin's concepts to literature.

The reflections in *Génies de France* (1942) date from the late thirties and early forties. In the essay called "Sur le génie de la France" Raymond tries to define the peculiarities of the French genius, accepting the view that French poetry is defined by its language and that the discoveries of authors are only possible within that language, but are still part of a collective reality just as language is. Raymond's choice of great writers is in some ways arbitrary. At first one might think that there is no continuity in French history. In his scheme, Louis XIV and the Jacobins are so extremely different that one might not think they came from the same nation. But a comparison of these figures reveals an undeniable resemblance. France now appears as a model of continuity and as a balance between two opposing forces, which Raymond decides is due to the mixture of races and to the late flowering of Christianity in the twelfth century, which he considers to be completely original in France. Raymond sides with what he perceives as the integral realism of the Middle Ages in France and sees a profound attraction to the real throughout French history. He views the "religion of poetry" as particularly French (39) and thinks that two principles in French literature have held true throughout the centuries. One is a complete integration, the success of the French in absorbing foreigners. The second is an admirable sense of balance, a faithfulness to things, an almost mystical desire to seize on nature and to see it as a harmony—something Raymond misses in other nations. More than any other people, the French have examined themselves and come to represent the human condition. While they are oddly provincial in many ways, they are also universally human, and this universality is one of the great appeals of the French nation and literature.

The essays that follow these reflections on the genius of France cover a large part of French literature. Raymond's early, rather tolerant detachment avoids any harsh criticism of traditional scholarship. In an essay on Montaigne's religious attitude, Raymond expounds well his mixture of Christian religion, philosophical skepticism, and moral paganism and argues that Montaigne was a fideist, who finally accepted the Catholic religion as an alternative to his basic skepticism. The first part of Raymond's essay on Agrippa D'Aubigné presents a selection of some of his often weird poetry, quoting particularly passages containing obvious paradoxes, such as "My fire embraced the damp bosom of the waters." In the second part of the essay on D'Aubigné, Raymond shows that he has discovered the German, and generally European, revival of the Baroque. Raymond agrees that the period between the decline of the Pléiade and the coming of Louis XIV should be called Baroque. He is obviously impressed by Wölfflin's work, but has doubts about its applicability to literature.

Another article praises La Fontaine's *Psyché* highly, though Raymond admits that it does not escape a complete aestheticism that exalts grace as more beautiful than beauty. The terminology here may seem odd: grace is the highest trait of beauty and is thus more beautiful than beauty itself. The essay on Racine's poetic discourse plunges immediately into a polemic against Henri Bremond, whose discussion of pure poetry was at that time very much in the public eye. Bremond identifies poetry with prayer, something that seems to Raymond a mystical heresy. Raymond tries to define the particular success of Racine in his musical and euphonic sense, without, however, being able to analyze it in anything more than impressionistic terms. He praises the harmony of technique and feeling, of intellect and music, and ends paradoxically by praising Racine's innocence. In an essay devoted to Montesquieu and his humanism, Raymond praises Montesquieu for his rigid rationalism, which however assumes a belief in eternal laws of morals and politics. This is followed by an *hommage* to Lamartine, who does not fit in well with Raymond's conception of poetry but whom he praises as a man of heart and for his Christian humanism.

The most important essay is that on Victor Hugo as a magician. Raymond shows that the concept of the universe as some kind of extension of man exists even in Hugo's early writings and that the mysticism that Raymond admires in his last, posthumous writings, *Dieu* and *La Fin de Satan*, pervades his whole work. Raymond quotes Péguy's witty paradox for Hugo, "a genius spoiled by his talent," and emphasizes his primitivism and even childishness. The essay on Baudelaire gives a convincing account of his conception of imagination and his belief in a basic unity of the whole (*Génies*, 198), in spite of his idea of a dualism between God and Satan. Baudelaire seems to Raymond to have a predisposition to mysticism in a savage state. But in the second part of the essay Raymond contrasts Baudelaire's yearning for a paradise or an age of gold with the horrible pictures of urban decay, suffering, and misery in *Les Fleurs du mal*. For Raymond the modernity of Baudelaire lies in his complete sincerity, a view that minimizes his poses and theatrical manners. In an essay on recent poetry Raymond describes Bergson as despairing of language, given its incompatibility with the spirit. Raymond admires Bergson's emphasis on the concrete and the visual, which seems to me not quite compatible with Bergson's emphasis on suggestion. Bergson, Raymond argues, disapproves of mysticism, but shares an interest in primitive poetry with the philosopher and ethnologist Lucien Lévy-Bruhl (1857–1939). For the first time in the book, Raymond mentions existential philosophy, as working against man's "slavery to time." Rimbaud and Proust are then invoked as "singers," as poets who recover eternity outside of duration.

This outline of the history of French poetry is greatly elaborated in other essays dating from the thirties and forties that were collected much later in *Etre et dire* (1970). The essays include comments on the stages of contemporary French literature (1935). Raymond connects the trends in French poetry with public events such as the Dreyfus affair and the world war. Among the more recent movements, Raymond distinguishes Unanimism, represented by Jules Romains, who preaches a Socialist morale, and Futurism, which seems to him pre-Fascist and pseudo-Nietzschean. On the whole, Raymond is skeptical about the "isms" of the twentieth century and the debates about abstractions. He admires actually the ambition to produce a work and approves even of Dadaism, which tries to be a knowledge of being. There is also a sketch of metaphysics in recent poetry, which Raymond sees as mainly influenced by Bergson. He distinguishes between attempts to change life, the dream of social, ethical action, and the other, mystical hope that poetry will allow man to transform things, to redeem nature as Rousseau and Novalis dreamed of doing.

In a long review of Béguin's *L'Ame romantique et le rêve* (1937), Raymond largely approves of the book and its exposition of the role of dreams and the unconscious, but he obviously has difficulties with Béguin's claim that poetry comes from dreams. Raymond finds that there is a gulf between a simple dream and poetry. The review shows that the two friends already had different approaches and philosophies, which however never spoiled their later, very amiable, relations. In another long essay, originally published as a pamphlet, "Le Sens de la qualité" (1946), Raymond argues that poetry differs sharply from science. Using even English texts such as Arthur Eddington's *Nature of the Physical World* (1928), Raymond shows the contrast between quantitative science and poetry, which is concerned with quality and, in contrast to the attempts of science to reduce everything to a simple Einsteinian formula, is caught up in the fullness of things. Raymond sounds here like the American John Crowe Ransom: poetry means participation in the world, identification of subject and object, and thus an all-embracing sympathy. The universal and the particular must both be emphasized, and in this is implied the unity of mankind—though Raymond recognizes that such a belief can also lead to conflicts. At the end, Raymond appeals to Vico. Poetry is faithful to the alliance between man and man through all centuries and civilizations, and to that of man with all things.

A piece on the poet and language (originally in *Trivium*, 1944) embraces, surprisingly, a mimetic concept of the role of poetry, referring to Aristotle and quoting the German dramatist Friedrich Hebbel (1813–63): "Man wird, was man sieht." Raymond praises imagination, very much in the sense of Coleridge, using the term *plasmatrice* and finally confessing that imagination is an unexplained mystery. He comments at length on what had become a preoccupation of modern criticism—the view (which he derives from Ferdinand de Saussure without naming him) that language is arbitrary and conventional. Raymond has doubts about this idea and tries to emphasize the remnants of onomatopoeia. He lists, for instance, words that contain "a" and suggest redness, though he then confesses that the French word *rouge* is itself an exception. Raymond agrees that words are not necessarily expressive in themselves but can be made so by the poet. He knows books such as Heinz Werner's *Grundfragen der Sprachphysionomik* and touches, at least vaguely, on the whole question of sound and meaning and their relation to each other. He praises Mal-

larmé's attempt to eliminate chance from language and has great sympathy for his ambition of giving poetry the task of coinciding with the real. But Raymond sees that this leads finally to a kind of myth, to the view that language is an ontology and that it tries to recover the power of the Word, in the biblical sense. It shows Raymond's reading in the psychological literature, but ends in a vague hope for an integral language that would grasp the essence of the world. Raymond approves of the idea of trying to determine the act of poetic creation as a specific act, but he cannot arrive at any solution except that we must assume some kind of harmony between man and nature.

Raymond demonstrates his interest in onomatopoeia and the whole question of imitation with sensitive comments on poems by Verlaine. Oddly enough, Raymond finds these sound-imitations extremely "classical" in their deliberate avoidance of direct expression of feeling.

The other essays go back to historical questions. There is a long piece on Ronsard and mannerism, in which Raymond discusses the whole new polemics about his position in the history of French poetry, showing a knowledge of the debate at the time and recent readings in E. R. Curtius. Raymond gives examples of Ronsard's poetry that could be considered manneristic, some explicit in their eroticism. This is followed by an article on the frontiers between Baroque and Mannerism, a learned and sensitive discussion of seventeenth-century French poetry, which draws on Raymond's thesis on Ronsard but now much more boldly claims for this poetry a value as high poetry. Raymond devotes two essays to Baudelaire. "Baudelaire et la sculpture," which contains many new and original observations, addresses the poet's concern with emaciated women and with skeletons. The other, more general essay sees Baudelaire as propounder of a romantic concept of the imagination, a view with which I fully agree (see this *History*, vol. 4). This second essay focuses on Baudelaire's attempt to analogize the whole of nature to man and to see the aim of poetry in the identification of object and subject. This imagination is more than real. On the whole, Raymond plays down the satanic and gloomy side of Baudelaire and thinks of him as "a perfect chemist and a saintly soul"— though the chemist, he agrees, is in part associated with Satan.

Mainly through his book *De Baudelaire au surréalisme*, Raymond established his authority over his followers, even though they were writing on very different topics. These eminent critics and some followers recognized Raymond as the head of a group paradoxically called the Geneva School, though, of the main figures, Albert Béguin came from the Jura and Georges Poulet was a Belgian who settled first in Scotland. *Critics of Consciousness*, the title of Sarah Lawall's book on the whole group, is a

more accurate description of their doctrine. In 1979 Poulet and a younger
group of friends and admirers assembled at Cartigny, the place of Raymond's retirement and death, and discussed for days his and Béguin's
work, though Raymond was too ill to attend. The proceedings were published after his death as *Albert Béguin et Marcel Raymond: Colloque de Cartigny* (1979).

ALBERT BÉGUIN (1902–1957)

I consider Albert Béguin's *L'Ame romantique et le rêve* (1937) one of the
finest productions, or even the finest, of French literary scholarship in
this century. I met M. Béguin in 1952 at Yale, where he was giving a lecture. We sat down in private and had a long conversation in German,
which he spoke fluently and gladly. He struck me as a modest, even
humble man, deeply religious, with a face that shone with spirituality. He
told me what he apparently told other interviewers, that in about 1926 he
was a clerk in a bookshop (I see from other accounts that the shop was in
Batignolles). He was often bored there and was intrigued by a large collection, covered with dust, on the highest shelf—German volumes with
the name Jean Paul on them. The name intrigued him, as it reminded
him of Rousseau and of an epigraph in *La Chartreuse de Parme* attributed
to Jean Paul (the epigraph was of course composed by Stendhal himself,
who followed the fashion of Sir Walter Scott by arbitrarily inventing epi-
graphs). Béguin found *Hesperus* on the shelf and started to decipher it.
He must have done a great deal of reading in German, much more than is
usually assumed, as he translated first an E. T. A. Hoffmann story, "Salva-
tor Rosa" (1926), and then Eduard Mörike's *Mozart auf der Reise nach Prag*
(1929), as well as the two volumes of *Hesperus* (1930)—an arduous task. By
that time, Béguin, who was studying in Geneva, had applied for a French
lectureship in Germany. He was assigned to the University of Halle and
spent five years there, learning and reading German. He and his wife
seem to have lived in almost complete isolation. It took him a long time to
discover what was going on in Germany after Hitler's seizure of power.
Béguin resigned in 1934; he was not, as has been stated, expelled from
Germany but simply felt he was spending time unprofitably in unconge-
nial surroundings. He returned to Geneva to study and to write his thesis
for the doctorate of letters, which became the book *L'Ame romantique et le
rêve*. It made such an impression that he was immediately nominated professor of French literature at the University of Basel. The war had broken
out, and Béguin more and more moved away from his German interests.
In November 1940 he converted to Catholicism, though he came from

a Protestant family in the Jura, where he was born in 1902. He gave up his academic career and went to Paris, where he became the founder and editor of the magazine *Esprit*. He died, unfortunately very early, on 3 May 1957, of a heart attack in Rome.

Béguin's thesis for the University of Geneva appeared in 1937 as two volumes in the series Cahiers du Sud. It was a small edition—only about nine hundred copies, which were soon sold out—and Béguin was persuaded to abridge it, drop all the elaborate references, and publish it as a single volume in 1946. This was the edition that secured his reputation. The later German translation, *Traumwelt und Romantik,* by Peter Grotzer (1972), has the great advantage of quoting all the German works in the original and tracking down the sometimes serious mistranslations of the French version.

The book begins with an elaborate discussion of dreaming and waking, conceived as parallel to each other. The main trouble of the whole book is precisely here. Béguin cannot quite distinguish (and this is not his fault) between night dreams and daydreams, or between invention and interpretation. He cannot face the inevitable dilemma that the dream world, whether described, reported, or analyzed, comes to us in the form of a text. Only through language can we know about these experiences or reports. This problem is put in the most drastic manner in Maurice Blanchot's writings, for instance, in the preface to *Faux pas* (1943), "De l'angoisse au langage." The paradox is that the poet wants to express the inexpressible and can express it only in language. Blanchot, quite logically, sees silence as the aim of literature, which at the same time is impossible. If writers were silent, there would be no literature. This deep anxiety about language later led to the nihilistic conclusions of deconstruction. There is, claim the deconstructionists, only text, with no relation to reality.

In the preface to *L'Ame romantique et le rêve,* Béguin recalls how in childhood he had read fairy tales and poems by Heine and Eichendorff and soon discovered surrealism and Rimbaud. He himself constantly felt that the borderline between "I" and "non-I" is displaced and even obliterated by poetry, but he tries to answer the question that the romantics asked, whether dreams are not vestiges of the golden age. Béguin quite openly denies that his study is objective in an academic sense: it is a personal inquiry and not a study of influences in any traditional comparative literature sense. He thinks of the relation between German and French romanticism as based on affinities among spiritual families rather than on actual reading and knowledge of the Germans by the French. Béguin strongly disapproves of the critics of the so-called Goethe-Zeit, who judged the romantics from a Goethean point of view. They fail because sympathy is the only method. The life of dreams is for Béguin and for the German romantics a life in which the memory of the golden age survives or is anticipated. In one passage he goes so far as to say that "our soul is an original pulsation with the stars." Béguin rejects psychoanalysis as opposed to romanticism: it is a rationalistic eighteenth-century point of view that obscures the true construction of a reality. Psychology uses the work of art only as a document and is irrelevant to the quality and impact of the poetry.

After this introduction, Béguin devotes a long section to the interest in dreams in the eighteenth century mainly among psychologists in Germany. He quotes an unknown writer, Ludwig K. von Jaholt (1795), that dreaming is involuntary poetry, and then goes on to study the writings of Georg Christoph Lichtenberg and Karl Philipp Moritz. Moritz's pedagogical novel *Anton Reiser* (1785–90) is said to anticipate Proust in the distinction between a sensation born of memory and an absolute memory. Moritz asked: "What is my existence? What is my life?" He tried to think without words, and the idea of existence (*Dasein*) seemed to him the limit of all thinking, of *la pensée humaine* (*ARR*, 32). Moritz believes that reminiscences in early states of mind predate the fragmentation of consciousness into individuals, an idea which anticipates Schopenhauer and Jung. Béguin then undertakes to explain what he calls the "reintegration of nature into man" in the writings of Herder, Goethe, and Schelling. He studies several often fantastic *Naturphilosophen* who assume a literal and, to my mind, absurd identity between body and nature. Franz Baader (1765–1841) speaks of a birthmark growing like a strawberry when spring comes. Béguin studies also all kinds of German speculations about the metaphysics of dreams. They often anticipate Bergson in the claim that dreams reach a supreme reality in which man tries to unify soul and being. In Paul Vitalis Troxler's (1780–1866) *Hymn to Nature* (usually ascribed to Goethe) body and soul are conceived as a unity, which, however, is dominated by spirit. Troxler makes to my mind an incomprehensible distinction between *Leib* and *Körper* (95). According to Béguin, the study of dreams leads often to a study of dream symbolism. The most famous book is *Die Symbolik des Traumes* (1814) by Heinrich von Schubert. In dreams the soul speaks another language. Dream language is poetry made out of symbols and metaphors. Troxler, for example, determined what colors mean: yellow announces mourning; red, joy (109). In dreams a storm announces deep suffering. The navel alludes to the native country and a shoulder to a bed companion. Schubert continues in this vein, identifying motifs in dreams with specific events in real life. The assumption is always that nature is a revelation of God and that we have to learn to read this alphabet of hieroglyphs. Schubert allows irony in the sense of Friedrich Schlegel, however, which permits him to look at dreams as often humorous comments on reality. He deplores the present practice of poetry, which he says has become prose. Béguin emphasizes that man is a double creature who lives in two worlds, which is always also interpreted as offering a choice between night and day, good and evil. All of this assumed dualism, of course, takes for granted the Fall of Man.

These elaborate and often learned introductory sections on the German *Naturphilosophen,* which I have sketched only in part, have been criticized for ignoring the actual philosophical background, and though Béguin often refers to Schelling, he discusses neither Fichte nor Schlegel in a philosophical context. Béguin focuses on the literary, in spite of his recognition that the aesthetic is only part of the "stream of consciousness," or the developing life of the mind.

The book definitely centers on the great German romantics in its next section. Jean Paul is the main hero. He is a poet of cosmic visions, for whom the whole universe is dissolved into sound and color. His visions include horrible faces without sight, battlefields drenched in blood, bodies from which hands and arms are severed. Béguin has compiled a whole table of dreams in Jean Paul's novels and admires him as the greatest of the German romantics, one who has a grasp of the kind of visions that are later articulated in French by Victor Hugo in his last works, *Dieu* and *La Fin de Satan.* The most famous of Jean Paul's visions is that of the death of God, where the dead Christ realizes that heaven is empty. This dream of the death of God, imagined as sightless with an empty eye socket, made a great impression on Mme de Staël, who quotes it in *De l'Allemagne* (1810), from which Nerval and Hugo derive the whole image. One should note that Jean Paul earlier had written a dream called "The Complaints of the Dead Shakespeare," and then substituted Christ in his novel *Siebenkäs* (1796–97). Dream and poetry evoke myths, which formulate the inexpressible center of our being. Everything is metamorphosed by the metaphysical imagination. Jean Paul sees a deep affiliation between dream and aesthetic experience and thinks of man as double: there are two "I" 's, the one who lives and dreams and the critical and satirical spectator who resists life and dreaming (*ARR,* 191). Béguin's characterization of Jean Paul is excellent but obviously ignores wide stretches of his work, particularly the humorous and the idyllic side.

The next chapter is devoted to Novalis. *Heinrich von Ofterdingen* (1802), Béguin notes, is much closer to allegory than anything in Jean Paul, and the dream in the novel, which has erotic overtones, is much nearer to popular tradition. Novalis was convinced that here and now we live in a higher world, that "the world becomes dream and the dream becomes world" (*ARR*, 195). He believed in a magic transformation of the world. Béguin discusses Novalis's relationship with Sophie von Kühn, who was only thirteen when he knew her. According to Béguin, she was not particularly intelligent and cannot be considered as a love object for Novalis, who later said, "I had religion for Sophie, but not love" (199). For Béguin Novalis is the real initiator of German romanticism. He hoped that poetry and philosophy would transform the earth and that an act of will would lift man above himself. Novalis believed that man had to reconstitute the world in its original unity and should be able to transform the world according to his will. It is the essence of a genius that he speak of imagined objects as real objects and treat them as such. The universe is an analogy of the human mind. The conscious and the unconscious must be in harmony, and Novalis envisages the end of history as a return to images of the golden age. Béguin admires *Hymnen an die Nacht* (1800) as a masterpiece of properly romantic poetry (211), and he discusses in detail the cult of night and its history.

Turning next to Ludwig Tieck, Béguin notes that Tieck created in his novels a hero who hesitates to recognize the reality of the external world. Béguin is surprised that Tieck uses Shakespeare as an example—mainly the Shakespeare of *The Tempest*. Tieck's essay "Das Wunderbare" argues that Shakespeare closely observed his own dreams and wished to live entirely in the dream world. The hero of *William Lovell* (1795–96) cannot comprehend reality. The next novel, *Franz Sternbalds Wanderungen* (1798), is merely another version of the same topic, and so are most of Tieck's stories and novels, which always involve anxiety and the punishment of erotic desire. In his later development Tieck more and more renounced his connection with dreams. Béguin thinks that he did not understand the new German romantic movement. The sentiment of reality, the taste for the nightscape, the attention to the imaginary emerging from the unconscious are constant motifs in Tieck, who, however, had neither the heroism nor the virile desire to triumph over his dream world. Possibly on purpose, Béguin ignores Tieck's later works, which became realistic in the sense of early genre observation and picturesqueness.

In the chapter on Achim von Arnim, Béguin has a good deal to say about his wife, Bettina, whom he seems to admire extravagantly despite her theatricality. Arnim presents the strange case of a man who lived a double life: he was an efficient landowner and agricultural expert in East Prussia, whose writings bear no relation to his ordinary existence or even to real life. Béguin admires particularly the preface to *Die Kronenwächter*, in which Arnim argues that the truth of poetry is higher than that of history. Poetry leads the alienated world back to external community. The poets are also seers, but interestingly, like Poe at the same time, Arnim disparages passion in poetry. Feeling, yes, but no passion. Béguin prefers the unfinished second volume of *Isabella von Ägypten* to the first; he thinks it an important, poetic book, whose strength lies in the internal life, the deep layers of the soul, where monstrous ideals and idols sometimes live, often illuminated by rays descending from the divine. Arnim belongs to those who express their secret life and have given up governing it. In many ways he anticipates surrealism.

Béguin's next chapter is devoted to Clemens Brentano, the greatest lyrical poet of German romanticism. According to Béguin, Brentano's only interest was the drama of his own soul, his weakness, his sins, his prayers, his humility. He never looked for explanations of such symbols. Though his mother was Protestant, his father brought him up in the Catholic faith, and he remained absorbed in the cult of the Madonna which, Béguin asserts, is one of the permanent images each of us has hidden in his soul (*ARR*, 274). The *Romanzen vom Rosencranz* is Brentano's best work, though he never published it, while there are many fine things in the posthumous writings, in the unlimited dreams, or in such personal poems as "Cries of a Distressed Soul" and "Reverberations of Beethoven's Music" (which Béguin thinks is not unworthy of the composer) (294). In his discussion of the novel *Godwi* (*Ein verwilderter Roman von Maria*), Béguin ignores Brentano's self-satirical and deliberate breaking of the artistic illusion: one may recall the passage where Godwi says, "Here is the pond in which I will fall on page 213, volume two."

The subject of the last chapter in this section is E. T. A. Hoffmann. Béguin makes much of his being a composer, one who would put us in touch with the invisible world. A dream is a substitute for life. Béguin rightly deplores Hoffmann's reputation as a *Gespenster-Hoffmann*, a descendant of the *roman noir,* who uses such romantic conventions as hereditary curses and the sudden, totally irrational actions of the court councillor, who behaves like the Devil, dancing and jumping around like a marionette. Tenderness and beauty often liven up this cauldron of sorcery, but in turn may be dispelled by sarcastic laughter. This aspect of Hoffmann obscures his originality, his victories over his own self. In *Der goldene Topf* Hoffmann displays a real knowledge of abnormal life and gives it vitality and vigor. Béguin is impressed by Hoffmann's handling of vampirism in several stories and of the *Doppelgänger* motif. He compares *Die Elixiere des Teufels* with the visions of Anselm in *Der goldene Topf*, as having common ground. Surprisingly, he fails to mention that *Die Elixiere des Teufels* is a close imitation of Matthew Lewis's *The Monk*. Béguin quotes Abraham the Magician in *Kater Murr* as saying that "nothing in the world occurs naturally." Man is related to everything. The dream in *Die Elixiere des Teufels* seems to him worthy of Dostoevsky (*ARR*, 301). Béguin criticizes Hoffmann for having little sense of his own personality and of personality in general. Hoffmann feels a stranger in the world, though there is a utopian hope somewhere in the distant future. Béguin notices that in *Die Elixiere des Teufels* Hoffmann avoids the word *God* completely. He does not seem to realize that this may well have been influenced by the English source, Lewis's *The Monk*, since in eighteenth-century England God could not be mentioned in print in secular contexts. Béguin is a great admirer of Hoffmann, particularly of the *Prinzessin Brambilla* and *Der goldene Topf*, which seem to him the climax of romantic art. Next to these two stories, only some poems of Novalis and Brentano are comparable. Hoffmann was, as Béguin emphasizes, completely absorbed by the claims of art, and by art as an inspiration for the act of cognition, which requires sacrificing earthly love. In his recently discovered diary Hoffmann expresses relief that Julia Marc, who was his supposedly tragic love in Bamberg, had finally married a philistine.

A new chapter called "Milky Ways and Meteors" returns to romanticism's general preoccupation with dreaming and then sketches rather quickly the representatives of the later generation in their relation to dreams. In Eichendorff there is constant allusion to the inexpressible, a theme of many of his novels. Béguin very briefly discusses Heine, whose work seems mainly the cry of a suffering individual, an elegy for his youth and lost innocence, but has a touch of modernism with its constant ironic interruptions. Béguin quotes the end of Heine's poem on bad dreams: "Bury the old and lying songs, the old and sad dreams, let us look for a big shroud. This shroud should be bigger than the wine barrel at the bottom of the castle at Heidelberg." Actually, Béguin admires Kleist most highly: he has works of greatness and perfection, but Béguin recognizes that the theme of dreams is only marginal for him, with the exception of *Das Käthchen von Heilbronn* (1810). Kleist's famous essay on the *Marionettentheater* is an apology for unconscious creation.

With a new chapter Béguin suddenly moves to France. He is of the opinion that in 1830 nobody in France knew anything about German romanticism, despite the fact that the slogan came from Germany through Mme de Staël. Béguin complains about the modern neglect of the flowering of French poetry in the nineteenth century, as well as of its background, the local and general tradition of occult or mystical worship. He mentions the eighteenth-century mystic philosopher Louis Claude

de Saint-Martin. Then come the masters of *rêverie:* Senancour, Charles
Nodier, Maurice de Guérin, and finally Proust. All of them derive from
Rousseau's "Fifth Reverie," which has "given all new poets confidence in
the revelation of the dark uncontested movements of time." Béguin discusses Nodier and his fairy tale *La Fée aux miettes* (1834), which pushes
its images so far as to acquire finally the strength of myth. Nodier must
see the images in their eternal reality and make them visible, saying that
"the life of sleep is more majestic than real life." Sleep "is not only the
most productive, but also the clearest situation in which we see reality."
Béguin then discusses Guérin's poem *Le Centaure* (1840) and particularly
the newly discovered *Cahier vert* (1861), which contains high praise for
German thought. But Béguin objects to Guérin's obsessive habit of self-
observation, for poetry disappears in such self-consciousness. Guérin tells
us, "I inhabit the interior elements of things. I retrace the rays of stars
and the current of rivers until I reach the bosom of the mysteries of their
generation." Béguin is taken by this harmonious text and Guérin's sense
of origins and the need to recover the past. Béguin comments that the
French spirit usually ignores what is familiar to the Germanic soul, noting
that the German language, even in ordinary usage, employs abundantly
the prefix *Ur* to designate the original, primordial state of things, beings,
and ideas. This is an essential difference, asserts Béguin in a passage
rare in his writings that speculates rashly on the difference between the
French and the German mind. That is why the Germans are committed
to "becoming," to evolution, and why they want to retrace the current
of incessant metamorphosis and contemplate the original state, the only
moment of purity, immobility outside of time, analogous to what will be
at the end of time. The French, not accustomed to considering the condition of becoming, are more inclined to see the condition of permanent
being. They are less tempted to oppose the infinite flow of life, a primordial state to which they could attach their nostalgia. This nostalgia is
apparently the main theme in Guérin's writings (*ARR,* 349). *Le Centaure*
is one of the few Dionysiac works of French literature, but Béguin prefers Guérin's *Méditation sur la mort de Marie* (1861), which seems to him
unique in French literature before Hugo. Guérin's is "the voice of cosmic
intoxication" (353).

Béguin then comments on Amiel and the sixteen thousand pages of
his diary. Amiel is a passive observer who depersonalizes himself. His
most famous pages of cosmogonic reverie reflect his feeling that he pos-
sesses the infinite. Béguin deplores his unfortunate distinction between
life and contemplation. Amiel lived in Geneva and of course had read
many of the Germans, for instance, the *Naturphilosophen* Heinrich von

Schubert and Carl Gustav Carus. He was inclined toward Buddhism and a kind of Indian mysticism. Amiel views the world as a dream of maya, the poet as a seer. Imagination, he says, is a form of knowledge.

Proust, usually seen as a depicter of French society, is actually, according to Béguin, one of the greatest mystics of modern times (*ARR*, 354). He achieves a victory over time, he has confidence in poetry as a means of escaping time. He admires Nerval and Baudelaire. All the chapters in the last volume of the great series, *Le Temps retrouvé*, reflect this neopantheism (384). There is nothing of this sort in Bergson. I agree fully with Béguin that the association of Proust with Bergsonism is completely mistaken.

The next chapter is called "The Birth of Poetry"—presumably only in France. Béguin asserts that modern aesthetics owes much to Nerval, whose discoveries are rather different from Senancour's experience of dreaming. *Aurélia* (1855) and some of the sonnets in *Les Chimères* (1854) are unique in French literature. Poetry is the tool for achieving truth, for opening the mystical doors that divide us from the world of the invisible. *Aurélia* is a dream-poem, whose plot is trivial: disappointment with an actress. Nerval believes that "in sleep we enter a new life, free of space and time, which is undoubtedly similar to what will happen to us after death." The dream is a prefiguration of eternal life. Much of Nerval's poetry has a tinge of despair and is concerned with pathological states; he admired Hoffmann's *Die Elixiere des Teufels*. Béguin regards *Aurélia* as a surprising and heroic work, but can find no possible explanation for the sonnet "El Desdichado." To my mind, only one line is incomprehensible: "The prince of Aquitania at the ruined tower" (*ARR*, 365). Even today nobody knows where this prince comes from, but it may have been the memory of a quite remote allusion and is in itself perfectly comprehensible. In Nerval there is plenty of synesthesia: the whole world appears as a network of correspondences.

In Béguin's view, there are three summits of nineteenth-century poetry —Nerval, Baudelaire, and Hugo. Then, twenty years later, came the great breakthrough: Rimbaud's *Une Saison en enfer* (1873). In Hugo only the last poems, *Dieu* and *La Fin de Satan*, create a new myth. Béguin describes Hugo's conversion to occultism and the strange hilarity among his ghosts, but he thinks that this late stage of Hugo is quite wrongly neglected (*ARR*, 374). The section on Baudelaire starts by describing his ambivalent relation to Hugo. Baudelaire differs from Hugo (and in this respect is closer to German romanticism) in his view that magic is a matter of will: one must will to dream. Poetry is an act of grace, of inner presence, of which man is not the master; but at the same time he must clearly show in poetry his defiance of the world and of God. There is a definite satanic edge

in Baudelaire: all nature is fallen. The customary emphasis on the sonnet "Correspondances" is mistaken, argues Béguin. Synesthesia is only a
minor theme in Baudelaire; he is more concerned with states of deperson-
alization and with nostalgia for a golden age, for the original unity (381).
Baudelaire is the main initiator of a tentative magic, a cult of images that
allows us to grasp the essence of the universe. The section on Baudelaire
is quite deliberately one-sided or fragmentary.

With Mallarmé we get to a poet who leaves the initiative to words,
whereas Rimbaud declared, "I assist at the bursting out, the birth, of my
thought." Mallarmé led a life of dreams, while Rimbaud dropped poetry
in favor of a life of action as a trader in ivory. Béguin's main admiration
and love go to the surrealists, particularly André Breton's novel *Nadja*
(1928); Béguin deplores, however, his later turn toward revolution. Paul
Eluard, the last poet Béguin describes, combines highest purity with sensual pleasure. A main motif of modern poetry is the restoration of an
improbable innocence, of a promised paradise. Béguin ends by quoting
a poem by Léon-Paul Fargue, which does not seem, however, in any way
surrealistic: "One day God will give us the happiness that he has promised" (*ARR*, 473).

After this historical survey of what he considers the main tradition
of genuine poetry in France, Béguin gives what seems to be primarily
his own creed of poetry. He rejects modern psychology, meaning largely
psychoanalysis, and appeals to the obscure feeling of regret which reminds us that man used to live in a deeper and more harmonious relation
with the world. Poets have a special ability to induce such a longing. An
obscure memory forces the poet to go far back into the past, to myth.
The soul is concerned with its transtemporal fate, with origins and possibly with a future in other spaces. The origins of man are in touch with a
higher reality, whether divine or cosmic, but certainly infinite and spiritual. Poetry is the absolutely real, higher than history. The poet brings
together things far apart in space and time, which correspond to real kinship. Poetry is the only possible answer to the *Ur-angst* of man locked in
his temporal existence. Poetry affirms the analogical conception of the
universe. It reasserts the deepest structure of spirit or of total being,
and its spontaneous rhythms are identical with the structure and great
rhythms of the universe. The dream is the model of aesthetic experience.
The poet arrives at the same contemplation without object, at pure inexpressible *présence* (a noun that corresponds to Heidegger's *Dasein*). It leads
to the total divestment of images, to a negation which is self-negation.
Romanticism recognized the deep resemblance between poetic states and
religious revelations. In poetry the word and the birth of poetic form re-

turn us to consciousness. A new marvelling induced by poetry restores objects to their first novelty and restores to the world its fairy-tale appearance. The poet names the objects—they say what they want to say. On returning to daily life everything is different. Places and faces have assumed the appearance they had in the eyes of a child: "From the dream I return with the ability to love life, people, things, and acts which I had forgotten and disregarded in quitting the child's paradise. The solitude of poetry and dream lightens our desolate solitude. From the depths of our sadness, which has turned us away from life, there rises a song of purest happiness." These are the last words of the book.

In 1957 Béguin published a collection of papers called *Poésie de la présence de Chrétien de Troyes à Pierre Emmanuel*. Many of the essays go back to the forties, and Béguin even reprints a whole chapter from *L'Ame romantique et le rêve*. The book is a sketch of the history of French poetry from the beginnings to the surrealists, following in its conception the model of Marcel Raymond's sketch in *Etre et dire*. Béguin differs, however, from Raymond by placing far greater emphasis on a mystical interpretation of the role of poetry. For Raymond, poetry is conceived as a way of knowing, not simply of the external or psychic world but also of the universe. Poetry supposedly restores the original unity between man and the universe or nature. In a literal sense, Béguin believes that we return to the unity of primitive man in myth and ritual. He does, however, distinguish sharply between mysticism and poetry. Mysticism aims at the abolition of the self, a union with God, whereas poetry is trapped in the paradox that it can express the ineffable only by words. Mysticism ends in silence, but poetry achieves the work of art, which has both aesthetic and moral value. The book differs also from Béguin's other writings in its emphasis on the "presence" of poetry. *Présence* seems an unnecessary and even obfuscating term for the work of art, its unity and coherence.

The essays in *Poésie de la présence* span the whole history of French poetry, seeing the beginning of real poetry in Chrétien de Troyes, whose every plot and character is interpreted as containing implicit symbolism. Béguin admires also the whole tradition of the quest for the Grail. Somewhat surprising is Béguin's dismissal of Wolfram von Eschenbach as representative of a people still bound up in "primitive paganism." *Parzival* surely cannot be reduced to such a category. In another article Béguin espouses the view that Maurice Scève's Neoplatonic idealism— the ideal somehow hovering above appearance—is comparable to that of Mallarmé. Béguin finds in Scève the same adoration of night and nothingness, the same mystical despair. Béguin's essay on Pierre Corneille is surprising in its emphasis on his optimism and lucidity. He praises the

Christian martyr in *Polyeucte* (1643) for his heroism of sanctity. Oddly enough, while his main emphasis is on this martyr drama, at other points Béguin exalts the comedy *Suréna* (1672), in order to combat the view that Corneille had declined in his later years. Béguin differs with Corneille in making much of the night images in Racine's *Phèdre* (1677). He admires and defends the famous *flamme noire*, the paradoxical image of "black burning," which is for him the example of the reconciliation of opposites.

A whole chapter of *Poésie de la présence* is devoted to the tradition of occultism in French poetry, which obviously descends from the Renaissance. Béguin shows that there was an undercurrent of irrational, possibly superstitious, belief in the occult throughout French poetry, exemplified in the famous dream of Jean Paul as used by Hugo, who admired it but misinterpreted it. The dream was available to him only through Mme de Staël's truncated translation, which speaks of the empty, black, and bottomless eye socket of God, ignoring or not understanding that Jean Paul himself put it into a context that denied such atheism. Hugo, using constantly the figure of Jean Paul and alluding to him even late, became a convert to occultism in his years on Guernsey, engaging in table rapping and communications with spirits. Béguin admires particularly Hugo's last poems, *Dieu* and *La Fin de Satan:* they seem to him a return to the proper concept of poetry, which he thinks had been deserted by both the eighteenth century and the sentimental rhetoric of French romanticism. The French romantics had no understanding and knowledge of the Germans, but early on resumed the true concept of poetry on the basis of their own traditions in folklore—as, for instance, in Nodier, to whom Béguin devotes a chapter praising *La Fée aux miettes*. Baudelaire is the real innovator of French poetry. Béguin discusses "Mon coeur mis à nu," rejecting the suggestion that Baudelaire became a convert to Catholic orthodoxy, whatever his behavior may have been in the final stages of his fatal illness.

The remaining essays in *Poésie de la présence* emphasize what Béguin considers true poetry, such as that of Verlaine, who returned to a poetry of feeling and rejected all the rest as *littérature*. This pejorative use of the word was very influential in France and still survives among critics like Roland Barthes. The last essays follow this trend as far as Pierre Emmanuel and even discuss Breton with considerable sympathy. The whole volume ends somewhat oddly with a quotation from Emmanuel, in which he hopes for a restitution of an earthly paradise. Béguin apparently kept his faith in a good God.

Many of Béguin's later writings return to *L'Ame romantique et le rêve* and comment elaborately on it, developing particular themes, like the religion of Novalis or of E. T. A. Hoffmann. Several essays were collected well after Béguin's death in *Création et destinée* (1973). The first essay in this collection is an amusing piece on reading that begins with a story about Albert Thibaudet: one of his students (who did not dare to introduce himself) saw Thibaudet on the train, pulling books from a big suitcase, cutting a few pages, and throwing all the books behind the *portière*. Béguin then tells the story of his discovery of Jean Paul in a bookstore in Batignolles. He himself recovers faith in a future life, in the presence of God in the universe, and in the union of romanticism and Christianity. The Germans knew this union of the unconscious and the conscious. While he admits that Goethe and Carus originated the view of organic unity, Béguin rejects the classicist interpretation of romanticism. He holds a very narrow conception of German romanticism, noting disparagingly that with the exception of "one or two negligible Schlegels, sick with theory," the only German romanticists are Novalis, Brentano, Arnim, and possibly Tieck. In this article, written in 1937, Béguin is greatly troubled by the new aggressive nationalism of Hitler that threatened to destroy European civilization. Béguin rejects the familiar idea that there are two Germanys—one materialistic and aggressive, the other spiritual and philosophical. One cannot deny, he says, that Arnim was a blind anti-Semite and a furious Gallophobe who hated Napoleon and his conquests (*CD*, 73). But it is also true that Germany consists of a shapeless mass of people, topped by a small cultivated class usually without social and political consciousness, whereas France is a unified nation permeated by a single spirit.

Béguin came to admire E. T. A. Hoffmann as the best artist among the German romantics. One of his last enterprises was a collection of Hoffmann's works, for which he wrote a long introduction (*CD*, 99–124) that gives a fairly detailed biography of Hoffmann and surveys his writings, with a constant emphasis on his theme of the relation of the artist to society. Unlike other German romantics, Hoffmann, we are told, tried always to accommodate himself to reality, though he never succeeded.

Béguin also wrote a good deal about contemporary critics, particularly Marcel Raymond, his master, whose interpretation of the history of French poetry Béguin greatly admires, though he has a less sober view of the achievement of modern French poetry. For Raymond poetry is a kind of knowledge, while for Béguin it is a way to faith. Béguin's comments on Charles Du Bos grossly overrate him, particularly his little book in English *What Is Literature?* (1940), which seems to me an extremely simple set of sentimental sermons. More justly, Béguin admires some of Du Bos's journals, which all attempt to analyze his embrace of the Catholic faith.

Béguin strongly sides with Du Bos in his refusal to accept orders from a Jesuit abbot who was a strict Thomist and tried to make Du Bos give up writing on spirituality in literature. Béguin defends human liberty, though he sees its risks for faith. This abbot forbade Du Bos to publish his translation of the *Aphorisms* of Coventry Patmore, which seemed to his censor to violate Thomist ideas, whereas Du Bos thought of his own writings as a very personal search for a creed.

The most interesting piece in *Création et destinée*, from the point of view of literary criticism, is an excellent article on *Madame Bovary* (*CD*, 205–11), ostensibly a review of the edition of the newly discovered drafts of the original much longer version of the book, which Flaubert had abridged and reshaped. Béguin discusses the differences between the two versions, much preferring the earlier one as freer and more courageous both in its metaphors and in its explicitness in sexual matters. He shows that Emma's boredom becomes in the later version more banal and deprived of its metaphysical nature. Flaubert appears as a writer who sacrificed his original inspiration to what Béguin calls "the flattening mill of his later style." He succumbed to the idol of "art for art's sake" and damaged irremediably his "poem of boredom."

Another author who preoccupied Béguin is Balzac, about whom he published a first book called *Balzac visionnaire* (1946). It expounds the view that Balzac is not a realist and must be seen as a visionary—the term Baudelaire applied to Balzac without further elaboration. Béguin, however, tries to fortify this view—that Balzac created another world, an absolute world of spiritual reality, which has nothing whatever to do with what could be called realism. Béguin studies the occult sources of Balzac's philosophy and emphasizes among his works the so-called philosophical writings, *Louis Lambert* and *Séraphita*, which introduce a supernatural world. Béguin never mentions by name the book that anticipates his whole thesis, Ernst Robert Curtius's *Balzac* (1923), except in the dedication to a "prince des Balzaciens," Marcel Buteron, where Curtius is listed alongside other French writers on Balzac (Alain, Ramon Fernandez, Fernand Baldensperger). In the actual text there is no mention of Curtius, unless one takes Béguin's carefully limited attacks on realistic criticism to refer always to French criticism, thus showing some sort of bad conscience about failing to acknowledge his predecessor. The general point of view seems grossly exaggerated: it is hard to believe that for years Balzac was so tied to his desk that he could think of his characters simply as creations of his mind, existing in a new reality. I know, of course, the anecdotes about Balzac saying, "Let's get down to something real. I want to talk about Dr. Bianchon [the doctor in the novel *La Peau de chagrin*]."

Fictional characters seemed to him more real than any friend. But surely the novels are nourished by a tremendous immersion in actual reality, even though it may have been largely one of memory.

The Balzac book was reissued in 1965, some years after Béguin's death, under the title *Balzac lu et relu*. The new version reprints the earlier book in its entirety and adds introductions that Béguin wrote just before his death for a complete edition of Balzac. These introductions to various works by Balzac are sometimes of considerable interest, as they develop many points in *Balzac visionnaire*, but the selection made by the editor of the volume is obviously quite arbitrary. All the pieces show Béguin's preoccupation with Balzac's road to faith, with his struggle between orthodox religion and some freer creed. Béguin is quite aware that one must distinguish between Balzac's conversion after his marriage and on his deathbed, where he accepted the last rites of the Church, and the views actually presented and enacted in the novels. Béguin, in spite of his concern with matters of faith, remained a literary critic of great perception, who could distinguish between the author and his work and yet see the unity in these two aspects of a man's endeavor.

In his later years Béguin wrote profusely on the figures of the Catholic Renaissance, such writers as Georges Bernanos, Julien Green, St. John Perse, Charles-Ferdinand Ramuz, Charles Péguy, and Paul Claudel, on the surrealists, and on more recent poets, such as Pierre Reverdy and Pierre Emmanuel. But certainly Béguin's leading preoccupation was always religion, and poetry was only a means to it. Still, Béguin was a genuine critic who had excellent taste and knew how to defend his choices. He was one of the few twentieth-century French critics who had a grasp of aesthetic values, even though late in life he allowed them to be overshadowed by his concern for religion.

GEORGES POULET (1902–)

In 1956 the *Yale Review* sent me a group of books on criticism for review, among them the English translation of Georges Poulet's *Etudes sur le temps humain*. I reviewed Poulet's book toward the end of the essay, favorably, praising the subtlety of his method and the learning displayed and expounding somewhat the philosophical background in phenomenology and existentialism. I concluded, however:

> The claim (not made in the body of the book) that the method will change the course of literary criticism is obviously mistaken. No literary value judgements can be made by his criteria, though M. Poulet offers them off and on, implicitly. A work of art is neither better

nor worse for showing a deeper or slighter grasp of the problem of time. At most, a subtlety on this point will indicate or parallel artistic complexity. But clearly no coherent work of art need be analyzed by this method and the method applies just as successfully to a philosophical treatise or to isolated aphorisms (such as Pascal's) as to a long novel (such as Proust's). M. Poulet is not a *literary* critic (at least in this book) but a philosopher, a historian of ideas and feelings who succeeds best with thinkers who have expressly dealt with his problem or with writers such as Proust who have felt it profoundly and reflected on it extensively. When M. Poulet discusses authors such as Molière or Marivaux he tends to impose his philosophical pattern and to violate the integrity of his texts. Sometimes he presses hard to extract a meaning suitable for his purposes from trite reflections, seeing "negative eternity" in comic types, or "anterior" and "posterior duration" in the simple fact that Racine's *Iphigénie*, in its plot, precedes the Trojan War while *Andromaque* follows it. M. Poulet also does not quite escape the dangers of much intellectual history. As he is bound to set off authors and periods sharply, he is apt to minimize or ignore common elements and to magnify differences. Many passages he picks on echo experiences common to all mankind in all times and places. The idea that youth looks ahead while old age looks back, the saying that nothing will matter a hundred years from now, could be exemplified by proverbs among, say, the peasants of Eastern Europe. We need no Rousseau or Benjamin Constant to tell us this. Occasionally M. Poulet's intellect obscures his common sense: his power of analysis becomes a skill of extracting something from nothing or almost nothing: virtuosity, time for time's sake. But at his best, M. Poulet has used the concept of and feeling for time as a central light which illuminates the recesses of the mind of many writers and thinkers and some of the obscurest processes of intellectual history.

M. Poulet then wrote me a long letter, dated 6 October 1956, in which he not only defended his method but expounded it more clearly than in the book itself. The most striking detail of his letter is its reference to his essay on Molière. He admits it failed, not because there is no Molièresque time, however, but because he was unable to grasp it. This assumes that every man has a particular individual relation to space and time, and that it is the task of literary criticism to discover it. In further correspondence with M. Poulet, I tried to argue that this is only a farfetched hypothesis. We can discover and grasp the conception of time and space in writers such as Rousseau and Proust, who were concerned with it, but comedy such as Molière's has nothing to say on these topics except for commonplaces such as Time flies or proverbs which do not require the testimony of a great writer. I found it incomprehensible that M. Poulet thought it necessary to speculate on the special relation to space and time of a man who has been dead for more than three hundred years and who left no record whatsoever of any such relation to space and time. Comedy has been an almost stable genre since Terence, and the quotation that M. Poulet produces in the essay on Molière on the difference between tragedy and comedy could have come from any writer in the tradition of Renaissance comedy or *commedia dell'arte*. This essay, then, shows the danger of the whole enterprise. It ignores individual works of art and looks not for aesthetic value, but for the assumed mysterious *Cogito*, a term Poulet derives from Descartes but actually uses quite differently, to mean simply the psyche of the author. Poulet would indignantly reject the idea that he is studying psychology in any scientific sense, but it is difficult to see how a history of the concepts of space and time can escape probing into the psychology of the author and the mental climate of his period. I must admit I admired M. Poulet's skill in characterizing the main authors and relating their conception of space and time to large historical changes.

I had to conclude that Poulet's work is not literary criticism, though most of his evidence is drawn from literature. It does not allow any judgment and does not consider a single work of art as a totality. The method is that of *Geistesgeschichte*, intellectual history, where intellectual does not mean reason but the general mentality of man, including his sensations and feelings.

It seems to me fair, before criticizing Poulet's main theories, to describe his actual practice as a critic. I shall not try to summarize Poulet's elaborate introduction to *Etudes sur le temps humain*, as I find his shifts from philosophical and historical considerations to generalizations about experience confusing and even obfuscating (possibly deliberately).

The book starts with an essay on Montaigne, who is described as living in the present, living from moment to moment. Poulet quotes a passage from the *Essais* (Alcan edition, 1:175): "I conceive we have knowledge only of the present, none at all of the past, no more of what is to come." This convincing account, however, ignores Montaigne's deathbed conversion, when he professed to have hope in personal immortality.

The next chapter is devoted to the dream of Descartes in 1619. It argues that "time does not exist in the consciousness of Descartes. And having excluded consciousness of time from his ideas, he finds himself all of a sudden in the presence of time in that part of ourselves where time cannot avoid being present: the affective part" (*SHT*, 57). Poulet argues that the dream is authentic and not an allegory. It is a dream of deliverance, of reconciliation, which Poulet compares to the atmosphere of Shakespeare's *The Tempest*. Poulet summarizes Descarte's actual philosophical conclusions (72) in a way that has nothing to do with problems of space and time, unless we consider the deterministic mechanism of nature, which is perpetual movement, to relate to the problem of the book. Otherwise, Poulet discusses theological and metaphysical questions without regard to space and time. The whole book constantly deviates into general characterizations of the authors discussed.

In the next chapter Poulet argues that Pascal considered time to be something we do not know by reason but only through the heart. Poulet sees the truth of feeling as a profoundly Bergsonian concept—time as affective duration—but the intuitive feeling leads also, according to Pascal, to despair. We never live, but we hope to live. Pascal has moments in which he believes in God's grace, but it is seen only as a possibility in the famous argument of the wager.

The chapter on Molière is quite disappointing. Poulet quotes Molière only once, from a preface, and his reflections on the difference between tragedy and comedy are so traditional, and even trite, that they could apply to any comedy from Terence to George Bernard Shaw.

The next chapter, on Corneille, seems to me hardly related to the questions of human time. Poulet rightly emphasizes Corneille's concern with the will, which he identified with being human. The continuity of the self rests entirely on a choice of the will, which Poulet thinks implies a nontemporal being. The argument that will implies a nontemporal being seems to hark back to Schopenhauer and is not convincing unless one accepts his general metaphysics.

In the chapter "Notes on Racinian Time" Poulet argues that in Racine the past continues into the present. Tragedy in Racine differs from all other tragedy in this emphasis on fatality and irreversibility. In Racine there are three parallel durations "as in the medieval thinkers: the discontinuous time of actual passions; the continuous time of the fulfillment of divine will; and finally this will itself in its pure nontemporality" (*SHT*, 126). Poulet, who is usually sober and rational, becomes to my mind commonplace and even silly when he makes considerable fuss over the fact that *Andromaque* was written before *Iphigénie*, while of course the events recounted in Homer and Euripides occur in the opposite order. Saying that Racine becomes a slave to "anterior or posterior duration," as Poulet does, is a pretentious formulation of the commonplace.

The chapter on Fontenelle claims that his conception of time anticipated the thought of Bergson and Valéry (*SHT*, 147).

In the chapter on Abbé Prévost, Poulet starts with a generalization that seems to me vague and applicable to many other novels, like the Greek romances or the Spanish picaresque novels. Poulet says that there is a rhythm of pure successiveness, a simple series of one adventure after another, but that in Prévost these adventures are held together by a unity of feeling.

The most elaborate chapter is devoted to Rousseau. Poulet expounds Rousseau's philosophy of history, describing early man and young people today as completely passive, living for pure sensation and the feeling of actual existence, which constitute happiness. In later life man becomes obsessed with his desires and ambitions. As Poulet explains, in *Rêveries* Rousseau himself finally achieves moments of grace when he becomes identified with nature; time means nothing to him and the present lasts forever. Poulet discusses Rousseau's view that feeling can never be mistaken and describes the role of affective memory. While commenting, for instance, on the episode of the periwinkle in the *Confessions,* the sensation reappears in his mind, in memory. He relives his past as if for the first time. This seems to me the most successful chapter, though much of it could be expounded without particular attention to space and time.

In the chapter on Diderot, Poulet stresses his incoherence but again sees the anticipation of Bergsonian thought in Diderot's distinctions between intuition and intellect and also in his affirmation of the total life of the mind. Diderot, we are told, argued that emotion paralyzes creation. Poulet barely alludes to the *Paradoxe sur le comédien,* which articulates in strong terms the divorce between actor and person. Probably Poulet recognized that this argument would undermine his theory of criticism as complete identification.

In his chapter on Benjamin Constant Poulet makes the surprising claim that in *Adolphe,* for the first time in the novel, the past appears to be a veritable past (*SHT,* 214). While Poulet asserts that without freedom no human time is possible, he notes that Constant always emphasizes obedience to time and resignation.

Poulet makes Vigny sound like an existentialist. Being is first of all consciousness, and consciousness is first of all measured in the triple internal experience of past, present, and future, which constitutes duration. Vigny sees the paradox of language; the life of feeling is of the heart, is actual, whereas the life of the mind is temporary. Insofar as one can trust an entry in his *Journal,* Vigny believes that silence is the true poetry, a conclusion reached also by some recent critics.

Poulet emphasizes the seriality of memory in *Madame Bovary* and the hallucinatory clarity of images by which Flaubert accelerates emotion. Poulet then spends a page comparing Flaubert and Balzac. While Flaubert is interested in a stairway of causes, "Balzac starts with an a priori creature, posits at the outset the existence of a law-force, of which there remains simply to express next in terms more and more concrete, the descending curve into real life. Balzac, novelist of the determining; Flaubert, novelist of the determined" (*SHT,* 260).

The next chapter, on Baudelaire, is a fine characterization of the poet with some emphasis on his feeling for "the horrible burden of time." The world is conceived of as lacking any coherence, without fixed relations, a world essentially transitory, a world of contingencies. Poulet deliberately ignores many aspects of Baudelaire.

The chapter on Valéry again emphasizes Bergson. According to Poulet, Valéry drew a pessimistic conclusion from Bergsonism: man is abandoned to the transitory present and to the single flux of duration, a double nothingness. Duration is, in Valéry, "something hard, closed in, a closed cycle" (*SHT,* 289).

The last and longest chapter in *Etudes sur le temps humain* is on Proust, with whom Poulet identifies. He describes the whole novel as that of an existence in search of its essence. Oddly, Poulet minimizes the effect of memory illustrated in the famous moment of Marcel's tasting of the *madeleine.* What is lost and what is found in Proust is not lost time but a fragment of time, to which clings a fragment of space. If the past confers on the present its authentic existence, the search for the essences of things is of course a search for timelessness. Poulet argues, I think convincingly, that "nothing is more false than to compare Proustian duration with Bergsonian duration. The latter is full, the former empty; the latter is a continuity, the former a discontinuity" (*SHT,* 316). The outcome of this debate seems to me quite unequivocally to argue against any Bergsonian influence, no matter how plausible it may seem on the surface. Poulet concludes by saying that Proust's work is a retrospective view of all French thought on time.

Poulet continued his studies of human time in a second volume under a different title, *La Distance intérieure,* published in 1952. I shall not try to discuss this volume, which in substance applies the same method used in *Etudes sur le temps humain* to new texts, but I want to single out the essay on Marivaux because it elicited an interesting polemic with Leo Spitzer. Poulet collects, to my mind convincingly, a great number of passages from Marivaux's comedies, along with an occasional quotation from his novel, *La Vie de Marianne.* Characterizing the Marivauxian heroes as living in single moments, constantly being surprised by new events, Poulet concludes: "In contrast to the Cartesian *Cogito,* the Marivauxian *Cogito* is purely negative. I do not know what I think, nor even if I think. . . . The Marivauxian personage is incomprehensible to himself. . . . He has lost the thread of his very existence" (*ID,* 6–12). He has no past to sustain him, "without identity, without memory, without origin, without temporality, fallen from the skies, the Marivauxian being lands upon an indescribable world. . . . It suggests nothing, recalls nothing, signifies nothing. . . . The play of love and chance can only engender a chaos" (12). For Marivaux, "the instant is all, for it is only within itself, and not in time, that something happens" (16). The Marivauxian being, like the Proustian being, "constantly loses himself along the way" (25). The time of Marivaux, in the manner of Bergson, is made of a "continuous flow" (26).

Fancifully, Poulet says that Marivaux is "both . . . the point and the line; a point that extends out, and prolongs itself, and is transformed into a line; an instant which exceeds and lengthens itself, and which is transformed into time" (*ID*, 27). He then speaks of Marivaux's language as spontaneous and chancy: "I say what occurs to me." Poulet feels this is essentially an anticipation of Mallarmé: "Both . . . seek to mime all the variations of being. The play of time and of chance becomes a marvelous 'play of words'" (28).

This essay seems convincing in its characterization of Marivaux, whose comedies I have not read. I was surprised by Leo Spitzer's long comment, reprinted in *Romanische Literaturstudien* (1956). Focusing on Marivaux's only novel, *La Vie de Marianne*, Spitzer tries to refute Poulet's interpretation as totally erroneous. Poulet and Spitzer were then colleagues at Johns Hopkins University, and Spitzer must have been personally offended, as he somewhat sarcastically refers to Poulet's allusion to his "lack of philosophical culture and affiliation." Spitzer shows in great detail that the heroine of *La Vie de Marianne* is an extremely well-organized, stable, continuously moral heroine, who by force of character overcomes all obstacles. There is nothing whatever of the point-by-point life of the Marivauxian hero as conceived by Poulet. Marianne is a genius of the heart, who triumphs over the vicissitudes of life. The novel has a continuous outline. It is, to use the figure made famous by Stendhal, "a mirror along the road" that reflects the puddles on the road, whereas Poulet wrongly argues that the mirror is empty. Poulet's attempt to make Marivaux a skeptic, a predecessor of Proust or even of Kafka, is completely mistaken.

Marivaux's novel is nourished by a strong feeling which Spitzer thinks of as rococo trust in human nature, in the firmness of an ideal character. Its heroine is a model in life, far removed from the nihilism that Poulet finds everywhere. Spitzer also shows that Poulet has taken many of the quotations, even from the comedies, out of context, often giving them a sense opposite to that a contextual reading would give. Spitzer favors philology in the reading of all texts, before making any philosophical deductions and speculations. Spitzer seems to me substantially right, but he does not confront the main problem. Poulet is not interested in the novel, or any single work of art, but cares only for the hypothetical *Cogito* of the writer. *La Vie de Marianne* as a novel or the heroine as a figure means nothing to him. He thinks he has discovered Marivaux's special relation to space and time.

The last book in which Poulet explicitly addressed the problem of space is *L'Espace Proustien* (1963). It starts with the striking thesis of a contrast between Bergson and Proust: "Bergson denounces and rejects the metamorphosis of time into space. Proust not only accommodates himself to it, but installs himself in it, carries it to extremes, and makes of it finally one of the principles of his art" (*PS,* 4). Poulet argues that Proust is in search not only of lost time but also of lost space. Abundant quotations show how characters in Proust are attached to parts of a landscape. But these fragments of space are always seen by Proust in isolation from the real world. Poulet cites several instances where a fragment of space is used, to my mind quite arbitrarily, to establish a new world in which persons and places are united and places can be called persons. Poulet thus explains and even defends Proust's snobbery not as an admiration for specific noblemen and noblewomen, but as an attachment to names and places of some worthy memory. All appear to Proust as individual, just as he defines and describes cities such as Venice and Florence as individuals and sees characters such as Albertine from different angles. Poulet then shows how these characters are represented as discontinuous. Proust speaks of a progress interrupted by gaps. Distance can be taken as a synonym of space, and many scenes and characters in Proust emphasize the frightful inner distances between people, the "intermittences of the heart." This interior distance leads to the conclusion that human beings are always out of reach of others and that the distance between them is absolute. Each of us is like an eternal stranger in an eternal absence. Proust says that everything that lives is closed up in itself, but this rigorous conclusion splits existence in two. Poulet shows that the constantly true way of the world is double. The distinction Proust always maintains between the Guermantes way and the Méséglise way can, according to Poulet, actually be erased.

In the following chapter, Poulet argues that whatever continuity appears is the same as discontinuity—it is the "infinite stream of the mind," a phrase that appears in Ernst Robert Curtius's essay on Proust (*PS,* 61). Earlier we are told that while Proust wanted to reconquer time he also attempted to reconquer space, but Poulet sees that he actually does not completely succeed. There is a parallelism between the dialectic of time and that of space but no real meeting of the two. Poulet modifies some of these observations by pointing out the great importance of travel. In Proust the metamorphosis of space is brought about by travel. Poulet appeals to old ideas of the coincidence of contraries and admits that in Proust each thing has rapport with an infinity of others. Each being, like each place, offers an infinite number of possible positions. Poulet uses this in commenting on such famous scenes as Marcel's attempted kissing of Albertine. Albertine multiplied tenfold is already "Albertine vanished." The true image is lost in the midst of a crowd of masks. Again Poulet elaborates the contrast with Bergson: experience for Proust is not at all the burial of the past under the present, but, quite contrarily, the resurrection of the past in spite of the present. The juxtaposition of things and places has the effect of freezing the position, as juxtaposition is the opposite of motion. Poulet singles out Proust's early description of Florence and other instances of two purely simultaneous events and things, claiming that it would be difficult to find an equivalent of this method of juxtaposition in any other modern novelist.

The whole of Proust's work is a series of themes cut from the cloth of reality. Time gives way to space but things and characters remain discontinuous episodes, like a gallery of pictures. The world of Proust is made of, and remains made of, distinct episodes. Time has taken the form of space, and thus Proustian time is directly opposed to Bergsonian time. Proustian time is spatialized and juxtaposed. A plurality of episodes makes way for and constructs its own space, which is the space of a work of art.

This late, little book seems to me a particularly successful example of Poulet's method, as he is discussing a work that is especially concerned with time and space and that speculates on them. Proust's work lends itself to the kind of analysis to which Poulet subjects it. At times his parallels and metaphors seem to me farfetched, particularly when they leave the realm of literature and appeal to pictorial analogues. I'm unconvinced by his elaborate attempt to compare the novel to a predella and a reliquary. On the whole, as often in Poulet, his ingenuity and very real learning carry him away into a realm of fancy. Though Poulet does succeed in characterizing an elaborate and extensive work, a reader of his book would hardly have any idea of the Balzacian social picture that covers so much space. He mentions the name Swann, I think, only once. The whole of Proust's book is reduced to a series of memories and meditations abstracted from the body of the work, which is, after all, much more concrete and realistic than it would appear from Poulet's account.

After his studies of human time and space, Poulet moved on to a new topic. Les Métamorphoses du cercle (1961) is again an ingenious way of discussing and characterizing authors from the whole history of French (and other) literature. But unlike his earlier attempts to use time and space, Poulet's effort to exploit the idea of the circle and its circumference seems to me removed from literature, though literature is used as the text in most examples. Poulet displays great erudition in collecting circles and circumferences from all over literature, but he seems to me to achieve only a kind of thematology. Actually, what is in the forefront of Poulet's mind is a history of ideas, a history of attitudes for which we use the circle, along with an idea of wholeness. This is often surprisingly ingenious. I shall not try to describe the book in detail but only illustrate a few points to indicate his method.

In the chapter on romanticism, for instance, we are told that "for the first time there clearly appears the consciousness of the non-identity which distinguishes the self-center from the circumreferential self" (*MC*, 92). This statement seems hardly verifiable. Even long before antiquity, people must have realized the difference between themselves and the world around them. Poulet makes much of the discovery of the historical sense by the Germans Herder and Fichte. Man is intelligible only if one grasps him in the gradual unrolling of his history, a well-known thesis for which, however, Poulet's metaphors seem to me quite irrelevant. He says that "the history of humanity is not linear. It is the history of a point that becomes a sphere" (98). All philosophies supposedly became, with the German romantics, a study of the similarities between center and circle, and even more, a study of their dependence on each other. Poulet then produces a quotation from Friedrich Schlegel's late lectures (see 369, n. 19). Goethe is the hero of this chapter, which adopts as a matter of course the French periodization that assigns Goethe to romanticism and ignores his classicism. In Goethe, supposedly, the opposition between subject and object is surmounted, the center "thinks" the circle, a phrasing which, put in more empirical terms, merely means that Goethe never loses sight of himself and studies himself as a central object.

Many other chapters are somehow fitted into this scheme. For instance, a long piece on Edgar Allan Poe merely describes his dreamworld and uses the *Colloquy between Monos and Una* to document Poulet's belief that the "intemporal soul stands on the threshold of the temple of eternity" (*MC*, 190). Poulet takes seriously Poe's occult fantasies.

A chapter on Henry James forces him into the same framework. Poulet collects quotations to show that in James the loss of self is in fact caused by an abundance of memories. The Jamesian novel is frequently divested of the past and the Jamesian character has little duration, a fairly obvious Bergsonian phrasing. James puts his characters in the present, and they go from Europe to America or from America to Europe to feel any change. Poulet emphasizes James's exploitation of the infinite possibilities open to the novel by his varying successive points of view. *The Awkward*

Age seems to him the most characteristic of James's novels, "consisting of a plurality of consciousnesses all aimed at the same object," but, Poulet asserts, one could also compare this space to that of an auditorium.

In a special appendix, Poulet discusses briefly three non-French poets: Rainer Maria Rilke, T. S. Eliot, and Jorge Guillén. The brief essay on Rilke seems rather trivial, contrasting the earlier poet's supposed concern with flat surfaces, such as the Russian steppes and Worpswede, with the later Rilke's absorption by "things," which have their own lives, as Rilke learned from the sculptor Rodin. The Eliot essay makes a good point by contrasting him with Proust. All Eliot's reflections depend on voluntary memory, a patient effort to recover the reassembled past and to adapt it to new conditions. He restores the past by using all his mental and physical powers. The past that Eliot most wants to recover is seen as a totality. Time doesn't heal anything and must be accepted with all its consequences. The new time is tragic, discontinuous; everything flees or seems to flee. Eliot values a time he calls "Christian," a time of sacrifice. We sacrifice our time, our passion, our pleasures, to allow us to accept the order of the past and finally the duties demanded by the future, a total submission to the central authority of being, "a fixed point around which the world turns." We thus acquire peace when our thinking detaches itself from the cycle of passions in order to adhere to the supreme law.

Poulet produced during the 1980s a three-volume history called *La Pensée indéterminée* (1985–90). In it he attempts to summarize his lifework by covering the whole history of French literature. The book assumes that it is important to write a history of what he calls "undetermined thought," which in practice means "reverie" and religious thought that is not rationally theological—mainly, thought about thought itself, thought that is "conscious of itself in its interior nakedness," thought that is "singularly free of the precise details of a determined life" (*PI*, 1:5–6). Poulet skims through French literature and a selection of writers in German and English. His ingenuity in describing the "indistinct reveries" contained in the writings of the main French authors from the very beginnings to Pierre Emmanuel is striking and convincing. I shall give at least one example illustrating his method, which singles out passages and even individual works that answer the description of "indistinct thought."

Discussing D. H. Lawrence, for instance, Poulet starts with a quotation from a letter of 1 February 1916, in which Lawrence describes the landscape and the rocks of Cornwall, which he says create an impression of "the original darkness before the Creation." Poulet then links this passage with one of Lawrence's late novels, *The Plumed Serpent* (1926), which includes a description remarkably similar to the feelings he experienced while looking at the landscape: "He . . . stood still, in pure unconsciousness, neither hearing nor feeling nor knowing, like a dark sea-weed deep in the sea. With no Time and no World, in the deeps that are timeless and worldless." Poulet considers these quotations to be central to Lawrence's understanding of the world and even human civilization. Lawrence lived in contact with the world without form before the Creation, which he usually calls "darkness" (PI, 3:209–13).

Poulet uses a similar method in describing Virginia Woolf. He concentrates on the late novel The Waves (1931), where the heroine, Rhoda, loses all distinctness, becomes "pure absence," dissolves almost completely into shadow. A simple freeing of oneself from oneself is accomplished without complaint and without noise. The novelist appears like a shadow behind her heroine (PI, 3:214–17). Likewise, though Poulet characterizes Hugo von Hofmannsthal by classing him with what is called symbolism, he thinks this categorization is quite misleading. Hofmannsthal picked fragments from contemporary poetry, which he presented as a composite in a multiplicity of forms without continuity. There are gaps. What we might think of as praise, calling the poetry "eternal," is actually reversed when eternity is identified with nothingness (3:232–34).

I could go on picking out these frequently hard-hitting descriptions of writers, but it may be most useful to concentrate on Poulet's rather rare comments on critics and criticism. I was surprised to learn that Henri Frédéric Amiel (1821–81) was in Poulet's view the most profound critic in the whole history of literature (PI, 2:123–35). Amiel is not, I am afraid, included in this History, as I relegated him to the category of diarists who may have literary opinions but no critical point of view. Poulet ignores Sainte-Beuve as a critic and pays attention only to the novel of his youth, Volupté (2:83–86). Poulet dismisses Hippolyte Taine, labeling him a Spinozist and complaining about his search for a "hierarchy of necessities" (2:164–65).

The one critic whom Poulet analyzes in some detail is his old friend and companion Marcel Raymond (PI, 3:148). Raymond is described in reference to Bergson, Max Scheler, and Maurice Merleau-Ponty and is presented as a writer who tries completely to identify with the author studied and even to imitate him in style and form. Raymond wants to reproduce the universe of the poet, to absorb it so completely that it becomes purely "subjective," meaning a complete absorption of the ego of the writer. Poulet relates Raymond to mysticism of the seventeenth century, Jakob Boehme, the German romantics, Victor Hugo, and of course Rousseau. He quotes from Raymond's journal, where he speaks of a nostalgia for the "first unity," of a desire to reintegrate himself "beyond all contraries, polarities, alienations," a desire for a "unity without object." Poulet contends that this leads to a doctrine of solipsism, which by a dialectical reversal means "nothingness." In order to accept being nothing, you arrive at a quietist mysticism, a complete effacement of the "I," an abolishment of the external world. But this temporary sacrifice of individuality, this quietism, related to that of Fénelon, is never complete and cannot be complete. It is mitigated by the attempt "to imitate the gestures and to repeat the words" of the authors studied. As a critic, Raymond entered the consciousnesses of the authors he studied and tried to submerge himself completely, but without success—it is precisely that failure which allows the act of criticism.

In the section on Ramon Fernandez, Poulet does not discuss his literary criticism, but only his brief book on personality. Fernandez here appears as an aggressive egotist compared with Charles Du Bos, so much admired by Poulet. Poulet makes much of Fernandez's criticism of Proust, whose "passivity is . . . condemnable." Fernandez demands concentration of the will and intentional organization and effort leading to action. The primitive, anarchic "I" must be transformed into a person, and a person must be directed to the future and thus to a critique of moral judgment. Fernandez would like to "reform" the author, become his moral guide (*PI*, 3:132–38).

These types of examinations and reflections are always acute and nourished by Poulet's wide reading and undeniable erudition. But sometimes one cannot help feeling that his isolation of particular motives, however convincing, distorts the image of a given writer. In the striking chapter on Chekhov (3:246–51), for instance, Poulet quotes Turgenev's description of the experience of the steppe, which gives "a sort of strange concentration of the mind on a single vision or on a single thought." The "vast silent uniformity" reduces the unique experience and makes existence an "entirely negative element . . . oppressed by the surrounding void." Poulet seems to consider this experience of monotony, where even the colors lose their freshness, as somehow characteristic of Russian literature, the search for a "negative equality," which he bolsters with quotations from Goncharov and Turgenev. He concludes by appealing to the Orthodox philosopher Berdyaev who, in describing the opposition in Dostoevsky between the light and an abyss of shadows, speaks of "the anxiety of being without certitude" and of being "incapable of determining oneself." By singling out the Chekhov story, however, Poulet completely distorts the main trait of Chekhov's writings, which certainly are not, whatever we might find in them, lacking in concrete experiences and even determined aims. Chekhov was a country doctor who traveled as far as Sakhalin on the Pacific Ocean, wrote in detail on the condition of prisoners there, and back in Russia became involved with other doctors in the struggle against cholera in the villages of his district.

There are several other instances where Poulet similarly distorts a writer's image by isolating a single motive. For instance, Poulet seems to accept without any criticism Rilke's dialogues with the angels and to approve of his observation that, like a painter, he tries in his poetry "to find the determined by painting the indetermined" (*PI*, 3:242). This is obviously also Poulet's final aim: to depict the history of man's thought or, better, "mentality" or *Geist* or mind, or whatever term excludes philosophical precision and argumentation. He hopes himself to come nearer to the original mystery, which is "always more or less indetermined" and which Amiel called "re-implication," meaning the "return of the mind to its original point of departure, often enveloped in shadow" (3:288). Poulet's book ends more definitely, with a religious emphasis on the ultimate mystery, which he wanted to approach by going through the whole history of literature, isolating the passages that answer his deep inner demands, concentrating on what he feels to be the highlights, however indeterminate, that he has found by listening to the inner movement. This desire to discover the center of a writer, which is by no means necessarily overt, ends finally in a complete subjectivity. Poulet asks us to believe in him and in his instinct. But "instinct" is the wrong word. Instinct is too biological, even too animal, to describe Poulet's aim. He wants to reach a transcendent aim on the way to divinity, a goal without form, "lost and as if submerged in the profound sea of Divinity" (1:14).

The enormous range of Poulet's work, which covers a great stretch of time and many topics, particularly from the history of French literature, makes him, to my mind, the most representative and impressive figure in twentieth-century French criticism. In looking more closely at Poulet's work, however, we have to conclude that he is not primarily interested in *literary* criticism. He uses literature mainly as a pretext or as a document for studying the changes in man's attitudes toward time and space, the ego and the subconscious, and other such topics that vaguely approximate philosophy. Poulet is a striking case of a man with a good rational mind who can interpret texts in their logical contexts but is strangely inhibited by his adherence to, or simply acceptance of, the philosophy of Bergson. Twentieth-century France is totally dominated by Bergsonian irrationalism, if not immediately connected with the philosopher himself, then simply drawn from the age-old tradition of irrationalism. Poulet is in constant conflict between his own rationalism and his conviction, however arrived at, that literature and the arts are irrational and even instinctive and subconscious. I have the impression that when the conflict became too obvious to him he took refuge in religion—a religion that is vaguely Catholic, but mainly a refuge for the arts and literature as the great treasures of mankind's feelings and sentiments. When this refuge becomes insufficient to handle some of the greatest poetry, Poulet is content with gestures toward the transcendental and the supernatural, feelings which ultimately remain simply mysterious and inexpressible. In this sense, one could say that Poulet fails as a *literary* critic. His commitment to religion was greater.

8 : ALBERT CAMUS (1913–1960)

ALBERT CAMUS IS MAINLY KNOWN for his three novels: *La Peste,* written during the war but published only in 1947, *L'Etranger* (1942), and *La Chute* (1956). Camus was no critic. Only his very occasional reviews have rightly attracted attention. When he reviewed Sartre's novel *La Nausée* in 1938 Camus was still in Algiers. The review is remarkable for praising the (to Camus) totally unknown author, for recognizing Sartre's position in a history of thought, and for criticizing the book quite severely as unable to reconcile straight storytelling with reflections on life and death, which according to Camus should be the main point of any novel. "A novel is never anything but a philosophy put into images," Camus writes. "And in a good novel, the whole of the philosophy has passed into the images" (*SEN,* 167). He recognizes Sartre's "remarkable gifts as a novelist" as well as his "most lucid and cruellest of minds" (167). But Camus does not find that these two sides, philosophy and storytelling, though "both equally convincing," are fused together in *La Nausée.* Camus, who studied philosophy, places Sartre in the neighborhood of Kierkegaard and Lev Shestov, Jaspers and Heidegger, and he notes the similarity between Sartre and Kafka, whom, he says, no one had yet mentioned in connection with *La Nausée* (168). Camus later moved to Paris and met Sartre. In March 1939 in an obscure Algerian newspaper Camus published a review of Sartre's collection of short stories, *Le Mur.* Again, Camus admires the "absolute mastery" of the telling and the pitiless way Sartre observes his often "ridiculous" characters. These characters are "free," but "their liberty is of no use to them." Man, Sartre demonstrates, "is alone, locked up in his liberty" (171). Sartre's dramatic universe is "garish and yet colorless." His message "involves a conversion to nothingness, but also to lucidity," Camus concludes. "And the image, which he perpetuates through his characters, of a man sitting amid the ruins of his life, is a good illustration of the greatness and truth of this work" (172).

Camus was a great admirer of Gide. In an obituary essay called "Rencontres avec André Gide" (1951) he tells of his early reading of Gide and how, later, he even occupied a studio in Gide's Paris apartment for a time, though never sharing more than the most ordinary conversations with him. "Gide's secret," says Camus, "lies in the fact that never, in the midst of his doubts, did he lose the pride of being a man. . . . He smiled at the mystery, and showed the abyss the same face which he had presented to life" (*SEN*, 177).

Another of Camus's literary enthusiasms was Herman Melville. In an essay written in 1952 Camus says that Melville "is first and foremost a creator of myths" (*SEN*, 179), and that his works "depict a spiritual experience of unequalled intensity" (178). He reflects that Melville is "at the farthest possible remove from Kafka" (180). In Kafka, the spiritual experience "overflows the modes of expression and invention, which remain monotonous," whereas, "like the greatest artists, Melville constructed his symbols out of concrete things, not from the material of dreams" (181). Camus contrasts Kafka's world, in which "the reality he describes is created by the symbol," with that of Melville, in which "the symbol emerges from reality." Melville, according to Camus, "never cut himself off from flesh or nature, which are barely perceptible in Kafka's work" (181). Camus praises in particular *Billy Budd*, a "flawless story which can be placed on the same level as certain Greek tragedies" (180).

Camus also admired William Faulkner. Camus himself made a dramatic adaptation of Faulkner's *Requiem for a Nun*, and in his program note for the production of the play in 1956 he commented that Faulkner's characters "belong to our own day, and yet they confront the same destiny that crushed Electra or Orestes" (*SEN*, 183). He sees a "human grandeur" in *Requiem* and in Faulkner's whole work and particularly admires his language. *Requiem* is, Camus asserts, "one of the few modern tragedies there are" (183).

Late in his life Camus gave a public lecture in Athens called "The Future of Tragedy" (1955). It has been greatly admired but, to my mind, is merely a reproduction of Hegel's theory of tragedy. Camus hopes for a revival of tragedy in France and sees signs of this renaissance in Greek studies and in Paul Claudel's adaptation of Aeschylus's *Agamemnon*.

Camus was killed in a car accident before he could fulfill the great promise of his early work, and we must be content with these reviews and occasional pronouncements in letters and journals. His power of introspection is remarkable. The self-portrait introducing a 1958 reissue of the little collection of essays called *L'Envers et l'endroit* is a marvel of clearly sincere self-examination and, possibly, self-torture. Camus concludes these reflections about accepting everything, "the whole radiance of the world," with a characteristic turn: "Death for us all, but his own death to each. After all, the sun still warms our bones for us" (37).

9 : JEAN-PAUL SARTRE (1905–1980)

JEAN-PAUL SARTRE is undoubtedly the most prominent figure in postwar French literature. He was an enormously versatile and prolific writer: somebody has estimated that his writings amount to five million words. The monograph on Flaubert alone, which is not even finished, runs to almost three thousand pages. Sartre was, of course, not only a literary critic, but also a philosopher, a politician, a journalist, a novelist, and a playwright—to mention only his main activities. In a strict sense literary criticism was, I believe, only a minor interest for Sartre, who used it often to illustrate or document his pet theories. The later critical works— the biographies of Baudelaire, Genet, and Flaubert—and the fragmentary book on Mallarmé all have a psychoanalytic slant, which Sartre tries to combine with Marxism. The leading concept of his criticism is always freedom and revolt—"freedom" understood in the sense of Husserl and Heidegger, first stressed in opposition to Marxism (see the article "Marxism and Revolution"). But later Sartre tried to combine his particular version of existentialism with Marxism, a difficult task which he never accomplished. Marxism is strictly deterministic, and Sartre's philosophy proclaims indeterminism.

From the biography of Sartre by Annie Cohen-Solal one can learn a great deal about his early career and views. In 1963 he wrote *Les Mots*, an account, attractive in many ways, of his early life. One has to label the book "retrospective fantasies"—one cannot take it as a reproduction or recall of actual dreams and imaginings, though obviously it contains a kernel of reality. Sartre completely conceals, for instance, his mother's remarriage and his family's move out of Paris. Sartre's early development is now much better documented from firsthand accounts: the war diaries kept during the so-called phony war in 1939–40, during his captivity in a German prison camp near Trier, and still later after he returned to Paris to live, taking part in underground associations. On the whole, one has the impression that until he lived in Paris during the last stages of the war, Sartre avoided political topics. Like almost every Frenchman, of course, he was opposed to the German occupation.

The early literary criticism, collected in the first volume of his *Situations* (1947), is almost devoid of political allusions or even implications. The earliest critical essay of any interest, "François Mauriac and Freedom," published in February 1939, precedes the war. It assumes freedom and indeterminism and a Bergsonian concept of time. Sartre begins by reflecting on Stavrogin in Dostoevsky's *The Possessed*. He rightly rejects the view that Stavrogin is a creation of the reader's imagination: "We decipher him, wait for him." Still, "the novel swells and feeds on the reader's time." The true novelist must, says Sartre, "draw the reader into a time in which the future does not exist, a time resembling my own." Thus Sartre rejects novels like those of Zola, where the future of the hero is determined in advance by his heredity and social milieu. Characters live only when they are free. Rogozhin is an example, because Christians are free and Dostoevsky is a Christian novelist (*S*, 1:8). Dmitry and Alyosha Karamazov are free; they struggle against themselves, but it is their own self-made nature.

All this is introductory to a discussion of Mauriac's then new novel *La Fin de la nuit*. The heroine, Thérèse Desqueyroux, is torn between reason and passion. Her destiny is determined by a flaw in her character and a curse that hangs over her acts. The idea of destiny, according to Sartre, is poetic and contemplative, but a novel is action and no novelist has the right to become a mere spectator (*S*, 1:11). Mauriac initially identifies with his character, but then abandons her to consider her from the outside like a judge, saying first, "I saw that she was trembling," and then that "she was astounded to hear the echo of her own words." Thérèse is thus both "she"-object, and "she"-subject (1:12). What is going on in her conscious mind gives the reader the right to judge or condemn her. Mauriac is vacillating: he moves from Thérèse-object to Thérèse-subject, sometimes in a single sentence. At times he even installs himself in another character, and there are occasionally an author's reflections. Mauriac in fact wrote that "the novelist is to his own creatures what God is to his" (1:14)—a view, I would add, shared by Flaubert and Joyce. Mauriac, Sartre concludes, is omniscient (as most novelists are). Bringing in Conrad, Sartre notes that we hear only through the mouth of another character that Lord Jim is a romantic, whereas Mauriac calls Thérèse "a cautious and desperate woman." Sartre states bluntly that Mauriac has no right to make these absolute judgments; there should be testimonies from the participants, whose point of view is relative to their position. The test is always what makes the reader most acutely aware of the dragging of time: "It is for the reader alone to establish the absolute reality" (1:15).

There is, then, according to Sartre, a twofold error of technique in

Mauriac: first, he presupposes a purely contemplative narrator, and second, he appeals to an absolute that is nontemporal: "If you pitch the narrative into the absolute, you snap the string of duration. The novel disappears" (S, 1:13). Mauriac fabricates the natures of his characters, as does Hemingway, who sees his characters only from the outside—but what is acceptable in Hemingway is apparently not in Mauriac, where characters are transformed into things. Things simply *are*, minds *become*. According to the law of fictional beings, the novelist is either a witness or an accomplice, but never both at the same time. The novelist must be either inside or outside, asserts Sartre. (One might ask why he can't be both.) The freedom in Mauriac's novel is nearly a discontinuous force that allows only brief escapes. His novel is really a story of enslavement (1:17). The ups and downs of the heroine, Sartre says, "affect me little more than those of a cockroach climbing a wall with stupid obstinacy" (1:18). Freedom for Mauriac differs from slavery in value but not in nature: "Any intention directed upward towards God is free, any will to evil is fettered" (1:19). This "will to evil" stifles freedom in fiction, and with it, "immediate duration, which is the substance of the novel" (1:19). Sartre complains that Mauriac does not bother to play upon the reader's impatience: no one has any secrets in the book. Mauriac has no liking for time, no fondness for the Bergsonian necessity of waiting. In Hemingway's *A Farewell to Arms* there are innumerable tiny obstacles, but Mauriac tries to economize in presenting conversation and even simply summarizes. There is no graver error in the book than this stinginess, this attempt at foreshortening. Mauriac treats only the essential events, as he is always in a hurry. Sartre complains of Mauriac's declamatory style, of his theatrical platitudes. He refers to Racine's *Bérénice* and even sees Mauriac in the mode of eighteenth-century comic writers. He prefers Dostoevsky, Conrad, and Faulkner, who resist generalizing; they make dialogue the fictional moment, the time when the sense of duration or process is richest (1:21). Sartre alludes to Mauriac's classicism as always rejecting the woolly and unclear. Classicism is rhetorical and theatrical, and *La Fin de la nuit* is actually made up of four scenes, each ending in a "catastrophe." Sartre contrasts it with George Meredith's novel *Beauchamp's Career*, where the outcome remains uncertain. It is a real novel, and *La Fin de la nuit* is not. A novel is made up of time and free minds. Mauriac, Sartre concludes, is not a novelist. Sartre finally appeals to the theory of relativity, to the cosmos of Einstein, in which there is no place for a privileged observer, just as there is none in a real novel. Mauriac has chosen divine omniscience and omnipotence, "but novels are written by men and for men. In the eyes of God, who cuts through appearances and goes beyond them, there is no novel, no art, for art thrives on appearances. God is not an artist. Neither is M. Mauriac" (1:23). This witticism seems an unconvincing argument for the complete absence of the author, the complete "objectivity" of the novel, an ideal postulate of Sartre's which is refuted by the main tradition of the novel from Laurence Sterne to our own day.

Sartre's article on Camus's *L'Etranger* (February 1943), compared to the Mauriac review, is far more obvious. He explains the term "absurd" as referring to the nature of the world as irrational and dark, to our own sense of its absurdity, and to its ultimate lack of meaning. Camus wrote *Le Mythe de Sisyphe* as an explanation of his views, with half-understood references to Jaspers, Heidegger, and Kierkegaard. *L'Etranger,* however, shows a classical temperament, a mind steeped in the sun of the Mediterranean. *L'Etranger* does not explain anything; it is rather a series of images. Camus sees art as an act of unnecessary generosity—it is Kant's "zwecklose Zweckmässigkeit." The figure of L'Etranger remains opaque (*S,* 1:32). Camus tries to be silent with words, and he quotes Heidegger's statement that silence is an authentic mode of speech. Camus, Sartre says, is wrongly compared to Kafka. Camus lacks transcendence, is very much at peace with the disorder of the world. The book has American technique (American here means Hemingway). Camus inserts a glass partition between the reader and his characters, a partition constructed so as to be transparent to things and opaque to meanings. Meanings are only those of a world of neorealism, parts of the immediate data. Camus's book is comparable to the tales of Voltaire and *Gulliver's Travels.* It is only a series of instances, and the discontinuity between the clipped phrases imitates the discontinuity of time. The sentences are like islands, and Camus bounds from one to another. He prefers the more fragmented *passé parfait composé* to the *passé defini:* he writes "il s'est promené longtemps" but rarely "il se promena." The relation between objects is external in Camus, as it is in neorealist epistemology. The dialogue is integrated into the narration. The world is stripped of all causality. *L'Etranger* is a classical work, an orderly work, written about the absurd and against the absurd. It substitutes the order of causality for chronological sequence, and therefore it is not a novel: "A novel requires continuous duration, development, and the manifest presence of the irreversibility of time." Rather, Sartre argues, the book shows the succession of inert present moments. For all the influence of the German existentialists and American novelists, the book remains very close to tales like *Zadig* and *Candide* (1:41).

Sartre was interested in the American novels that were being translated in the late thirties. The first he commented on was Faulkner's *Sartoris,* in February 1938. Sartre praises the beginning of *Light in August,* which seems to him a hermetic thing, like a mineral or a stone or a tree. In contrast, however, *Sartoris* betrays the author. The dogmatic assumption everywhere at that time was that the author must be totally absent. *Sartoris* is all strange illusions. The minds of Faulkner's characters are always empty and evasive: he does not tell us what is inside their consciousness. "The book," asserts Sartre, "is verbose, has a pompous, sickening monotony." The essence of the novel is in its actions, but Faulkner does not even mention actions; they are only suggested. They are beyond language, undecipherable acts of violence that are later changed into general stories: the Civil War, the First World War. Sartre reflects on the twofold origins of Faulkner's technique in *Light in August* and *The Sound and the Fury*, which he obviously greatly prefers to *Sartoris*. There is a technique of disorder in these two novels, an irresistible need to interrupt the action in order to relate a story, which seems to Sartre characteristic of lyric novelists; on the other hand, there is a half-sincere, half-imaginary faith in the magical power of stories (*S*, 1:76). When Faulkner wrote *Sartoris* he had not yet mastered this technique, according to Sartre. His hero is fixed and immutable, he is obstinate like a stone or rock, a thing opaque, a solidified spirit behind consciousness. The men Faulkner likes—for instance, Joe Christmas in *Light in August* and Sartoris—are men who have secrets and keep quiet. This dream of silence, a silence outside us and a silence within us, is the futile dream of a puritan ultra-stoicism. "Is he shamming? What does he do when he is alone?" (1:78).

The article on *Sartoris* was followed by one on *The Sound and the Fury*, subtitled "Time in the Work of Faulkner" (July 1939). According to Sartre, nothing happens in the book, the story does not unfold. What interests us is Faulkner's handling of time. Sartre makes here the fundamental and principal declaration about his criticism: "A fictional technique always relates back to the novelist's metaphysics. The critic's task is to define the latter before evaluating the former." It is immediately obvious that Faulkner's metaphysics is a metaphysics of time. Time is our misfortune. Faulkner's present is essentially catastrophic. There is never any progression, never anything that comes from the future. Faulkner has seized upon a "frozen speed at the very heart of things." In *The Sound and the Fury* everything has already happened. Sartre formulates this as "Je ne suis pas, j'étais." The present is a chaotic din, the future is past. The present is not: it becomes. In Faulkner the order of the past is the order of the heart.

Sartre compares Faulkner with Proust: they seem to be similar, unspeakably present, subject to the sudden invasion of the past, to an emotional order rather than an intellectual or volitional order. The "intermittences of the heart" are obvious parallels, but there is a difference: Proust looks for salvation in time itself, for the reappearance of the past, whereas in Faulkner the past, unfortunately, is never lost. It is always there, an obsession. Proust's fictional technique should have been Faulkner's. Faulkner is a lost man. Proust is a Frenchman and a classicist; he keeps at least a semblance of chronology. Sartre asserts that most modern authors—Proust, Joyce, Dos Passos, Faulkner, Virginia Woolf—distort time. Proust and Faulkner have simply decapitated it—they have deprived it of its future, of its dimensions, of its acts and freedom (S, 1:84). Faulkner's heroes never look ahead. For instance, Quentin thinks of his last day as in the past, as if he were someone who is remembering. There is no intuition of the future. This explains everything, particularly the irrationality of time. Man spends his life struggling against time, and then the speech of Macbeth is quoted which ends "full of sound and fury, signifying nothing." Consciousness can exist with time only on condition that it become time, it must become temporalized, it must project itself into the future. Here Sartre first mentions Heidegger: man is not the sum of what he has been, but the totality of what he has not yet become. According to Sartre, a historian who writes to explain the past must first seek out its future (1:87). The absurdity that Faulkner finds in human life is one that he himself put there. Faulkner uses his art to describe our suffocation and the world dying of old age. "I like his art," Sartre concludes, "but I do not believe in his metaphysics" (1:87). Sartre apparently focused on the section called "Dilsey," where, one could argue, the future is closed; he did not or could not consider the other parts of this great and difficult book.

In 1938 Sartre also published an essay on John Dos Passos and his book *1919*. Sartre presumes that Dos Passos held the old view of the novel as a mirror, an obvious allusion to Stendhal's well-known saying. Dos Passos put on the garb of populism, the pretense of complete realism. Still, his scenes are discreetly queer and even sinister, as in a nightmare. This world is not real, it is a crowded object: "I know however none, not even Faulkner or Kafka, in which the art is greater or better hidden" (S, 1:89). Again Sartre reflects on time: we live in time and the novel, like life, unfolds in the present, but in a present with aesthetic distances. Man is free, he develops before our eyes, but the tale (*récit*) develops in the past. This clear-cut distinction is derived from Ramon Fernandez. In Dos Passos there is really no narrative, as "narrating means adding." The lives he tells about are all closed in on themselves. Capitalist society is unrelievedly stifling: "Men do not have lives, they have only destinies." His writing is in the style of a statement to the press, a behaviorist style, with attention to public opinion. It reproduces the abject consciousness of Everyman, of what Heidegger calls "das man." Dos Passos believes in a statistical determination: nothing can interfere with the regularity of births, marriages, and suicides. One is not quite sure whether Sartre is simply trying to write a pastiche of Dos Passos or a parody when he invents a passage beginning: "And they ordered two beers and said that the war was hateful." Dos Passos's man is a hybrid creature, an exterior-interior being. He vacillates between individual consciousnesses or becomes diluted in collective consciousness. Sartre quotes a passage about Joe's death and concludes rather surprisingly that Dos Passos's world, "like those of Faulkner, Kafka, Stendhal, is impossible because it is contradictory, but therein lies its beauty. Beauty is a veiled contradiction." He then abruptly ends: "I regard Dos Passos as the greatest writer of our time." Sartre must have changed his mind about the eminence of Dos Passos, as he obviously admires Faulkner more.

Two essays are devoted to contemporary French writers: Jean Giraudoux and Maurice Blanchot. "Giraudoux and the Philosophy of Aristotle," published in March 1940, begins with the rather surprising generalization that "the world is a soft pasty substance, traversed by waves, a world without a future." In contrast, however, rest and order come first in Giraudoux (at least, in *Choix des élues,* the novel Sartre is describing). Giraudoux sees the species only in individuals: Jacques, for instance, is an artless little boy. Giraudoux, however, is not a Platonist; his forms are not in the heaven of ideas, but right in our midst. Nor are they simply concepts; they are norms and canons rather than general ideas. Sartre occasionally calls them "archetypes" (*S,* 1:45). There is no causality, no determinism, but there is some change, which comes in stages: "Transitions take place behind the scenes." Giraudoux's world is one with an air of schizophrenia, "a world without a present indicative" (1:46). There are actually two presents in Giraudoux: the ignominious present of the event and that of the archetype, which is in eternity (1:47). Time is discontinuous. Reading the book is like turning the pages of a family album; the changes are sudden and instantaneous. His people share a metaphysical chastity, like the film stars that Jean Prévost called "glass-skinned women—their bodies are as thoroughly scoured as a Dutch kitchen and their gleaming flesh has the freshness of a tile floor" (1:48). Giraudoux constantly draws analogies between acts and things. He writes something like natural history, but his natural history is pre-evolutionary—Linnaeus and not Lamarck. Anything like bewilderment, evolution, disorder, or novelty is wholly banished. The writer is like a real estate clerk, comfortably installed, everywhere at home. Giraudoux says that "man's character does not really differ in any way from the essence of a pickle." What he wants is characterology and the art of physiognomy. Man realizes his essence spontaneously; he conforms to his own archetype, out of his own free will: "Man is constantly choosing himself as he is" (1:52). Thus there is a very thin line between freedom and absolute necessity. Giraudoux has an ethics: "Man must freely realize his finite essence and in so doing freely harmonize with the rest of the world." He then receives his reward, which is happiness. Sartre says that he now perceives the character of Giraudoux's famous humanism: it is a pagan eudaemonism.

The philosophy of Aristotle is behind it all, imposing conformity between man and thing. Only sudden revelations disturb this static world. On a stroll through the streets of Paris things suddenly seem to stand still. On a certain little street in Montmartre, time has stopped. We experience a moment of happiness. It is a revelation, but it has nothing to teach us. It is unproductive. A Marxist would define this view as urbane rationalism and would explain the revelation in terms of the triumphant rise of capitalism at the beginning of the twentieth century. Giraudoux's urbanity thus would be attributed to his special position within the French bourgeoisie, his peasant origins, his Hellenic culture, and his career. But Sartre is not convinced: this discreet and self-effacing author remains a mystery (S, 1:55).

In his article "*Aminadab,* or the Fantastic Considered as Language," Sartre begins by characterizing Blanchot's novel as Kafkaesque. It has the same minute and courtly style, though Sartre recognizes that Blanchot denied having read Kafka before writing the book (S, 1:57). Sartre then reflects on the fantastic in literature. "Things suffer and tend towards inertia without ever attaining it," he writes. "The debased, enslaved mind unsuccessfully strives towards consciousness and freedom. The fantastic then represents a reverse image of the union of body and soul. We have to indulge in the magical mentality of the dream, the private and the child" (1:58). Sartre refers to Salvador Dali and Giorgio De Chirico, who reveal to us a nature that is haunted and yet has nothing supernatural about it. For Dali, the only fantastic object is man. Sartre finds the same to be true of Blanchot, and he emphasizes the fact that fantastic literature, like the books of Kafka and Blanchot, takes place outside of nature, in urban surroundings. None of the heroes ever gets a glimpse of forests, plains, and hills; if they did, the fantastic would immediately vanish. The fantastic world is stratified like a bureaucracy, and the technique is to take a man who is right side up and transport him miraculously into an upside-down world. Sartre comments on Kafka's fantastic novel *The Trial* as *Erziehungsroman* and goes on to argue that Kafka perfected this technique in *The Castle:* the hero himself is fantastic—we know nothing about him except his incomprehensible obstinacy in remaining in a forbidden village. Blanchot uses the same method. His hero, like Kafka's heroes—

Samsa or the surveyor in *The Castle*—is never surprised. Sartre sees the
fantastic author writing the fantastic book, choosing to paint the world
upside-down. He views this as an attempt to force the reader to identify
with an inhuman hero who soars above the human condition and sees it
from the outside—a contradictory world in which mind becomes matter.
Here Sartre suddenly drops Kafka, stating: "I have nothing more to say
except that he is one of the greatest and most unique writers of our time"
(1:69). Kafka shows us human life troubled by an impossible transcendence. Blanchot has considerable talents, but he comes after Kafka, and
the artifices he employs are already familiar. Deeply experienced themes
become, with him, literary conventions. He does not succeed in ensnar-
ing the reader in the nightmarish world he is portraying. Kafka cannot
be imitated. But by having unwittingly imitated him, Blanchot delivers
us from him. He brings Kafka's methods into the open; they are now
categorized, classified, and useless, no longer frightening. Kafka, Sartre
says, was only a stage: "Through him, as through Hoffmann, Poe, Lewis
Carroll, and the surrealists, the fantastic pursues the continuous process,
which should ultimately reunite it with what has always been" (1:72). I
presume this is a history of a genre called "fantastic": Kafka and Blanchot
appear only as stages in a describable progression—an odd conclusion
which seems to devalue both writers.

Qu'est ce que la littérature? (1947) is by far Sartre's best-known book of
literary criticism. It established the literary term "engaged" and served as
a battle cry for many authors. The first chapter—"What Is Literature?"—
oddly enough makes not the slightest attempt to answer that question. It
is an important polemic against any parallelism among the arts. Although
Sartre recognizes that the arts have influenced one another, he denies
that painting and music have any meaning, any signification. They are not
signs, they are things. Verbal art signifies, whereas the other arts transform everything into imaginary objects—*imaginary* used here in Sartre's
sense of "image." Colors and signs are not a language. In a note, Sartre
concedes that the painter Paul Klee, for example, tried to make painting
both a sign and an object, but he maintains that this was an error: painting cannot be both. The yellow rift in the sky in Tintoretto's *Crucifixion*
in Venice, according to Sartre, does not signify anguish or provoke it,
it *is* anguish and the yellow sky at the same time. It is an anguish made
thing, an anguish which has turned into a yellow rift of sky. The nature of
painting prevents the painter from expressing this anguish. Sartre pursues his argument by saying that a painter creates an imaginary house on

the canvas and not the sign of a house. Painting is apparently ineffective: Sartre says that Picasso's *Guernica* has never won over a single person to the Spanish cause. Picasso's *Long Harlequins* are emotion become flesh, but the emotion is unrecognizable. One cannot paint significations, one does not put them into music. How can one then require the painter or the musician to engage himself? Painters and composers are exempt from such social demands.

Turning to literature, Sartre decides that it is divided into two sharply distinguished realms: poetry and prose. Poetry is grouped with painting, sculpture, and music. Sartre protests that he does not detest poetry—he just thinks of it as totally outside the world of action: "Poets are men who refuse to *utilize* language" (*WIL*, 12). A poetic attitude considers words as things and not as signs. Each word, each term is analogous to an expression on a face, to the sad or gay meaning of sounds and colors. For the poet language is a structure of the external world. He maneuvers words from within; he feels them as though they were his body. He considers words as if they were a trap to catch a fleeting reality. A word represents, rather than expresses signification—*represent* meaning simply "presenting." The poet creates an object: the words/things are grouped by magical associations of fitness or incongruity like colors and sounds (16). To Sartre it seems foolish to require of a poet any political engagement. Emotion, even passion, is at the origin of the poem, but not expressed there as in a pamphlet or a confession. Emotion has become a thing and has the opacity of things.

A poet, asserts Sartre, has hardly anything in common with a prose writer. Prose is in essence utilitarian: "I would readily define the prose writer as the man who *makes use* of words. . . . Jourdain made prose to ask for his slippers, and Hitler to declare war on Poland" (*WIL*, 19). A writer is a speaker: he designates, demonstrates, and so forth. Prose is an attitude of mind. It is like a sixth finger, a third leg, it is a pure function. To speak, then, is to act: "In writing, I go beyond the present situation towards the future" (23). The prose writer has chosen a method of action which we may call action by disclosure. The writer should never say to himself, "I'll be lucky if I have three thousand readers," but rather, "What would happen if everybody read what I wrote?" (23). The function of the writer is to act in such a way that nobody can be ignorant of the world and that nobody may say he is innocent of what it is all about. Silence is also a moment of language. If a writer has chosen to remain silent on any aspect of the world, one has the right to ask: Why have you spoken of this rather than that? Why have you chosen to change this rather than that? The implication is that the writer must speak on every subject, as Sartre did all his life, and that silence means a divestment of responsibility. Yet Sartre can suddenly say that "style makes the value of the prose," but it "should pass unnoticed" (25). He strongly disapproves of Giraudoux's statement that the only concern is finding the style and that the idea comes afterward. New social and metaphysical requirements must continuously engage artists in finding new language and new techniques. Obviously content precedes form. Sartre strongly condemns the theory of art for art's sake (27). In his opinion, pure art is the same thing as empty art. Aesthetic purism was a brilliant maneuver by the nineteenth-century bourgeoisie, who preferred to be denounced as philistines rather than as exploiters. Their embarrassment would have been extreme had Fernandez not invented the notion of "message." Even pure art, according to Fernandez, has a message.

Sartre ridicules critics who are "cemetery watchmen"—an image derived, by the way, from Sainte-Beuve. The only thing the dead have done is to write: "They have long since been washed clean of the sin of living, and besides, their lives are known only through other books which other dead men have written about them. . . . All that remains are the little coffins that are stacked on shelves along the walls like urns in a columbarium" (*WIL*, 28). A critic can always enter his library, take down a book from the shelf, open it, and let it give off a slight odor of the cellar. The strange operation that the critic has decided to call reading begins. He lends his body to the dead so that they may come back to life. He persuades himself that he has entered into a relationship with an intelligible world. During the time he is reading his everyday life becomes an appearance. The critic has chosen to have relationships with the defunct, as it is absolutely necessary to have relationships with our fellow creatures. Sartre speaks then of archetypes of human nature, but everything becomes remote. Sade is hardly scandalous and Rousseau's "Letter on the Theater" keeps no one from going to the theater. The *Social Contract* can be explained by the Oedipus complex and the *Spirit of the Laws* by the inferiority complex. That is, the critic fully enjoys the well-known superiority of live dogs over dead lions. Sartre ridicules relativism, alluding to Rousseau and Gobineau, who sent us messages, and the critic—I suppose Fernandez—who considers them with equal sympathy. If they were alive, he would have to choose to love one and hate the other, but what brings them together is that they are profoundly and deliciously wrong and, in the same way, dead. The message, when all is said and done, is a soul made into an object. One contemplates it at a respectful distance. What is called literary art is the assembly of treatments which make it inoffensive, which guarantee it to be without risk. Who can take seriously the skepticism of Montaigne, who was frightened when the plague ravaged Bordeaux, or the humanism of Rousseau, who put his children into an orphanage? The critic will inform us that French thought is a perpetual colloquy between Pascal and Montaigne. In doing so, he has no interest in making Pascal and Montaigne more alive, but in making Gide and Malraux more dead. Thus ends this diatribe against criticism, relativism, and literature that is concerned only with the past or that uses the past to deaden the present. In his radical distinction between prose and poetry, putting poetry together with music and painting as irresponsible arts, Sartre has not defined what writing is or what literature is. The next chapter tries to answer the question Why write?

Again Sartre does not actually provide an answer. "Why Write?" is an elaborate discussion of the role of the reader in reading. We are treated to some difficult arguments about what amounts to epistemology. Sartre recognizes that there is an external world, but we set up a relation between, for instance, this tree and that bit of sky. Our feeling is essential in the relation to the world. Oddly enough, he claims, "I cannot reveal and produce at the same time" (*WIL,* 39). I am puzzled by sentences like "The writer cannot read what he writes." "The operation of writing," claims Sartre, "involves a quasi-reading which makes real reading impossible." Later he says that reading is a "synthesis of perception and creation" (43). The literary object, though "realized *through* language, is never given *in* language"—a passage that anticipates Sartre's lack of interest in linguistics and in the surface of sounds. Again, paradoxically, we are told that the literary object "is by nature a silence, an opponent of the word" (44). Sartre speaks of the "height of silence": silence is really the author's goal, and in the interior of the object there are more silences. This view of silence seems to be a metaphor for the inexpressible underlying a work, still linked to the conclusion that reading is directed creation, that "Raskolnikov's waiting is *my* waiting which I lend him" (45).

Then, rather suddenly, Sartre asserts that all literary work is an appeal to the reader that leads into objective existence, the unveiling of which the author has accomplished by means of language. Sartre resolutely rejects any explanations by anterior data, by sources and influences. He says, to use his terminology, that the writer appeals to the reader's freedom to collaborate in the production of the work. The argument here shifts constantly: the work of art has no end, it *is* an end, it has a value because it has an appeal. But obviously the work of art is also pure presentation from which the reader must make a certain aesthetic withdrawal. This is what Théophile Gautier foolishly confused with art for art's sake

and the Parnassians with the *impassibilité* of the artist. In lending the feeling to a character, we freely assent to a belief in the story. Sartre here
paraphrases what Coleridge called the "willing suspension of disbelief."
The reader, he says, renders himself credulous: "Raskolnikov . . . would
only be a shadow, without the mixture of repulsion and friendship which
I feel for him and which makes him live. But . . . it is not his behavior
which excites my indignation or esteem, but my indignation and esteem
which give consistency and objectivity to his behavior" (*WIL*, 50). This is a
strange proposal, which assumes in the reader's mind judgments and
opinions of a figure carefully presented in Dostoevsky's novel. Further,
this lending or sharing of our feelings is something like an exercise in generosity, a new appeal to the freedom of readers. Sartre devotes a whole
page to the way we organize a landscape, harmonizing the greens and
blues within it, as an example of the gift we give to the objective world. In
nature tree and sky harmonize only by chance. We organize it and so does
the painter. Sartre uses Cézanne, Vermeer, and Van Gogh as examples of
how the creative act aims at the total renewal of the world. Each painting,
each book is a recovery of the totality of being. Then comes Sartre's most
famous formula: "The goal of art is to recover this world by giving it to
be seen not as it is, but as if it had its source in human freedom" (57).
This view of the aim of art was anticipated by Friedrich Schiller in his
Letters on Aesthetic Education, who would not, however, have included the
skeptical reservation "as if."

Sartre somewhat surprisingly recognizes the existence of aesthetic pleasure. The recognition of freedom is itself a joy. To write is thus to dis-
close the world and to offer it as a task for the generosity of the reader.
This term "generosity" has its difficulties. It seems already to suggest
what Sartre's later arguments will demand—hatred for the injustice in
the world. Sartre asks the reader to help make himself responsible for
the whole world, for which the reader clearly bears responsibility. As a
moral imperative, which is at the same time an aesthetic imperative, I
must see that the imaginary representation of the world demands human
freedom. There is, according to Sartre, no gloomy literature. The only
literature possible is that which asks that the world be always impregnated with more freedom. He denies that there could be a good novel that
denounces Jews, blacks, workers, or colonial peoples, as the novelist has
only one subject: freedom. He comments at length on Drieu La Rochelle,
who finally fell silent even though he had long served the Germans during the war. The art of prose, says Sartre, forgetting about long stretches
of history, is bound up with the only regime in which prose has meaning—democracy. Sartre sees all writing as engaged writing, as defending
freedom. Thus he dismisses Julien Benda's *La Trahison des clercs*.

The next chapter, "For Whom Does One Write?" (again, without quite answering the question), indulges in an elaborate argument for the historicity of all writing. Every piece of writing occurs in a concrete situation: the author decides on his subject by choosing his reader. The image of the reader is constantly in his mind. There is an elaborate discussion of Vercors's *Le Silence de la mer*, which Sartre quite rightly places at a particular moment in 1941 when the French were being told that some Germans were good and decent. But once the situation changed, when the Germans were retreating, devastating the French countryside, and the Allies had invaded Germany, the conflict between Germans and French again became stark. That Vercors's work quickly became out-of-date leads Sartre to the extreme conclusion that "works of the mind should likewise be eaten on the spot" (*WII.*, 74). Yet he does not agree with Taine that the milieu produces the writer; rather the public calls to him and puts questions to his freedom. In *La Critique scientifique* (1888) Hennequin had similarly, long before Sartre, considered the reader as the power that forms a writer.

This section concludes with a long discussion of the readership of the black writer Richard Wright. Sartre argues convincingly that Wright does not write for the blacks in the South, but "has his audience only among the cultivated blacks of the North and the white Americans of good will (intellectuals, democrats of the left, radicals, CIO workers)" (*WIL*, 78). Literature, Sartre says, is not paid for, no price can be set on its value. The writer, he remarks extravagantly, consumes and does not produce—*produce* apparently referring here to economic goods. The writer is really not paid; he is fed, well or badly, according to the period. His activity is considered useless and even sometimes harmful for society, but conservative societies occasionally like to be given a guilty conscience. The writer is a parasite of the governing elite, but functionally he often moves in opposition to those who keep him alive. Sartre refers to Beaumarchais's *Mariage de Figaro*, which though harmful to established interests apparently was welcomed by conservative forces who liked self-criticism. But only in a classless society, one whose internal structure would be "permanent revolution," can the writer be "a mediator *for all*" (82). Sartre obviously does not share the Marxist hope of a final peaceful stable condition at the end of history. He suddenly switches into remote history and describes the role of clerics in medieval society. He violently constrasts the clerical propaganda of orthodox beliefs with the ignorance of the illiterate barons who pillaged and burned everything, even though the whole Christian ideology was ultimately intended for them. It was communicated to them by images, the sculptures of cathedrals and stained-glass windows. The Middle Ages "realized, in effect, the ideal of Benda"—but this was possible only because the whole population was illiterate and the only public of the writer was the college of other writers: "The good conscience of the medieval cleric flowered on the death of literature" (86).

Sartre's next example of this involvement of the writer in society is seventeenth-century France, where the writers became parasites of a parasitic class. Grouping themselves into a symbolic college, the Académie Française, they addressed a strictly limited public, which actually exercised permanent control over them. They knew neither the pride nor the anguish of being different. In short, they were classical: "There is classicism when a society has taken on a relatively stable form and when it has been permeated with the myth of its perenniality" (WIL, 91). The writer did not even suspect the importance of economic, religious, metaphysical, and political factions in the constitution of his audience. Satires were allowed, but they were, so to say, internal, physiological satires. Something beautiful was assumed to be made out of glass—aesthetic distance put it out of reach. It was a moralizing art, but one based on the premise that man should transcend the psychological toward the moral because all religious, metaphysical, political, and social problems had been solved. In the eighteenth century, the governing class lost control of its ideology. The rising middle class became more and more dominant, but the writer was not yet wedged between the dying ideology of the declining class and the rigorous ideology of the rising class. The aristocracy was still pensioning the writer, but it was the bourgeoisie who was buying the books: the writer was collecting at both ends. Sartre tells anecdotes of the status the great writers had acquired: Diderot, in the heat of a philosophic conversation, pinching the thigh of the empress of Russia until blood flowed; Voltaire's extremely stormy relationship with Frederick of Prussia. Sartre seems to share the view that the eighteenth century had no historical sense and believed in the universality of reason. He praises Voltaire for his impassioned sense of the present and sees the whole eighteenth century as a single polemic against the aristocracy—the constant, almost the only, subject of writing. Eighteenth-century optimism is expounded as a denial of the mere existence of evil. Bourgeois man can be recognized by his denial of the existence of social classes, in particular that of the bourgeoisie. Literature became increasingly subservient to the ideology of the bourgeoisie, to whom writers sold their products while despising those who bought them.

This fundamental conflict between the writer and his public was, for Sartre, an unprecedented phenomenon. In the seventeenth century the harmony between the man of letters and the reader was perfect. In the eighteenth century the author had two equally real publics at his disposal and could rely on one or the other as he pleased. Romanticism vainly attempted to avoid an open conflict by depending on the aristocracy rather than on the liberal bourgeoisie. This situation, Sartre would argue, applied to Chateaubriand but company but was totally inapplicable outside of France. Elsewhere Romanticism was identified with liberalism. Sartre of course sees that there is liberalism and even socialism in writers like Hugo, Michelet, and others who were given their status by the bourgeois university. Here I think Sartre makes unjustifiable judgments. The bourgeois university awarded recognition to Michelet, an authentic genius and prose writer of great talent, and also to Taine, whom Sartre calls only a cheap pedant, as well as to Ernest Renan, whose fine style nonetheless offers all the examples one could want of meanness and ugliness. Sartre comments on the rise of the proletariat. Proudhon saw the relation between the demands of the lower classes and the principles of the art of writing, as did Marx, though neither was a man of letters. More and more, the writer did not know for whom he was writing. He was speaking only of his solitude and concocted the notion that one writes for himself alone or for God.

Sartre then attacks Flaubert for his disgraceful abuse of workers. Flaubert did not even notice that the bourgeoisie was an oppressing class. Sartre describes the newer artists who thought of themselves as a communion of saints, who belonged to a symbolic society based on the image of the aristocracy of the old regime. He seems to be thinking mainly of Baudelaire—"I have complete contempt for trade"—and he plays up their use of alcohol and drugs. These transformed the universe into pure beholding. Sartre refers to Rimbaud's "systematic deranging of all the senses" and finally the "icy silence" of Mallarmé (WIL, 130). He briefly alludes to symbolism as discovering the close relation between beauty and death—as if nobody had discovered it before (what about Tristan und Isolde?). Sartre refers to surrealism, quoting André Breton's declaration that "the simplest surrealist act consists of going down into the street, revolver in hand, and firing into the crowd at random as long as you can." Then came the principle of total irresponsibility, automatic writing. This writer wanted to preserve the social order, however, "so that he could feel that as a stranger there he was a permanent fixture. In short, he was a rebel, not a revolutionary" (135). Summarizing, Sartre argues that no matter how cynical and bitter it may have been, nineteenth-century narrative technique offered the French public "a reassuring image of the bourgeoisie" (136).

Sartre, always interested in the question of time, argues that the novel is almost always written in the past tense, whereas the epic, which is of collective origin, is frequently in the present. Sartre then comments at length on how nineteenth-century authors begin their stories by describing the audience to which they are addressed. The audience represents order, the calm of the night, the silence of passions—everything concurs in stabilizing the bourgeoisie, who think that nothing more will happen and who believe in the eternity of the capitalist system. There is always an internal narrator, an ideal universal man of experience, and the tale is laid in the past. Although Sartre draws his examples from Maupassant and Daudet, he realizes that new methods have been invented and refers to the novel written in dialogue form, naming Gyp, Lavedan, and Abel Hermant— all pupils of his. He comments perceptively on stream of consciousness, recognizing that the method implies a certain amount of faking: a stream of consciousness is necessarily a succession of words, even deformed ones. The so-called internal monologue is a rhetoric, a poetic transposition of the inner life, which has become one method among others for the novelist. Sartre does not know Benito Pérez Galdós, but clearly knows Joyce and even his supposed forerunner Valery Larbaud. The bourgeois novel of the nineteenth century seems to Sartre a betrayal of the proletariat. By clarifying and supporting the claims of the proletariat, the writer would attain the essence of the art of writing. Marxism would have triumphed, but in actual reality Marxism, for lack of contradiction in itself, lost its life. It became a church. Sartre again harps on the historicity of all writing: "being situated" is an essential and necessary characteristic of freedom. He returns to history, saying that the twelfth century offers us the image of a concrete and alienated literature. One learns there to write only about God. It is unreflective, in contrast to our twentieth-century literature, which has cut all bonds with society and no longer even has a public. He quotes Jean Paulhan's extravagant remark that "everyone knows that there are two literatures in our time, the bad, which is really unreadable (it is widely read), and the good, which is not read" (WIL, 153). While literature is in history and tied to a specific situation, it always appeals to an abstract universality, even such books as Vercors's Le Silence de la mer and the writings of Richard Wright, which will be forgotten when the situation has changed: "Actual literature can only realize its full essence in a classless society. Only in this society could . . . literature . . . really be anthropological" (156–57). "Anthropological" is here used, I suppose, in the sense of "all human." A writer, a "clerk," however, is always on the side of the oppressor, whether or not he identifies himself with the good or divine perfection, with the beautiful or the true. He is a watchdog or a jester—it is for him to choose. Benda chose the cap and bells, and Gabriel Marcel chose the kennel. Sartre dreams again of a literature in a classless society, which would be a festival. It would be the subjectivity of the society in permanent revolution. In a society without classes, literature would end by becoming conscious of itself. Sartre recognizes that this is all utopian, and in the last chapter he considers the writer in 1947.

"The Situation of the Writer" begins by contrasting the French writer, who is supposedly the only one who has remained a bourgeois, with the American, who has often taken up manual occupations before writing his books. The American writer's vocation seems to be on the ranch and in the shop on a city street. He does not see literature as a means of proclaiming his solitude, as does the Frenchman, but as a means of escaping it. The American writer muses less about glory than he dreams of fraternity (*WIL*, 161). He rarely appears in the work and has no solidarity with other writers; nothing is more remote from him than a university or an official job. For a while he is feted, then lost and forgotten. Sartre gives the example of Nathanael West, whose publisher had no idea of his identity or even of his death in a car accident. Sartre doubts that there is a bourgeoisie in the United States. He then comments on the situation of the writer in England, where writers form an eccentric and slightly cantankerous caste that has little contact with the rest of the population. They are, however, considered quite harmless. Among themselves they never speak about literature, and they live in a freely chosen isolation. In Italy, the bourgeoisie has never counted very much, and the condition of the writer is very bad. He is needy, badly paid, lodged in dilapidated palaces too vast to be heated or even furnished, at grips with a princely language too pompous to be supple. Finally Sartre passes to the French: they are "the most bourgeois writers in the world" (163). One cannot write in France without being at least a bachelor of arts. French writers are all involved in literary explications and the heritage of texts. Centralization has grouped them all in Paris. Exaggerated pictures abound of the writer as a kind of prophet: the French all have images of the writer from Romain Rolland's *Jean Christophe* or Zola writing for Dreyfus, or they may choose the death of Nerval, Byron, or Shelley. The writer seems to the French magnificent (166-67).

Sartre distinguishes three generations of modern French writers. First are the authors who produced before the First World War. They all had either independent means, like Proust, Gide, and Mauriac, or a stable job, like Paul Claudel, a diplomat, and Georges Duhamel, a doctor. What they wanted was to be as individual as possible. Sartre quotes a writer saying: "One should do what everyone else does, but be like no one else." It is a kind of alibi-literature. The second generation came of age after 1918: Jean Cocteau and Marcel Arland were the heroes, surrealism the magnificent rocket. These young bourgeois wanted to ruin culture because they were cultivated. Sartre comments on surrealism, on automatic writing, which seems to him the destruction of subjectivity, and for illustration draws even on Marcel Duchamp and Dali's effort to discredit totally the world of reality. But in fact the surrealists destroyed nothing at all. The world was simply put in brackets. They were actually parasites of the human race, and their preoccupation strictly prohibited them from finding a public among the working class. Though they preached "permanent violence," they arrived at complete quietism. They offered themselves to the Communist party, but surrealism was only a temporary ally. The surrealists had no readers in the proletariat; they remained parasites of the class they insulted. Sartre ridicules Paul Morand, the world traveler, and Drieu La Rochelle, the Fascist sympathizer.

Last comes the new radicalism of the most recent generation, which has no history, no historical sense. In terms that to me are not comprehensible, Sartre distinguishes between the writers associated with the radical socialists and those connected with the ralliés, who seem to be the Gaullists. He gives no examples. This new literature has become a literature of action. Malraux and Saint-Exupéry, for example, write about war and construction, heroism and working, doing, having, and being. Because of war and then death we have no choice but to produce a literature of historicity. Our time has seen horrible events—Sartre alludes to Oradour, Dachau, and Auschwitz. He reflects on torture and concludes that evil cannot be redeemed, but always honestly asks himself, "Suppose I were tortured, what would I do? Would I be as abject as many became?" So we have now to create a literature of extreme situations, create circumstances that reconcile the metaphysical absolute and the relativity of historical fact. Sartre again speaks of the influence of Kafka, whom he refers to as a Jew in Eastern Europe. Americans writers move us not by their cruelty and pessimism, but because they manage to render their stupor and forlornness in the midst of incomprehensible events. We want to achieve, then, a literature that will hurl the reader into the center of the universe, where our books may exist just as things, plants, and events exist. We want to drive providence from our world; we should no longer define beauty by form or matter but by density of being. Sartre dismisses the literature of the Resistance as nothing to be excited about, yet appeals again to a new literature of action, a synthesis of historical relativity and of moral and physical absolutes—a total literature.

Sartre actually thinks that literature is dying. The writer's public is collapsing and disappearing and he no longer knows for whom to write. Sartre alludes to the new media, to newspapers, to the radio, to the movies, concluding again and again that the fate of literature is bound up with the working class, but not necessarily with the Communist party. He gives a skeptical and even ironic picture of what happens to a Communist writer who must pretend to please all readers as well as the authorities within the party, and thus commits himself to dishonesty. Sartre finds only one genuine writer among the Communists, Francis Ponge. It is no accident that he writes about mimosa and beach pebbles. Much of what Sartre has to say here is dated and even wrong, for instance, that in the United States the word *communist* designates any American citizen who did not vote for the Republicans (a statement made during the presidency of a Democrat named Truman). There are four mystifications: Nazism, Gaullism, Catholicism, and French Communism. Sartre monotonously repeats that the fortuncs of literature are tied up with the coming of socialist Europe, but he concludes on a strange downbeat: "The world can very well do without literature. But it can do without man still better" (*WIL*, 297).

Looking back on Sartre's early criticism, one must, I think, single out his essays on the novel. They contain interesting analyses of time, dogmatically assuming that a novel must move in a linear progression toward a future aim. He condemns novels with no sense of time or with a special way of curtailing the time scheme. Thus the hero of Faulkner's *The Sound and the Fury* supposedly has no future, and in Dos Passos there is only the present. Another of Sartre's dogmas is that the novel must be completely objective, with no interference by the author. Thus Sartre criticizes Mauriac for judging his characters, or "playing God."

These early essays are understandable without existential philosophy or any other philosophy. *Qu'est ce que la littérature?* is an eloquent plea for engagement or commitment and has played a great role in making literature in France once again political and polemical. It presents an interesting, though possibly too boldly designed, history of the relation of the writer to his audience. In the Middle Ages, according to Sartre, there was no audience. During classicism there was an audience identified with the writer. In the eighteenth and nineteenth centuries the gulf between writer and audience grew wider and wider until today the writer is an isolated figure in rebellion against his society. Sartre's discussion is based on doctrinaire and ultimately indefensible theories about two issues. Literature, he asserts, is totally different from the other arts. The other arts present images, whereas literature presents ideas and symbols. Sartre takes this view to extremes, denying any kind of rational or objective meaning to painting or music. The Swiss artist Paul Klee is the one exception Sartre seems to recognize, though he disapproves of an artist trying to present symbols as meaning. Most surprisingly, Sartre considers all poetry to be devoid of rational meaning, and he postulates a harshly formulated contrast between poetic and literary language. Sartre traces the history of lyrical poetry, rapidly sketching its development toward symbolism in the sense of Mallarmé, where words lose their dictionary meaning and become mere free images. Sartre detests surrealism, as it reduces the poet to an automaton and deprives him of freedom. Freedom is the one existentialist concept that pervades this and Sartre's later books, but it frankly means nothing more than the assertion of the possibilities of choice and a summary dismissal of determinism. As everybody is utterly free to choose, this allows Sartre to ignore tradition and sources and influences. Yet the novelist is a completely separate creature who is necessarily obliged to commit himself on political and social issues. He cannot escape them. Sartre's view is anti-aesthetic. Beauty is evil and thus poetry is also evil, or at least an escape from responsibility and from society. The concept of "literature," confined to the novel, "requires a morality of generosity, of sociality, of the recognition and promotion of freedom in other people's freedom." Literature, then, is the will to intervene in the real, whereas poetry is the will to escape it. Evil is also simply called the imaginative. There is an equation: beauty is evil, but it is also freedom. Sartre extricates himself in insoluble contradictions by condemning beauty as evil and at the same time wanting a literature that achieves something good, or at least aims at some ultimate good.

Qu'est ce que la littérature? was Sartre's most successful critical book, which made the concept of an engaged or committed literature enormously popular at that time and gave rise to much discussion. Some of Sartre's statements are so extreme, at least in their formulation, that they must never be understood in a literal sense. But one cannot but admire the passion with which he defends freedom—freedom in the very widest sense, not only political.

Sartre's biographies, which he calls psychoanalytical, all seem to be modeled on his own experience: his early life in harmony, almost incestuous, with his mother, and his terrible disappointment when she remarried and broke that bond. He sees the same pattern everywhere, in Baudelaire, in Mallarmé, in Flaubert, though varied somewhat from case to case. Baudelaire was six when his father died, and his mother remarried when he was ten. This second marriage was the deepest shock: "When one has a son like me one doesn't remarry." The justification for his existence had disappeared. In Sartre's conception, Baudelaire then had to choose the sort of person he would be—"that irreversible choice by which each of us decides in a particular situation what he will be and what he is" (*B*, 18). He wanted to make himself another person, totally unique, a man who never forgot himself. But Baudelaire, according to Sartre, was a man without immediacy—he faked his whole attempt to become another person. He was, however, exasperated at his own lucidity, his ability to look upon himself as though he were another person. He became obsessed by a profound sense of his own uselessness, a feeling that life was nothing but an absurd game. He became indifferent, lazy, and, in an odd way, resigned to his dependence on a committee of guardians whom he hated but at the same time was unable or unwilling to free himself from. This basic attitude of indifference or ennui prevented Baudelaire from carrying out any lengthy undertaking. His freedom and his gratuitousness and his abandonment frightened him. Sartre speaks of his "dryness of heart," of his laziness and his abuse of narcotics, and of his puerile ideas of morality, which he derived from other people and never questioned. In the trial over *Les Fleurs du mal*, Sartre notes, Baudelaire did not even attempt to defend the contents of the book—he simply presented it either as a diversion or as a work of edification that was intended to induce horror of vice.

Sartre has a low opinion of Baudelaire's Christianity and of attempts to view him as a Christian. He rejects the opinion of the Catholic critic who claimed that Baudelaire was a Catholic. Baudelaire professed atheism at least as early as 1847, and Christ seems to have been unknown to him. Though in constant revolt he was in no way a revolutionary and always showed signs of a bad conscience. When he revolted against his stepfather it never occurred to Baudelaire to destroy the idea of family. In Sartre's view, Baudelaire remained a child. His parents became hateful idols but he could not escape them. He hated to be alone, even for an hour. He wanted to horrify his parents, but Sartre is not convinced that he had an Oedipus complex in the sense of desiring his mother. He never challenged the sacred character of his judges. His mother was certainly the only person for whom Baudelaire felt any affection. He liked to arrange clandestine meetings with her in museums, and he constantly presented himself, says Sartre, in the guise of a guilty person. Baudelaire "was an eternal minor, a middle-aged adolescent who lived in a constant state of rage and hatred, though under the vigilant and reassuring protection of others" (*B*, 66). Sartre emphasizes Baudelaire's desire to be free, but free within the framework of a ready-made universe. Baudelaire believed in creation, in poetry which is evil—the "flowers of evil": "Hell is very well for the crude smug sins, but the soul of a man who desires evil for evil's sake is an exquisite flower" (74). He regularly sinned in public and then condemned his sinning, which he thought of as evil: "The supreme and unique pleasure of love lies in the certainty that one is doing evil." He had a physical horror of the sexual act because it was natural and because it was a form of communication with another person. According to Sartre, Baudelaire thought of evil only in the form of eroticism; thousands of other forces of evil—treachery, baseness, envy, brutality, avarice, and so on—remained completely alien to him.

More and more, Sartre tells us, Baudelaire wanted to turn himself into a thing. He lived in bad faith and even the initial choice was made in bad faith. He never completely believed in anything he thought or felt or in any of his suffering or in any of his guilty pleasures. Baudelaire's feeling had an inner emptiness. Such a fundamental inability to take oneself seriously goes with bad faith. Paradoxically, Sartre notes, in Baudelaire the remorse preceded the sin. He had such a violent horror of himself that his life can be seen as a long series of self-inflicted punishments. He set out to make himself odious—for instance, he left no stone unturned to make people believe he was a pederast. He once said: "When I have aroused universal horror and disgust, I shall have conquered solitude." Sartre regards Baudelaire's living in squalor with prostitutes and contracting syphilis as one stage in his self-punishment. The happy man, according to Baudelaire, has lost spiritual tension and has fallen. Baudelaire would never have achieved happiness because he considered it immoral. Suffering, he said, is nobility. His suffering enabled him to adopt the pose of not being in this world. His spirituality was completely negative. He identified himself with Satan, but Sartre thinks that Satan is nothing but a symbol for disobedient, sulky children.

Sartre harps on Baudelaire's belief that the natural behavior of man is evil and that goodness is always a product of art. He belongs to the whole nineteenth-century movement of anti-nature, which included Mallarmé and Huysmans. Baudelaire disliked naturalistic novels and even orderly landscapes and plant life: he professed to be "incapable of getting worked up over plants." He hated the abundance and warmth of nature and eulogized sterility, manifested in his attraction to minerals and jewels and anything sparkling and metallic: "How wrong to eat, sleep and make love like everyone else" (*B*, 110). Detesting abandon, from dawn to dusk Baudelaire never for a moment let himself go, which explains his dandyism and his precision in language. He was a fetishist, worshiped women's shoes, and had a cult of rigidity, sterility, and coldness. The moon became for him a symbol of frigidity. Sartre gives examples of his erotic preferences, his preoccupation with harlots of the lowest class. Baudelaire was horrified at the idea of giving pleasure. I suspect that many of these observations are based on Sartre's construction or guesses and on interpretations of poems or prose pieces like the very early *Fanfarlo* (1847). Sartre stresses Baudelaire's fascination with rape and murder. He constantly vacillated, however, between masochism and sadism, between lunar metal and corpses.

One would assume that Sartre has a low opinion of Baudelaire as a man, making him appear childish and perverse and cruel, but suddenly, though he rarely expresses judgments in the book, Sartre says: "Baudelaire's nobility and greatness as a man are due in large measure to his horror of drift" (*B*, 134). Baudelaire, Sartre argues, had no spontaneity: the dandyism was ceremonial, a cult of ego. He cultivated a special aura and thought of himself as a member of an elite, like Flaubert, Lautréamont, Rimbaud, and Van Gogh. Sartre cites Flaubert as a case in point, who laid down as an a priori condition that he should escape from the bourgeoisie and join some kind of fictional parasitic aristocracy. Baudelaire, too, thought of himself as justified and consecrated by the writers of the past, particularly Edgar Allan Poe. For Baudelaire dandyism represented a higher ideal than poetry. Dandyism to him was a suicide club, the execution of some sort of "permanent suicide." He dyed and curled his hair, wore pink glasses, and displayed a feminine taste in clothes. Baudelaire is supposed to have been a man of the city, of the crowds, but actually he had a horrible fear of crowds. He was extremely shy and always failed as a lecturer. But he nonetheless thought of himself as a *déclassé*, as a bohemian; he set himself not above but below the bourgeoisie. Baudelaire made himself up and travestied himself in order to take himself by surprise. Comparing Baudelaire and Rimbaud, Sartre decides that Baudelaire was a prime creator of form who merely travestied and ordered things, whereas Rimbaud was a creator of form and matter. Sartre returns constantly to Baudelaire's obsession with his mother's remarriage, noting that Baudelaire even added ten years to his father's age: "That is what comes of being the child of a mother of twenty-seven and a father of seventy-two. Because of them, I'm falling to pieces." Sartre thinks that at every moment Baudelaire, though still alive, was already on the other side of the grave. The die was cast very early, when he contracted venereal disease at the age of twenty-one. *Fanfarlo* seems to Sartre to confirm all the ideas of the later Baudelaire: he did nothing but repeat himself. The idea of progress was hateful to Baudelaire, as it snatched him away from the contemplation of the past and compelled him to turn his eyes toward the future. He thought that the world was coming to an end and predicted the destruction of the Western peoples. He constantly tried to live in the past; only the past had value. To drift meant to fall, to live in the present was to fall, and he felt free because he was guilty.

Sartre's main theme—that Baudelaire was an inauthentic person who had a horror of nature and tried in his poems to achieve a union of being and existence—is expressed in terms that are obviously those of Sartre and not of Baudelaire, who himself had a romantic idea of the identification of object and subject in the poetic act. He had a horror of life and wanted to be accursed. He completely lacked charity and generosity and had no end other than himself, but he cultivated sufferings which were, in his feelings, identical with his pleasures. He constantly flirted with the idea of suicide yet never seriously attempted it, as he wanted to be a survivor, a contemplator of his own sufferings. Suffering for Baudelaire had the intimate structure of pleasure. Living always in the eyes of others, he chose to live for himself as he existed for others. He accepted the society of his time, refusing experience: nothing from the outside could change him, he learned nothing. His story is that of a very slow, very painful decapitation. Sartre ends with the paradoxical conclusion that "the choice a man makes for himself is completely identical with what is called his destiny." In retrospect, one is struck by Sartre's violent denunciation of Baudelaire as a person, based primarily on *Fanfarlo* and extracts from his letters and occasional quotations from the poems. There is no literary criticism in the sense of a discussion of the poetry, and it must remain a mystery how a man as despicable as the one Sartre depicts could have produced poetry of such monumental quality.

Among Sartre's early literary biographies was the one on Stéphane Mallarmé. Hundreds of pages that Sartre had written on Mallarmé apparently disappeared from his Paris apartment when it was bombed by right-wing activists. Sartre rewrote the manuscript in 1952, but never developed it fully. This manuscript, though unfinished, was printed for the first time in 1978, in a special issue of *Obliques* (no. 18–19). An enlarged version, entitled *Mallarmé: La Lucidité et sa face d'ombre,* was published in 1986, after Sartre's death, by Gallimard and incorporates as its third section an essay, also written in 1952, that was first published in volume 3 of *Ecrivains célèbres* (1953) and later reprinted in volume 4 of Sartre's *Situations.* This little book has not attracted the attention it deserves, as it represents his most ambitious and clearest statements on the nature of poetry and on the history of French poetry and *Weltanschauung.* The work is divided into three parts: the first is an account of French poetry before Mallarmé; the second is a psychoanalytical study of Mallarmé's mental condition; and the third is an attempt to define the special nature of Mallarmé's poetry. Sartre thought of Mallarmé as the greatest French poet, and obviously felt a considerable kinship with him, evidenced by the title of Sartre's early book *L'Etre et le néant* (1943). For him, Mallarmé is the "poet of nothingness."

The first section, "The Aesthetic Heritage," is really an attempt to explain the whole history of France and of French poetry by what happened in 1793, the cult of reason during the Terror. According to Sartre, in spite of many devout people and even movements, atheism became victorious in the nineteenth century. He examines the main French poets and accuses them, in fact, of hypocrisy. They only pretend that God is not dead and write as if the old creed were still universally accepted and believed. Sartre is strongly antireligious and refers to the story of Christ as an "absurd legend propagated by the diehards of Christianity" (*M*, 24). While the early poets, such as Musset, Leconte de Lisle, and Lamartine, then, are hypocrites, later poets simply turned to a cult of form and technique. Sartre ascribes great importance to the influence of Poe's "Philosophy of Composition," to which Baudelaire constantly referred and even paraphrased. The new cult of beauty is for Sartre another example of that retirement and avoidance of atheism. He finds the emergence of the *poète maudit* significant. Sartre also reflects on contemporary affairs, the whole revival of Christian philosophy, and even the Absolute in the philosophy of René le Senne and Simone Weil. He speaks of Weil's doctrine that "God's omnipresence is the same as His universal absence. This should not be viewed as merely attesting to the virulent spread of disbelief" (29). Sartre thinks that religious poetry failed, paralleling the failure of socialist poetry. As usual, Sartre satirizes the French bourgeois and their ridicule by the poets, who after all are nourished by the objects of their contempt. It is hard to see how he can say that literature from 1860 to 1900 goes on a "silence strike." In a fairly interesting digression Sartre discusses the use of troubadour poetry, of which again the bourgeoisie is considered to be the origin. Seventeenth-century preciosity is a similar reaction to the bourgeoisie. Sartre emphasizes the poverty of poets— with the one exception of Hugo, who earned a lot of money, supposedly 180 million francs, a staggering sum by modern standards. All the others were ignored, in which they took a princely pride. The ruin of poetry becomes emblematic of our personal failures. Sartre quotes Verlaine's atheistic declarations and sees a universal negation, which the poets called "dream." He comments interestingly on the whole impact of science on poetry and on the poet's preference for the myth of decadence over the bourgeois myth of progress. Art appears to be no more than an opiate, a bogus substitute for religion.

Sartre makes some interesting remarks and employs apt quotations, but ultimately he generalizes far too sweepingly, as in his somewhat Marxist explanation that "the overly strenuous negation of the bourgeoisie is directly inspired by the bourgeoisie itself" and that "there is a trick to persuading the oppressed that there is no oppression" (*M*, 30). The entire section seems almost a diatribe against the bourgeoisie, which obsessed Sartre all his life. But of course he is also very critical of the enemies of the bourgeoisie. He is shocked at Flaubert's regret that the entire Commune was not shipped off to the galleys and at Leconte de Lisle's outrage that the painter Courbet could not be lined up in front of a firing squad (57). Even Zola does not escape Sartre's condemnation. The poets refuse to take part in the human enterprise, and the experimental novelist refuses to accept "the hopes and values of this curious species of the ant which builds its anthills in the open" (50). Sartre remains an admirer of progress and technological expansion. He concludes the section by attributing everything to the effect of historical events—the Commune, the long reign of Napoleon III, the new rule of the bourgeoisie—and ends with a quotation from Marx: "Ideas have no history of their own" (65).

The second section begins with a psychological sketch of Mallarmé's marriage, which has little interest for a history of criticism. I cannot substantiate his low assessment of Mme Mallarmé as a dumb German whom the young husband refashioned into a domestic angel (*M*, 70). I find it difficult to justify using verses out of context as if they were statements of the poet himself. Sartre convincingly elaborates the gloom of Mallarmé, who was often near suicide, who read in nature the decadence of poetry and the imminent death of man, and yet the following discussion, which plays up Mallarmé's ancestry in the legal bureaucracy, sounds very doubtful. Sartre overstates the significance of Mallarmé's father and uncle having been members of the recorder's office. Mallarmé is supposed to be living in childhood, which can, however, contain a hell in the likeness of man. It can be deciphered like a dream, without taking its poetic or common meaning into account. Sartre quotes Charles Mauron's book on obsessive ideas in poetry, a work that had a wide response in England also, as Mauron lived in London. Sartre tries to see Mallarmé as being increasingly obsessed by the image of shipwreck and creates a gloomy and absurd picture of the poet and his so-called friends, who apparently were often sarcastic and satirical observers of what they considered a pathological phenomenon. Sartre at that time could not know Mallarmé's projection of Bible-reading, the bible consisting in an anecdote of his own which would be read and re-read to an enormous audience. It is, to my mind, a really paranoid, naive, and at the same time frightening image of Mallarmé's decay. Sartre sees this without any concrete prophecy of his own. From his sixth year Mallarmé is a child who thinks of being in the world as exile and believes that his life will be an experience of failure. I shall not try to unravel Sartre's account of Mallarmé's relationship with his mother and with his widowed grandmother, nor do I care to speculate as to why he seems never to have referred to his new stepsister. Even Sartre thinks that that question cannot be settled until the publication of Mallarmé's complete correspondence; in any case, the letters may not necessarily contain references to a person whom he hardly knew and obviously disliked, as she was the first child of his father's second marriage. In Sartre's view, Mallarmé convincingly embraced purity, which equals nullity; his life is the embodiment of sterility, which reflects on itself and sterilizes him. Sartre is so convinced of this purely negative interpretation of Mallarmé that he rejects any attempt to read his ideas, such as the famous passage about the bouquet of flowers ("I say, 'a flower!' and . . . musically it arises, the sweet idea itself, missing from all bouquets"), as some kind of Platonism: "Those who carry on about Mallarmé's Platonism are either dupes or rascals" (123).

The last section, "Requiem of a Poet," originally written as an independent essay, focuses on the poetic rather than on the psychoanalytic aspect of Mallarmé. Sartre suggests that for Mallarmé writing poetry in the early years was a way of obliterating his detestable background. His writings testify to the fact that he kept the universe at a distance, and even his finest poems have no other subject than poetry itself. Sartre considers Mallarmé a materialist who recognized that all poetry, certainly his own, was simply reminiscence. Sartre dismisses Mallarmé's constant complaints of impotence as theological in origin. Although the death of God imposes the obligation to replace Him, Mallarmé felt he had arrived too late—everything had already been said. Mallarmé was therefore driven to complete despair and seriously contemplated suicide. He apparently was of the opinion that his suicide would destroy the universe—a view anticipated by Kirilov in Dostoevsky's *The Possessed*, though Mallarmé did not, of course, know the novel. Mallarmé's despair goes so far that he feels there is no reality left; it has evaporated into writing. Meaning has completely disappeared. Again Sartre harshly condemns any attempt to speak of Mallarmé's so-called Platonism. Mallarmé was not interested in ideal or intelligent structures of reality. He thought of a poem as a "hole pierced in Being"—it produces "the total absence of the world" (*M*, 141). Sartre recognizes that this conception contains something regrettably mystifying; though he does not use the term, he suspects Mallarmé of charlatanism. But, then again, Sartre seems to admire Mallarmé as hero, prophet, and tragedian, who experienced the death of God far more profoundly than Nietzsche did. Mallarmé felt, like Camus so much later, that suicide was the fundamental issue facing man. Still, Mallarmé was a poet to the core, wholly committed to the critical self-destruction of poetry. Sartre closes by quoting Mallarmé. While knowing perfectly well that his art is an imposture, Mallarmé also seems to be saying: It might have been the truth.

Sartre's essay is finally disappointing. His remarks about Mallarmé's ancestry and marriage, though highly speculative, are good, but he does not really discuss the poetry, except in a most general way relating to Mallarmé's idea of poetry as nothingness and silence. Perhaps a portion of what was once a more complete manuscript would have come closer to literary criticism, but what is preserved belongs definitely to Sartre's psychobiographies, of which the Baudelaire is by far the most successful.

10 : PAUL VALÉRY (1871–1945)

THE POETIC THEORY OF Paul Valéry can be seen as almost the direct opposite of that of Benedetto Croce: in Croce we find the most complete identification of the author's creative act with the work of art and the response of the reader, the most emphatic devaluation of what ordinarily is called for in favor of sentiment, the strongest feeling for the historicity of literature. In Valéry we are confronted with a theory that asserts the discontinuity between author, work, and reader, emphasizes a most extreme regard for form and nothing but form divorced from emotion, and takes poetry completely out of history into the realm of the pure and the absolute.

Valéry expounded his poetics in a systematic fashion only once: in the course on poetics he gave at the Collège de France from 1937 to 1945. He published only the introductory lecture, and the meager notes published in *Ygdrassil* by Georges Le Breton covering eighteen lectures between 25 December 1937 and 25 February 1939 add little. The introductory lecture moves in the confines of preliminary philosophical considerations. A study of the mass of notes accumulated by Valéry during his so-called silence (from 1892 to 1917)[1] and a complete transcript of the course hardly change what we already know from Valéry's considered pronouncements in his published essays, collected mainly in the five volumes of *Variété* (1924–44) and in *Pièces sur l'art* (1931), in the essays in *Poësie* (1928), in "Réflexions sur l'art" (1935), in scattered prefaces and addresses, and in the great number of aphorisms throughout volumes such as *Mélanges* (1941) and *Tel quel* (2 vols., 1941–42). Valéry is not a systematic philosopher or aesthetician: he propounds a number of insights which are sometimes, at least superficially, contradictory; he is, within a very limited range, a practical critic and above all a practicing poet who examines the creative process or speculates about his craft. He implic-

1. See page 347 for this and subsequent notes.

itly raises fundamental questions without often claiming or attempting to solve them within a consistent framework.

Much of the interest of Valéry's thought lies precisely in its tentativeness, in its suggestiveness, in its extremism which, however, is held only provisionally, often for the sake of a specific argument or as a contradiction to accepted opinions, in order to surprise or shock, to experiment with a thought, to see where it will lead.

Valéry, like many other theorists, sharply distinguishes between the author, the work, and the reader, but he goes further than any other writer I know in doubting the continuity and even the desirability of continuity among the three. He complains that in most aesthetics one finds "a confusion of considerations some of which make sense only for the author, others are valid only for the work, and yet others only for the person who experiences the work. Any proposition which brings together these three entities is illusory." He would assert more positively that "producer and consumer are two essentially separate systems" (*O*, 2:801, 1: 1346; *CW*, 14:391, 13:96) and most boldly that the "art, as value, depends essentially on this nonidentification (of producer and consumer), this need for an intermediary between producer and consumer" ("Réflexions," 64; *CW*, 13:143). Valéry summarizes:

> In short, a work of art is an object, a human product [*fabrication*], made with a view to affecting certain individuals in a certain way. The phenomenon Art can be represented by two perfectly distinct transformations (it is the same relation as that in economics between production and consumption). What is extremely important to note is that the two transformations—the one which goes from the author to the *manufactured object* and the one which expresses the fact that the object or the work modifies the consumer—are entirely independent. It follows that one should always consider them separately ("Réflexions," 63; *CW*, 13:142).

Thus, art is *not* communication, certainly not direct communication between authors and readers: "If what has happened in the one person were communicated directly to the other, all art would collapse, all the effects of art would disappear" ("Réflexions," 64; *CW*, 13:143). Art the producer and the consumer, their ignorance of each other's thoughts and needs is almost essential to the effect of a work" (*O*, 1:1348; *CW*, 13:98). But it is hard to see how such a theory can be upheld in its extreme formulation: if the gulf between creator, work, and reader were unbridgeable, there would be no works and the works (if existent) would be completely incomprehensible. But although Valéry tries out the theory without quite seeing its consequences, he is right when he emphasizes the difficulties of these relationships: Has the work anything to do with the author? Has the reader's interpretation of a work anything to do with its supposed "real" meaning? Valéry answers "very little," but to my mind he can hardly answer "nothing at all."

If we isolate the three factors and begin with the author, we can see that Valéry has the courage of his conviction and is really not so much or not primarily interested in the product, the work of art, as in the process of production, the creative process independent of its result. As a matter of fact, if one wanted to explain the psychological or genetic origin of Valéry's theory, one would probably find that it started with his interest in the creative process and was motivated by it. Valéry is interested in this activity in itself and thus creates the somewhat monstrous self-caricature, Monsieur Teste: he writes elaborately about Leonardo da Vinci, the universal man. When, in a formal, rather empty anniversary speech, Valéry praised Goethe in the terms he had used for Leonardo, he implicitly praised himself or rather the ideal he had set up for himself. Goethe is the potential creator, who has the genius of transformation, of metamorphosis; he is Orpheus, Proteus (O, 1:534, 538; CW, 6:151, 156–57). Goethe's speculations on metamorphosis and evolution attract Valéry more than his poetry. He admires the combination of scientist and poet. Valéry's thought moves so much on this very general level of human creativeness that he can assimilate artistic creativeness and scientific creativeness by some general term such as *speculation*. The essay on Edgar Allan Poe's *Eureka* is inspired by such an identification (or by the hope for such an identification) of science and poetry through the common element of imagination, though Valéry avoids the term (O, 1:154–67; CW, 8:161–76).

If one is interested in the creative process as such, one will disparage the work of art. This is what Valéry does, both in words and in deeds. During his many years of silence, he obviously felt that he was elaborating his ideas and his personality and that expression and especially publication were purely secondary to this inner activity. "The Great Work for me is knowing work as such—knowing the most general transformation, of which the works are only local applications, particular problems." Thus the work of art is conceived as existing only in the act. "Poetry is essentially *in actu*" (O, 2:1516, 1:1415; CW, 15:302, 13:69).

> A work of mind exists only in action. Outside of that act, nothing is left but an object which has no particular relation to the mind. Transport a statue which you admire to a country sufficiently different from ours and it turns into a meaningless stone, a Parthenon

into nothing more than a small marble quarry. And when a piece of poetry is used as a collection of grammatical difficulties or examples, it ceases immediately to be a work of the mind, since the use that is made of it is utterly alien to the conditions under which it came into being, while, at the same time, it is denied the consumption value that gives it meaning (*O*, 1:1349; *CW*, 13:100).

Implicitly, of course, the discontinuity is here deplored or considered as a condition to be overcome under ideal circumstances, but the emphasis remains on the act of composing, not on its result. Thus Valéry could tell an interviewer that a work of art is never finished, that we deliver it to the public only under the pressure of external circumstances (Lefè-vre, 109). We can only abandon it. Valéry always assumes that a thought comes first and then its artistic dress, or rather shape or form. Too ready a communication of the thought would prejudice the artistic process.

It is not surprising that Valéry has given us several minute introspective accounts of the composition of his poems and that he excels in this analysis. But whatever the specific interest of these "marvels of introspection," as T. S. Eliot calls them, Valéry of necessity arrives at very little for theory, since his introspection leads to the conclusion that there is no direct relation between a specific state of mind of the author and the work itself. Indeed, there might be a considerable distance between the original idea, the germ of the work, and the finished product. He rejects the organic analogy of begetting, growing, and being born: there is no continuity between the act of conception and the work produced. The germ of a work of art can be anything: "Sometimes a certain subject, sometimes a group of words, sometimes a simple rhythm, sometimes (even) a prosodic scheme. . . . It is important to remember that one germ may be as good as another. . . . An empty sheet of paper; an idle moment; a slip of the tongue; a misreading; a pen that is pleasant to hold." Anything might suggest the germ of the poem. The poetic state is "perfectly irregular, inconstant, involuntary, fragile . . . we lose it, as we obtain it, *by accident*." One could call this a theory of inspiration, but Valéry is reluctant to admit inspiration: "I believed and still believe that it is ignoble to write from enthusiasm alone. Enthusiasm is not a state of mind for a writer." Inspiration is no guarantee of the value of the product: "The spirit blows where it listeth: one sees it blow on fools" (*O*, 1:1415, 1321, 1204–05, 1490; *CW*, 13:69, 7:60, 8:71, 7:131).

If poetry or art in general is not inspiration, it is obviously not dream. In an age in which surrealism, Freudianism, and symbolism asserted the kinship of poetry and dream, Valéry repudiates it emphatically, though he recognizes that "the poetic universe bears strong analogies to the universe of dreams," and that as a historical fact, this confusion between poetry and dream has been understandable since the time of romanticism. But "the true condition of a true poet is as distinct as possible from the state of dreaming. In the former I can see nothing but voluntary efforts, suppleness of thought, a submission of the mind to exquisite constraints, and the perpetual triumph of sacrifice. . . . Whoever speaks of exactness of style invokes the opposite of dream" (O, 1:1363, 476; CW, 7:198, 11).

Though Valéry recognizes some initial irrational suggestion, such as two rhythms insisting on being heard, as he describes them in "Mémoires d'un poème" (O, 1:1464–90; CW, 7:100–32), all the practical emphasis falls on the share of rational speculation after the moment of conception, on the poetic calculus, on the poet's exercise of choice among possibilities, his clairvoyant, highly conscious pursuit of a sport or game. Valéry loves to think of the art of poetry as "a sport of people insensitive to the conventional values of common language." He says, in slightly different terms, that a poem is "a game, but a solemn, regulated, significant game" or "a kind of calculus" or an algebra. Thus "every true poet is necessarily a critic of the first order," but, of course, this criticism by no means makes the poet a philosopher. Valéry, surprisingly enough in view of his intellectualism, sharply divorces poetry from philosophy, not as an act, but in its result. "Every true poet," he admits, "is much more capable than is generally known of right reasoning and abstract thinking." Still, philosophical poetry is impossible, is not even a possible idea. Valéry disparages poet-philosophers such as Alfred de Vigny: "To philosophize in verse, was and still is the same as if one wanted to play chess by the rules of the game of checkers" (O, 2:1530, 546, 1515, 1:1335, 1335–36, 2:667; CW, 15:324, 14:96, 15:301, 7:76, 77, 14:235).

What Valéry demands of poetry is always something pure, something sui generis, and thus poetry cannot be continuous with the personality of the author; it is and must be impersonal to be perfect. "Perfection eliminates the person of the author," or even more strongly: "I don't see what something that keeps reminding me of the man behind it has to do with art. . . . The writer's duty, his proper function, is to fade out of the picture, to obliterate himself, his face, his personal concerns, his love affairs. . . . What makes a work is not the man who signs it. What makes a work has no name." What Valéry admires in poetry is the effort of men such as Victor Hugo and Stéphane Mallarmé (a surprising pairing) "to form non-human ways of discourse, absolute discourse, in a sense—discourse which suggests a certain being independent of any person—a divinity of language" (O, 1:453, 2:801, 635; CW, 7:289, 14:390–91, 209). Valéry minimizes the

continuity between author and work and especially resents or rejects the
emotions of ordinary life as themes of art. "Our most important thoughts
are those which contradict our feelings," says Valéry repeatedly (*O*, 2:
642, 764; *CW*, 14:218, 347). "All emotion, all sentiment indicates a defect
in adaptation." Valéry resents the emotional effect of art. He complains
that as a young man reading Stendhal's *Lucien Leuwen,* for example, he
felt the illusion so strongly that he could "no longer distinguish clearly
between my own feelings and those which the artifice of the author communicated to me. . . . *Lucien Leuwen* brought about in me the miracle of a
confusion which I detest" (*O*, 2:866, 1:555; *CW*, 14:470, 9:177). Needless
to say, Valéry has no use for confessional literature and looks coldly at the
criterion of "sincerity" or "good intention":

> Everything that aims at sensibility . . . romances, Musset, beggars,
> the poor of Victor Hugo, Jean Valjean arouses disgust if not anger
> in me. Pascal playing with death, Hugo with poverty, though they be
> virtuosos on their instruments, are basically repugnant to me. The
> calculated effort to draw tears, to break hearts, to excite by some-
> thing too beautiful or too sad, makes me merciless. Emotion seems
> to me a forbidden means. It is an ignoble act to make anybody weak
> (*O*, 2:1533; *CW*, 15:328).

Thus nothing seems to him more absurd than "to confide one's sorrow
to paper. . . . What a quaint idea! That's the origin of many bad books, and
of all the worst ones." The essay on Stendhal, though not unsympathetic,
sees him as an exploiter of sincerity: "The will to be sincere with oneself
is inevitably a principle of falsification." Such an author is an actor who
arrives at cynicism out of desperate ambition: "When we no longer know
what to do in order to create a stir and to survive, we prostitute ourselves,
we expose our *pudenda,* we offer them to public view." In telling the history of his return to poetry, Valéry somewhat ruefully admits that "the
majority of writers have tried, and the greatest poets have miraculously
succeeded in the task of reproducing the immediate emotions of life."
But he always resented literature that tried to convert and persuade him:
"I dislike picturing, across the page I read, a flushed or derisive face, on
which is painted the intention to make me love what I hate or hate what
I love" (*O*, 2:866, 1:572, 565, 1471–72; *CW*, 14:469, 9:199, 190, 7:109).
This is the task of politics and eloquence but not of poetry and certainly
not of the poetry Valéry wants to write. He wanted to go a different way
and did. He has a clear conception of a work of art constructed by the
intellect, free from personal and emotional admixtures, pure, or as he
sometimes says, *absolute* poetry.

Valéry early on uses the phrase "pure poetry," old as such, in the preface to Lucien Fabre's *Connaissance de la déesse* (1920) to suggest the ideal of the symbolists, which will always remain an ideal, though Valéry recognizes that it is only an abstract ideal.[2] It is a tendency toward the utmost rigor in art, "toward a beauty ever more conscious of its genesis, ever more independent of all *subjects*, and free from the vulgar attractions of sentiment as well as from the blatant effects of eloquence." It is "the perfect vacuum and the absolute zero of temperature—ideals neither of which can be attained, and only approached at the price of an exhausting series of efforts." It is "pure in the sense in which a physicist speaks of pure water" (*O*, 1:1275–76, 1451; *CW*, 7:46–47, 185). Pure poetry is a "poetry which results, by a kind of *exhaustion*, from the progressive suppression of the prosaic elements of a poem. By prosaic elements we mean everything that *without damage* can be said also in prose; everything, history, legend, anecdote, morality, even philosophy, which exists by itself without the necessary co-operation of song" (Lefèvre, 65–66). The purity of poetry is obviously for Valéry a standard of judgment: "A poem is worth as much as it contains of pure poetry." At times, Valéry thinks of it as a kind of admixture of pure gold among foreign matter: "What one calls a poem is in practice composed of fragments of pure poetry embedded in the substance of a discourse" (*O*, 1:1453, 1457; *CW*, 7:180, 185).

But what is this pure gold, how can it be distinguished from prose? Poetry, first of all, cannot be paraphrased, cannot be reduced to its prose content. Valéry condemns in strongest terms the heresy of paraphrase: "Nothing beautiful can be summarized. . . . Homer and Lucretius were not yet pure. Epic poets, didactic poets, and their like, are impure." The "absurd school exercise which consists of putting verse into prose . . . implies the belief that poetry is an *accident* of the *substance* prose. But poetry exists only for those in whose eyes such an operation is impossible and who recognize poetry by this very impossibility." The impossibility of paraphrase logically implies the impossibility of translating poetry: "Translations of the great foreign poets are architectural blueprints which may well be admirable; only they make the edifices themselves, palaces, temples, and the rest disappear" (*O*, 2:638, 1:1509, 2:638–39; *CW*, 14:213, 7:156, 14:213).

But why cannot poetry be reduced to prose, or to thought or theme? Valéry has several answers: one, which he repeats many times, is that prose language perishes when it is understood, whereas poetry demands repetition, demands and suggests a universe. Prose is practical, it presupposes a realm of ends: "As soon as the aim is reached, the word expires." But the universe of poetry is "a universe of reciprocal relations analogous to the universe of sounds within which the musical thought is born and

moves. In this poetic universe, resonance triumphs over causality." The
poem must "maintain itself in a condition as remote as possible from that
of prose." Furthermore, "the poetic universe arises from the number, or
rather from the density of images, figures, consonances, dissonances, by
the linking of turns of speech and rhythms—the essential being continually to avoid anything that would lead back to prose" (*O*, 1:1501–03; *CW*,
7:146–47). Valéry here resumes old motifs of aesthetics: the contemplative isolation of poetry, its divorce from the world of ends, its creation of
a new world. This last can be achieved only by exploiting the resources
of language to the utmost, by removing its world from that of ordinary
speech through sound and meter and all the devices of metaphorics.

Valéry stresses the poet's intimate relation to language: he repeats
the famous anecdote about Edgar Degas, who complained that although
he was full of ideas, he could not write poetry, to which Mallarmé an-
swered: "My dear Degas, poetry is not written with ideas. It is made
with words" (*O*, 1:1324 [cf. 1:784]; *CW*, 7:63 [cf. 8:324]). For Valéry,
the poet has a kind of "verbal materialism": "You know that only the
words and the forms are the real discourse." Poets are combiners and ar-
rangers of words. "One must adjust these complex words like irregular
blocks, speculating about the chances and surprises which such arrangements prepare for us, and give the name of 'poets' to those whom fortune
favors in this work." The real greatness of poets is that they are able to
"grasp strongly with their words things of which they have had but fleeting glimpses in their minds." Literature, apparently all literature, "is in
truth only a kind of speculation, a development of certain properties of
language." The poet creates his own special language, a language within a
language: "Like a political power [he] mints his own money." Ultimately,
"the problem is how to extract from this practical instrument [everyday
language] the means of realizing an essentially nonpractical work" (*O*, 1:
1456, 2:113, 483, 1:1423, 2:640, 1460; *CW*, 7:183, 4:108, 14:17, 11:88,
14:216, 7:189).

If poetry is words, it is, of course, not words in isolation, but words
in a pattern, words formalized. One could collect from Valéry the most
extreme formalist statements. He quotes the Provençal poet Frédéric Mistral with approval: "*There is nothing but form* . . . form alone preserves the
works of the mind." He approves of Mallarmé, with whom "the material
is no longer the *cause* of the 'Form': it is one of the effects." Content is
"*nothing but an impure form*—that is to say a *confused* form." Valéry praises
Hugo because with him "the form is always master. . . . Thought becomes
with him a means and not the end of expression." And he says of himself:
"I subordinate 'content' to 'form' (the nearer I am to my *best* state)—I am

always inclined to sacrifice the *former* to the *latter*" (*O*, 1:584, 710, 657, 589, 2:1515; *CW*, 7:253, 8:298, 289, 7:258, 15:301).

Valéry complains that "the philosopher does not easily understand that the artist passes almost without distinction from *form* to *content* as from *content* to *form*." The form, he says with an inversion of usual imagery, is "the skeleton of works: but some works have none. All works die, but those that have a skeleton last much longer than those that were soft all through." This formalism extends to the origin of the poem: "A delightful, touching, 'profoundly human' (as the dunces say) idea sometimes arises from the need to link up two stanzas, two developments of a theme." Once Valéry even said that "the principal personages of a poem are always the smoothness and the vigor of the verse" (*O*, 1:1245, 2:679, 635, 1:485; *CW*, 8:124, 238, 14:209, 7:22). But on the whole Valéry rarely goes to such extremes of formalism, which could be matched only by that of the Russian group.

Much more frequently Valéry thinks of poetry as a collaboration of sound and sense, a compromise between the two. He conceives of sound and sense as "two independent variables," between which there is absolutely no relation (*Bulletin de la Société française de philosophie* 31 [1931]: 118; *CW*, 13:142). Words are arbitrary signs: there is no natural relation between sound and sense. The doctrine of the *mot juste* has no justification: "Flaubert was convinced that for every idea there exists a single form. . . . This fine doctrine unfortunately makes no sense." Thus the union of sound and sense established by the poet is arbitrary but indissoluble: "The value of a poem resides in the indissolubility of sound and sense. Now this is a condition which seems to demand the impossible. There is no relation between the sound and meaning of a word. . . . Yet it is the business of the poet to give us the feeling of an intimate union between the word and the mind." This union must resist dissolution: "If the sense and the sound (or the content and the form) can be easily dissociated the poem *decomposes*." This union of sound and meaning is song, but not quite song. We must remember that Valéry also said that poetry is calculus, sport, exercise, even a game. But apparently song (*chant*) in Valéry's mind is not literally song (*carmen*); it is also enchantment, incantation, charm, magic. Valéry called a collection of his poems *Charmes;* and he means it also as a suggestion of the original function of poetry: "There is a very ancient man in every true poet; he still drinks from the very springs of language." But this primitivism is reconcilable with the greatest refinement. Mallarmé, "the least primitive of poets, gave . . . the magic formula" (*O*, 1:1476, 1333, 1505, 651, 649; *CW*, 7:114, 74, 150, 8:281, 279). The poet is the Orpheus who brings all nature to life (*O*, 1:651; *CW*,

8:282), who has the animizing power of ancient man. Thus all poetry will be and must be metaphorical: "The poet who multiplies figures is only rediscovering within himself language in its *nascent state*" (*O*, 1:1440; *CW*, 13:86).

Poetry is figurative and incantatory and, of course, metrical. Valéry has little use for free verse. He always praises the merits of strict metrical schemes and of all poetic conventions: "The demands of a strict prosody are the artifice that confers on natural language the qualities of a resistant matter." In verse, as Valéry interprets it, there must always be a clash between speech and metrical pattern, and even the most artificial rules of French metrics are good (though arbitrary), just as any kind of restraint is good. Even a small vocabulary is considered a good thing: "A restricted vocabulary, from which one knows how to form numerous combinations, is worth more than thirty thousand words which do nothing but embarrass the acts of the mind." Valéry defends stanzaic forms and is enraptured by the sonnet. He would like to encounter its inventor in the underworld. However bad his sonnets might have been, Valéry wants to tell him: "I set you in my heart above all the poets of the earth and the underworld. . . . You have invented a *form*, and the greatest have accommodated themselves to this form." The constant argument is the value of convention, of restriction, even of chains: "Restriction can be achieved only by the arbitrary." Valéry thus revives one of the oldest doctrines of poetics, that of difficulties overcome. This "difficulty overcome" is for Valéry a criterion of value: "Every judgment which one wants to make of a work of art must first of all take into account the difficulties which the author has set up for himself to overcome" (*O*, 1:480, 1137, 1254, 590, 1279; *CW*, 7:16, 10:128, 7:160, 14:150, 7:51). We hardly need to point out that Valéry prefers classicism to romanticism: classicism is superior because of its set conventions.

All these elaborate conventions, the dance, even the dance in fetters, are there for a purpose: to achieve that ideal art work—unified, antirelative, nontemporal, imperishable, eternal, something beyond the decay of nature and man, something absolute. The poem, Valéry says, is "a closed system of all parts in which nothing can be modified" (quoted in Charles Du Bos, *Journal 1921–23* [1946], 222). Beauty, Valéry defines, is precisely "the sentiment of the impossibility of variation." Moreover, "what is finished, what is complete gives us the feeling of our being powerless to modify it." "What is not entirely finished does not yet exist," he says paradoxically, especially in view of his constant insistence on poetry as an act, as a continuous activity and on the impossibility of finishing. But this is precisely the distant ideal of perfection for which Valéry finally has to give up finding words. Beauty is ultimately inexpressible. It implies an effect of ineffability, indescribability, it signifies "inexpressibility": "Literature attempts by words to create the state of a lack of words." Thus a central obscurity in poetry is justified: "What is clear and comprehensible and corresponds to a precise idea does not produce the effect of the divine." In the end, "everything that is beautiful, generous, heroic is in essence obscure, incomprehensible. . . . Whoever swears faithfulness to clarity, renounces thereby being a hero" (*O*, 2:714, 1:374–75, 2:893, 773; *CW*, 14:282–83, 562–63, 505, 359).

This curious criterion of resistance to transformation is central to Valéry's ideal of poetry. Racine's *Phèdre*, Valéry discovered, resisted attempts to change it: "I learned by direct experience and immediate sensation what is perfection in a work" (*O*, 1:508; *CW*, 11:195). A lack of this resistance is what Valéry considers the main objection to the novel:

> As a reader of novels and histories I could not help observing all the freedom which these writings left me to modify [them] at my pleasure. . . . Novels demand passivity. They claim to make you take them at their word. They should be careful not to awaken the faculty of invention which, as to details, is in all of us at least equal to that of the author, and which can be, at every moment, exercised diabolically and can amuse itself with modifying the text, with bringing in an infinite number of possible substitutions which every narrative allows without noticeable alterations of its theme. . . . That is why I admire those novelists who tell us that they live (as one says) their characters and live them to the point of being rather lived by them than living them. I am convinced that they speak the truth as I myself have once or twice in my life experienced something analogous, I think, to such a sort of incarnation. But how can one gloss over the fact that everything ends on paper, that however intense and intimate the illusion of the author may be, it is translated into words, into phrases fixed once for all for everybody, exposed to our view, to the reactions and maneuvers of a mind which may be an active mind?[3]

Valéry can rewrite a novel in imagination, and that is why it is "a naive genre," ultimately inferior to poetry. But this is not the only reason for Valéry's depreciation of the novel. The novel is also "historical," based on truth and memory, and neither truth nor memory means anything in art for Valéry. He does not care for memories. "I certainly shall not search for lost time," he says, alluding to his difference from Proust. Just as he does not care to remember his own past, so he does not care for history. "I am antihistorical," he says bluntly, and he often regrets the effects of historiography: the inciting of national passions, the keeping alive of old grievances and illusions (*O*, 2:1530, 1506, 1530; *CW*, 15:324, 288, 324).

His other objection to the novel is its claim to "truth": "Whereas the world of poetry is essentially closed and complete in itself, being purely a system of ornaments and accidents of language, the universe of the novel, even of the fantastic novel, is joined to the real world—just as a painted background merges imperceptibly into real objects, among which a spectator comes and goes." Valéry finds this appeal to truth puzzling. How is it that "a collection of details which are insignificant in themselves, and valueless one by one should produce a passionate interest and the impression of life?" "The novel," he says elsewhere, slightly varying the thought, "is possible because of the fact that this truth costs nothing . . . like air or sunlight. It lends itself to an infinity of compositions of equal probability." Besides, the novel is, of course, prose in Valéry's sense. "Unlike poems, a novel can be summarized; in other words, its plot can be told. It can be shortened without materially changing the story; . . . it can also be translated without losing its value. It can be developed internally and prolonged indefinitely." The same is true of epic poetry, of any long poem. It "can be summarized. . . . A melody cannot be summarized," says Valéry, to his mind devastatingly, as statement and truth are excluded a priori from his definition of poetry (*O*, 1:770, 771, 2:1515, 1:771–72, 2:638; *CW*, 9:296, 297, 15:1302, 9:297–98, 14:213).

It is merely consistent that Valéry does not know what to do with drama, although he himself wrote dramatic scenes, dialogues, and what he calls "mélodrames."[4] "Everything that is dramatic in life, in history, etc., seems to me of secondary interest. . . . This indifference to violent and spectacular incidents explains to me why I am not a novelist, a historian, or a dramatist" (*O*, 2:1524; *CW*, 15:314–15). He is frankly puzzled as to why man finds pleasure in tragedy. He recognizes that

> man likes to feed on the sight of the misfortune of others. Two centuries ago, ladies went to see people put to torture. In any case it seems that the tragic genre is completely opposed to the production, in the soul, of the highest state which art can create in it: the contemplative state—the state of sensuous knowledge in which all the notions and emotions which cannot enter into the composition of a harmonious, though momentary life are abolished at the same time. (preface to Lucien Fabre, *Dieu est innocent* [1946], xiv–xv; *CW*, 7:239)

Still, surprisingly, Valéry recognizes that Greek tragedy has accomplished the impossible:

> In putting on the stage the most atrocious stories in the world, they have imposed upon them all the purity and perfection of a form which insensibly communicates to the spectator of crimes and evils

an indefinable feeling which makes him regard these horrible dis-
orders with a divine eye. . . . [He can] always come back from the
emotion to comprehension, from excess to measure, from the exceptional to the norm, and from nature overthrown to the unchangeable
presence of the profound order of the world. (preface to Fabre, *Dieu
est innocent*, xv; *CW*, 7:239–40)

One cannot help reflecting that Valéry might have admitted the same
transforming power of art in other cases, even in the epic or the social
novel. He himself admits that there is, "in the order of the arts, no theme
and no model which execution cannot ennoble or degrade, make a cause
of disgust or pretext for enthusiasm." In his own practice he more and
more insisted on only one theme of poetry: that of "the life of intelligence
[which] constitutes an incomparable lyrical universe. . . . There is an immense realm of the intellectual sensibility," hitherto neglected by poetry
(*O*, 2:1329, 1:796; *CW*, 12:109, 9:18). It was Valéry's right to insist on this
discovery; every artist recommends the art he himself practices. Every
artist is an apologist for his own art, and that is, in part, the interest of
his criticism. But as a general theory of literature it seems an extremely
narrow, exclusive, puristic view, a specialty hardly applicable beyond that
unique closed system of Valéry's "civilized mind."

Valéry's ideal of poetry remains absolute, almost frozen into the grandeur of a "pure form." Such a hard structure presumably would have to
be apprehended by its audience as purely as it was conceived, as imper-
sonally as it was created. But here Valéry's strong sense of the discontinuity between author and reader interferes. A work of art to his mind
is open to many interpretations, has only a loose relation to its audience.
A work of art is essentially ambiguous: "It is an error contrary to the
nature of poetry and which could even be fatal to it, to claim that to
a poem corresponds one single, true meaning which conforms to or is
identical with some thought of the author" (*O*, 1:1509; *CW*, 7:155–56).
Valéry, with a sort of mischievous courtesy, wrote introductions to Gustave Cohen's commentary on *Le Cimetière marin* and to Alain's commentaries on *Charmes*, which manage to praise the authors without accepting
a single one of their interpretations (*O*, 1:1496–1506, 1507–14; *CW*, 7:
140–52, 153–58). "My verses have the meaning which one gives to them,"
he says bluntly. "There is no true sense of a text. The author has no authority. Whatever he wanted to say, he has written what he has written."
The last part of this pronouncement is entirely defensible: it reasserts his
suspicion of good intentions. "Bad verses are made of good intentions."
Valéry is quite right to say, "when a work has appeared, its interpretation by the author has no more value than its interpretation by someone

else. . . . My intention is only my intention and the work is the work" (*O*, 1: 1509, 1507, 2:678, 557; *CW*, 7:155, 152, 14:236, 109).

This insight into the detachment of the work from the author, into the "intentional fallacy," does not dispose of the problem of interpretation. All interpretations are not equal: there remains the problem of correctness. Valéry seems nearer the truth when he says: "There is no very fine work which is not susceptible of a great variety of equally plausible interpretations. The richness of a work is the number of senses or values which it can receive while still remaining itself" ("Un Eloge de la virtuosité," *Centenaire de Paganini* [1940]; reprinted in *Vues* [1948], 357). The accretion of meaning in the process of history is a fact: great works of art have proved their vitality by this variety of appeal. Valéry recognizes the effects of history on the meaning of a work of art: "The change of an era, which is a change of reader, is comparable to a change in the text itself, a change which is always unforeseeable and incalculable." Valéry echoes a phrase used by Coleridge when he says that "certain works are created by their public. Certain other works create their public" (*O*, 1:494, 2:478; *CW*, 7:33, 14:10). But Valéry indulges in dangerous paradoxes when he asserts the role of "creative misunderstanding" ("Réflexions," 64; *CW*, 13: 144) or gives us this little dialogue: "I understand this text badly. . . . Don't bother. I find fine things. It draws them out of me. It matters little that I know what the author said. My error becomes the author" (*O*, 1: 373–74, 817; *CW*, 14:562, 9:44). Here the way would be opened to extreme caprice and anarchy. The break between work and audience would be complete.

But we must not make too much of irreconcilable contradictions and paradoxes in Valéry's thought. In discussing Descartes he warns that "every system is an enterprise of the mind against itself. . . . If one tries to reconstruct a thinking being from an examination of the texts alone, one is led to the invention of monsters who are incapable of life in direct proportion to the strict carefulness that one has devoted to the elaboration of the study" (*O*, 1:817; *CW*, 9:44). We must not try to force unity on Valéry's thought, we must not invent a logical monster. Let us be content to have shown the main motifs of his thought on poetry.

The preceding discussion is a reprint of the lecture I gave on Valéry in a series of lectures at the University of Washington, Seattle. It was written to contrast with a lecture on Croce, who linked author, work, and reader almost completely, while Valéry argued for discontinuity between author, work, and reader. I am aware that my exposition of Valéry, which fully documents these views, can be criticized for producing ambiguous statements from the enormous number of his writings. I must also admit that Valéry's emphasis on "intention" subverts the idea of a complete gulf between author and reader. Intention, one can argue, presupposes an author and cannot be, as it often is by Valéry, assumed to be floating in the air as a bridge between author and reader, a bridge that Valéry would dismiss as not needed at all.

But Valéry was an enormously prolific author whose collected writings, now available in the Pléiade edition, fill two volumes of 1669 and 1829 pages, respectively. These volumes, of course, are by no means only literary criticism. They range as Valéry's interests range, all over French culture, with excursions into other literatures as well, particularly the classics, like the work of Goethe, and touching on all kinds of issues, social and political. In these writings, Valéry meditates about the state of our civilization generally, not only in France.

Valéry, born in 1871, studied law as a young man and later got a job with the government, in an office of statistics. But he established a reputation mainly as a host to young people, with whom he engaged in conversation. Everybody knew of his close friendship with Stéphane Mallarmé, and after the poet's death in 1898 Valéry assumed Mallarmé's reputation and position as a kind of oracle. He published two short monographs which discuss the poetic process, using Leonardo da Vinci and Michelangelo quite loosely to propagate a cult of genius. But after these two little books, Valéry fell silent as an author until 1917, when at the age of forty-six he published a poem called *La Jeune Parque*. After the First World War he began to write essays, mainly on literature, though not exclusively so.

The first of the five volumes of his *Variétés* (1924) begins with an essay entitled "Villon and Verlaine," which seems to me a masterpiece of characterization and narration. François Villon is coolly described as a robber and a murderer. Valéry makes much of the pardon that King Charles VII issued in 1455 for the death of a cleric whom Villon had killed with a dagger to the groin. "It is a remarkable thing," says Valéry, "that this express act of clemency should have been based entirely on Villon's version of the affair," and that his excuse of self-defense was accepted without challenge or judicial investigation (*CW*, 9:243). Villon is then contrasted with Verlaine, whom Valéry, as a young man, used to see limping along the streets near the Sorbonne: dirty, in an old robe and straw slippers, he yet composed the subtlest, most refined, most personal, sometimes sentimental, poetry in the French language. The essay argues, by example, that a man's life has nothing to do with the ethical value of his work. Villon was a felon, Verlaine a bohemian beggar. Their poetry, however, lived and will live when all the details of their lives are completely forgotten.

This opening essay is followed by a long series of literary studies which, however, are at first glance quite misleading. Valéry appears to be writing something like a history of the writer and his relations to his work. He takes up, for instance, La Fontaine and his verse epic *Adonis,* contrasting it with Racine's *Phèdre.* Both these writings seem to Valéry to have nothing whatever to do with the lives of their authors. *Phèdre,* he argues, is perfect, and so is *Adonis,* and they are not tainted by the supposed love affairs of Racine or the riotous life of the jester La Fontaine. Then Valéry settles down to a surprisingly elaborate account of seventeenth-century spiritual canticles, which he chooses with fine taste. He then suddenly turns to a satirical discussion of Voltaire, a satirist himself. Valéry ridicules the inscription on a little church at Voltaire's estate at Ferney, DEO EREXIT VOLTAIRE, and quotes the wish of Joseph de Maistre "to have a statue raised to him—by the public executioner" (*CW,* 9:136). The whole of the eighteenth century strikes Valéry as "unpoetic," conforming too much to the "detestable notion of d'Alembert, who had the audacity to say that the best verse is that which is closest to good prose" (9:137). The whole of the nineteenth century, meanwhile, seems to him a time of the decay of poetry. Nothing is gained, according to Valéry, by "sentimental lying," which he finds in Chateaubriand, and he makes much of what he considers the completely faked vision of the world presented by Balzac. Then comes the great figure of Victor Hugo, whom Valéry considers a pure formalist, quoting Mistral, the Provençal poet: "Only form preserves the works of the mind" (*CW,* 7:253). But even Hugo, though necessarily recognized as a poet of wide-ranging influence and power, is finally ridiculed as a vulgar philistine.

Valéry dismisses, then, the entire nineteenth century in favor of one figure—Stéphane Mallarmé. In numerous essays and reminiscences Valéry defends Mallarmé against the accusations of obscurity, preciosity, and sterility. These discussions have their comic moments, as when Valéry tells of his encounter with one man who, "with a sort of grief and desperate indignation," said to him of Mallarmé's poetry: "But sir, I am a doctor of letters and I cannot understand a word of it!" (*CW,* 8:261).

Valéry's admiration for Mallarmé, whom he visited frequently, up to a few days before his death, leads to the question of symbolism. In "The Existence of Symbolism," an address given at Liège in 1936 to celebrate the fiftieth anniversary of symbolism, Valéry quite rightly expounds the strangeness of celebrating 1886 as the birth of symbolism, even though "nothing written, nothing remembered by the survivors, existed under that name at the date assigned": "We are constructing symbolism; we are announcing its birth today at the happy age of fifty." It is marvelous, says

Valéry, "to think that we are celebrating the existence fifty years ago, of something that was absent from the universe of fifty years ago," and he professes himself "happy and honored to take part in the generation of a myth, in broad daylight" (*CW*, 8:217). The old question of the name *symbolism* bothers Valéry greatly. He tells an anecdote of the famous astronomer Arago, director of the Paris Observatory, who in 1840 received a visit from a member of the royal family. Arago invited his visitor to look through the great telescope at "the finest star in the sky," telling him: "That, Monseigneur, is Sirius." The prince gazed at the star for some time, then said: "Between you and me, Monsieur le Directeur, are you quite certain that this magnificent star really calls itself Sirius?" (8:216).

Valéry sees that between 1860 and 1900 there existed an aggregate of works and authors that is today called symbolism, but, like Arago's prince, he is "not quite certain that this is its real name" (*CW*, 8:217). Once we have classified the works of that period as classical, romantic, or realist, we are left, says Valéry, with a fourth category of unclassifiable writings—like the *Illuminations* of Arthur Rimbaud or Mallarmé's *L'Après-midi d'un faune*. These works are not similar at all; they have nothing in common with one another. Symbolism is nothing but "the identical gesture that separates each of them from our first three piles" (8:218). There cannot be anything like a symbolist aesthetic. The secret to the symbolists' cohesion, argues Valéry, lies elsewhere, and he tries to show that the only common thing we can find among them is their suffering, their lack of, and disdain for, public approbation. Everyone the symbolists admired had suffered. Edgar Allan Poe died in utter poverty, Baudelaire was prosecuted, Wagner was hissed down at the Paris Opera, Verlaine and Rimbaud were vagabonds and suspicious characters, Mallarmé was ridiculed by the lowest papers.

Symbolism, concludes Valéry, was not for the wider public, but only for the "happy few." It was not a school. It might perhaps be called "mystical," since "it satisfied and sustained more than one heart as effectively as a formal creed" (*CW*, 8:224). But if symbolism had become a matter of religion, it was a highly individualistic religion, and Valéry feels that the symbolist "tries to be himself by means of himself" (8:226). He notes that Baudelaire, for instance, considered music "both diabolic and sacred" (8:230). Valéry thinks of the symbolist poets as forming a religious gathering that resembles an orchestra more than a church, and argues that Mallarmé, seeking "to win back for poetry the empire that had been seized by the great modern composers," approached literature as no one had ever done before (8:231–32). Valéry discusses the whole debate about French free verse, without, apparently, making up his mind.

He then concludes his address, in a way which seems to me extreme, by declaring that "never did the Ivory Tower seem quite so high" as with the symbolist poets (8:239).

In a 1944 essay on Mallarmé, Valéry makes much of Mallarmé's view that "the world has been created so as to end in a beautiful book" (*CW*, 8:296), his mystical, almost biblical, conception of language, "the Word." In religion we have prayer, invocation, and incantation, but for Mallarmé language becomes also an instrument of "spirituality," an instrument of "the direct transmutation of desires and emotions into presences and powers that become 'realities' in themselves" (8:296–97). Mallarmé came more and more to take the view that the subject is not the cause of the form, it is one of its effects: "Each line becomes an entity having physical reasons for existence. It is a discovery, a sort of 'intrinsic truth' that has been wrenched from the domain of chance. As for the world, all reality has no other excuse for existence except to offer the poet the chance to play a sublime match against it—a match that is lost in advance" (8:298). This adoration of language applies only to a later stage of Mallarmé's oeuvre, but it began quite humbly, as we already know, for instance, from the anecdote Valéry tells of the painter Degas, with his frustrated ambitions to be a poet and Mallarmé's admonition to him that "poetry is not written with ideas, but with *words*" (8:324).

As a leading member of the League of Nations' Permanent Committee on Arts and Letters, Valéry was invited in 1932 to be the main speaker at a ceremony commemorating the hundredth anniversary of Goethe's death. The Goethe centennial had become a great political event. The president of the Republic, Paul Doumer, was in the audience, and Valéry began his "Address in Honor of Goethe" by expressing the hopes of men of culture for a European union, prophesying boldly that the original European civilization, which, like that of the ancient Greeks, combined knowledge and beauty, was now decaying. In the address Valéry takes some time to mention Goethe by name, and then he admits that German is "a language which I have the misfortune not to understand" (*CW*, 9:148). He notes somewhat apologetically that he can view his subject only as a stranger, from the outside, adding that Goethe is today "a personality transfigured by fame and, so to speak, become one with his own glory" (9:149). Valéry then retreats somewhat, calling it naive to seek to "define" someone. "An attempt to re-create a writer," he argues, "is an attempt to re-create a capacity for works entirely different from his own, but nevertheless of such a kind that *he alone* could have written them" (9:150)—an odd demand, to replace the complex and voluminous work of a Goethe with some kind of intellectual fake. Valéry claims that we say "Goethe" just as we say "Orpheus" and that "his name immediately, irresistibly, conjures up in our minds a prodigious Figure, a monster of comprehension and creative power, a monster of vitality, a monster of varying moods, a monster of serenity." After "transforming into immortal works everything that the experience of one human being could in the course of his existence grasp," this monster "is himself in the end transmuted into a *myth,* for he compelled posterity to create, to exalt forever that incomparable GOETHE we now observe rising again, after a century, to the highest zenith in the Heavens of the Mind" (9:151).

After this rather strange, meteorological definition of Goethe's fame, Valéry turns to more mundane or ordinary reflections. Goethe's fame, says Valéry, is partly owing to his very long life and to his constant observations of himself. His long life embraced "the whole gamut of reactions, both conflicting and harmonious, which everything he came into contact with was capable of provoking" (*CW,* 9:152). Goethe had the good fortune to live at "the end of an age, and the beginning of another." Valéry briefly sketches the joys of civilized life in the eighteenth century, the elegance, sentiment, and cynicism that were there combined: "The salons brought the geometers and the mystics together with the ladies. . . . Goethe certainly had his share of the good things of life" (9:153). Valéry alludes to the fact that as a child Goethe learned French from Count Thorane, who was quartered in the Goethe home in Frankfurt, a supposedly free town, during the Seven Years' War. Later Goethe witnessed the changes brought about by the French Revolution, which awoke nations to a "consciousness of the full resources of their strength" and composed "the noisy overture to the new age" (9:153).

But Valéry describes Goethe as being less affected by the turmoil of the Revolution than by the upheavals happening in literature. Shakespeare, whom Voltaire had made a European author, was now said to have killed tragedy—meaning French tragedy, particularly Racine and the plays of Voltaire himself. Herder revived the Germanic tradition and announced the exhaustion of French art. In Germany, "the august fathers of nineteenth-century thought," Kant, Fichte, and Hegel, and those who were to become "the sublime fathers of music" lived and worked not far from Goethe's home. In Goethe's time, Pompeii and Herculaneum were recovered, the theories of Newton and Laplace reigned in the field of science, and "electricity from Volta to Ampère was explored and recognized as the basic phenomenon of the universe" (*CW,* 9:154). The science of chemistry was founded. Goethe himself, while he had no use for mathematics, became a subtle and profound researcher in biology. Valéry says that Goethe had a "genius for transformation" and calls him "Poet and Proteus." He mentions Weimar, where Goethe became "courtier, confidant, minister," finding time to manage the Weimar theater even while conducting various experiments in botany. In Weimar Goethe "breathed an engaging atmosphere of freedom." He was, says Valéry, "perhaps the last man to enjoy Europe in its perfection" (9:156).

But such freedom has its disadvantages. Proteus must preserve what is unique beneath the many forms he assumes. Valéry alludes to Jove changing himself into a bull, a swan, or a shower of gold: "he must not remain bound to one of them forever, caught in the trap of his own seductive designs—in short, transformed forever into a beast." Goethe, like Jove, never let himself be caught. He had a "genius for disengagement and flight," a strong instinct for liberty. He passed through passions and circumstances without ever being caught. In matters of the heart, "his highly lucid Demon bade him love," but he always escaped. According to Valéry, Goethe "sacrificed every woman to the Eternal Feminine" (*CW*, 9:158), which is a weird misapplication of the last chorus of the second part of *Faust*. Goethe's "Demonism" is a form of pride, a pride rising to a metaphysical level that Valéry thinks makes it "the equivalent of an infinite modesty" (9:159). Demonism is a principle of nature, which he judges to be quite neutral. "The tiniest leaf had more meaning for him than any word," argues Valéry, "and on almost the last day of his life he was still saying to Eckermann that no speech was worth a drawing, even one tossed off casually. He was a poet who disparaged words" (9:160). (After sixty-six years I have re-read Johann Eckermann's *Gespräche mit Goethe* from A to Z and cannot find any passage that remotely resembles this pronouncement ascribed to Goethe.)

Valéry then compares Hamlet's attitude toward a skull with that of Faust. Hamlet holds the skull, speaks of his horror of the void, and "his gorge rises": he throws it away in disgust. But Faust coldly picks up "the fearful object." He knows that brooding leads nowhere, only to "that future past, which is death." He examines the skull with great attention and compares this concentration to "the effort he had made in the past to decipher ancient manuscripts," ending in a meditation on the skulls of men and beasts (*CW*, 9:160). Goethe's imaginative faculty is content with the "study and representation of the visible world." Valéry alludes to the famous song of Lynceus, "My happy eyes, what you have seen is beautiful!" and quotes Goethe's claim, "I have never thought about thought." He thought only about the appearance of things. Still, Valéry recognizes that Goethe is not content with simple observation but rather pursues

or seeks to discover the design of nature through botany and anatomy—
one more proof, according to Valéry, "of the diversity—and what might
almost be called the ordinary incompatibility—of gifts which is essential
to minds of the highest order" (9:162). But Goethe does not see natural reality as static, but as a metamorphosis. Valéry praises him as one
of the founders of "transformism," or the theory of evolution, adding
that Goethe, like Rousseau, was one of the first to react against the whole
analytical mechanics derived from the laws of Newton.

Valéry argues that there are two sides to Goethe: classical and romantic.
He was a scholar and scientist, but he was also a mystic, "a mystic of an unusual kind, entirely devoted to the contemplation of the external world"
(9:167). He tries to arrive at a conception of nature which is neither that
of Newton nor of God, or at least not of the God "propounded by the different religions." He rejects the idea of a single Creation, because he views
the evolution of organisms as overwhelming refutation of it. Goethe, declares Valéry, was "hope itself." He rejected everything that could weaken
his will to live and "did not recoil before any apparent contradiction if the
contradiction was likely to enrich his mind" (9:167). Valéry compares
Goethe to "that monstrous god revered in Rome, the god of passage, of
transition, who contemplated all possible things with his two faces looking in opposite directions: Janus *bifrons*." Goethe has one face "turned
toward the century which was drawing to a close, the other . . . toward
us"; in the same way he offers Germany "a face classical in its beauty" and
France "another entirely romantic" (9:168). Valéry develops this motif
of contradiction further. Goethe's lyrical soul, he claims, alternates with
the botanist; he is a scholar and a gallant; he combines nobility and can-
dor with the cynicism of Mephistopheles. Above all, "he reconciled at will
Apollo and Dionysus, Gothic and Classic, Hell and Hades, God and the
Devil, in the same way that his mind reconciled Orphism and experimental science, Kant and the demoniac, and everything in general with
something else which contradicted it" (9:168). Goethe's main concern is
freedom—freedom from Hegel, from Fichte, from Newton.

At this point Valéry turns to a decisive encounter which impressed
Goethe deeply: his meeting in 1808 with Napoleon. Goethe always
thought of that meeting as "his greatest memory and his crowning pride"
(*CW,* 9:169). Valéry calls Napoleon "Faust with a crown on his head."
He appears as "the emperor of the mind and even of literature," while
Goethe appears as "the embodiment of the mind" (9:171). Napoleon,
who knew that man's future depends on the reputation he leaves behind,
greeted Goethe by saying: "You are a Man"—that is to say, he treated
Goethe as an equal. Valéry thinks that Bonaparte would make an ideal

figure for a third part to *Faust*. (Valéry's dialogue *Mon Faust* has nothing directly to do with this idea, however.) The constant analogies are elaborated. Napoleon, possessed by the ideal of "Complete Action," action that is "imagined, constructed in the mind with incredible precision down to the least detail, then executed with the promptness and force of the spring of a wild beast," is compared to Caesar, in his capacity for "understanding and manipulating all the peoples of the world" (9:172). Likewise Goethe "enlisted, assembled, and manipulated Euripides and Shakespeare, Voltaire and Trismegistus, Job and Diderot, God Himself and the Devil." He is "capable of being Linnaeus and Don Juan." Both Napoleon and Goethe yield to the seduction of the East, Bonaparte appreciating "the simple and martial religion of Islam" and Goethe being "carried away by Hafiz," while both admired Mohammed (9:173). "But what is more European," asks Valéry, "than to be attracted by the East?" Napoleon and Goethe both profess contempt for ideology: Goethe does not want to think about thinking; Napoleon detests abstract designs that do not demand verification or execution. Both are similar too in their attitude toward religion, wavering between respect and contempt.

Napoleon, however, was a passionate man who put everything into action, who accepted "a sort of volcanism applied to the art of war, and even practiced it in the realm of politics, for his aim was to remake the world in the space of ten years" (*CW*, 9:174). And here Valéry sees the great difference between the two men. Goethe "did not care for volcanoes." He had adopted "the profound notion of imperceptible transformation" and believed in "the maternal slowness of nature." Goethe is a "sage"—with, says Valéry, "a dash of the devil for completeness' sake, and enough of what was absolute and inalienable in the freedom of the intellect to make use of the devil, and in the end to outwit him." He is the "Pontifex Maximus," a great builder of bridges between the centuries and the forms of cultures. Among his antiques, his herbals, his engravings, and his books, Goethe, exercising "a magistracy of the European mind," grew to become "a supreme and lucid Jupiter of ivory and gold, a god of light." He lived for ten years after the death of the emperor, in his little Weimar, which Valéry calls "a sort of delicious St. Helena," comparing Müller and Eckermann to the two Frenchmen who served Napoleon and kept records of his last days. "What a noble sunset!" concludes Valéry, "What a view of the plenitude and glory of life. . . . Faust could now say: 'Moment, thou art so beautiful. I consent to die.' But when called by Helen he appears, *saved*, elevated by universal consent to the first place among the Fathers of Thought and the Doctors of Poetry: PATER AESTHETICUS IN AETERNUM" (9:175).

"Address in Honor of Goethe" disappoints, because it obviously shows little knowledge of Goethe's works and does not even attempt to describe them. Valéry's emphasis is always on Goethe's biological observations, although Valéry is not the only critic to see Goethe's residence at Weimar as the end of his sincere and spontaneous poetry or to prefer the scientist or the minister to the poet. This speech illustrates in an odd way Valéry's main conception, his preoccupation with creativity as such and with the audience and the effect of the fame of a work. But the speech moves too quickly from a generalized creativity to very concrete discoveries in botany and anatomy to conceal the bridge which cannot be denied: author and work cannot be separated, except by the new nihilists of deconstructionism.

We must be aware, of course, that Valéry gave this address in an official capacity (as vice-president of the French committee to honor the Goethe centennial) and before different audiences in diverse places: one at Frankfurt, which was celebrating noisily this anniversary, one at Zurich at the university, and possibly others elsewhere. He thus was obliged to give a laudatory account of Goethe both as a man and as a writer. All the same, while praising Goethe and allegorizing him as a series of Greek and Roman gods—Proteus, Jove, Janus *bifrons*—Valéry manages to lead up to a somewhat ambiguous conclusion. Goethe is reduced to his fame and influence and finally evaporates into a myth, which Valéry cleverly analogizes with the "myth" of symbolism. When we celebrate the fiftieth anniversary of the birth of symbolism even though we cannot find any texts to document the use of the term by poets and critics fifty years before, we are present at the creation of a myth: and Valéry suggests that this is the case with Goethe as well. His was a great presence, but we are not sure that he was more than his fame. Valéry seems to say that, like the origins of symbolism, Goethe is also in some way a fiction. In the end, Valéry allows Goethe to be a sort of patron saint of aestheticism. Quoting the final scene of *Faust*, where the *Pater ecstaticus* appears in the mountain ravines, Valéry distorts or parodies this vision by speaking of Goethe as *Pater aestheticus*, the patron saint of art, remote and unreal.

11 : PROSPECT

I HAVE DECIDED TO CONCLUDE the section on France with the approximate date of 1950. It allows me to ignore the new trends that did not begin to flourish in France until the fifties and sixties. Without discussing the new "isms"—existentialism, structuralism, and the rest—I am content to say that the atmosphere in Paris changed with the arrival of a young talent, Roland Barthes (1915–80). Barthes's little pamphlet *Le Degré zéro de l'écriture* was almost completely neglected when it was published in 1953, but his next book, *Sur Racine* (1963), became the center of a controversy between the defenders of the older views and what Barthes claimed as the New Criticism. I realize, of course, that writers like Poulet and Sartre who began to publish before 1950 are discussed in the body of this book often up to quite recent date. With Barthes, however, as he himself argues, "the whole of literature, from Flaubert to the present, has become the problematics of language"—and that is a new story.

PART II   ITALIAN CRITICISM
1900–1950

12 : BENEDETTO CROCE (1866–1952)

IN A SPEECH AT ZURICH in 1925 Rudolf Borchardt, then a highly visible German essayist, spoke of Croce as dominating the twentieth century as Cicero did the first century B.C., Petrarch the fourteenth, Leibniz the seventeenth, Voltaire the eighteenth, and Goethe the nineteenth.[1] Croce, no doubt, did dominate at least the cultural life of Italy at that time so fully that one could speak of his "intellectual dictatorship."[2] Today, however, Borchardt's assertion or prophecy sounds exceedingly strange. Natalino Sapegno, professor of Italian literature at the University of Rome and an eminent and prolific literary historian, who should know such things, stated fairly recently that "the young people of today no longer read Croce."[3] Even among scholars and critics, Croce students, not to speak of adherents, have become rare. There is the *Rivista di studi cro-ciani,* and new monographs and surveys have multiplied since his death, but the general readership seems to have deserted him. Something has happened. It is not merely the usual slump in the reputation of a writer after his death, the common feeling that his lesson has been absorbed, but something much more serious: his philosophy and its assumptions, and even his aesthetics, have become almost incomprehensible. He was not refuted, though early on many objections were voiced. Rather he was simply passed over, left by the wayside. At least in aesthetics and literary criticism, to which I shall confine myself, totally different and diverse movements have ignored Croce's work. Just glancing at twentieth-century developments in criticism and aesthetics—the Russian Formalists, the Prague school, French structuralism, the Geneva critics of consciousness, the new German hermeneutics and *Rezeptionsaesthetik,* semiotics, and the deconstructionism of Derrida and his followers, not to mention old adversaries such as the Marxists—one can see that Croce is considered irrelevant. He is not referred to or quoted, even when he discusses the same problems and gives similar solutions.

His considerable influence in his time was almost entirely confined

1. See page 349 for this and subsequent notes.

to the early *Estetica*. Outside of Italy it was, surprisingly, strongest in England and America, where he found not only excellent expounders of his doctrines but independent thinkers who used, modified, and assimilated his views. In England, Robin G. Collingwood was a philosopher of distinction in his own right whose *Principles of Art* (1934) draws heavily on Croce, and in the United States, John Dewey's *Experience in Art* (1934) develops an aesthetics in many respects similar to Croce's in spite of totally different philosophical presuppositions.[4] But Croce's aesthetic ideas were most effectively expounded in the United States in a somewhat watered-down version in the writings of Joel E. Spingarn.[5] Through him and possibly the philosopher Wilbur M. Urban some of Croce's ideas filtered through to the so-called New Critics. Explicit references are rare, but John Crowe Ransom, who gave the group its name, quotes Croce and so does the very different R. P. Blackmur.[6] There is a substantial chapter on Croce by William K. Wimsatt in his and Cleanth Brooks's *Literary Criticism: A Short History* (1957), and a solid monograph by the Italian émigré Gian N. G. Orsini, *Benedetto Croce: Philosopher of Art and Literary Critic* (1961), which remains one of the best expositions, not only in English.

In Germany, several Romance scholars were deeply impressed by Croce. Karl Vossler, whose published correspondence with Croce illuminates the agreements and conflicts of the time,[7] Leo Spitzer, whose "stylistics" must not, however, be described as Crocean,[8] and Erich Auerbach, who translated *La Filosofia di G. B. Vico*, spread a knowledge of Croce. But Croce's influence was rather strictly confined to the academic world of philologists, and his aesthetics was sharply rejected by the then leading exponents of the discipline: Max Dessoir and Johannes Volkelt.[9] Croce's echo in France was weak, though Jean Lameere produced a good book on the aesthetics (1936). There were, of course, other references, often unfavorable, but the silence of the central figures in French criticism— Paul Valéry and Albert Thibaudet—is deafening.[10] In Spain, Dámaso Alonso was clearly influenced by Croce.[11] Not unexpectedly, Croce's effect in Russia was negligible, even before and certainly after the Revolution. There are, however, striking similarities between his theories of language and those of Aleksandr Potebnya, explainable by a common ancestry in Wilhelm von Humboldt's views, but casual references among Formalist writers such as B. M. Engelhardt and Viktor Vinogradov are uniformly unfavorable. What might sound Crocean in Viktor Shklovsky actually comes from Bergson.[12]

Croce's dominant position in Italy in the first half of the twentieth century is, of course, due not only to his aesthetics, but to a combination of all the activities of a man who excelled in almost every branch of humane learning. As a philosopher Croce devised a whole scheme in which logic, economics, and ethics have their coordinate places with aesthetics. Croce was also deeply immersed in the theory and practice of historiography and in political and moral theory. After some wavering he sided against Fascism and became the symbol of liberalism. Most important for our purposes, starting with the foundation of his periodical *La Critica* in 1903, Croce became a highly influential critic of contemporary Italian literature and later of the great classics, Italian and foreign, and an immensely erudite scholar in literary and intellectual history, often in the remotest bypaths. In the whole history of criticism only Sainte-Beuve, Wilhelm Dilthey, and possibly George Saintsbury can rival him in this respect, and Croce might, I believe, surpass them. They have their obvious limitations: Sainte-Beuve in his almost exclusive concern with French matters, Dilthey in his German angle of vision, and Saintsbury in his arbitrary selectiveness.

In focusing on Croce's aesthetics, his theory of poetry and literature, and his literary criticism, one must inevitably look at his general philosophy. Croce always denied that he had a rigid system. He thought of it as offering "provisional and dynamic systematization" (*FiSto*, 64), and he changed his mind on many issues, developing, elaborating, and sometimes repudiating old positions while holding firm to his basic outlook. Within his system, though "indefinite, because in motion" (64), the place of aesthetics is never in doubt: "The philosophy of art or aesthetics . . . is not really comprehensible and accessible to thought [*pensabile*] except within the whole of which it is a part, that is, in relation to the philosophy of all the other forms of the spirit" (*P*, 114).

Croce's basic assumption is that of a complete idealist monism. Nothing exists except spirit, or rather the activity of spirit in history (and thus in time). Croce in his later writings preferred not to speak of idealism, but called his philosophy *storicismo assoluto*. Yet Croce's *storicismo* must not be confused with the use of "historicism" in German, French, and English, where it implies relativism and finally skepticism. In Croce there is no dualism of being and value, body and soul, nature and mind. Nature is resolved into one of the forms and products of the spirit. External reality is a myth. History, the only reality, moves on with no utopian or final stage in sight. Within this universal mind Croce distinguishes four aspects, or moments: the aesthetic and the logical, which are both theoretical, and the economic and the ethical, which are practical. He insists that unlike Hegel, with whom his scheme was often wrongly identified, he conceives these aspects not as contraries or triads but as distinctions (*distinti*) and that they are the only categories within which the spirit moves in a circular fashion. This is not the place to discuss the intricacies of Croce's system, but most today will have difficulty with the denial of nature except as a form of "economics," or "praxis," and with the expansion of the category of economics to encompass every daily activity of man, including his feelings and volitions. Be that as it may, some understanding of the scheme is necessary as it has bearing on Croce's aesthetics.

The aesthetics, widely quoted and referred to, seems simple in its radicalism but is still easy to misunderstand. A full study would have to distinguish between four phases of Croce's career, represented by *Estetica* (1902), *Breviario di estetica* (1912), "Aesthetica in nuce" (in *Ultimi saggi*, 1928), and *La Poesia* (1936). In addition, the pre-history of Croce's thought is formulated in *La Critica letteraria* (1894), and a close study of many essays, lectures, and reviews would show that changes embodied in the main pronouncements were anticipated more or less casually before. Elaborate arguments have been made to show that Croce radically changed his views, that one cannot even speak of a single aesthetic, but it seems wiser instead to recognize his additions and possible modifications and concessions, which should not obscure the basic continuity of his thinking. The original *Estetica*, which Croce later described as suffering from "youthful radicalism" (*P*, 35), contains concessions to a dualism of form and matter Croce would not condone in his mature writings. *La Poesia*, on the other hand, shows a tolerance, a spirit of conciliation toward different concerns and methodologies absent in the early writings. One can find contradictions in Croce, but he would not admit them or tolerate them: "I have always tried to think, and perhaps to link up or preserve my judgments in rigorous accord of unity" (*CC*, 3:200). If he discovered an error, he would want to solve it, correct it, revise his thinking. Even his later writings, in which Croce asserts the primacy of ethical action and implicitly rejects the dialectics of the distinti (see *Storia* 1938, 42ff.), can be reconciled with his general scheme as an assertion of his basic faith in life and his moral inspiration.[13]

The main thesis of Croce's aesthetics, as is well known, is that art is intuition. One must, in order to understand Croce's term, forget about mystical intuition (there is no transcendence in Croce) and about Descartes's use of the word to mean immediate evidence and many other uses by modern philosophers. In Croce *intuition* means "representation," the German *Anschauung*. It is not "sensation," which in Croce's early terminology would be mere formless matter, and it is not "perception," which is always the apprehension of something real. It is "the undifferentiated

unity of the perception of the real and of the simple image of the possible"
(*E,* 6). Intuition is thus a far wider category than what we ordinarily call
art. Although Croce's aesthetics is concerned exclusively with the realm
of art, it assumes a total continuity between ordinary representation, also
when remembered, of any individual objects—for example, "this river,
this lake, this brook, this rain, this glass of water"—and art (26). Croce
expressly denies that one can draw a line between intuitions called "art"
and those which are vulgarly called "not art." Here is a problem he seems
not to have resolved.

But we have failed to understand Croce's definition if we do not immediately add his identification of intuition with expression: "What does
not objectify itself in an expression is not intuition or representation, but
sensation and naturalness" (*E,* 11). Expression in Croce is not necessarily
verbal expression: it might be expression by line, color, or sound. Verbal
expression need not be speaking aloud or, of course, writing: an intuition may be expressed (but even this dualism is false, because intuition
is simply expression) without any outward action. Expression can occur
within the mind alone, but it is still expression, since for Croce there is no
thinking without speaking, though speaking need not be speaking aloud.
Thus all language is intuition-expression, and hence a part of aesthetics
in the wide sense Croce gives to the term. Croce's intuition-expression
is the activity of the spirit which precedes that of conceptual knowledge.
Still, it is knowledge—not practical activity but theoretical—knowledge
of things in their concreteness and individuality.

Once we have understood the term intuition-expression, we shall not
be surprised by the conclusions Croce draws. Art (that is, this intuition-
expression, an activity and not an object) cannot be a physical fact: neither
a stone nor a canvas nor a piece of paper with ink marks on it, whether
letters or notes. There cannot be any natural beauty and hence there are
no canons of female beauty, no golden sections, no laws of the beautiful in nature. The lady who decided that the Gulf of Naples is, after all,
une cuvette bleue, a "blue washbasin" (*US,* 21), was right, as all beauty is
in the eye of the beholder. Neither can art be an imitation or mirroring
of reality, as there is no reality outside the mind. Realism is quickly dis-
posed of as an impossible concept, though art does express reality, "the
only reality, which is the soul, the spirit" (*P,* 198). Poetry can never be
realistic, for it "belongs to the soul and not to the *res,* that is, to all things
seen and considered externally" (*PoSc,* 1:166). Art thus cannot be history,
as history refers to factual reality. The historical existence of a fictional
character is irrelevant. Verisimilitude, often required from art, is only
another term for coherence of images.

Art is also not pleasure. The experience of pleasure and pain belongs to the realm of the practical. Pleasure does not distinguish aesthetic acts from other acts. Pleasure may be sexual, visceral, and so on; it may accompany all activities of man, but does not single out the world of art. It is impossible to discover any specific aesthetic pleasure. To define art by pleasure (one of the oldest doctrines) is like defining fish by the water in which they swim.

Neither can art be an outpouring of immediate emotions, which belong to the realm of the practical. They must be transfigured in art, contemplated, distanced, rather than suffered or undergone. This is catharsis, the liberation from passion, the calming property of art (US, 8).

Nor can art be simply "the play of imagination," the inventiveness of a spinner of yarns or a teller of tales, which Croce always distinguishes from *fantasia*, the creative imagination of the English tradition (where the terms are ranked in reverse: imagination is the higher, fancy the lower faculty).

Moreover, art is not morality, as morality is a practical act which follows intuition and conceptual knowledge. But it is a gross misunderstanding to think of Croce as an aesthete who denies the moral and social responsibility of the artist. He would make such a claim only for that inner act: "The artist is always morally blameless and philosophically irreproachable, even though his art may have for subject matter a low morality and philosophy: insofar as he is an artist, he does not act and does not reason, but composes poetry, paints, sings, and, in short, expresses himself" (NSE, 62). But the reproduction and diffusion of the artistic intuition is a practical act and can be regulated by society. Croce would censor pornographic literature and admits that "as practical works . . . they lend themselves to being locked up in a closet or in a cupboard, and even to being burned at a 'stake of vanity' *à la* Savonarola" (62–63). Nobody is more violent than Croce in his condemnation of aestheticism as it was understood at the end of the nineteenth century. This attempt to make the aesthetic the standard of morality was an illegitimate encroachment from one category to another. D'Annunzio and Marinetti prefigure immoral Fascism; Stefan George, Croce suspects, helped the rise of Hitlerism (NPS, 2:116).

But rhetoric, persuasion, and didacticism cannot be art either, for this would subordinate it to a practical end, move it into the category of the economic in Croce's wide sense. Most important, art for Croce is neither science nor philosophy. Croce insists that art is not conceptual knowledge, does not represent abstract ideas or universals, that "he who begins to think scientifically has already ceased to contemplate aesthetically" (E, 41). Conceptual knowledge is always knowledge of the real and unreal, whereas intuition means "indistinction of reality and unreality, the image in its value as mere image, the pure ideality of the image" (*NSE*, 15–16). Thus Croce considers all intellectualistic theories of art that make art symbolic of reality—all theories that put the aim of art into the creation of the typical or generic or make art a version of religion and myth (in Croce, these are mistaken forms of rudimentary philosophy)—to be another "confusion of realms." Hence Croce establishes the autonomy of art, which, however, has nothing to do with art for art's sake but rather constitutes a defense of poetry and art against the encroachments of conceptual thought, mere personal pleasure, social utility, and externally imposed moralism. The outlines of a critical methodology emerge in these negations: Croce's criticism will consist of his pointing to the transgressions and incursions from the other moments or movements of the spirit.

The identification of intuition and expression has other striking consequences. If this is a single internal act, there cannot be any distinction between content and form. Content for the early Croce would be, at most, brute matter preceding the act of intuition. But we could not say anything about it: "The aesthetic act is, therefore, form, and nothing but form" (*E*, 19). Croce's aesthetics of intuition could also be called "aesthetics of form" (*NSE*, 34). Thus Croce is often convicted by his own words of being a formalist. But this is quite misleading, as Croce always condemned academic formalism, sharply criticized the formalist school descended from Johann Friedrich Herbart, and had no use for the formal analyses of Heinrich Wölfflin in the history of painting or for those in narrative technique he read about in J. W. Beach's *Twentieth Century Novel* (*TPS*, 2:61–63). Croce consistently criticized the whole movement of "stylistic criticism" as a renewal of antiquated rhetoric (*PS*, 1:108), leaving us "a miserable heap of inanimate fragments" (*P*, 124), manipulating "little images and little words without connection or without the profound connection which is of the soul, and with only the possession of what we call 'devices'" (*Letture*, 304)—the *procédés* of Valéry or the "devices" of the Russian Formalists. Nor does Croce have any use for prosody or metrics as an abstract science. In the rare instances when he comments on the ottava rima of Ariosto or the free rhythms of Goethe (*ASC*, 44; *G*, 1: 89–90) only the specific aesthetic effect is noted. Croce even admits that what he calls form could just as well be called content, "because it is always understood that the content is formed, and the form is filled, that the sentiment is a figured sentiment and the figure is a felt figure" (*NSE*, 34). *Form* as Croce uses it is a generic name, since "any spiritual act consists in the form which is proper to it and not in the subject matter" (*P*, 226).

If there is no distinction between content and form, then each work of art is indivisible, forms a unity, an organic whole that cannot be divided. Each work of art is an individual: "The single expressive facts are so many individuals, one not interchangeable with another except in the common quality of expression. . . . The impressions vary, as do the contents; every content is different from every other, because nothing repeats itself in life" (*E*, 76). Hence a work of art cannot be properly translated (though Croce himself did poetic translations from Goethe): only a new work of art can be created. There is no need for such a concept as style, as there cannot be any divorce between the verbal surface and the core of meaning. At most, style is a synonym for successful expression: "In the aesthetic fact there are none but proper words; and the same intuition can be expressed in one way only, because it is intuition and not a concept" (81). As every work of art is simply successful expression, Croce can dismiss not only traditional rhetorical categories but all such concepts as the tragic, the sublime, the comic, and the humorous. They are handed over to psychology: they are empirical, descriptive terms derived from an aesthetics of sympathy which is nonaesthetic in Croce's scheme.

The theory so far hangs together and is coherent once we have understood what it is about: the intuition-expression. One might think that in practice it would lead to a critical paralysis, as we are deprived of the majority of terms and concepts with which criticism works and has worked. Indeed, Croce's theory of criticism (at least, in its early stage) was highly untheoretical. It merely said that the critic must reproduce the work of art in himself. Creator, work, and auditor (or reader) are more closely identified than in any other system. Nothing could be more foreign to Croce's mind than a view such as Valéry's, which divides the creator from the work and the work from the audience and compares the process of creation to manufacturing: the baker is not even similar to the bread and the man who eats bread does not care about the baker. In Croce, the identification with the creator means that there is no difference between genius and taste, and that there is no special artistic genius at all. Instead of *poeta nascitur*, we could say *homo nascitur poeta* (*E*, 18). Croce formulates this required identification in the most extreme fashion: "To judge a work of art is *to remake it,* and in remaking it we are artists: helped artists, but artists. When I penetrate to the innermost sense of a canto of Dante's, *I am Dante*" (*PE*, 155). Elsewhere he recognizes that "empirically, of course, we are not Dante, nor is Dante we; but, in the moment of contemplation and judgment, our spirit is one with that of the poet, and in that moment we and he are a single thing" (*E*, 133). Croce quite logically rejects critical absolutism, which judges according to canons or models that would be intellectual concepts. But he also rejects critical relativism, which would deny the possibility of such an identification. His scheme, which has to recognize the frequent failure of this meeting of minds, assigns great importance to historical and philological scholarship, as able to achieve the restoration of the conditions that make this identification possible by removing obstacles to comprehension. Croce considers erudition, however, to be strictly auxiliary. Croce carried on a long fight against what he termed the *allotria* of scholarship, the irrelevance of much "research," though he himself often indulged in the minutiae of antiquarianism, perfectly aware of its subordinate place. While using these tools, criticism thus calls into existence an internal activity, aesthetic reproduction, which is fundamentally the same as the intuition-expression of the artist.

The work of art as an object is considered the result of a volitional act of externalization, whereas the creative act is purely internal. But "when we have fixed an intuition, we always have still to decide whether or not we should communicate it to others, and to whom, and when, and how; all these deliberations come equally under the utilitarian and ethical criterion" (*E*, 128). This externalization is the artist's device to prevent the loss of his spiritual labor "and to render possible and easy, for himself and for others, the *reproduction* of his images" (*NSE*, 38). These practical acts require knowledge and technique. Technique is thus something external. Hence Croce can dismiss all classifications of the arts. He is quite violent about it: "All the books about classifications and systems of the arts could be . . . burned without any loss whatever" (*E*, 126). If Croce opposes classification of the arts (as distinct from practical knowledge useful to the artist about casting bronze or mixing colors or the conventions of harmony), needless to say he rejects the concept of literary genres. These have, at most, a purely classificatory function such as, for instance, the Dewey decimal system in a library: "Who can deny the utility and the necessity of such arrangements? But what should we say if someone began seriously to seek out the literary laws of miscellanies or of eccentricities, of the Aldine or the Bodoni collections, of shelf A or shelf B, that is to say, of those altogether arbitrary groupings whose sole object was their practical utility?" (44). Artists have always ignored the so-called laws of genres: "Every true work of art has violated some established kind" (42–43). The three traditional kinds—drama, epic, and lyric—are not really distinguishable: in every lyric there is epic and drama, in every drama lyric and epic, in every epic drama and lyric. No lyric is purely subjective. It is addressed to others, and every epic and drama expresses the author. Croce does not bother to argue with the details of genre theories: "No intermediate element interposes itself philosophically between the universal and the particular, no series of kinds, or of species, of *generalia*" (*NSE*, 48).

Croce's view of the externalization of the intuition-expression as a practical activity, and its corollary, which denies the aesthetic relevance of technique and the distinction of the arts and of genres, has aroused the most opposition to his theories. But Croce's position can be and has been misunderstood if we think it assumes that the artist has an internal vision which is unique and undifferentiated and is then translated, in a second practical act, into a painting, a statue, a poem, or a piece of music. Croce sometimes speaks in a manner that is open to this misinterpretation. But we must always remember that intuition is not just inner vision but also expression. He argues that "when the intuition has been distinguished from the expression, and the one has been made different from the other, no ingenuity of middle terms can succeed in welding them together. . . . In reality we know nothing but expressed intuitions" (*NSE*, 35). There are no ideas without words, no musical imagination without sounds, no painterly imagination that is not colored. In a curious passage Croce speaks of words running through our organism, "soliciting the muscles of our mouth and ringing internally in our ears: when music is truly music, it trills in the throat or shivers in the fingers that touch ideal notes; when a pictorial image is pictorially real, we are impregnated with lymphs that are colors, and maybe, if coloring matters were not at our disposal, we might spontaneously color surrounding objects by a sort of irradiation, as is said of certain hysterics and of certain saints who caused stigmata to appear upon their hands and feet by means of an act of imagination!" (36–37). With this odd idea of irradiation and colored fluids Croce can accept the view that Raphael would have been a great painter even had he not possessed hands, a paradox alluded to in a scene of Lessing's *Emilia Galotti*. Still, this inner intuition-expression is different from the externalization, from technique. There are great artists who use bad techniques: painters who use colors that deteriorate rapidly, architects who build with unsuitable materials. But the only example for literature Croce can think of is a poet who corrects his proofs badly. For Croce recognizes that "if we take away from a poem its meter, its rhythm and its words, there does not remain beyond all this, as some think there will, the poetic thought; there remains nothing. Poetry is born of words, of rhythm and of meter" (37–38). Nonetheless, the complete unity of the arts raises insurmountable difficulties. A poem and even a symphony may be composed in the mind, but a painting comes about in the act of putting the colors on canvas. A poem in the mind may be a bird in hand; a painting in the mind remains a bird in the bush. Irradiation and colored fluids do not convince. But whatever the difficulties of Croce's general system, we should recognize the coherence of his position. To state that "what is called *external* is no longer a work of art" (*E*, 57) is irrefutable on his terms. The work of art is put into this inner activity, but Croce, like every other student of art, has only the artifacts as the unique evidence from which to infer the inner processes.

In the later stages of his thinking Croce modified some of his extreme positions. In his early pronouncements intuition-expression was purely cognition of the individual. In later writings Croce asserts the universalizing character of art, for which he invented the term *cosmicità*. While still insisting on the difference between art and conceptual knowledge, intuition and abstraction, he says that "poetry ties the particular to the universal" (*P*, 9). This universality is praised in almost hymnical terms. In poetry, "the particular palpitates with the life of the whole, and the whole is in the life of the particular; and every genuine artistic representation is itself and the universe, the universe in this individual form, and this individual form as the universe. In any accent of the poet, in any creature of his imagination, there is the whole of human destiny" (*NSE*, 122). But this universality of art has no specific determination (*NPS*, 2:70) or is merely a synonym for the "total and undivided humanity of the poet's vision" (*P*, 10), and it is even comfortably identified with "artistic form" (*NSE*, 124). In practice it is used to argue against purely personal confessional literature and against irony and satire, violations of the "total vision of reality, which, ultimately, is always serious" (137). It is thus not a requirement for totality in an extensive way or for a common humanity: it comes near the Hegelian concept of the concrete universal or even a common use of the term *symbol*. Croce, however, always dismisses symbol and symbolism—if symbol means something transcendent, it is false, and if it means the unity of the particular and the general, which is the very nature of intuition-expression, it is superfluous.

Croce soon discovered that his early aesthetics was misunderstood as recommending emotionalism, spontaneity, and expression, even the "overflow of feeling" of the Romantics. His vocabulary often contributes to such a misunderstanding when he speaks of the need for passion, sincerity, and personality. He was proud of having introduced the term *liricità* and argued that all poetry is lyrical. But neither the etymology of the word nor its use in modern languages prepares us for Croce's peculiar use, which identifies *liricità* simply with poetry itself (*Dante*, 26). It is passion, but not violent confused passion, and it is not restricted to the romantic passions of love and despair. Passions can express "security of thought, calm firmness of will, moderated energy, virtue, faith, and the like" (24). Art is always the theoretical expression of sentiment, sentiment transformed into an image. But the term *liricità* suggests the purely subjective.

Croce, hailed at first as an advocate of impressionism, expressionism, aestheticism, and so forth, actually came to exalt what he called *classicità*. It must not, of course, be confused with classicism. He always remained opposed to art too obviously mere craft, too obviously intellectual or oratorical, too obviously dependent on models and technical traditions, though in his writings on Italian writers and poets of the sixteenth century he treated these issues with surprising leniency and even sympathy. *Classicità* is simply poetry "in its perfection, in the full resolution of passional matter in a beautiful form" (*TPS*, 2:6).

In his theory of criticism Croce also modified his early demand for a simple identification with the author. Later Croce saw that criticism is rather a translation from the realm of sentiment into the realm of thought: "It is our firm conviction that poetry should be *poetic,* but that criticism, on the contrary, should be *prosaic* [*prosastica*], and not hope for any greater effect than that of reducing to logical and reasoned form genuine impressions of taste" (*G*, 1:142). Thus Croce rejects impressionistic, "creative" criticism and reminds critics of the prohibition he had seen posted in some German concert halls: "Das Mitsingen ist verboten" (*NSE*, 222). Criticism is part of philosophy because "criticism is *judgment,* and judgment implies a criterion of judgment, and a criterion of judgment implies thinking of a *concept,* and thinking of a concept implies a *relation* with other concepts, and a relation of concepts is, finally, a *system* or *philosophy*" (201). The theory of impressionism, which boasts of its enmity to philosophy, Croce argues is itself a philosophy: skepticism. He points out that Lemaître, Brunetière, and Sainte-Beuve implicitly embrace philosophies: sensualism, naturalism, positivism. The history of criticism belongs to the history of philosophy. Croce criticizes Saintsbury's *History of Criticism* as "wholly lacking in method and definite subject. What is lofty Rhetoric and Poetics, the theory of Criticism and of literary taste, if not simply Aesthetics?" (*E*, 537–38). Croce counters the objection that criticism in the new conception moves into a sphere completely remote from art by arguing that thought is the beginning of a new sentiment and act, and that better understanding means deeper enjoyment (*NSE*, 224). Still, the history of criticism is necessary, as there is no criticism except criticism of criticism (*PNP*, viii). This is why Croce often introduces his discussion of an author with a history of the criticism about him, whether he be Shakespeare, Ariosto or Corneille, Hölderlin or Dante.

This change to a more theoretical ideal of criticism nevertheless is not complete. The original act of identification remains intact. The aim of criticism is the *caratteristica* of the individual work and of the author's mind, and such characterization, even at its best, will always end by "wandering around the ineffable," a phrase he takes from Wilhelm von Humboldt (*P*, 126). The critic, Croce argues, can do only two things. First, he can decide whether a work is poetry or non-poetry, a decision Croce calls "the constant *leitmotiv* of my criticism" (*CC*, 3:199). Saying that something is poetry means recognizing that it belongs to the category of the beautiful. It cannot be qualified further: "The beautiful insofar as it is beautiful allows no distinctions and divisions." All such descriptive terms as "harmony," "truth," "simplicity," "unity in variety," "sincerity," and "sublimity" are only synonyms for the one concept of "beautiful expression" (*P*, 121). But the critic can, secondly, define the "generating motif of poetry," the "content or fundamental motif" that can be put into a formula, though Croce advises treating it with wise skepticism. Croce acknowledges that he asks the critic to be a psychologist and moralist as well as a philosopher, to have a knowledge of the human heart, to be a critic of persons and of the life depicted by them (124–25; cf. *NPS*, 1:222). He arrives here at a new dangerous dualism: evaluation cannot do more than declare the presence or absence of poetry, and characterization can only discuss the content of poetry—content of course not being merely the plot or theme preceding a work of art but the feelings, sentiments, and attitudes expressed in it. Criticism has been split into two parts: one a simple declaration about belonging or not to the category of art, and the other a psychological and moral definition of the personality of the artist. Aesthetic criticism, which one would think was Croce's original aim, has fallen between two stools. But we shall see that things are not so simple or disastrous.

We are first confronted with the problem of personality. Croce always insists that we must not confuse the empirical or "practical" person with the poetic personality, and he waged a long fight against the sins of *biografismo*. In his essay on Shakespeare he attacks the fantasies of such biographers as Georg Brandes and Frank Harris. The book on Goethe (1917) owes its success, in part, to Croce's resolute divorce between biography and work, a divorce that even scholars in Germany aware of the problem have not managed to accomplish. Croce criticizes Friedrich Gundolf's book on Goethe for its "mystical concept of the personality," which fails to appreciate "that the history is always of the work and not of the person" (*G*, 2:167). Croce himself nevertheless admires Goethe also as a person, for his "quiet virtue, serious goodness and judgment, wisdom, balance, good sense, sanity, and, in short, everything that is usually derided as being 'bourgeois'" (1:2).

Croce allows and even demands a poetic or spiritual biography, which for him is the only genuine evolutionary history: "One should always have an eye for the personal life of Goethe, but only in order to understand how this life prepares in the various periods the various forms of his art, or how it interferes with it, and sometimes disturbs it" (*G*, 1:9). Such a biography is not static and naturalistic, but intrinsically genetic and historical: "About an artist, for example, it will show how at his beginnings he tried to imitate the preexisting art, be it near or far, now consonant with his own temperament, now discordant and even opposed, and in these imitations he appears the more awkward, and the more contradictory elements he introduces the more energetic is his personal temperament, until he becomes aware of how he differs from others, until he finds himself and raises himself to original production" (*NSE*, 171). But Croce totally rejects the possibility of an evolutionary history of poetry. There are only poets—persons and their work—and they do not form an order, a chain or series. Only monographs and essays are allowed. Literary histories are kept alive only by the need of students and scholars for encyclopedic information. In a letter summarizing a conversation I had with Croce in the year of his death, he reasserted his rejection of literary history. If one asked to put a series of monographs and critical essays into some order, he would answer: "Everyone can put them in whatever order pleases him" (letter to René Wellek, 5 June 1952). There is no real continuity (except an external one) between Dante, Boccaccio, and Petrarch, or even between Pulci, Boiardo, and Ariosto. Each is completely different, unique, even though they may treat the same general theme: the matter of France.

It follows that Croce, from the time of his first contribution to literary theory, *La Critica letteraria,* published a decade before *Estetica,* should criticize the various types and methods of literary history. He considers the whole tradition of nineteenth-century literary historiography to be "sociological" and deterministic, both the romantic type exemplified by the Schlegel brothers, who conceive of literature as the expression of a national spirit, and all positivistic histories, which either make literature reflect a specific ideology and judge it accordingly, as Brandes did in his *Main Currents of Nineteenth Century Literature*, or explain literature in terms of race, milieu, and *moment,* as Hippolyte Taine tried to in his *Histoire de la littérature anglaise* (*NSE*, 259ff.; on Taine, see also *Storia* 1943, 187ff.). The anti-Semitic, racial, or grossly nationalistic histories of German literature by Adolf Bartels and R. M. Meyer are simply the perversions of a wrong conception (*NSE*, 181ff.). Croce recognized the immense advance of nineteenth-century historiography over the purely erudite accumulations of eighteenth-century learning, but he objected that they made literature the product of something else, that they confused art with philosophy and morality and with the presumed national aspirations of a people. Even Francesco De Sanctis, whom Croce saw as a precursor, whose fame he did much to reestablish, and whose aesthetic and critical views anticipated many of his own, did not escape criticism for the historical scheme of the rise, decadence, and rebirth of Italy that frames the *Storia della letteratura italiana* (*P*, 139; also *Una Famiglia di patrioti*, 300–301). Croce on principle rejected the concept of causality in history: "it cannot be a principle of knowledge" (*NPS*, 1:153). For instance, he refuses to search for the causes of the Baroque (*Età*, 34) or for the causes of the comparative inferiority of Latin poetry during the Renaissance. Latin, though then a living language, did not have a poet comparable to Ariosto or Tasso, but this is simply a fact which must be accepted as such (*Ppo*, 446).

Since Croce disputes a historical explanation of the course of literature, he must equally question attempts to account for works of art by studying literary tradition and specific literary sources. He would at most grant that "no poet creates his poem outside definite conditions of space and time," that "the historical situation is given to him" (*FiPrac*, 114–15). But to reduce Ariosto to a sum of his sources, as Pio Rajna attempted in *Le Fonti dell'Orlando furioso* (1876), seems to Croce futile doubting of Ariosto's deep originality (*LNI*, 3:389–90; also *Primi saggi*, 132). Likewise, Croce is not convinced by attempts to trace Shakespeare's art to predecessors and stage conventions. Nor can he be sympathetic to what was or is usually known as comparative literature. In reviewing the newly formed *Journal of Comparative Literature* (1903) edited at Columbia University, Croce asked, "What is comparative literature?" If it means the comparative method, it obviously goes far beyond literature and is constantly used even in the study of a single author. If it means tracing literary themes and influences, it is confined to "merely erudite investigations which in themselves do not lead us to understand a work of literature and do not make us penetrate into the living core of artistic creation" (*PE*, 73). Such investigations refer only to the after-history of a work, its reputation, translations, and imitations, or to materials that have contributed to its origin. If we define comparative literature as the study of all the antecedents of a work of art, philosophical and literary, then it is identical with all literary history and the word *comparative* is really a pleonasm. The only choice is between mere literary erudition and a truly historical and interpretive method.

External erudition was always a target of Croce's criticism, though he himself, especially in his youth, engaged in archival research on such subjects as theaters in Naples and literary and cultural relations between Spain and Italy. He was not averse to tracking down even trivial details of Goethe's stay in Naples or the fortunes of Goethe's teacher of Italian. But thematology, *Stoffgeschichte*, in literature seems to him particularly useless. Reviewing a German thesis on two dramas, one based on the story of Mary, Queen of Scots, and one on the theme of Sophonisbe, Croce disparages the idea that a historical fact is an aesthetic theme with a law of artistic representation. There is no such continuity among the different versions of the Mary Stuart theme or any theme, historical or mythological. Although comparing different handlings of such subject matter may throw light on changes in political or religious ideas and sentiments, in short, may contribute to cultural history, it will never produce a genuine history of poetry (*PE*, 84–90).

Croce also does not ascribe much importance to the study of a poet's drafts and sketches (*scartafacci*), a study that became quite a specialty, particularly in Italy. Croce argues that authors may make changes without putting them on paper; furthermore, if they do use the pen, they may well write something which in the very act of writing they know will eventually be rejected or reversed (*NSE*, 1:190–91).

What matters is only the final outcome. Everything that precedes a genuine work of art is absorbed in a totally new act, or, in Croce's striking image, "in the same way as we can cast into a melting furnace formless pieces of bronze and choicest statuettes. Before there can be a new statue, the choicest statuettes must be melted just like the formless pieces" (*E*, 24). Here the function of quotations, allusions, aphorisms, conventional themes, and traditional motifs is implicitly denied: the statuettes, however exquisite, will be melted down alongside the junk. Quite consistently Croce refuses to consider the question of plagiarism as literary at all: it would be only a moral, civil transgression (*PE*, 67–70). He defends D'Annunzio, not a favorite of his, against the accusation of borrowing, since "a work of art is an organism and has no other measure than itself" (499). Croce even produces the curious case of a love sonnet by Luigi Tansillo, which was literally transcribed, without acknowledgment, by Giordano Bruno in his *Eroici furori* (1585) and given a philosophical meaning, in order to argue that there may be "two works of art living in the same body" (135). On the other hand, Croce allows the possibility that "a single artistic personality can be divided between several biographical individuals, and that two or more diverse artistic personalities can succeed one another and alternate within the same biographical individual" (*NSE*, 229). He cites collective epics such as the Finnish *Kalevala* and theatrical collaborations as examples of the first instance and an anomalous and inferior play by Corneille as an example of the second.

If one thinks these pronouncements through, one has to recognize that the usual view of Croce as a defender of personality, sincerity, spontaneity, and *liricità* is misleading, as it does not apply to an empirical person at all. For Croce, "the poet is nothing other than his poetry" (*P*, 147). In such formulations Croce seems to deny the individual soul and to imagine some suprapersonal activity—poetry—working in history. But elsewhere Croce speaks of a writer's physiognomy, of his spiritual signature, and denies that an artist can have more than one psychic content. Discussing D'Annunzio, he asserts that "there have never been artists who have two or more distinct psychic contents" (*LNI*, 4:25), though he admits that Dante and Goethe (and possibly others) reveal two divergent but fundamental states of mind: the Dante of the *dolce stil nuovo* being unlike the Dante of the *Divine Comedy*, and the Goethe of *Werther* and the *Urfaust* contrasting with the Goethe of the *Iphigenie* and the later classicist writings (*P*, 149).

The work of art is called a monument and not a document (*US*, 31), but "monument" seems misleading if taken to mean an artifact like a building: Croce uses the term only to protest against the reduction of a work of art to the role of witness—to other things, to its time, to the life of the author, or to the state of society. Actually he considers the work to be a spiritual act immediately accessible here and now. A work of art must be appreciated "*tête-à-tête*, in an intimate colloquial manner" (*TPS*, 2:8), as it is "a movement which accomplishes itself in us, a particular posture of our soul" (*NPS*, 1:198). Thus Croce rejects the usual historicist argument that we must judge a writer by the criteria of his time. To speak of Dante, he says, "requires treating the poetry of Dante not according to Dante, but according to truth" (*Dante*, 22). Homer must be discussed not according to the presumed poetics of the rhapsodes of his time, but according to the eternal truth of poetry. Trying to think Aristotle with Aristotle, Dante with Dante, "we engage in a desperate torment, in the impossible effort to mutilate our soul and our mind, which rather remakes or rethinks the ancient, but only so far as it overcomes it" (22). But by resolutely facing up to the presence of the poet, however remote in time and space, Croce does not deny its historicity. On the contrary, he constantly identifies criticism with the history of poetry, as every judgment is for him a historical judgment, a judgment of a past event (*P*, 2:251ff.; *LNI*, 4:207–08). He stresses that "every work is well interpreted and well re-evoked only in its historical situation" (*P*, 130). Croce recognizes that a poet lives in his world, with a given tradition of language, syntax, metrics, and psychology. But a real poet will always make of it a new image, a new work, and the tradition of language, syntax, metrics, and psychology will belong to externals, to technique (*CC*, 3:141–42). In discussing "the preceding artistic history" Croce can, like any good source hunter, give a long list of phrases from Vincenzo Monti echoed in Ugo Foscolo and Giacomo Leopardi (5:148ff.), apparently revoking the image of the melting down of the bronze statuettes. But Croce distinguishes between the act of creation—original, spontaneous, unique—and the parallels and quotations visible in the external technique: a troublesome dualism which is not that of intuition-expression or form-content but raises the same dilemma.

Croce rejects both extremes. "The opposed upholders of a mere historical judgment of art (*storicisti*) and those of a mere aesthetic judgment (*estetisti*) are equally mistaken" (*US*, 29), the first because they reduce a work of art to its conditions, the second because they want to judge it outside of history. Croce rejects the view that Dante is the expression of the Middle Ages, Ariosto of the Renaissance, Tasso of the Counter-Reformation: "Every one of those poets is uniquely himself and in himself universal humanity, and they rise above the particularity of the epochs and the peoples to which they belonged" (*PoSc*, 2:254). But this does not mean that Croce approves anachronistic interpretations. For example, Melchiore Cesarotti's Homer—with his wig, pigtail, flowered waistcoat, and sword—seems to Croce as absurd as the Decadent readings of the late nineteenth century (*P*, 83–84). Commenting on *Lazarillo de Tormes,* Croce sees that we cannot understand it fully without knowing something of sixteenth-century Spain and the meaning of such simple terms as *hidalgo* and *caballero* (*NSE,* 226), just as we could not understand even the first line of Ariosto's *Orlando furioso* if we did not know the meaning of *donna* and *cavaliere.* Croce seems to side with the historicists when he says "we have always most firmly held the view that aesthetic criticism is nothing more than the same historical criticism of art" (226). But this is a delusion. The main decision, the judgment, that is, of poetry versus non-poetry, happens here and now.

We have to come back to the crucial question: how do we now recognize poetry? Croce admits it to be a "delicate and subtle task" (*FiSto,* 23) but thinks of it as self-evident. Poetry has "an eternal unmistakable accent which echoes through the most diverse times and places and in the most diverse materials" (*P*, 36). In repeated variations he tells us that poetry can be recognized by the identifications postulated in his aesthetics: intuition and expression, content and form, individuality and universality, sentiment and image. This suggests the jibe, best known in Giovanni Papini's formulation (in his *Stroncature* [1932], 135), that Croce's system "amounts merely to a hunt for pseudonyms [or rather synonyms?] of the word art, and may indeed be stated briefly and accurately in this formula: art = intuition = expression = feeling = imagination = fancy = lyricism = beauty." So-called ordinary-language philosophers argue that Croce insists merely that the word *art* be restricted to the kind of intuitions he describes, though normally it is not: "'Art is Intuitive Knowledge' becomes, in this interpretation, *a priori* true, irrefutably true" (Beryl Lake in William Elton, ed., *Aesthetics and Language* [1954], 107). Often, I think, one has to concede to such critics that we are reduced to Croce's ipse dixit, to his pointing to passages as examples of poetry without further argument. He indulged in this anthologizing particularly in the later, somewhat leisurely collections of essays such as *Letture di poeti* (1950), but also in the earlier books devoted to Italian literature of the sixteenth, seventeenth, and eighteenth centuries. Croce read even minor and minimal authors and selected what could be called "poetic moments." He defended Poe's view that "a long poem does not exist," or rather that a "long poem is, in fact, merely a succession of brief ones" (*Letture*, 212), stating further that "a great poem needs to contract itself into an exclamation of joy, of pain, of admiration, of regret" (*PE*, 23). It follows from his original decision that the distinction between a simple intuition and a complex work of art is merely empirical, so that he could ask: "An epigram belongs to art: why not a simple word? A short story belongs to art: why not a journalistic chronicle? A landscape belongs to art: why not a topographic sketch?" (*E*, 17). Croce was thus misunderstood to favor *frammentarismo*, a slogan exploited by Ardengo Soffici and Renato Serra. Croce protested against this "modernistic deformation" of his aesthetics (1915; *PS*, 1:389–91). Though he admired Poe, Croce took exception to what he thought the simplistic quantitative idea that a poem must be neither too short nor require a reading of longer than half an hour (*Letture*, 212). Croce stresses that "poetry . . . consists not only in a few single pieces, but circulates through the whole" (*P*, 97), and he recognizes that "one cannot have Homer without his lists of warriors and his often monotonous descriptions of battles, nor Dante without all his theology, his politics, his violent passions which fill the *Commedia*, nor Shakespeare without his being both playwright and an actor himself" (*Letture*, 314). Croce seems to reaffirm the organic unity of a work of art, retracting his attempts to break it up by distinguishing between poetry and non-poetry.

Croce used three procedures alternately or successively. The earliest and most persistent is the mode of eliminating works from the realm of poetry—already implied in the negations of his early aesthetics. It is best systematized, however, later in *La Poesia* (1936), where Croce excludes sentimental or immediate expression, the prosaic (that is, didactic expression), and oratorical expression from genuine poetry. Earlier, in his lecture "Per una poetica moderna" (1922; *NSE*, 315), Croce constructs a scale of evaluation that begins with the highest classical poetry, descends apparently to romantic or sentimental, to impressionistic, intellectualistic, cold (that is, imitative) poetry, then to didactic, psychological, sociological, descriptive, oratorical, tendentious poetry, and finally to merely agreeable, commercial poetry or, on another scale, to rude, refined or mannered, disharmonious, and fragmentary poetry. He seems to be proposing a new typology, though he reasserts his rejection of genre theories and actually never followed up this scheme. But these exclusions allow Croce many severe judgments, particularly in *Poesia e non poesia*. Most notoriously, his essay on Manzoni declared *I promessi sposi* to be a work of oratory and persuasion, a judgment that caused much offense, though Croce did not deny its greatness. Oddly enough, in 1952, without any real argument Croce suddenly retracted his old classification and declared *I promessi sposi* to be a work of poetry. He beats his breast, speaks of *mea culpa*, of "an error or at least a gross distraction," and explains it by the "ferocious intolerance I have always shown for the confusion that artists and critics make between Poetry and Oratory" (*TPS*, 1:129). But it is not clear that assigning *I promessi sposi* to the category *poesia* invalidates Croce's perfectly accurate observations about the dominance in the work of Catholic piety and historical information, which in turn do not deny the imaginative power of many scenes and the vividness of many characters. In the case of Manzoni the classification concerns a single large work: Croce always considered his verse drama *Adelchi* to be poetry. Croce uses the same method of elimination with Leopardi's poems, excluding the oratorical and patriotic poems as well as the philosophical, didactic poetry and prose: only the idylls are identified as genuine poetry.

But early on Croce made the distinction between poetry and nonpoetry also within a single work by introducing the term *struttura*. Structure (used quite differently than in French structuralism) is the nonpoetic scaffolding. Croce's book on Dante (1921) caused an enormous debate by distinguishing between *struttura*, the "theological romance," and the poetry. Croce imagines the poem as "a robust and massive framework over which a luxuriant vegetation clambers and spreads and adorns itself with pendulous boughs and festoons and flowers, covering it up so that only here and there does some wall-space show its rawness or some angle its hard line" (*Dante*, 59), and the episodes in the *Inferno* are declared to stand by themselves and each to be a lyric by itself (58). But Croce pleaded innocent to destroying the unity of the *Divine Comedy*, which he

claimed was to be found in the poetic soul of Dante and not in his allegorical and didactic devices (*Discorsi*, 2:44). Croce expressly condemns
"cutting 'structure' and 'poetry' like two slices which appear on two different plates" (*Letture*, 15), while restating that "structural parts, more or
less heavy or sometimes even the lightest, are in all poems and in all works
of art" (13). He argues that he has not reduced the *Divine Comedy* to fragments, but that the great episodes are "living organisms which the genius
of the poet generates" (6) and that in Dante "'structure' and 'poetry' do
not interpenetrate and do not contaminate each other, but rather they
alternate and are juxtaposed" (12). Croce assumes that a curious division
exists within Dante's soul: between the man of the Middle Ages and the
man of the early Renaissance, between the man who devised the journey to the other world which yielded the matter for the structure and
the man who represented human life "in all its tones, sublime and low,
tragic and grotesque, tormented and glorious—that is, in his 'poetry'"
(11). It seems a dubious, oddly schematic divorce, where structure and
poetry are associated with historical periods. In other contexts, for instance when pressed by Mario Fubini to see that the didactic moments
of the poem are intimately connected with the poetry, Croce assents that
"reducing a poem to fragments is nothing other than a relief we give
to purely poetic moments over those which are instructional, oratorical,
affective or whatever else: but all of these, if the poet is also a genuine
artist, form a unity which cannot be broken. . . . To have an eye for such
moments is the principal task of the aesthetic critic" (*TPS*, 1:126). Croce
obviously believes that he has developed this eye.

The test case is Goethe's *Faust*. Croce, like many critics, denies the unity
of the poem and condemns the numerous strained philosophical attempts
to find such unity of both parts in certain abstractions. Croce goes further
in making distinctions within the two parts; the poem appears to him as
an album in which Goethe entered his feelings at different periods of his
life. Croce recognizes an early Faust figure who expresses striving, dissatisfaction, and Titanic aspirations that have been called Faustian; then the
quite separate tragedy of Gretchen, in which Faust plays only the role of
a common seducer. Then comes Goethe's attempt to fill the lacuna with
the wager, which to Croce, in spite of incidental beauties, seems an artificial remedy. The second part is totally independent: "This second Faust
is certainly damaged by being joined to the first as a second part, with
the air of forming with it a single work" (*G*, 1:112). It is a loose series
of scenes—operatic, allegorical, fantastic—among which Croce isolates
the early *Helena* fragment as dating back to 1800 before the rescue of
Faust. The last scene of *Faust* seems to him half-jocular, ironic in tone,

decorative, a play of the imagination. Recent commentaries, without ever referring to Croce, have seen this: for example, Herman Meyer's fine essay *Diese sehr ernsten Scherze* (1970). Croce, of course, does not deny that Goethe tried to impose a unity on these fragments, but views it as a mechanical unity compared to the group of living creatures within. Intentions, mere plans do not matter in poetry: "The good old rule that with poets one must look not for what they wished or asserted they were doing, but only for what they did do poetically, is doubly valid and useful for Goethe" (*G*, 1:16). Croce rejects the accusation that his method has decomposed and destroyed an organism created by the poet. Just the opposite is the case: "The poet, by a reflective method, has fashioned a mechanism, enclosing and compressing into several diverse living organisms, to which the critic, by that process, restores their former liberty" (1:52). Croce is often considered an "intentionalist" because of his emphasis on expression, personality, and *liricità*. But this is quite mistaken. He had always known that "the *intentional world* of the poet is one thing and his world of *sentiment* and *fantasy*, that is, his *poetry*, is another" (2: 101). Croce always disapproved of concern with "poetics," programs and manifestos. In a reference to my and Austin Warren's *Theory of Literature* (drawn secondhand from an article by Mario Praz in *Comparative Literature*, 1950), Croce rebukes us, quite wrongly, for diverting attention to poetics, "the most miserable manifestation of literary life, which are the programs and ambitious tastes of schools and little schools" (*Indagini*, 256), because "what matters is not what the poet proposes or believes to make, but only what he has actually made" (*P*, 297). In the case of *Faust*, Croce's argument seems basically successful, though one may have doubts on specific points: for example, the wager must have been present very early and cannot be isolated so easily. On the whole, Croce succeeds in the case of *Faust* because *Goethe-philologie* enables him to date the different stages in the writing of *Faust* over a period of almost sixty years. Thus he can assimilate it to a spiritual biography of Goethe, which shows not only a poetic but also a moral and intellectual development. It is easy for Croce to show that *Wilhelm Meisters Lehrjahre* represents an artificial unity between the *Theatralische Sendung* and a later educational novel, a unity welded together not without some visible seams. Though this is hardly new and was evident even before the discovery of the manuscript of the *Theatralische Sendung*, it lends support to Croce's general thesis and here justifies the distinction between structure and poetry.

Croce assumes always that most works are composite works which contain elements that are not poetry: "The critic and the historian must rediscover and point out the poetic part of works, however much or little it may be, and give a reason for the rest" (*PoSc*, 2:235). But finally Croce came to realize that these structural non-poetic parts, which function within a work as scaffolding or framing or as giving relief to the poetry, exist independently throughout the wide realm of literary production and fulfill an important role in society. In *Poesia* (1936) and in later pronouncements, Croce developed a much more positive concept of "literature," considering it not merely as a contrast to poetry, as non-poetry, as the ugly, but as a realm by itself, in "praxis," in civilization. Within this broad realm Croce distinguishes "literary expression" as using the sentimental, the oratorical, and the "prosaistic" to achieve a harmony which is not that of poetry but has its own function as "one of the branches of civilization and education" (*P*, 33). Croce now celebrates "literature" as the great civilizing power that has led man out of the state of barbarism to true humanity. Suddenly even rhetoric is given a place, and there the old dichotomies of content and form, bare and ornate prose and style are readmitted. Croce draws a parallel between rhetoric and Aristotelian formal logic, which he considers useful, at least as a theory of error (though false compared to idealist logic). So Croce now praises rhetoric as implying a theory of literature and explains that his early aversion to rhetoric was "because it was always introduced or allowed to penetrate into the sacred inner realm of poetry" (*TPS*, 1:38). Croce's basic motivation has been called anti-rhetoric, and it is true that his own style aims at lucidity and simplicity and shuns the inflated emphasis of the rhetoric which he felt dominated the Italian tradition. But Croce has his own rhetoric of exposition, his own stylistic devices of persuasion, which I have not seen investigated in detail.

In practice, Croce's new tolerance toward "literature" in his sense allows him to discuss questions of literary history with terms he had previously rejected. He writes chapters on tragedy and on comedy in the Renaissance, on the *commedia dell'arte* and other genres, though he insists that these are purely empirical groupings. Even problems of periodization and typology are not completely dismissed. Before, he had deplored the dichotomy between classical and romantic as an illegitimate bifurcation of the concept of poetry and had advocated the term *classicità* as a term of "poetry" as such in the old sense of excellence. But later he discussed romanticism as a movement within time limits, distinguishing it as a literary phenomenon from moral romanticism, the *mal de siècle*, and philosophical and political romanticism (*PE*, 292–98)—distinctions similar to those made more recently between positive and negative romanticism. Croce advocates rigorous and correct definitions of such terms as "romanticism," "classicism" and "Baroque." He defines Baroque as "a vice of artistic expression which puts in place of beauty the product of the surprising or the unexpected" (*Storia* 1943, 132), and he uses the term as a criterion by which to recognize neo-Baroque elements in a particular artist or age, "because in every man there is the whole of man" (132). Croce sometimes uses Baroque as a type, seeing elements in Victor Hugo, D'Annunzio, and other moderns, and sometimes he sets chronological limits from the first decades of the sixteenth to the end of the seventeenth century (*Età*, 33). Still, he objects strongly to special tribunals for each epoch, "when the unique and eternal tribunal is that of the unique and eternal concept of art" (38). He does, however, acknowledge the historical sequence of periods, the irreversibility of time. The Enlightenment cannot be understood without the Reformation, rationalism, and empiricism, but, he argues, Ariosto's *Orlando furioso* needs no *Divina Commedia* or *Stanze* of Poliziano to be understood and judged for its poetic value. At least in works that Croce can consign to "literature" or to the "theater," forms of practical life, he sees their involvement in history and can even guess at causes. Thus he denies that the *sacre rappresentazioni* died for literary or political reasons, as adduced by their student, Alessandro D'Ancona, and states that their disappearance was instead due to the effect of the "true reality of what happened then, of the exhaustion of the fervid and ingenuous religious sentiment" (*PoSc*, 1:339).

Croce even speaks of the progress of literature, though he recognizes that Homer has never been surpassed formally. A new work surpasses him only by enshrining in images and words the experience of post-Homeric humanity (*FiSto*, 36). With a slight variation, Croce states that there is progress in "matter, life, which always grows of itself and therefore progresses (which does not yet mean that it runs toward a fixed term or ideal model). Goethe is not aesthetically a progress over Sophocles, . . . [but] Goethe would not have started out without the Sophoclean Iliad, or, better yet, without all the history that preceded him" (*CC*, 5:248–49). Not only literature but poetry is here implicated in the process of history, since for Croce history is the only existent and historical judgment, the only judgment.

Although this general progress is cumulative and inevitable, there are also specific periods of decadence. Though he criticized De Sanctis's scheme of the rise, decline, and rebirth of Italy, Croce actually put the decadence of Italy where De Sanctis and everybody else had: into the seventeenth century, the Baroque age. Italy was then dominated by foreigners—Spaniards and Austrians—and the Counter-Reformation made Italy an intellectual backwater. In the arts Italy produced the Baroque, which Croce always defines as a form of the ugly, an "artistic perversion"

(*Età*, 33), out for "the effect of the unexpected and the stupefying" (25), displaying "aridity of imagination and artificial and impotent intellectualism" (*NPS*, 2:62). Croce had a long-standing passionate interest in the period and, in spite of all his disparagements, a considerable taste for and even enjoyment of its literature, as witnessed by his early collection, *Lirici marinisti* (1911), and its introduction, "Sensualism and Ingenuity in the Lyric of the Seventeenth Century," as well as his translation of Giambattista Basile's *Pentamerone* from the Neapolitan dialect into standard Italian and his profuse learned commentary on it. Later he insists strongly, however, on the "silence of great poetry," dismissing the "pseudopoetry" of Giambattista Marino, whom he labels a mere witty sensualist, and noting the sporadic gleams of poetry in poets such as Achillini, Artale, and Lubrano. Croce has read everything. One may agree with him that Italian seventeenth-century poetry is inferior compared to Tasso, but not be convinced that this negative judgment applies to all other countries. Croce makes it easy by excluding French and English literature from the Baroque as well as the German mystic Angelus Silesius, but with Góngora, to whom he pays attention, he confronts the same problem under the name of *cultismo*, which is not so different from Marinism. But Croce declares Góngora to be a genuine poet, praises his early *romances*, and shows that the French translator L. P. Thomas, skillful though he is, makes Góngora sound like Mallarmé (*PoAMo*, 285–304). Nonetheless, Baroque always remains for Croce synonymous with non-poetry. Victor Hugo is "a fundamental Baroque writer," empty, exhibiting "much ado about nothing" (383–84), and D'Annunzio has Baroque features.

Baroquismo is only one element of the modern decadence. Like Bourget and Nietzsche, Croce takes the term in the widest sense and applies it far beyond its original use: Nisard's attack on the French romantics, Baudelaire's proud application to himself, the little group in Paris who called themselves Decadents. In poetry, Croce sees the origins of decadence in Baudelaire, whom he nevertheless admired with reservation. He gives a sympathetic account of Baudelaire's personality, praises his views on art, and considers him a great poet: "His inspiration, in the obscene, sad and bestial matter that he usually treats, is highly serious; and, confined in a world of sensuality which he cannot overcome, he manages to make it colossal, tragic, sublime" (*PNP*, 255). Reviewing some of the "pièces condamnés," Croce strongly stresses Baudelaire's part in the illness of late romanticism (*PoAMo*, 395–406), and he protests against a book by Benjamin Fondane that interpreted Baudelaire's experience of the abyss as having lifted him into a higher realm than art, "which is not a thing superior to poetry but an unachieved poetry, a living and unconquered torture, a sentiment that is not made serene" (*NPS*, 2:108). The standard of serenity, of Goethe's *Heiterkeit*, seems peculiarly out of place in any discussion of Baudelaire.

For Croce, Baudelaire is only the ancestor of what is the main source and model of poetic decadence, the movement of pure poetry: Rimbaud, Mallarmé, and Valéry. Croce judges Rimbaud with extreme harshness, even with distaste. He praises some of Rimbaud's early verse for precocious virtuosity, though "Bal des pendus" shows "stupid inhumanity" (*P*, 207), but considers all the later writings to be failures. *Les Illuminations* is "a document of a sterile attempt" (*Pagine sulla guerra*, 200). Rimbaud's only serious and virile act was his renunciation of poetry (*Letture*, 270). Croce discusses Mallarmé far more extensively. What excites Croce's polemical fervor is the whole concept of pure poetry, in which words are conceived as sound and music, in which "suggestion" takes the place of expression and willed obscurity violates the ideal of clarification, which is also moral purgation. Croce finds the claim that pure poetry is an entirely new kind of poetry particularly annoying. Mallarmé's theory seems to him a confession of impotence, sterility, and aridity, which he finds confirmed in the reports about Mallarmé's abortive project, an Ultimate Book (*PS*, 2:286). Several times Croce wonders whether to call him a "placid maniac," a poseur who is "not free of a conscious or unconscious charlatanism" (*Letture*, 285). He quotes some of Mallarmé's early poems and the set pieces such as *Hérodiade*, but finds them preoccupied with sensuality and vague longings: "No sky unfolds over his head which would invite him in: he has no sense of a larger human life" (*PNP*, 318). Later Croce examined "L'Après-midi d'un faune," contrasting it with a somewhat comic Latin poem by the famous Italian humanist Pietro Bembo (1470–1547) on the same theme in order to repudiate an allegorical interpretation by Albert Thibaudet. Croce is convinced that Mallarmé "remains a prisoner of crude sense" (*Letture*, 173), an obviously false conclusion if one knows the essays in *Divagations*.

Valéry, as a follower of Mallarmé, is not considered as a poet at all, but condemned for his poetic theory. Croce ridicules the public that listens openmouthed to Valéry's "poor, and often twisted and distorted, pseudophilosophical sentences" (*Letture*, 285). Elsewhere he protests against Valéry's view of poetry as a game or ritual with arbitrary rules: "The construction, the full intellectual consciousness and the accident of invention are the three elements of this so-called poetry-as-game" (*TPS*, 1:228). It seems to Croce a shocking obtuseness toward the power of the imagination. Nor does he have any use for Valéry's view of language as sign or emotion: "Valéry ignores that which is the only and true word . . .

the word which, dominating the emotions and objectifying them before itself, converts them into images; that is, directly through the spiritual virtue of the word, on the road of poetry" (*PNP*, 321n).

Croce considers French modern poetry, what would usually be called the symbolist tradition (and Verlaine is included in a harshly phrased essay condemning his morals, his conversion, and his poetry, except for the early Parnassian collections [*Letture*, 174–87]), the model for modern Italian poetry. He ignores or condemns wholesale all of hermeticism: only Guido Gozzano and Francesco Gaeta get some favorable notices. In the early essays Croce gives a balanced account of D'Annunzio, defending him against narrow moralistic attacks and charges of plagiarism but defining him as a "dilettante of sensations," a virtuoso moving in a narrow circle of sensuality and sorrow. Later, surely with the knowledge of D'Annunzio's war exploits and politics in mind, Croce becomes much more severe. He bluntly says that D'Annunzio is no poet, accuses him of lacking humanity, and reiterates that he remained the same all his life, "a mere juggler, a virtuoso, a technician with rare moments of simple charm" (*LNI*, 4:7–71, 6:247–61). D'Annunzio is, however, merely the most conspicuous figure of the period Croce labeled "decadent." Croce also severely criticizes Fogazzaro and Pascoli and later added Pirandello to his dislikes. Croce uses the term so broadly that in Italy it has become almost a synonym for all modernisms. Without at that time using the term, in his 1907 essay "Di un carattere della piú recente letteratura italiana" (*LNI*, 4:188–206) Croce made bold generalizations about the differences between the period dominated by Carducci and *verismo* and the new period beginning in 1885 or 1890 dominated by D'Annunzio, Fogazzaro, and Pascoli. Carducci remained for Croce always the great poet of the near past, "a Homerid," expressing "a dream between furor and ardor and melancholy" (4:189). Croce rejects verismo as a confusion of science and art and disapproves of positivism, which, he argues, was needlessly accepted by the historical and philosophical scholarship of the late nineteenth century. Although Croce is thus far from uncritical toward the period preceding his own working life, he formulates sharply his objections to the new time. He feels a "wind of insincerity" (4:189) engaged in "the great industry of the empty" (4:195). The new period's three representative figures are "the imperialist [Marinetti], the mystic [Pascoli] and the aesthete [D'Annunzio]," and all three are insincere, not necessarily in the sense of lying, but lacking in inner clarity. Megalomania, egocentricity, and *istrionismo* are the modern maladies. Croce sees, of course, that this is not only an Italian phenomenon but a European disease. Throughout the rest of his life Croce could not fail to observe the growing symptoms of decadence. Fascism was an obvious confirmation, as Croce soon saw through its claim for a revival of ancient virtues. At the end of the war he played a short-lived political role as premier in the Badoglio government. Post-1945 Italy also disappointed him. Croce gave up writing on contemporary poetry, novels, and plays and followed only philosophical, aesthetic, and historical writings, both Italian and foreign, with undiminished zest and vigor. His sharp comments on existentialism and on the new Marxists are as pungent as ever. But he must have felt that he had better be silent on poetry, novels, and plays as he did not even understand the contexts anymore.

Croce occasionally asserts that his criticism is an exemplification of his theories. As he formulated it, "so much of my literary criticism is informed by a desire to illuminate, *per exempla*, the skeleton of literary criticism" (*Carteggio Croce-Vossler*, 19 October 1911, p. 149), and "in every individual I propose to resolve a universal question" (*PS*, 1:211). But this cannot be true literally. Long before Croce formulated his aesthetic theory he wrote literary criticism, even as a schoolboy. His early articles in *La Critica*, moreover, show little of his theoretical apparatus. The motivation of the essays is often quite occasional or practical. Croce wanted to influence public opinion outside the little circle of students of aesthetics. He was preoccupied with the decadence of Italy and Europe. The isolation of criticism and theory in Croce is admittedly artificial. There was a constant interchange: the essays are neither completely devoid of theory nor simply exemplifications of a theory. They range between these two extremes, never reaching either. Often the essays do what any critic, including one who has never heard of Croce, would do. He asks: Is the work original or imitative? Does it treat a topic of general interest or is it limited to a private predicament? Does it present a coherent whole? Is it well written? Does it represent life accurately? Croce might rephrase this last demand, as he cannot believe in any "mirroring of reality." If we look at the essay on Verga (*LNI*, 3:5–32), however, we see that Croce rejects the creed of verismo and doubts its dogma of impersonality, as many others have, and otherwise simply retells some of the novels and stories, praising the main scenes in *I Malavoglia* as "striking in their simplicity and truth" and Verga's personality as "made of goodness and melancholy" (3: 28–29). The one critical perception about the difference between Verga's early society novels and the later writings set in Sicily is too obvious to be new. Much later Croce also would write essays that are hardly more than series of quotations or, in the case of a foreign author, of literal translations, retellings of plots accompanied by sensible reflections that could have occurred to almost anyone. There is something admirable in the fact that Croce could, in 1936, take the trouble to translate many of Gerard Manley Hopkins's difficult poems, but the comment in the essay is meager. There are two polemical asides: Croce defends the obscurity of "The Windhover," ascribing it to excessive condensation and lack of transitions, unlike the willed obscurity of Mallarmé and his followers (*PoAMo*, 436); he praises Hopkins's feeling for nature as having nothing to do with the "impressionistic disintegration that is usual today" (431). But the essay hardly fulfills even its modest aim, as Croce's faithful interlinear versions—with remarks on the exquisite rhythm and meter or on "traces of distortions and oddities" (446)—cannot even suggest what matters in Hopkins: the language, the syntax, the "sprung rhythm," the sound schemes. Croce's anti-stylistic and anti-rhetorical views prevent any closer engagement with these texts, which he knew mainly from Italian translations.

Another essay typical of Croce is the polemic preceded by criticism having little or no contact with the work itself. The essay on Hölderlin is an egregious example. Croce was upset by the fanatical devotion of the Germans to Hölderlin and the enormous claims made for him, particularly during the Second World War. To combat it, he quotes Dilthey (from an essay dating back to 1867, revised in 1905), who voices some reservations (hardly a convincing authority, for Dilthey could not then know the great late hymns since discovered). Nor can the condescending judgments of Goethe and Schiller that Croce quotes carry much weight, as they refer only to two of Hölderlin's early imitative poems (1797). Croce dismisses any philosophical claims made for Hölderlin, apparently unaware of his theoretical writings, and he comments irritably on Heidegger's *Hölderlin und das Wesen der Dichtung*, pointing out that the sayings Heidegger focuses on are either echoes of Vico (rather, Hamann and Herder) or yearnings for a primitive world Croce could not approve. He easily undermines any claims to greatness for Hölderlin's later odes and hymns by quoting German and French writers who hailed him as a religious prophet, thus relegating him to a province outside of poetry. Croce's one direct comment, that the poems are "emphatic, full of exclamations, poor in images, without freshness, abstract and conventional in the language they use, badly designed and sometimes formless" (*Discorsi*, 1:63), seems quite mistaken, as is the conclusion, which associates Hölderlin with Schopenhauer, Nietzsche, Bachofen, and Klages (who is not mentioned by name) as propounders of the soul against the spirit, with irrationalism, decadence, and dark mysticism. No Crocean aesthetics, only a general distaste for irrationalism and Teutonism, was needed to write the essay.

The Hölderlin essay is an essay on criticism rather than on poetry and has an ideological target. The essay on Rilke, the only non-Italian poet of the twentieth century Croce discusses at length, focuses on the actual texts to condemn him as a phenomenon of decadence—feminine, morbid, obsessed by death. The essay starts as many of Croce's do, with a long series of literal translations of poems from quite different periods of Rilke's life accompanied by some praise and some complaints about impressionism and vagueness. But then Croce accuses Rilke of intellectual impotence: not a single observation, thought, or sentence illuminates the nature of art. The *Briefe an einen jungen Dichter* (1929) contains only advice about the moral dignity of a writer. The book on Rodin accepts Rodin's false idea of the study of "things," as for Croce there are no things and the poet can only "dig into his spirit which is the document of documents, the key of all documents" (*Letture,* 199). Quite illogically, Croce comments, Rilke preaches the obsolete romantic concept of art as religion and as the essence of death or about angels who are nothing but a voice and a vague appearance. Rilke fought only the image of death and envied children and animals for their lack of consciousness. To chide Rilke for his "longing to become a beast" (201), Croce quotes the eighth Duino elegy, the notorious verse "O Glück der Mücke" ("O happiness of the gnat"). Finally Croce recognizes that one can be a great poet without being a great intellect, but Rilke is denied even this. The *Duineser Elegien* are pronounced didactic and compared to Lucretius's *De rerum natura.* Lucretius, Croce argues, has the advantage of a firm texture of concepts, a system derived from Epicurus, whereas Rilke has only a web of images that tears the moment we touch it. Croce quotes at length from the second and third elegies to demonstrate the tone of *Angst* and desperation, concluding that Rilke was a fine artist but not a poet in Croce's exclusive sense (206). Croce's distaste for the irrational, his preference for an intellectually coherent system like that of Lucretius (however much he would disagree with it), is obvious. Croce's dislike of primitivism and mysticism brings out his belief in serenity, intellectual coherence, and a kind of stoic optimism not achieved by Rilke. But Croce neglects wide areas of Rilke's work. He does not even mention *Malte Laurids Brigge* and ignores Rilke's contact with Kierkegaard (his Epicurus). It is straight ideological criticism, its conclusions not dissimilar from those reached by Hans Egon Holthusen (*Der unbehauste Mensch*) from a Protestant theological point of view.

In another group of essays Croce very deliberately applies the standards devised by his theory. The collection *Poesia e non poesia* in particular yields many examples, besides the essays on Manzoni and Leopardi. The essay on Schiller starts immediately with a judgment: Schiller belongs to a second class of poetry, is a mere man of letters. Croce buttresses this view by referring to a 1905 *enquête* in which German writers agreed about the decline of Schiller's fame. Croce also plays up the fact that an English writer (not mentioned by name but actually the ignorant Irish novelist George Moore) confessed never to have read a line of Schiller and joked about his name. We are then treated to a harshly critical survey of Schiller's tragedies: the crudities of *Die Räuber* with its imitations of *King Lear* and the contrivances of *Kabale und Liebe*, redeemed only by the figure of Musicus Miller. Croce sympathizes with Schiller's turn to a more refined manner in *Don Carlos*. Schiller shows the gifts of a moral apostle and of a psychological reflexive dramatist. According to Croce, Schiller's espousal of "inner freedom" rather than sympathy for the French Revolution does not matter in poetry, but his preoccupation with aesthetic theory and history is a sign of poetic impotence. The later plays are all contrived to exemplify concepts: Mary Stuart depicted sowing death by her charms, Joan of Arc suddenly moved by feelings of love, the Knights of Malta unable to live up to the pure spirit of their order. Schiller's attempt with *Die Braut von Messina* to combine Greek tragedy and Shakespearean drama, to introduce a chorus that would not betray the feelings of the author, anticipates the false ideal of pure poetry. The Switzerland in *Wilhelm Tell* has the look of a Christmas manger. Croce completely ignores the *Wallenstein* trilogy, feels "nausea" at the "sweetnesses" (*PNP,* 34) in *Die Jungfrau von Orleans,* and concludes that he prefers the philosopher to the poet. He sympathizes with his arguments against the rigorism of Kant's ethics but rejects Schiller's theory of naive and sentimental poetry, as he did any genre theory (and had done so before in the historical part of *Estetica*). The essay concludes with a reference to Schiller's "Gedanken Dichtung," which as "didactic poetry is therefore not real poetry" (37). Curiously enough, Croce drops the argument that Schiller's drama is modeled on Voltaire's and thus belongs to the "Latin" tradition—an argument Croce had embraced in a review of John G. Robertson's *Schiller after a Century* (1907; in *PE,* 455–61). Perhaps he came to see that it could not withstand closer inspection, or maybe he thought that it clashed with his admiration for Corneille, whom he declares a genuine poet, though he seems vulnerable to the same criticisms as Schiller. But Croce exempts Corneille from charges of being a rhetorician working with mechanical contrived plots, or rather forgives him these sins, because he was dominated by a ruling passion Croce calls "deliberate will" (*ASC,* 225). One would think that Croce might have been able to feel the breath of passion in Schiller, too.

The essay on Heinrich von Kleist comes to even more negative conclusions. Croce depicts Kleist as a man dominated by raw emotion and "instinctive, bestial and mechanical motion" (*PNP*, 48). *Penthesilea* is absolved, however, from being inspired by "libidinous, sanguinary and horrifying pleasure." Rather, Croce says, it is "vain boasting of a high ideal and desperation at not having been able to reach it" (48)—without telling us how he or anybody else could know this. Then he condemns the pathological patriotism of *Hermmannsschlacht* and *Das Käthchen von Heilbronn*, distorted by superstition, hysterics, and somnambulism. Even Kleist's short stories, of which two are retold, he finds "curious and terrifying, but not really tragic or moving" (49). Croce detests *Amphitryon* as "a trifle in bad taste" drowning in a "slime of erotic physiopathology" (50). *Der Prinz von Homburg* is a melodrama which does not avoid "banality and superficiality and puerility in its handling" (50) and *Der zerbrochene Krug* is "an incredibly and pedantically drawn-out farce" (51). Kleist is no poet at all, at most an orator, and "possibly there is not a single passage in him that is truly poetic" (51). Croce was obviously irritated by the claims for Kleist at the time of naturalism and the hunt for a "crude Germanic drama." He prefers Ibsen, "a much higher artistic spirit" (52), and appeals to Goethe's and Hegel's unfavorable opinions of Kleist. He says nothing whatever about Kleist's best story, *Michael Kohlhaas*, while he refers to *Die Marquise von O* . . . only by title and completely ignores the essay on the puppet theater. But behind what seems to me the gross underestimation of Kleist, the Crocean standard is asserted: his distaste for "the colossal, the noisy, the roll on the drum between the blasts of the trumpet, that uproar in the midst of which true poetry is suffocated like Cordelia, who has a subtle voice and few words" (52).

The essay on Heinrich Heine is less sweeping but also banishes him almost completely from the realm of poetry. Croce, quite rightly, dismisses Heine as a philosopher and does not think highly of his adherence to the general ideal of liberty, fraternity, progress, and reason. He was, at most, "an ally of bad faith" (*PNP*, 169). Heine's fundamental "mentality" employs *celia*, jesting, and persiflage, which produces rhetoric but not poetry. Croce admits having argued that any kind of subject matter could be poetic, but jesting is not "a sentimental and passional disposition" (170), merely a practical act aimed at amusing and making us laugh. Heine belongs to the "artists" and not to the "poets," a distinction Croce had repudiated when drawn by De Sanctis for Ariosto and Metastasio. Croce quotes examples of Heine's wit and inventiveness, but then grants him a vein of genuine poetry, which he calls "poetry of childhood." He finds it not only in nostalgic pieces but also in the love lyrics, which conceive love always as a pleasurable game. Irony, however, "the tone which is that of a malicious boy, of a candid song" (177), prevails, and poetry, even in the last poems, never returns. Heine is there an *Arlecchino doloroso:* pain is felt too immediately, not poetically enough. The "cleft foot" (179) that he shows all too frequently is not the attribute of a poet. Again a strangely narrow concept of poetry emerges. "Poetry . . . has something of the religious," asserts Croce (170). The poet "fixes his sight on the depths within himself and forces himself to depict what he there discovers and to bring out an aspect of the universe in the trembling of becoming." "Poetic disposition should be serenity, joy, happiness" (170), but not persiflage, jesting, even humor or satire. The concept rules out vast stretches of what is normally called poetry.

Croce resents the charge that he is "categorizing," classifying, labeling. He rightly asserts, "I never classify! I am the most radical enemy of classifications and pigeonholes (of genres, of the arts, of rhetoric, and of whatever else may be known of that kind) who has ever appeared in the aesthetic camp" (*LNI,* 4:219). His only aim has been to understand and thus not to criticize. But the examples given (and they could easily be augmented) show that Croce works by assignment, if not to categories in his sense or to genres, then to psychological types he considers incapable of creating poetry. In at least two cases, the long essays on Ariosto and Shakespeare, Croce is able to surpass this procedure because he is confronted with poets of such scope and universality that a simple assignment, a simple recognition of a fundamental motive, would not work. Actually, Croce tries it even with Ariosto, first by sorting out the usual labels. He is not a representative of art for art's sake, unless we mean by that the trite idea of total devotion to his art. He is not objective in the sense of indifference, as there are no things outside the spirit (*ASC,* 8). He has no particular wisdom, nor is it true that the dissolution of chivalry is the main theme of his work. Croce disputes the notion that Ariosto was in love with the Middle Ages and denies that he aimed at absolute beauty, a Neoplatonic ideal that leads to mysticism, quite foreign to Ariosto's mind. The so-called irony of Ariosto is not romantic irony at all, nor is *Orlando furioso* epic, as it lacks ethical elements and the characters are figures without relief and roundness. They are never frivolous, and in spite of all the moving scenes there is no tragic catharsis. Croce comes up with a solution. Ariosto loves "the pure rhythm of the universe, Harmony" (24): here is his principal accent. But Croce rejects the fatuous belief that his formula is equivalent to Ariosto's poetry. Quoting Goethe, "Individuum est ineffabile," he concludes that after all the harmony is not harmony in general, "but an *Ariostoesque harmony*" (57). We are put off with a tautology: Ariosto is Ariosto. In passing, Croce sensitively comments on many individual passages and praises his ottava rima. He mentions Pulci and Boiardo to emphasize their complete difference from Ariosto. Pulci's *Morgante* is a "picaresque romance" lacking "a single dominant inspiration" (61). Boiardo's *Orlando innamorato* is inspired by a "passion for the energetic and primitive," which becomes monotonous and arid (65): "Pulci and Boiardo . . . should not, then, be placed either below or above Ariosto, because they are not even *akin* to him" (68). Croce brings out the individuality of each poet, and his circumlocutions, exclusions, denials, and display of passages somehow manage to convey the flavor of Ariosto and certainly the love and admiration Croce felt for his favorite poet. It is evident that his concept of poetry is not only serious, melancholy, and serene, as other pronouncements suggest. It also has scope. One feels this in Croce's discussion of Shakespeare.

The Shakespeare essay opens with a sharp attack on the biographical fallacy, ridiculing vain conjectures and identifications, hunts for models, hypotheses about Francis Bacon as the author of Shakespeare's plays, and so on. Faced with the usual task of defining the leading sentiment of his author, Croce equivocates: "No particular emotion or order of emotions prevails" (*ASC*, 86), hence the claim that Shakespeare is universal, objective, impartial, and sometimes cold. He is not a poet of moral and political ideas. Rather he has a strong sense of life as perpetual discord "in its bittersweet, in all its contradiction and complexity" (88). Croce rejects the "caricature" propounded by Taine. Shakespeare's view of life is not one of blind disgust. He believes that goodness and virtue are stronger than evil and vice, although they never come together in a superior harmony: "The world of Shakespeare is a world in which these contrasts are not resolved" (90). As Ariosto did with divine irony, Shakespeare achieves a kind of equilibrium after a struggle, and this struggle is his poetry. However, there is a constant obscure "consciousness of a divinity" (89), "the trepidation for the Unknown" (92). Shakespeare, Croce stresses, is no philosopher. He asks questions but does not provide answers. One can still define his presuppositions. He is outside Catholicism and Protestantism, even outside Christianity or any religious conception. He knows no other life than the earthly and, around and above it, the shadow of the mystery. Still, although he knows no asceticism or mysticism, "the delicacy of his conscience, his humanity, carry strongly the imprint of Christian ethics" (96). Shakespeare, however, lacks the concept of a rational course of things or of a governing Providence. He does not accept the determinism of the individual character, which would be a version of Fate; he recognizes the spontaneity and liberty of man and lets it clash with necessity (97). Croce deplores that Shakespeare does not anticipate the modern theodicy—history—as he lacks a historical concept of life and therefore must lack a true political creed and passion. Shakespeare's vigorous feeling for cosmic contrasts finds, in Croce's view, its logical complement in speculative idealism, dialectics, an anti-ascetic morality, romantic aesthetics, realistic politics, and a historical conception of the real. Croce's Ariosto has been called a "poetic Hegel," but it is much more applicable to his Shakespeare. He prefigures Hegel and Croce, or rather, Croce has shaped him according to his own image. Many of these generalizations about Shakespeare's attitudes are, to say the least, extremely controversial.

Croce groups the plays according to their sources of inspiration. The first group is the love comedies, which includes even *Romeo and Juliet,* "a tragedy in a minor key, a tragedy, so to say, of a comedy" (*ASC,* 109). The second group Croce calls *il romanzesco,* which includes works of literary inspiration: the poems and the sonnets. The third group is inspired by "the interest for practical working-out," which allows a discussion of the history plays. They lack an "epic sense" because Shakespeare "did not subscribe to one or another political or religious banner" (125). The plays are not properly historical: they show no nostalgia for the past. They concern action, its obstacles and triumphs. They reflect a purely formal interest in politics in the sense of Machiavelli. Mostly Croce sees the plays as a portrait gallery: he criticizes Falstaff's rejection as an "aesthetic denigration" (135), in much the same terms as A. C. Bradley's essay. The fourth group comprises the tragedy of good and evil: the major Shakespeare. *Macbeth* is almost allegorized. Its characters are more than individuals; they are "eternal positions of the human spirit" (137). Croce celebrates Macbeth for his greatness of soul "in that passion, in that creative act that asks of a man a resolute dedication of his entire self, total boldness" (138)—a strange view of the murderer of Duncan. Macbeth dies "austerely, representing a sacred mystery, covered with religious horror" (141). Croce sees *King Lear* also as a spiritual triumph, even in the death of Cordelia. Though defeated, she grows in beauty, "evoking ever more disconsolate desire until she is finally adored as something sacred" (144), an interpretation that seems glib in the face of that final horror. In *Othello,* Croce is interested in Iago as an artist in evil, similar to Coleridge's view. The fifth group is the tragedy of will. *Antony and Cleopatra,* while poetically great, is morally low, a strange dualism for Croce. Brutus is another tragedy of will, and Hamlet is "a song of anguish, desperate and desolate" (157). The sixth group is called "Justice and Indulgence": "the song of conciliation, of the reconciliation of contrasts, of inner pacification, of the restoring of serenity" (158), represented by *The Tempest.* Croce recognizes that he has construed an ideal development of Shakespeare: a particular tonality presupposes a more elementary one, a pessimistic and philosophical song of love and sorrow presupposes a simple song of love. But it is only an ideal development. Croce does not succumb to the temptation of ordering it into thesis, antithesis, and synthesis, and he knows that it is not necessarily a chronological order. There are returns and relapses as well as anticipations.

Having sorted out the characters, the physiognomy of the sentiments, Croce feels required to say something about the art of Shakespeare. But he immediately banishes "technique" from aesthetic criticism. Croce considers Otto Ludwig's *Shakespearestudien* (written before 1865) the most intelligent book, but in quoting it, he tries to show that Ludwig can only enumerate traits that belong to every genuine poet. Everything in Shakespeare is individualized, a totality, based on experience, time and space are ideal, the plays have a sonata form, and so on. But all these are synonyms or metaphors for the one poetry. Croce allows that one may comment on the individual plays scene by scene, pointing out beauties, but all this has only a didactic value. It may elucidate reading, but it is not the main task of criticism, as Shakespeare is "one of the clearest, most evident, most comprehensible poets, even for men of little or elementary education" (*ASC*, 173), a view which seems belied by modern Shakespeare interpretation in general, and not just philology.

Croce then makes a rather superfluous effort to refute old classicist and naturalistic (Voltaire's and Tolstoy's) objections to Shakespeare. He also dismisses the realistic criticism of Rümelin, who saw a dualism between Shakespeare's creaky plots and his glorious poetry, similar to Croce's interpretation of Dante. But Croce asserts that "we can neither differentiate nor contrast them as characters and actions, discourses and dialogues" (*ASC*, 176), though his own discussions are almost all centered on characters taken out of their context: Falstaff, Brutus, and Shylock in particular. Croce sketches the history of Shakespeare criticism, distinguishing *critica esclamativa, critica immaginifica* (what we would call impressionistic), and criticism by biographers, philologists, and moralists, who read philosophical, moral, political, or historical lessons into Shakespeare and allegorize him. Finally there is "objectivist" criticism, criticism of characters, which Croce disapproves of, as they are torn from the "generative center" of the drama. A last chapter, "Shakespeare e Noi," expounds the view that Shakespeare was more highly appreciated during the romantic period than in the present, when naturalism and positivism have buried the dialectics and idealism which he suggested and, in his way, represented. Now (and Croce was writing during the First World War), "the distinction between freedom and passion, good and evil, nobility and wildness, refinement and sensuality, between the high and the low that is in man," is obscured (203).

The Shakespeare essay has been praised to the skies. Undoubtedly it has its virtues. Croce resolutely reverts attention to the poetry, away from biography, theater history, and other *allotria*. But the essay has grave defects, or rather, limitations. It is confined to an evocation of the prevalent moods of the plays and traits of the main characters. Although it has, it seems to me, a good sense of Shakespeare's moral outlook, this is illegitimately made to appear to harmonize with the kind of idealism Croce embraced. The essay suffers as well from its total disregard of the aesthetic surface of the plays—their imagery, their style, their language, and their involvement with the theater. Croce read Shakespeare mainly in Italian translations and could rarely have seen the plays performed. His image of Shakespeare is ultimately conventional, dependent in its general conception on the Germans of the nineteenth century and on the English writers he alludes to briefly: Edward Dowden, A. C. Bradley, and Sir Walter Raleigh. The essay illustrates what seems to me the main defect of Croce's criticism: his inability to overcome the dualism he would deny, between the simple judgment of what is poetry and what is not and the descriptive psychology with which he characterizes the authors and works, defining their ruling sentiments. The decision about poetry or non-poetry leads ultimately to a definition of Croce's taste, which is necessarily time-bound and limited, and the characterizations, vivid and perceptive as they often are, remain unsystematic applications of an intuitive psychology. It seems to me significant that Croce once tried to systematize these psychological terms, giving a long list in his paper "Per una poetica moderna," but never returned to this scheme. It is deeply ironic that Croce, defender of the autonomy of art, aesthetician, a man endowed with a great sensibility, good taste, and judgment, was finally unable to develop a theoretical and analytical scheme of criticism and had to be content (like many other critics) with defining his own taste, selecting his canon of classics, and persuading others that he was right. He was successful only for a time. But this is the fate of every critic, even the greatest, and only confirms Croce's own belief in history.

13 : THE FOLLOWERS OF CROCE

CROCE SUPPOSEDLY EXERCISED an intellectual dictatorship over Italy in his time, at least as aesthetician and literary critic. But this cannot have been true. The first eminent students of aesthetics and practitioners of criticism who came under his influence soon revolted against him. Giovanni Gentile (1875–1944) contributed to the early volumes of Croce's *La Critica,* but soon broke with Croce, not only for political reasons. Their relations were by no means merely those of teacher and disciple. In fact Gentile must have been effective in making Croce overcome his early aestheticism. Much of Gentile's later writings were open polemics against Croce, at least after 1909, though Gentile contributed to *La Critica* as late as 1922. But a full study of this relationship is not my concern here. Alfredo Gargiulo (1876–1949) also was an early contributor to *La Critica* who moved away from his master. His book *D'Annunzio* (1912) is still Crocean in its attempt to distinguish the creator of nature myths and the singer of lyrical landscapes from the decadent poseur. But Gargiulo later developed a theory of "expressive means" that allowed him to reintroduce into aesthetics a classification of the arts and of the concepts of medium and genre dismissed by Croce. Gargiulo's *Scritti di estetica* (1952) were collected only after his death but contain pieces that date back to the twenties and thirties. Giuseppe Borgese (1882–1952) proved an equally unfaithful disciple. He started with a book that could be called Crocean, *Storia della critica romantica in Italia* (1905), which propounded the paradoxical thesis that Italian romanticism is actually good classicism. But Borgese soon became a prophet of art as the "transfiguration of man and figuration of God," who proclaimed the meaning of Italian art to be "sacred, eternal and celestial," phrases that run counter to anything Croce stood for. Borgese's later collection of essays, *Poetica dell'unità* (1934), sharply attacks Croce and his denial of an evolutionary history of poetry, as Borgese embraced a romantic collectivistic view of literature.

Thus the generation immediately following Croce's revolted against their master. The devoted orthodox followers were younger, many of

whom played a great role in Italian academic life and remained faithful
propagators of Croce's gospel. Three established an independent eminence that singles them out for special consideration: Luigi Russo, Francesco Flora, and Mario Fubini. All three, however, deviated from Croce
in taste and theories, though only Russo was later "excommunicated" by
Croce, in 1949, in part because of a trivial disagreement over the interpretation of a sonnet by Petrarch ("Movesi il vecchierell"), but more
profoundly for political reasons, when Russo deserted the Liberal party
and joined the Communists, becoming a senator. Croce's harsh comment
on Russo (in *Terze pagine sparse* [1955], 2:161–62), "Delirî di cattiva filosofia" (Ravings of bad philosophy) defends his own distinction of *poesia
e non-poesia* and his concept of *esteticità* without mentioning the political
rift. Flora was from 1924 on the responsible editor of *La Critica* and never
broke with Croce, though his tastes, preferences, and methods led him
far afield. Fubini, who was located at Turin and did not live in personal
intimacy with Croce as the two southerners had in Naples, kept an affectionate memory of conversations with the master (see *Saggi i ricordi*,
1971). All three critics wrote extensively on Croce. Russo's three long
chapters in volume 1 of *La Critica letteraria contemporanea* (1942) are a
remarkable feat of lucid exposition, which should be supplemented by
his critical discussion of Croce's book on Dante in the third volume, by
some early defenses, and by the late bitter reply to Croce's rebuff (reprinted in *Prose polemiche*, 1979). Flora wrote a little expository book on
Croce (1927) and discussed and referred to him many times, in addition to the chapter in volume 4 of *Storia della letteratura italiana* (1947).
Fubini, besides the reminiscences and many references in his theoretical and historical writings, gave a balanced account in a commemorative
lecture at the Accademia Nazionale dei Lincei in 1966, "Croce critico."
The three commented and criticized each other freely: Russo reviewed
Flora several times, and both Flora and Fubini contributed to a special
issue of *Belfagor*, Russo's journal, devoted to his memory. All three were
professors of Italian literature who mastered the whole range, from the
beginnings to the present, almost systematically, though all three agreed
with Croce's rejection of a collective evolutionary literary history and
wrote monographs, comments, and portraits rather than histories. When
Russo and Flora wrote books called histories of literature they actually
collected a series of essays. Flora's *Storia della letteratura italiana* (3 vol.,
1940–42; expanded to 5 in 1947) is almost an anthology of Italian literature, a series of quotations commented on enthusiastically, often in
colorful metaphors. Russo, late in his life, started the *Storia della letteratura
italiana* (1957) with a volume ranging from St. Francis of Assisi to Savona-

rola. Although the history was never completed, Russo's work can hardly be considered unfinished, for the many essays collected in *Ritratti e disegni storici,* together with the monographs on Boccaccio (*Letture del Decameron,* 1956), *Machiavelli* (1945), *Metastasio* (1915), the book on Manzoni (*Personaggi dei Promessi sposi,* 1945), *Francesco De Sanctis e la cultura napoletana* (1928), and the smaller works, *Carducci senza retorica* (1957), *Salvatore di Giacomo* (1921), and *D'Annunzio* (1939), constitute an almost complete survey. Only Fubini did not write a book professing to be a literary history, though his studies of the eighteenth century cover almost every aspect of the age. He is also an exception in having written on French literature, specifically on Vigny and the history of Racine criticism.

LUIGI RUSSO (1892–1961)

Starting from Crocean positions, Russo held to them tenaciously, on some points at least, long after he had diverged from his master on other matters. Russo acknowledged freely Croce's decisive early influence. He describes himself as a "barbarian" (*PP,* 196) from a little town in Sicily when he arrived at Naples: "My mental orientation was clearly toward Croce, but a Croce directly rooted in De Sanctis, with all the corrections that Croce, with his persistent speculation, had brought into the great work of the Master from Irpino [the birthplace of De Sanctis]. And in this vocation I could not be other than faithful" (*PMC,* 300). Russo's thesis on Metastasio, an author "quite foreign to my taste and my temperament" (300), was strictly Crocean, and even the book on Verga (1919), his favorite writer, he later viewed as suffering from "too petulant and rigid Croceanism" (*PMC,* 302). Still, in a speech at the Congress of Literary History in Budapest in 1931 Russo expounds a *storicismo assoluto* and the concept of literary history of a monographic type as individualizing, a history of personality, in good Crocean terms (*CLC,* 1:98). Every work of art, he asserts, is individual and "autogenetic." He rejects formalism, moralism, and sociologism. In 1931, Russo declared, all nationalistic and all racist conceptions of literature are "in disuse and disparaged" in Italy. Poetry, he proclaims, alluding to Gentile, is not a "symbolizing of the philosophical concept" but a "symbol solely of itself" (1:104). Russo exalts the role of criticism: "The work of art exists, has its own reality, in criticism, the criticism of the poet himself or of his eternal reader"— an idea Russo was to repeat several times (for example, 2:19). The critic is a philosopher and "also creator of a new cosmos no longer poetic but logical." Even this does not satisfy the claims for criticism. The critic, he says somewhat contradictorily, "enters into a relation solely with himself, with the artistic world lived and absorbed from inside, and he does not only make clear the art of the other, but attempts to clarify himself and to respond to his own problems" (1:108). Russo goes so far as to say that "the critic enfolds the art of the other into the simple matter of his own philosophizing and his own judging" (1:108). At times, repeating the idea that "the critic is in relation only with himself" (1:182), Russo sounds like Anatole France on criticism as autobiography. He speaks of his own struggles at self-clarification in portentous tones. He asks for "internal coherence," not "extrinsic adequation of the critic to the text" (1:109), apparently denying any obligation to objectivity, correct interpretation, or truth. But these claims are deceptive. Actually Russo was a close reader, a faithful interpreter of his texts, who believed that he had grasped their genuine meaning in history. Impressionism, he would say, is only the first step to criticism (1:120). Aesthetic and psychological criticism are, he admits, still pedagogical, still *didascalia* (1:123). There is (and Russo indulged in it frequently) an "oratory of taste" (1:126), but all, in the end, must arrive at what he calls "science" (1:124), aesthetics in Croce's sense. No wonder Croce praised this speech for its exactitude and insight (*Pagine sparse* [1941], 2:185), as it is still fairly orthodox if one disregards the *hybris* about self-definition.

But Russo had long before begun to argue against some of Croce's most cherished positions, for he considered the early *Estetica* to be subservient to the old concept of beauty and *fantasia*. Probably under the influence of Gentile, Russo argues against the Crocean and Vichian concept of art as the "naïve and dawning [*aurorale*] life of the Spirit" (*CLC*, 1:109), replacing it with what, after all, was Croce's later view: art is never naive but only becomes naive. Like Croce, Russo arrives at "order, education, tradition, historical experience, self-conscious culture, harmony, literature, in a word, *classicità*" (1:112). Russo had come to disapprove of the dichotomy between poetry and non-poetry, the isolation of the poetic moment, though in practice he did precisely this. In discussing Leopardi's poems, for example, he says bluntly that one should "mentally amputate the first six stanzas" from "Sopra il Monumento di Dante" (*RD* 1946, 1:247) and that "Al Conte Carlo Pepoli" is "totally devoid of poetry, at least until the next to last stanza" (1:307). He also boasts that "we have isolated the verses that succeed in being all-poetic" from "Inno ai Patriarchi" (1:282). But in general Russo not only protests against "a pedantic fidelity to the canon of poetry and non-poetry" (1:282), but tries to overcome it by introducing such terms as "*animus* poetico" and, more insistently, *poetica*. Croce's Dante book did not satisfy Russo. In a generally highly sympathetic exposition of Croce's development, he speaks of

him as being at that time "philosophically a little tired" (*CLC*, 1:206) and
alludes to a "nodding Homer" (1:208). In "Dante Criticism and the Experiments of *Storicismo*" (1927), Russo makes an elaborate argument for
a dialectical unity of poetry and structure. While he recognizes that this
is also Croce's position, unlike Croce, he assigns priority to poetry—"but
it is always the poetry that generates its own structure" (*CLC*, 1:22)—a
reversal that allows him to call the structure "the Poetry, the philosophy,
the religion of the poet." Russo asserts that one cannot write a history of
Dante's poetry without also writing a history of Dante's philosophy and
without tracing his whole intentional world. To extract the poetry from
the poetics, or the structural part from the work of art, seems to him
the pursuit of an abstract possibility (2:34; similarly in *Storia*, 246). The
structural parts are actually generated by "a fundamental poetic *animus*"
(*CLC*, 2:36). In short, Russo tries to arrive at a unitary conception of
the *Commedia* without denying the presence of structural, that is, purely
intellectual or schematic, devices.

Russo does the same in his arguments about *I promessi sposi*. "Alessandro
Manzoni, poeta an orator?" (*RD* 1946, 2:124ff.) is a response to Croce,
who at that time labeled the novel a work of oratory. Russo maintains
that the novel's basic animus is poetic, that the idea of Providence and
the feel of the seventeenth century provide a unified inspiration but that
one can distinguish three moments in the book: the imaginative or lyrical, the meditative and historically illustrative, and the more specifically
hortatory. The solution seems sensible enough. Russo himself admits it
to be "eclecticism," but as an outsider to this debate I find it difficult to
conceive why it is so important to call *I promessi sposi* poetry: obviously it
cannot be through and through and there is nothing wrong with that.
In good Crocean terms Russo insists that the characters in a novel and
in *I promessi sposi* in particular cannot be abstracted from their context:
"They are only one of the many infinite and most noble fictions of the
sentiments of the poet, a kind of diaspora of the state of his soul" (*PPS*,
20). Or, phrased differently, "the unique and sole protagonist is always
the sentiment of the writer" (23); we hear many times of "the absolutely
individual and autogenetic character of the work of art" (*CLC*, 1:102). But
whatever Russo's protestations that "the personage is a lyrical pretext for
the poet" (*PPS*, 12), the chapters devoted to four characters in the novel—
L'Innominato, Cardinal Borromeo, Don Rodrigo, and Fra Cristoforo—
actually provide psychological portraits of these four as well as regular,
standard literary history, through comparisons with the earlier version
of the novel and with the historical sources or models. Russo studies
L'Innominato as a psychological case, by examining the stages prepara-

tory to his conversion, and constantly seeks support from the intellectual biography of the author: in his allegiance to the Enlightenment and to Jansenism. Manzoni is actually for Russo the model realist. Russo considers *Il Discorso sul romanzo storico* to be the manifesto of Realism (*N*, 18) and Manzoni the fountainhead of the Italian narrative tradition, which culminated in Russo's favorite author, Giovanni Verga. Russo's early book on Verga (1919; reworked in 1933) exalted his greatness. The tone is often strident, the claims for his eminence, in my view, inflated, but the detail is convincing: the way Russo sees the early society novels as protests against the fashionable world and the way he establishes a continuity between these novels and the Sicilian stories and novels in their predilection for the "defeated" (*i vinti*). Russo argues that *verismo* as a theory merely freed Verga, that he was a realist before, by instinct so to speak, but one could hardly deny the theoretical and practical model of the French novel of the time without using the Italian name for it. Russo's concept of Verga's attitude changes somewhat: in the earlier writings he sees Verga as a poet of the humble, as "the melancholy adorer of a *Christus patiens*" (*PMC*, 319), whereas a late essay (1952) corrects this to: "the poet of the poor people" whose work is "a cry of protest, a cry for freedom from misery for so many poor oppressed people" (*TL*, 518). Verga may not prophesy a new social order (Russo knows that Verga was a conservative and a nationalist and no revolutionary), but he indicates its coming as a fated necessity. The Marxist conception of an "objective evolution" comes in handy. Russo regards Verga as peculiarly Italian and Sicilian, a regional writer, and explores and welcomes the paradox that Italian literature was all-national before the unification but became rooted in provincialism after it. Russo considers Fogazzaro, Pascoli, and even D'Annunzio to be provincial authors rooted in their regions, and he especially loves Salvatore di Giacomo as a poet writing in dialect. In his valuable survey of the enormous output of Italian novelists since Manzoni, Russo recognizes a new Europeanizing, a cosmopolitan tendency in which the later D'Annunzio plays a leading role, but he sees it with jaundiced eyes. Russo cannot quite deny the merit of this airing of Italian literature, but neither can he help detesting D'Annunzio for his aestheticism and his politics and seeing him in the context of decadence, in Croce's sense of insincerity and moral emptiness. Russo also condemns Pirandello for his *atomismo assoluto*. Still, "we feel that they are estranged from our national tradition" (*N*, 28–29). The whole of recent Italian literature excites no interest in Russo: only Montale is exempt.

Russo's endorsement of Realism is not truly an acceptance of the dogma of the "mirroring of reality" and certainly does not exclude highly styl-

ized and imaginative art such as Alfieri's, Foscolo's, or Dante's. Rather it is
a protest against the Italian tradition of the *letterato,* of the writer remote
from civic concerns. In an essay originally written in 1919 Russo welcomes
il tramonto del letterato, the "twilight of the man of letters," and he used
the phrase again as the title for his last collection of essays in 1960. Russo
asserts the ethical commitment of "modern idealism" (Croce) and disparages not only futurism and decadence, but Giovanni Papini and even
Renato Serra. What Russo is looking for is "the transcendental politicalness" of Italian writers, where *trascendentale* seems to mean "implied, not
necessarily overt," "objective" in the Marxist sense. The poet, in Russo's
view, should be political: "A poet who appears free of politicalness is
either a poor poet or a flaw in our narrow sense of history, that we do not
manage to see his more hidden political logic" (*TL,* 214). But this must
not be interpreted, Russo hastens to add, as recommending that poetry
become a "servant of politics." In many interpretations, particularly those
of Alfieri and Foscolo, Russo tries to define their position in an ideal
history of poetic politics: the conflicts between individualism and historicism, nationalism and cosmopolitanism. Russo actually engages in what
could be called intellectual history, or rather *Geistegeschichte,* locating the
main Italian writers in a grid of general period-concepts. Thus he defines Petrarch's position as "eternally suspended between the ancient and
the new, between the transcendentalist Medieval and naturalistic Humanism, between heaven and earth, between the heavenly Jerusalem and the
earthly Jerusalem" (*RD* 1960, 1:259–60). Russo proclaims Boccaccio to
be the founder of "the new modern religion, the religion of the wisdom
of man, of his genius, of his cunning," having opened up the world "not
only of humanism but of all the later centuries" (1:421). In very simplified ways Russo sees the process of history as one of secularization and
enlightenment, though in spite of his violent anticlericalism he speaks
rightly of Boccaccio's "strong religious vein" (*PMC,* 309) and refers to his
"Christianity" or "neo-Christianity" (*CLC,* 3:271, 275).

Here and in many contexts Russo gives up the Crocean individualizing,
and he himself recognizes that he embraces a new "sociologism," but of
an immanent type (*CLC,* 1:286, 296) which he insists differs both from
romantic sociologism and from what he calls formalistic sociologism.
Romantic sociologism assumes a national mind, the formalistic an evolution of forms. Russo is always emphatic in condemning what he considers
abstract formalism: he calls linguistic criticism a myth (1:303), dismisses
a history of rhythms, modulations, and intonations (1:223), and harshly
attacks close reading as a mere revival of old grammatical criticism. But
in spite of this Crocean insistence on the irrelevance of the linguistic

surface, Russo in his own way did study the language of some writers, most fully in his chapters on Verga and Machiavelli, but also in incidental remarks on Tasso and Leopardi and in innumerable comments on individual words and their connotations. What interests Russo is not stylistics in the sense of Spitzer or Contini, but the clash of linguistic traditions in the diction of a writer. But linguistic traditions reflected in the work of a writer imply stylistic traditions, genre traditions, and relations to other writers. At times, Russo asserts that "poetry is a high thing because one can link up one poet with another" (1:225) and that "works of art, being individual, original, are also unclassifiable" (1:289). He holds fast to Croce's rejection of genres, denying that genre exists as a philosophical category. Russo reintroduces genre, however, as a "historical formation that is born, grows, decays like everything that is historical" (N, 17), for example, the Italian nineteenth-century novel or chivalric poetry, which is "a concrete historical formation, and not an abstract literary genre" (CLC, 1:295). Similarly, in spite of Russo's assertions of individuality—which deny the possibility of transferring the criterion of value from the world of one poet to that of another (Belfagor, 775)—he reopens the whole question of literary history as a continuous stream of forms, devices, theories, tastes, institutions, and so on by his use and reinterpretation of the term poetica. It is for him a replacement for non-poesia, or even struttura, an all-inclusive term that allows him to connect poet with poet. He finds it "in thoughts about art, in thoughts about the life of proper sentiments, in the confession of amorous idols and polemics of the mind" (CLC, 2:59), and he uses it to study interrelationships among poets: "In the realm of poetics we find infinite connections between one poet and another who are historically close" (2:65). By defending his attention to a poet's theories and intentions, Russo defies Croce, quoting Croce's own references to the German Sturm und Drang and to Rousseau in his discussion of Alfieri (2:59–60). Russo concedes that poetica is not aesthetics and is not simply the complex of a poet's aesthetic ideas, but "the world itself and that of aesthetic theories, and of passional, moral, political myths, which constitute the humus from which his poetry grows concretely, and which detaches itself from his poetry" (2:66). In practice poetica links the poet "to the taste of his times and to the fraternal fate of kindred and close spirits" (1:177). Taste and sensibility are historical (1:265). In a Crocean manner, Russo distinguishes between the individualizing characterization and judgment of poetry as an expression of personality, and the "poetics," which is another name for history, literary history, history of taste, and so on. Russo, of course, would not admit a gulf between the two. The term storicismo simbolico or even storicismo lirico-simbolico (2:58) allows a reconciliation between them, and we are expressly told that "the history of poetry is in urgent dialectical relation with the history of poetics" (2:65). As poetics is conceived as "a historical aura, the style and the conscience of an epoch" (*RD* 1960, 1:250), the way is opened to a study of literature in its historicity and in its historical setting, though Russo always rejects a simple determinism. Croce, who had no use for poetica and insisted on misinterpreting it as the mere world of manifestos and good intentions, is abandoned for what Russo saw as his return to De Sanctis.

In his early, well-researched book *Francesco De Sanctis e la cultura napoletana (1860–1885)*, Russo had studied De Sanctis closely as a "political educator," as a reformer of the University of Naples, and as a man deeply involved in the ideological struggles of his time. Russo uses De Sanctis's late paper "La Scienza e la vita" to make him a model of activism, of a reconciliation between scholarship and life. De Sanctis is seen also as a defender of realism and even Zolaesque naturalism, though Russo knows that De Sanctis was not an initiator on this point. Russo perceptively analyzes De Sanctis's autobiographical fragment, *La Giovinezza,* to show that he belonged to "realistic writers of his period" and shared their poetics (*RD* 1946, 2:231). Russo even assimilates these nostalgic reminiscences to the provincialism he so much admires in Verga (2:231). Not surprisingly, Russo has a good word to say for the role of positivism and the "historical school," against which Croce had launched an attack when he restored De Sanctis to his rightful position. Russo admires Michele Barbi, the Dante scholar, whom he regards not only as a meticulous textual critic but as a defender of a new philology that allowed the subjectivity of the editor some leeway in construing a critical text and fostered the study of language and the times. Russo appreciates the argument that every work requires its own approach, that there is no single orthodox method (*CLC*, 1:81). He sees no conflict between criticism and philology: "Because poetry is not only a question of vocabulary, a question of ancient and modern Italian, but is also imagination, humanity, exaltation" (1:85). This is the combination Russo himself practiced: the minute comments, sometimes at the bottom of the page, in his numerous editions of the Italian classics or the expositions that often closely mimic the style of the author discussed; and the strongly phrased, often polemical, often metaphorical, and linguistically inventive disquisitions that have the personal tone of a sturdy, combative moralist. While Russo preserved allegiance to some of Croce's basic insights, he returned in practice to the old literary history, purged of its often mechanistic and deterministic preconceptions. Russo properly belongs to the "historical school," because he recognized that a historical critic, while characterizing an individual work or writer as well as judging him in some symbolic relation to his time, need not embrace the obfuscating positivism of the later nineteenth century. It seems a pity that as a result of the Fascist experience Russo felt persuaded to welcome Marxism—historical materialism—after the war. He discovered Antonio Gramsci, who in his diaries favorably describes Russo as one of the "most remarkable thinkers of contemporary Europe" (*TL*, 502). Fortunately, this repudiation of his earlier idealism did not affect his historical writing. The *Storia della letteratura italiana* often reproduces his older views almost verbatim and in no way denies what its preface asserts, that he is and was a "pupil of De Sanctis, of Croce and of Gentile" (*Storia*, xi). Early on Russo had called himself "obsessed with liberty" (*PMC*, 299), and to the end he served the cause of freedom in criticism and scholarship. His review *Belfagor* is eloquent testimony to this broad tolerance.

FRANCESCO FLORA (1891–1962)

Like Russo, Flora started from Crocean positions. From 1920 on he was an assiduous visitor to Croce's house in Naples, and in 1924 he took over the legal editor's responsibilities for *La Critica*. He wrote frequently on Croce, expounding his views in a little book in 1927, in a long chapter in *Saggi di poetica moderna* (1949), and again in *Scrittori italiani contemporanei* (1952). The expositions are always from the inside, uncritical, except for comments on Croce's style. Croce also permeates Flora's independent work. His aesthetics is a development of Croce's in a direction Croce himself did not move, and his taste, from the very beginning, differed from Croce's. He had undergone the experience of modernism in the broad sense and did not feel the ethical revulsion Croce felt against decadence. Flora's first book, *Dal romanticismo al futurismo* (1921), seems to have evolved from Croce's essays on recent Italian literature. Like Croce, Flora sees Carducci as the last classic, but he sees him as a remote figure, "a curious chaser of butterflies beneath the arch of Titus" (*RF*, 10). Also like Croce, Flora contrasts Pascoli and D'Annunzio as the initiators of the new Italian poetry. Here and in later writings on these two poets (a book on D'Annunzio, 1926, and one on Pascoli, 1959), Flora comes to much more favorable conclusions than Croce had. In *D'Annunzio* Flora makes a distinction between the "orator of concupiscence" and the genuine poet, whose dominant tone is that of music, and he defends the intellect and learning of Pascoli, even if he deplores his lack of lyrical fire. And unlike Croce, Flora shows some sympathy for Futurism in this early book. Futurism is for him synonymous with the new literature: a far broader definition than that suggested by Marinetti. Flora argues that Futurism, while wrong to reject the past so brutally, accomplished something positive: it made us conscious of the ills of our age and gave us the will to recover from them. Flora welcomes "the principle of novelty" (*RF,* 79) and the collaboration and even confusion of the arts that he sees widely used in recent poetry. Music is the central metaphor in poetry: "There are poets whose word is dissolved and liquefied in music" (118). In good Crocean terms, Flora declares that each poem is radically different from every other. He acknowledges no evolution of literature; even the evolution of a single poet is only a mechanical abstraction (141). No work of art derives from previous works, but from the experience of the poet and the life around him: "Real history is that which . . . feels its individuality in relation to the whole" (145). Flora hails the new amalgamation of the arts and expressly rejects Lessing's sharp distinction between painting and poetry (125). Poetry is not the expression of society: reality, nature, and the world are "only its expressive aspiration" (149). Futurism at least destroyed the old rhetoric, the sentimental worship of women, and opened up new technical possibilities. Flora even envisages an art of touch and smell, *tattilismo* and *olfattismo* (190). The second half of this fervently youthful book takes up individual writers: Marinetti, Pirandello, Papini, whom Flora harshly condemns, and Borgese, who receives surprising praise. The book culminates in a paean to Croce, who discovered "the highest aesthetic truth: the lyric character of art." But *lirico* is used so generally that Flora also says and will say for the rest of his life: "All the arts are music" (370).

Here in germ are the outlines of Flora's later position, which he worked out in many books, particularly *I Miti della parola* (1931) and *Orfismo della parola* (1953). *I Miti della parola* starts with charming reminiscences about how, as a child, he imagined the palace of Don Rodrigo or the house of Don Abbondio in *I promessi sposi* to look in order to show that words suggest images and imply myths that vary from person to person (*MP,* 15). Flora develops Croce's identification of language and art. Physical nature disappears: "From moment to moment time is transferred into space and there it spreads out and there it annuls itself" (47). The beauty of things is a reflection of the poetry diffused in the common language (52). Metaphor, analogy, and similitude are the methods of all art. Flora repeats again and again: "The word of the poet is musical metaphor. . . . What is poetic language is a totally musical expressivity, the pure melodic and symbolic equilibrium of the human spirit" (119). This poetic language is not, of course, the poetic diction of the Italian tradition, which Flora amusingly ridicules for using *speme* for *speranza, speglio* for *specchio,* and so on (118). It is rather a "melodic transcription of the imagination," which contrasts with the practical language of everyday communication (112n). All this remains vague and fuzzy: Flora never gets beyond the implied claim that the critic can recognize this musicality, distinguish in Crocean terms between *poesia* and *non-poesia*. Language is expression, language is art, Flora says repeatedly, but later in the book he does discuss the role of tradition—how the past lives in the style (145), how a writer is shaped by the classics (148), what role imitation plays in the history of poetry. He always concludes, however, that what matters in art is only the individual creation. Poetry does not grow from poetry, but out of life influenced by poetry (169).

Orfismo della parola opens with a prolix, repetitious hymn to the word. *Word* is used in such a wide sense that it includes inner discourse as well as mathematical symbols, nature, and reality—all creations of the word: "The word is the everlasting truth in which man institutionalizes himself" (*OP*, 23). We should say, alluding to Descartes, *Loquor ergo cogito et sum* (18). It is thus impossible to conceive of a thing outside of the word: "Things are ineffable and therefore not really thought out" (19). Painting, sculpture, dance, and music also "recognize themselves ultimately in the word that defines them" (21). Flora asserts the Crocean rejection of realism in the strongest terms: "The artist never reproduces nature, but the soul, with which he regards and feels nature, that makes an object of itself." The only material for the artist is "the soul of the artist" (30).

Like the later Croce, Flora recognizes the difference between poetry and criticism. Criticism is simply aesthetics (*OP*, 37), and thus poets are not necessarily good critics. Criticism is a method of qualifying the object, inscribing it in its historical relation (39). The critic has to find again "the ideal voice of a poet and make it resound in us, repeating genesis and development" (40). Flora praises philology as preparatory to criticism, but he dismisses stylistics and the study of drafts and variants as irrelevant: "The history of a poem is collected whole, and only, in the finished work" (57). The main task of criticism is to recognize the poetic word, "distinguishing it from the lie, or anti-word" (60), a new word for non-poetry, the world of raw sentiment and oratory. Like Croce, Flora defends a criticism of criticism, as the critic should not repeat what has been said before. He ends with a burst of oratory about the dignity of criticism as "the custodian of the human in the word, which is truth" (61). *Humanitas* is essentially the word (26).

Taken by themselves, these pronouncements seem often inflated and vaguely general, but the encyclopedic *Storia della letteratura italiana* shows that Flora is more than a rhetorician of a new verbalism and more even than an impressionistic discerner of the word and the anti-word. The *History* is an admirable achievement, simply if judged as a firsthand reading of the whole of Italian literature from the earliest beginnings to the end of the nineteenth century. Flora covers twentieth-century literature only in the seventh edition (1953), replacing a volume by Luciano Nicastro; but in many other publications—*Poesia ermetica, Saggi di poetica moderna, Scrittori italiani contemporanei,* and others—Flora wrote at length on the twentieth century. The trouble with the voluminous *History* is that it tries to serve too many masters: it supplies a plethora of information on biography, bibliography, cultural background, and intellectual history and retells many of the plots, events, and scenes of epics, stories, novels, and plays. It is something like a huge anthology of Italian poetry, Flora picking out poetic, characteristic, or simply appealing passages. In a number of cases only specialists would ever have heard of the poets he selects, particularly those of the seventeenth century. The criterion is always Croce's *poesia e non poesia,* though Flora avoids the term and replaces it with his "music," "verbal magic," or simply "tone." What he always looks for is essentially the Crocean *liricità,* the poetic moment, or "the rhythm itself of the soul in the moment of creation." While these terms remain mere metaphors for the indefinable *quid* of poetry, they serve to define Flora's taste, which runs to the metaphorical and fantastical, and allows him to find beauties in Baroque poetry that Croce would have dubbed "ugliness." The chapter introducing Baroque literature engages in fanciful and quite unverifiable parallelisms between the arts. To say that "music is the true and infinite originality of the time" (*SLI,* 2:628) seems defensible, but to assert that "Baroque architecture makes music out of rock" (2:628) is sheer fancy derivative from Schelling's bon mot that "music is frozen architecture." Flora then draws the most farfetched comparisons between Italian music and the new science of Copernicus and Galileo (2:639). Elsewhere he constructs a parallel between Ariosto and Bach— the court poet of Ferrara and the Protestant organist—a comparison that makes sense only on a level of abstraction in which "a divine virtuosity of images" in Ariosto is somehow identified with "a series of sonorous numbers" in Bach's fugues (2:102). One may ask what is achieved by preferring Erminia, "a figure-landscape" in *Gerusalemme liberata,* to Beethoven's *Pastoral* Symphony (2:543)?

But it would be entirely unjust to dwell on the curlicues with which Flora decorated his volumes. His discussion of Baroque, in spite of some flights of fancy, comes to sensible conclusions: Flora rejects the all-inclusive use of the term by Eugenio D'Ors in *Du Baroque* (1935) and sees that "none of the contrasts between classical and baroque, if the difference is not placed in temporal limits, carries the slightest promise" (*SLI,* 3:636). Baroque is not a category but "a contingent fact" (3:638), and Flora rightly argues

that there are enormous qualitative differences between works called
Baroque: "The baroque of Bernini is not at all that of Churriguera, nor
is that of Shakespeare the baroque of Marino, nor is that of Carissimi the
baroque of Benevoli, nor is that of Magalotti the baroque of Emanuele
Orchi" (3:638). Actually, Flora's discussion of Marino is far from uncritical, and in many ways it repeats Croce's objections: "Literature in the
manner of Marino is a vice, no more nor less than morphine and other
drugs" (3:658). But the "epidermic sensuality" that Flora considers unpoetic, a mere practical act, is balanced by what he calls "literary sensuality, through which Marino becomes enamored of his own or another's
verse" (3:660). Marino is a virtuoso in all kinds of relations with poetry's
past. Flora is far from denying the attraction in describing Marino's particular mood as "a vein of sensual optimism, a most languid idyll of the
senses" (3:666).

Flora is at his best characterizing such poets as Tasso, Ariosto, and
Petrarch. He describes his own intuitive method: "To read Tasso with
the soul of poetry, with that divination of the exact tone, without which
art is not understood" (*SLI*, 2:550). Tasso's characters appear as "melodic
symbols in which the poet composes the ideal story of his soul," as "lyrical myths of the soul" (2:533): Rinaldo feels "the profound sadness of
fate" (2:544), Tancredi and Clorinda "form the high elegy of love and
death" (2:545), a theme Flora feels to be conceived with deep religiosity.
But beyond this search for the leading sentiment, Flora selects motifs
of night and sun, reminiscences from Vergil, epithets, verse forms, and
small stylistic details. He is never quite able, however, to integrate these
observations, except as support for his general sense of the poet's leading sentiment. Flora is equally good in trying to modify or supplement
Croce's definition of Ariosto as the poet of cosmic harmony. Flora notes
especially the sense of liberty, the "tone of joy" (2:96), and the contrast
"between a motive of intense gravity and a style of frantic hurry," which
seems to him the secret of Ariosto's charm. Similarly, Flora, more than
any critic before him, emphasizes Petrarch's "impalpability," his secret
virtue, his ethereal elusiveness, which Flora calls extravagantly "destruction of the word" (1:245, 249). The stress is again on the "verbal and
musical rhythm of the verse" (1:246), but this music must obviously not
be confused with mere euphony. Flora refuses Metastasio true musicality.
"He was a poet for music. . . . Limpid, exact, metrical, he was not really
musical" (3:894) compared with Petrarch, Ariosto, Tasso, and Foscolo,
whose *Grazie* Flora exalted as the high point of the poet's achievement
and a "supreme lyric poem" (4:80). But Flora also admires and characterizes very different kinds of poetry. He edited and studied Leopardi

closely and saw him almost as the opposite of his musical poets. His tone is "a kind of privation: he takes away from the word all flavor and color and smell of practical communication, and pronounces it as an inwardly transcribed metaphor which has lost its earthly sense and is more pure, conserving internally its form" (Giacomo Leopardi, *Tutte le opere* [1940], xliii). Surprisingly, Flora also makes an excellent defense of Dante's *allegorismo* as a kind of poetic language (*SLI*, 1:94).

Flora seems to me greatly inferior in his handling of prose writers. He is often content to summarize plots, to describe characters, to order motifs without analytical power. He does not have the tools to discuss narrative techniques. The discussions fall to pieces, unlike those of the poets, which are held together by the search for "tone." After expressing critical reservations about Verga—his "elementary tone of sentiments" is artificial, his style is often "apersonal and as if petrified," he lacks "the gift of music" (*SLI*, 4:527)—Flora produces a lyrical outburst on "la mesta cantilena siciliana" (the mournful Sicilian song) and evokes the novelist's hardly relevant, remote Greek heritage. Verga "found again a fate of primitive religion: he reunites with the Greeks. The fate of Aeschylus, in this Sicilian who has the spirit of a kindred Greekness, was in modern and Christian terms the same anxiety of living" (4:555). To a sober mind all this seems not only farfetched and unverifiable but positively absurd.

Flora's treatment of intellectual history and cultural background also is oddly unintegrated. In theory, he sees that Leonardo, Machiavelli, Ariosto, Palestrina, Michelangelo, Cellini, Tasso, and Bruno had each a very different relation to his time, and he asks us to construe "this real story which lives in the soul of the authors" (see "Abbozzo per un ritratto" [Sketch for a portrait] in *Letterature moderne* 10 [1960]: 450). In practice, however, Flora hardly succeeds in carrying out this program. His sketches of the different ages, of their *Zeitgeist,* are strangely dilettantish and lack firm outlines, or any real grasp of intellectual history. The strength of the *History* lies in its characterizations of the poets, seen in isolation from one another but as saying or rather singing the same hymn to beauty through the ages.

Late in life Flora took on a new project, the *Guida alla poesia,* which began with volumes on the poetry of the Bible (2 vols., 1960) and of Egypt and Mesopotamia (1960). He then jumped to a little book called *Poesia e impoesia nell'Ulisse di Joyce* (1962). Flora, who as a student of Italian literature rarely commented on anything foreign (I know only of the article on Tolstoy's *Resurrection* in *Saggi di poetica moderna*), discovered that "poetry oversteps all linguistic barriers" (*Letterature moderne* 10 [1960]: 451) and felt free to speak of works he could not read in the original. The book on Joyce's *Ulysses* obviously is based on the Italian translation. *Impoesia* (a term derived from Pascoli and roughly equivalent to Croce's *non poesia*) in Joyce is the whole scaffolding of the Homeric parallel and the quest for the father. Flora defines his purpose: "It is necessary to free it from the superstructures of a useless and tedious symbolism, from the pseudo-Homeric to the psychoanalytical, in order to restore it to poetry" (*PIU*, 254). He does this thoroughly, trying to isolate Joyce's "decadent lyricism" (16), to bring out the "dramatic communion and unity of the individuals" (254), the humor, the satire, and the parody, while dismissing too easily the symbolism and the psychoanalysis. Psychoanalysis was always a *bête noire* of Flora. His essay "Congedo a Freud" (Farewell to Freud) is completely negative. Psychoanalysis, according to Flora, "constructs uniform romances for the divine diversity of every human situation" (*CN*, 185). Freud propounds a mistaken theory of the word, a bad aesthetics, and a bad theory of history (217). There is, we may conclude, something appealingly ingenuous about Flora. He differs from both the dour, polemical, sturdy Russo and the solid, levelheaded, acute Fubini.

MARIO FUBINI (1900–1977)

Mario Fubini, the youngest of Croce's followers, was primarily an immensely learned, solid historian of Italian poetry and criticism. Due in part to Croce's lack of interest, the technical study of style, of metrics, and of genre traditions had been comparatively neglected in Italy. Fubini cultivated them with great success, particularly in his later years. He several times appealed to a little-known passage in Croce's preface to Cesare De Lollis's *Saggi sulla forma poetica italiana nell'Ottocento* (1929; reprinted in Croce, *Conversazioni critiche*, 3:348–50), in which Croce recognizes that "poetry . . . is like a chorus that continues through the centuries, and the new voice cannot resound as new if it does not listen to and welcome in itself the preceding voices, and respond to them, and take up from them the song and continue it in its own and at the same time in their manner" (*CC*, 3:349). In open or often discreetly concealed disagreement with Croce (whom he admired immensely as a person and whose views he accepted on many questions), Fubini engaged in a long defense of stylistics, of the close study of an author's linguistic system and of the relation it may have to different linguistic traditions, and of an author's use of sources, imitations, allusions, and parodies. While granting Croce's criticism that such studies must not be taken in isolation or considered the only right way of studying literature, Fubini argues that by studying the different versions of a book or variants in a text we come to know and understand it better. He demonstrates this enhancement of our understanding in many concrete studies: for example, his minute and acute comparison of the stylistic differences between the first and second editions of Vico's *Scienza nuova* (in *Stile e umanità di Giambattista Vico*, 1946), his studies of Italian metrics (*Metrica e poesia: Dal Duecento al Petrarca*, 1962), and his examination of such apparently trivial points as Foscolo's use of punctuation in his translation of Sterne's *Sentimental Journey* (see volume 5 in the Edizione Nazionale of Foscolo's works).

Fubini appeals not only to the flourishing of stylistics in other countries, quoting Leo Spitzer on the philological circle and Albert Thibaudet on Mallarmé's meter, but also to the native Italian tradition that paid attention to these supposedly merely formal matters. Neither Carducci nor Russo, who studied the language of Verga and Manzoni, could be suspected of decadent sympathies, to which Croce had ascribed the new interest in such matters. Fubini always kept his own point of view. He rejects Spitzer's psychoanalytical approach, since for him words are not "symptoms of a more hidden reality, but total reality, full reality, which declares itself" (*CP*, 115). He disapproves also of the purely linguistic stylistics of Giacomo De Voto (125) and remains committed to the view that stylistic studies must be integrated into a total study of a work. Although such a study ignores Croce's emphasis on the central inspiration, on the leading sentiment, the tone of a work and the *affetti* expressed in it, Fubini denies that these affetti are the only reality. In a curious exchange of letters with Croce dating from 1946, Fubini comes implicitly to reject Croce's "monistic realism": "It does not seem to me that one can assert that the 'sentiments' [affetti] are the reality, because the reality is the work of art, in relation to which the 'characteristic' which one gives of a poet, of his *ethos* and his *pathos*, contains something narrow and prosaic" (103). Croce, of course, remained unconvinced, reaffirming his rejection of any dualism, whereas Fubini defended a provisional separation of form and content in the study of literature, quoting with approval a passage to this effect from my *Theory of Literature* (113–14).

While on such matters as style and meter Fubini struck out on his own, conducting empirical, fully documented, and acutely observed studies, in other matters he stayed within the confines of Croce's system. He accepts Croce's invalidation of genre distinctions, acknowledging at most the existence of different stylistic traditions, but firmly insisting that genre theories lead inevitably to mistaken normative conclusions. Fubini's long treatise, "Genesi e storia dei generi letterari" (1948), argues, very much in Croce's wake, for the mere "instrumentality and not substantiality" of genres (*CP,* 138). In a historical survey of genre theories that traces mainly the antecedents of Croce's rejection of the whole concept, Fubini, usually extremely erudite and well informed, is surprisingly perfunctory about Aristotle and antiquity. He dismisses speculative or schematic, largely German attempts to find a theory of genres that would be descriptive of historical traditions and avoid any normative claims.

Fubini is also a good Crocean in his acceptance of the view that aesthetic activity (intuition-expression) is preconceptual and that the distinction between the beautiful and the ugly, between poetry and non-poetry, is a categorical judgment. Fubini defends the Crocean view of a universal aesthetic activity of man against Guido Calogero, who in his *Estetica, semantica, istorica* (1947) limits the aesthetic experience to rare moments, to the "Sundays" of our life. Fubini rejects the view that art is applicable only to specific "passional situations" and thus inferior to a more universal philosophy (*CP,* 274). As a learned historian of criticism, Fubini traces and judges critical conceptions of the past always from this Crocean point of view. He highlights, for instance, Leopardi's exaltation of the lyric to the center of poetry (in "L'Estetica e la critica letteraria nei Pensieri di Giacomo Leopardi") and Giuseppe Baretti's polemics against the unities of place and time and against literal illusion in his *Discours sur Shakespeare,* ignoring, however, Baretti's complete dependence on Dr. Johnson's identical arguments (*Dal Muratori al Baretti,* 145; cf. this *History,* 1:141–42).

Fubini is also a good Crocean in searching for the definition of emotion, for the tone, the unifying sentiment. He did so in his early monographs *Alfred de Vigny* (1922) and *Jean Racine e la critica delle sue tragedie* (1925) and very fully in the monographs *Alfieri* (1937) and *Ugo Foscolo* (1928) and in his edition of the *Operette morali* of Leopardi (1934), which, in opposition to Croce, attempts to assimilate Leopardi's works to the concept of "poetry." In all these writings (the Foscolo book seems the best), Fubini aims at a psychological profile of the author. While avoiding anecdotal, external biography, Fubini always traces the evolution of the poetic personality, drawing on all available evidence: Foscolo's correspondence, Alfieri's manuscripts, or the textual changes in the different editions of *Le ultime lettere di Jacopo Ortis.*

Fubini consistently displays a large tolerance for diverse methods and approaches, not shirking even the accusation of eclecticism, noting that "all roads lead to Rome" (*CP,* 101). He is suspicious of dogmatism, formulas, and panaceas and makes no grand claims for criticism. Giving examples from history, he reflects on the "conditionedness" of much criticism, its inspiration by contemporary issues, and comes to skeptical conclusions about the whole labor of criticism, which seems to him necessarily time-bound and thus transient (18). He does not believe in any supercriticism, any "absolute and integral criticism" (34), and recommends modesty to the critic, *Ehrfurcht* before the great masters (35). Fubini was upset when Croce, in a late paper, ascribed only pedagogical values to characterization, limiting the role of criticism to judgment. Fubini would like characterization to avoid all *filosofismo*. Personally he disclaims any originality in aesthetics and disapproves of criticism that would try to rival the poet: "creative" criticism and particularly "hermetic" criticism, which seems to him a *contradictio in adiecto*, as criticism is to him elucidation, clarification (84). The critic should let the reader feel the constant presence of the poetry (75), should search for the version that is "the most authentic or the nearest to 'authenticity,' or better, to prepare readers to understand it in its original tone" (323).

Fubini differs from Croce most markedly in his concern for the study of external form, which, he argues, is particularly pertinent in what Croce calls *letteratura*. Letteratura, rather than *poesia* in Croce's narrow sense, was the subject of many of Fubini's writings, and he rejects Croce's view of letteratura as simply "practical activity," for "literary works are a conspicuous testimony of aesthetic consciousness" (*CP,* 329). There is a continuous interchange between poetry and literature (331). Fubini, after all, studied with special devotion the Italian eighteenth century, the poets of the *Arcadia* such as Parini, who is self-consciously learned and professedly derivative. Vico, too, cannot be understood without studying the history of philosophy. Fubini makes no claim to a special aesthetics or even to a poetic theory. His theory of criticism allows him to include formalistic investigations, but he always conceives of criticism in service to an understanding of the writer. Fubini is an excellent interpreter, a reader and re-reader who teaches others to read correctly, and as a historian of literature he fosters a better understanding of old texts, their historical location and meaning, rather than the construction of historical schemes and developments. Within these limitations, Fubini has great merits: good sense, meticulous erudition, sensitivity to shades of meaning, analytical skill, and an admirable modesty and sobriety. One cannot ask for more.

All three Croceans—Russo, Flora, and Fubini—went through the experience of Fascism, which marked them and forced them into hiding or exile for a time. Croce was their rallying point politically as well. Flora wrote in 1960 that Croce "represented then all the highest values of the Resistance" (*Letterature moderne* 10 [1960]: 448), but Russo repudiated Croce's liberalism after the war by joining the Communist party. All three nonetheless moved and worked within the precinct of Croce's aesthetic and historical conceptions, though each in his own way tried to supplement or go beyond them: Russo with his robust realism, Flora with his musical sensibility, and Fubini with his much more technical attention to style, meter, and form.

ATTILIO MOMIGLIANO (1883–1952)

A generation of Italian college students were fortunate to have studied the *Storia della letteratura italiana* (1932) by Attilio Momigliano. Used as a textbook throughout the early years of the Fascist regime, it was dropped only when Italy adopted racial laws, which applied to Momigliano as a Jew. The book sold thousands of copies. This really distinguished performance bears, however, the stamp of its time. Momigliano, whether out of caution or conviction, completely neglected social and political implications in his history except those too obvious to be ignored. Momigliano always gave a sober factual account of events, as he did of the biographical details of writers, though in theory he disagreed with *biografismo,* the emphasis on biography.

The book is a combination of rather straightforward literary history and descriptive accounts of the main books of Italian literature. But it would be unjust to accept this general impression at face value, as the author obviously intended. In fact the book contains real literary criticism in the sense of characterization and judgment. Momigliano's characterization of authors is largely psychological, and the judgments are mainly based on his personal impressions. Like every Italian, he pays enormous attention to the great classics—Dante, Petrarch, and Boccaccio. But more distinct is his treatment of the two great poets of the Renaissance, Ariosto and Tasso. Momigliano is an inveterate user of the method of comparison and contrast. He draws an elaborate comparison between Ariosto and Tasso and particularly praises Ariosto for the way his art gives an illusion of "truth and life" (160). Ariosto is a great master at bringing in "things" that are surrounded by their natural atmosphere. Everything has "as much air and light as allow the reader to take it in comfortably." Similarly, Momigliano appreciates the very different truth of Verga, which surprisingly he combines with praise of Carducci: "Without romantic appearances he has a sadness which Carducci does not know." Momigliano generalizes rashly that modern literature is "mainly sad and morbidly joyous" (548).

Momigliano has no particular prejudices, but one senses that he dislikes the common-sense rationalism of the eighteenth century and that he identifies the great tradition of Italian literature in the sublime and the tragic mood. Foscolo's *Sepolcri* and Leopardi's poems are for him the key texts of modern Italian literature. Momigliano interprets Leopardi in an original manner: not as a nihilist or a deep pessimist, but as a poet who "makes people and their traces disappear in the infinity of time, in the eternal and solitary realm of nature," from which Momigliano perceives a mysterious soothing power that "descends into the hearts of men." Leopardi has the serenity of a poet who "speaks with himself and who has made the simple and immense mutation of his heart the motive of his life and of his desperate comfort" (445–46). Momigliano also devotes considerable attention to Manzoni as a central figure, not only for his great novel but also for his morals and religion. Although the tenor of the book is deliberately restrained and even detached, one feels throughout Momigliano's strong attachment to his country and even to the particular landscape. His taste obviously tends toward nineteenth-century realism. The book stops with the 1890s and does not, except for short references to D'Annunzio, engage the literature of the new Italy, which Momigliano viewed as decadent and deeply immoral. Within its limits the book provides substantial information, fine characterizations, and a warm sense of sound morality—that of a scholar who reads his texts with love but also with a certain detachment. Other literatures would be lucky to claim such an excellently informed, judicious, and well-written textbook.

14 : THE AESTHETICIANS

GIUSEPPE ANTONIO BORGESE (1882–1952)

GIUSEPPE ANTONIO BORGESE was one of Croce's first adherents. Borgese came from Sicily, somewhere in the neighborhood of Palermo, and studied at the University of Florence, where he wrote his thesis, *Storia della critica romantica in Italia* (1905). It stirred up a good deal of controversy because Borgese defended the paradoxical view that romantic criticism as such does not exist in Italy and that what is called romantic criticism is really classicist. The young Borgese was drawn into the circle around Croce and contributed to the first numbers of the newly founded *La Critica*. Borgese soon became involved in the polemics of the time and moved slowly into a position that can be described as anti-Crocean. He became an extremely prolific reviewer and polemicist, contributing to the periodicals *La Ronda* and *La Voce* of the group in Florence. His first book to make any impression was a discussion of D'Annunzio, whom Borgese both admired and frequently criticized. Borgese's writings are extremely miscellaneous and range widely over all of Italian literature, some French and (when we consider that he wrote also on Heine and Goethe) German. For a number of years Borgese was professor of German literature at the University of Rome and from 1917 to 1930 at the University of Milan. In 1931 he left Italy for the United States and after a stint at Berkeley became professor of Italian at the University of Chicago, where he was active from 1936 to 1947. Except for occasional journalism, however, he soon gave up literary criticism and became more and more involved in propaganda for the formulation of a world constitution, an idea that caused considerable stir. Borgese returned to Italy in 1947 and died in Fiesole in 1952. Late in his life he married Elizabeth Mann, the youngest daughter of Thomas Mann.

In 1934 Borgese collected a number of his more general articles under the title *Poetica dell'unità*. The preface to the volume contains a long, highly self-conscious discussion of his relation to Croce. It quotes Croce's favorable references and different formulations of Croce's theories before *La Poesia* in 1936. Borgese quotes finally Croce's comment on a book by Adelchi Attisani, *Interpretazioni crociane.* According to Borgese, Croce completely gave up his own position and accepted Borgese's view, though without mentioning him by name. In this preface Borgese feels completely vindicated and condemns strongly the polemics against him, quoting a saying of Georges Sorel: "The polemic genre is the shameful genre." In any case, Borgese develops what he calls a "poetics of unity," which he thinks of as the solution to all problems. He alludes only casually to the German antecedents of his views.

Borgese's self-conscious and self-approving account of his relation to Croce is then followed, however, by a serious and in many ways impressive exposition of his aesthetic. The first section, "Personality and Style," discusses the principle of progress and that of personality in literature. Borgese argues that progress and personality are new phenomena in the history of criticism. Progress is accepted simply as a fact of life, but no modern art is produced without the concept of "originality." In other ages imitation was acceptable and plagiarism even glorious; to describe a work as imitative was to praise it. Horace thought that he had erected "a monument more durable than bronze" when he adapted Greek metrics to Roman poetry, and Tasso died hallowed for having counterfeited the *Iliad* in *Gerusalemme liberata.* Dante asserts that he has imitated Vergil (though Borgese thinks that Dante does not resemble Vergil as a poet at all). Croce has destroyed rhetoric, but rhetoric reasserts itself in his distinction between the beautiful and the ugly. The concept of originality, however, is undermined if it becomes simply a synonym for beauty. Borgese condemns this romantic principle of originality and brings it together with the problem of style and symbol. But style and symbol have no sense without the universal, without the "asceticism of humanity." Style is the negation of the individual in favor of humanity.

Another section is a discussion of the unity of the history of poetry and the other arts. Borgese was taken up, as was fashionable in the twenties, with comparisons among the arts. One of his favorite examples is the supposed parallel between the eighteenth-century garden and picturesque and idyllic poetry. Borgese must have read a great many German books that compare the arts, often in a loose and arbitrary manner. (I have developed my objections in an essay, "The Parallelism between Literature and the Arts," *English Institute Annual 1941* [1943]; reprinted in *Literary Criticism,* ed. W. K. Wimsatt [1974], 44–65.)

A chapter called "Figuration and Transfiguration" discusses inspiration, vision, enthusiasm, genius, fantasy, and so on, arriving at the view that art is a "figuration and sensible representation of the absurd"—a phrase that reminds Borgese of the Hegelian "sensible shining of the idea." He argues that inspiration is not a useful concept, that one has to acknowledge technique but worry about the authenticity of the original vision. He discusses the concept of the tragic, which seems to him possible only in terms of a revolt against the shackles of fate and pain. Art is conceived of again as the transfiguration of the real, inspired by an intimate and universal model that ultimately has a religious dimension.

The poet wants "to perpetuate his products." Although. Borgese defends the value of the fragment, the glimpse of art, and even the "childishness" of art, he wants it replaced finally by prayer, transfiguring the reality to a higher reality worthy of adoration. This turn to religion is a novelty in Borgese's thinking. He strikes one as definitely secular throughout his life until this last, totally unexpected conversion to religion.

In his summary of the history of criticism Borgese is extremely biased against romantic excesses and also is critical of what he considers "humanism," meaning a worship of ancient texts and thus the wrong adoration of the word as such. In a way that must be derived from Croce, Borgese emphasizes the revolutionary role of Giambattista Vico, who is quoted as saying that "fantasy is the more robust the more reasoning is weak." Borgese focuses attention on Lessing's *Hamburgische Dramaturgie* and the whole of what we might today call pre-romantic sentimentalism, but he treats Kant and Schiller separately, and later the Danish critic Georg Brandes (1842–1927). The section on the nineteenth century is strewn with the most diverse names, referred to so briefly that it is difficult to judge how well Borgese could have understood their historical position. An outsider always wonders at the enormous emphasis given to Edgar Allan Poe's theories of what Borgese calls "poésie pure," even though Poe never used the term and did not develop its concept. These pages on the later nineteenth century are too hurried not to be superficial and mistaken in details. Still, Borgese accomplished what he wanted—to expound his poetics of purity, which in practice is the poetics of German romanticism.

ALFREDO GARGIULO (1876–1949)

The most effective theorist who can be labeled anti-Crocean was Alfredo Gargiulo. Gargiulo came from Naples and was one of Croce's first assistants on *La Critica*. From 1904 to 1910 Gargiulo edited and contributed to the journal, but he gradually moved away from Croce. In 1912 he published a favorable essay on D'Annunzio and was part of the Florentine group involved with the magazine *La Ronda*. During his lifetime Gargiulo published a collection of his reviews of books and figures in current Italian literature as *Letteratura italiana del Novecento* (1940), but his most important writings appeared only after his death under the title *Scritti di estetica* (1952). It contains articles written largely in the thirties and forties devoted primarily to problems of aesthetics in painting, sculpture, and architecture. Gargiulo's main quarrel with Croce was precisely over the question of the unity of the arts. He totally rejected the notion of a unified art and the view that the classification of the arts is unimportant, as it was for Croce. Gargiulo, on the contrary, was a firm believer in the distinct aesthetic formation of the individual arts.

In an early article that dates back to 1927, Gargiulo criticizes Croce for his deficient attention to "expressive means." This topic appears again and again in Gargiulo's writings, particularly in his elaborate review of Croce's book *La Poesia* (1936), called "Crisi di un'estetica," which is an acute and closely argued refutation of Croce's attempt to reduce all the arts to a single category. Unlike Croce, Gargiulo does not consider unity of the arts to be one of subjective experience. He finally concludes that Croce is actually discussing taste and that taste is always individual and in some ways uncontrollable. He is particularly shocked by Croce's attempt to make poetry a matter of pure sound and prose a matter of pure style, as they are if one ignores their content. Gargiulo is a strong defender of the mimetic power of art, the use of the present landscape by painters or of the human body by sculptors. Gargiulo puts his finger on the main difficulty in Croce's system: Croce cannot distinguish his intuition from artistic intuition. His intuition is so general that it embraces not only all language, but every kind of human expression.

Gargiulo sharply separates *lirismo* from the use of narrative and social entities in the novel. He draws interesting distinctions between reading and re-reading, between our construing a figure in our imagination and our recognizing it in such literary forms as autobiography and the historical romance. He raises—I don't know if for the first time in Italy—the crucial difference between aesthetics and *Kunstwissenschaft,* a distinction he derives from Max Dessoir. Most of his writings are about the different arts and their peculiar expressive means. As a consequence he rejects Croce's idealism and embraces what amounts to the psychological positivism of Taine and his contemporaries. This rejection of idealism separates him also from the philosopher Giovanni Gentile, who criticized Croce from a point of view that could be called Neoplatonic.

Gargiulo's essays are the most coherent and persuasive statement of an empirical study of the main features of the different arts, with the unforeseen result that lyric poetry becomes merely sound and rhythm and the epic and the novel become merely content. This simplistic and even crass theory obviously is defined in such a way that the great classics of realism—Balzac, Dickens, George Sand, George Eliot—remain as models. Gargiulo, however acute his criticism, is trapped in the old duality of content and form. He thus belongs, we must conclude, to an obsolete past.

15 : CRITICS CONCERNED WITH ENGLISH AND AMERICAN LITERATURE

DURING THE EARLY twentieth century, English and American literature became a topic of debate, admiration, and often harsh criticism in Italy. English literature had been influential in the eighteenth century, mainly through Milton and later Ossian. By the nineteenth century, however, with the exception of the dominant figure of Byron, English literature had receded into the background and certainly always was overshadowed by the French tradition. Italian literature vaguely followed the main trends of Western European literature, with poets like Carducci and novelists like Manzoni, but with the 1870 conquest of Rome and later the expansion into Libya and Ethiopia, which clashed with the interests of the British Empire, English and American literature became a great topic of debate. Thus all through these decades concern with English and American literature had a political tinge.

CESARE PAVESE (1908–1950)

Cesare Pavese had considerable merit as the first prominent Italian author to translate and comment on American literature. One must always bear in mind the Italian political situation. Under Mussolini, translating American literature was in itself apparently considered suspicious, and Pavese's writings, which exalt American literature, were considered definitely anti-Mussolini, though the main essays, written before his fall, studiously avoid any direct allusion to the Italian situation.

Pavese's first essay in the posthumous collection *La letteratura americana e altri saggi* (1951) was on the American novelist Sinclair Lewis. Though we may find it difficult to see why Pavese admired Lewis so highly and thought him worthy of lengthy discussion, the article caused something of a sensation when it appeared in the Turin review *La Cultura* in 1930. Pavese was a student in Turin and had access to all Lewis's books through a bookseller who imported every one of his works. The essay is a quite sober exposition and description of Lewis's many writings, with extracts and summaries of plots, praising Lewis as a great writer but by no means uncritically. Many of Pavese's remarks could be considered damaging, not only to the writer but also to the topic in question. The key passage is obviously the paragraph where Pavese describes the "thirst" of Lewis's characters: "Ultimately, the thirst of these characters is for one thing only: freedom, freedom for the individual confronted by the irrational restraints of society. It is the national malady of America, a country, if there ever was one, of impertinent moralists; but not, let it be understood, of supermen—poor creatures, rather, even when they possess genius" (*AL*, 5–6). This to him is the whole novelty of Lewis. Pavese describes well the "amused and mocking tone" of *Babbitt* (1922): "Usually [Lewis] wants to make of all the characters a series of whimsical little men and women, slightly ridiculous, slightly sad" (6). Pavese sees all the characters as topographical types, as faces of the same ego. Lewis "smiles and laughs, but always in the end caresses the victim with a sorrowful glance" (6). For this reason, *Babbitt* turned out to be his masterpiece: in Babbitt, better than in any other character, Lewis "fused the preposterous puppet with the human brother whom we must feel sorry for" (6).

Although Pavese is aware of and agrees with the satire of Lewis's books, he is more concerned with Lewis's sympathies and antipathies, his "uncertainties of judgment" (*AL*, 7). He looks for touches of poetry, for indulgent amusement, and sees more or less the same theme in all of Lewis's books. "Babbitt," he argues, "affects us precisely because he shows us how being an average man, a common man, a normal man, is like being a puppet." Pavese then asks: "What reader of the novel, while reading it, has not every so often squirmed, asking himself how many times he himself has been a Babbitt?" (17). Pavese admires *Babbitt* as a paradoxical book. A virtual "phonograph record of American vulgarity" is always the raw material for a synthesis that is poetry, where all the characters become functions of Babbitt. It is "a realism so little realistic and instead so full of poetry that, if for a moment the figure of Babbitt is removed, we can see how all the fragments of that vaunted realism no longer themselves say anything, how they no longer reflect any reality except (imperfectly) that of the missing hero" (17–18). Somewhat surprisingly, Pavese takes the later books, like *Arrowsmith* (1925) and *Elmer Gantry* (1927), very seriously and defends them. He describes Elmer Gantry, surely a repulsive caricature, as "a grandiose mind" (23). Pavese even accepts such a trivial person as Dodsworth.

In addition to his predilection for Sinclair Lewis, Pavese became a propagator and admirer of Sherwood Anderson, describing his books as mainly autobiography. *Dark Laughter* (1925) appeals most to Pavese, and in his 1931 essay on Anderson he somewhat indignantly rejects the idea that it was influenced by Joyce. Above all he admires the book's "sensual but healthy passion . . . for words and poetry," as expressed in the singing of "the Negroes with their 'red tongues'" (AL, 40). Pavese also got very interested in Edgar Lee Masters's Spoon River Anthology (1915) and in 1931 translated several vignettes from it, grossly overrating this highly local and pedestrian work. Pavese dismissed Gertrude Stein, on the other hand, as "unbearable" (39) and was also badly shocked by William Faulkner's novel Sanctuary (1931), which was filmed in Italy under the title Perdizione. Pavese retells the story of Faulkner's novel, making it seem even more violent and repellent than it is, and concludes that the book is little more than a "too ambitious thriller," and that Faulkner himself is merely "a bad pupil of Anderson" (145).

Pavese's most important and laudable discovery for Italy was Herman Melville. He translated Moby Dick, which must have been quite a job, and commented at length on Melville, whom he tries to see both in the context of earlier American literature and as a tremendous dark moral tragedy, a great spiritual power. Moby Dick is for Pavese an image of "the powerful thirst for inner freedom, for the beyond, the unknown, which gave life and traditions to these colonies" (AL, 59). Discussing Melville's style, he quotes Sir Thomas Browne and Coleridge, as well as the Neoplatonists and mystics of the seventeenth century. He gives some account of the early Melville and his travel books, which to him reflect the American yearning for the primitive. But otherwise he makes no attempt, though he has obviously read them, to defend the later books like Mardi and Pierre, except for Melville's story "Benito Cereno," which he greatly admires.

Pavese also was interested in John Dos Passos, who in Italy became famous through a film by King Vidor called The Crowd (Folla), drawn from Dos Passos's novel Manhattan Transfer (1925). Pavese, quite upset by what he considered a complete distortion or parody of the book, deliberately described Manhattan Transfer in a 1933 essay on Dos Passos as independent of the movie version. Among Dos Passos's other works, Pavese particularly admires The 42nd Parallel (1930) and 1919 (1932). He emphasizes Dos Passos's technique of using such extra inserts as "newsreels" and "camera eyes," devices that allow the author to pronounce indirectly his views while the actual narration is kept deliberately factual and dry.

Pavese also could not ignore Theodore Dreiser. He rightly sees that Dreiser embraces an abstruse and pseudoscientific chemistry to explain his characters in materialistic terms. Pavese also sees the odd contrast between Dreiser's loquacious scientific or pseudoscientific theories and his powerful ability to evoke situations and write dialogue. He is not impressed by Dreiser's polemics against supposed American Puritanism; these were all anticipated by Mencken and Sherwood Anderson and what Dreiser has to say is nothing new. But he has become important as an embodiment of the Middle West, of Chicago and the prairies, his deliberate provincialism clashing at times with his ambitions for universal humanity. In his other writings on American authors Pavese tries always to find a central situation or character, and he reduces all of Dreiser's characters to that of "the self-made man, the unscrupulous *arriviste*" who, however, has not yet produced "the antisocial exaltation of the superman" which Pavese deplores in Europe (*AL,* 114). Pavese retells *An American Tragedy* (1925) quite coolly, remarking that this tragedy has "no moral conclusion" (116). But he reverses himself at the end: "The miracle of human pietà revealed in the complex and interminable 'equations of emotions' is enough to make it one of the greatest books of these recent times" (116).

Besides writing about the most prominent American novelists of the time, Pavese was interested in an author the American literary historians ignored, O. Henry, who was translated and widely propagated in Italy. Pavese sees him as a literary "trickster," as a writer who achieves great success by devices of sudden surprises and solutions of puzzles.

Pavese's main critical interest is, of course, the novel, particularly the Russian novel. But among his many scattered essays is a sizable study of Walt Whitman, which shows that Pavese had read a good deal of American poetry and essays like those of Emerson. He admired Whitman not as a creator of "poetry appropriate to . . . the newly discovered land," not as a spokesman for this poetry of discourse, but rather as a poet who "made poetry out of making poetry" (*AL,* 122), an observation which may be worth elaborating.

Pavese later became well known for his novel *La Luna e i falò* (1950) and for his role in the resistance against the Republic of Salò, as well as for his love affair with the American actress Constance Dowling, with whom he lived for several years. When she suddenly left him and returned to America in 1950, Pavese committed suicide. After his death Pavese's diaries were published under the title *Il Mestiere di vivere* (1952), which includes many reflections on his works and on his working during his banishment to Brancaleone in Calabria. The book is of interest mainly as a source for a biography of Pavese, but it also contains a good many references to and reflections on literature and shows his considerable reading. It also reveals his ambitious attempt, when interest in Freud was still a novelty in Italy, to apply psychoanalysis to himself and to his friends. But little of this can be called literary criticism.

Pavese's occasional remarks on books show his taste quite clearly: the

early enthusiasm for D'Annunzio, for instance, and later the obvious rejection. I am surprised that Pavese read all kinds of Elizabethan and
Jacobean plays like Beaumont and Fletcher's *The Maid's Tragedy* (1609)
and *Philaster* (1608). He thinks *Philaster* "has a fine, colorful group of characters and an air of good theater, for which, I should say, the credit is due
to Beaumont," but it "lacks Shakespeare's ironic, significant construction;
the plot is sentimental and melodramatic (though it has points of similarity with *Cymbeline* and *The Winter's Tale*); and that is due to Fletcher"
(*BL*, 188). There are plenty of similar short judgments on English drama.
Shakespeare's *Richard II*, for instance, is "far better" than Marlowe's
Edward II, which "makes no attempt at imagination or wit or any play
on words, but rushes straight on, merely talking about passion" (181).
Throughout these jottings about different plays, mostly Shakespearean,
Pavese assumes that all this belongs to a mythological world. He speaks,
for instance, of a "mythological spot" which is "not one particular unique
place, a shrine or something similar . . . but a universal common denominator, *a* glade, *a* wood, *a* grotto, *a* seashore, which by its very vagueness
evokes all glades, all woods, all grottoes, all seashores" (174). He finds in
Italy particularly a taste for rustic mythology. He sees a mythic "consecra-
tion of individual places"; this "individuality, this *uniqueness* ascribed to a
place, is part of that broader, general assumption that an action or fact
is unique, absolute and therefore symbolic, which is characteristic of a
myth" (173). He considers Dostoevsky and Stendhal as writers with mythical themes: in Dostoevsky, that of "a man lowering himself to the level
of the complacent herd," and in Stendhal, "the isolation of prison life"
(173). The journals also contain often odd reflections on Italian poets,
who supposedly "like great constructions made up of very little chapters,
short, savory passages, the fruit of the tree (Dante's short cantos; Boccaccio's short stories; Machiavelli's brief chapters in his great works; Vico's
aphorisms in *Scienza Nuova;* the thoughts of Leopardi in *Zibaldone;* not
to mention the sonnets)" (181). The Italians, unlike Russian and French
novelists, are "intellectual and argumentative" (181).

In general, Pavese's journal is personal and hardly constitutes a chapter
in the history of criticism. Though the concept was still a novelty in Italy,
by the time the diaries were published in 1952 Pavese's discovery of myth
in literature opened doors that were already open.

MARIO PRAZ (1896–1982)

When I was at Oxford in the spring of 1927 I met, at Brasenose College, Cesare Foligno, the Professor of Italian at the university, and told

him of my project: a monograph on Andrew Marvell, which I was preparing as a second thesis for the *venia docendi* at my home university, Prague. He expressed surprise that I did not know Mario Praz, who had published a book, *Secentismo e Marinismo in Inghilterra,* in Florence in 1925 and was teaching at the University of Liverpool. I had just read (with great effort due to my deficient Italian) Praz's book but had no idea that he lived in England. I admired the book greatly. It was actually two independent monographs: one on John Donne and one on Richard Crashaw. The Donne part, with its contrast between the young rake and the older preacher, showed Praz's mastery of physiognomic portraiture and psychological sympathy; the Crashaw part displayed learning in Continental poetry and the emblem literature of the time, which I envied as I needed it sorely for my Marvell project. Foligno gave me—and I must always be grateful to his memory—an introduction to Mario Praz, and we soon met in London, staying in one of the dreary boardinghouses near the British Museum. We talked and talked in the evenings and read in the Library during the daytime. I learned from Praz, who was my senior by seven years and was steeped in the literature and the arts of the seventeenth century. I had caught the enthusiasm for the Baroque from the architecture in Prague, (which Praz later saw, admired, and described in "Praga barocca" [1968], reprinted in *Il Giardino dei sensi* [1975]). I had shared in the revival of interest in both Czech and German Baroque poetry before I first came to England in the summer of 1924 and saw the tomb of John Donne in his shroud at St. Paul's, read him and the other Metaphysicals, and was charmed and puzzled by Andrew Marvell in particular. I wanted to show Marvell's deep involvement in Continental poetry, French and Latin, and remove him from his usual association with Puritanism. Except for a fine short essay by T. S. Eliot and a thin biography by Augustin Birrell, nothing worth reading had been written about him: there was not even a decent modern edition. It was thus a blow to my plans when I heard that H. M. Margoliouth, Secretary to the Faculties at Oxford, had a critical edition almost ready for the Oxford University Press. On a visit to Mr. Margoliouth, I was dealt a second blow. He told me of a forthcoming large French thèse by Pierre Legouis, a nephew of the famous French historian of English literature, Emile. I obviously could not go on with my project without knowing these books. That year I went for the first time to America, to Princeton on a fellowship, and under the impact of the new environment I abandoned my Marvell project and worked on what would be my first book in English, *Immanuel Kant in England.* Because of what I deemed his desertion and almost betrayal, I made no effort to contact Mario Praz during the three years (September 1927 to June 1930) I spent in the States. Back in Prague, after the publication of my book on Kant, I sent a copy to Praz, and he wrote a friendly report on it for *La Cultura* (April-June 1932; no. 297 in Gabrieli, *Bibliografia*). In June 1932 I received a copy of *La Carne, la Morte e il Diavolo nella letteratura romantica*. I reviewed it in the main Czech professional journal, *Časopis pro moderní filologii* 21 (December 1934), together with the English translation by Angus Davidson, which gave it what I have always thought a misleading title, *The Romantic Agony*. In my review I mentioned Praz's earlier writings and indicated that I knew he had just that autumn moved to Rome. I expounded there Praz's introductory discussion of the term *romantic,* his clear delimitation of the scope of his book to one topic: erotic sensibility. I endorsed his view that *romantic* is an approximate term, an empirical category applicable to the whole of the nineteenth century. I agreed with his rejection of attempts to make it an unhistorical type occurring at every stage of civilization. I recognized Praz's commitment to what is usually called "historicism." Praz expounded the view that the critic must avoid anachronism: "Tendencies, themes and mannerisms current in a writer's own day provide an indispensable aid to the interpretation of his work." He rejected interpretation by later theories and tastes as a "corrosive patina spread over by critics" (*Agony,* 2) and gave examples of unhistorical readings. The assumption is that the artist's intention decides, and not the interpretation of the reader. Praz wanted to set himself off from the overwhelming authority of Benedetto Croce. The introduction rejects the Crocean view that criticism is an immediate judgment of the "here" and "now," as it would leave the critic "no other alternative but a mystical admiring silence" (2). Praz defends the use of empirical categories and of the concept of genres, which Croce had rejected. In an addition to the introduction that appeared only in the English translation, Praz defended his emphasis on romantic sensibility. Croce had criticized his book (in *La Critica* 29 [1931]: 133–34), complaining that Praz neglected the romantic movement's role in philosophy, aesthetics, historiography, and philology. Praz, after all, did pioneering work in the history of sensibility. There were plenty of histories of ideas but at that time hardly anything on the development of sensibility. Possibly such German books as Paul Kluckhohn's *Die Auffassung der Liebe in der Literatur des achtzehnten Jahrhunderts und in der Romantik* (1922) and Walther Rehm's *Der Todesgedanke in der deutschen Dichtung* (1928) or André Monglond's study *Le Préromantisme* (1930) could qualify, though Praz probably did not know the German books at that time. Praz's book mapped out a new territory explored only superficially by such a crude polemicist as Max Nordau in his *Entartung* (1892). The emphasis on the often subterranean impact of the marquis de Sade (whom Praz fortunately does not overrate as a writer or thinker) was particularly new, and new also was the careful tracing of such key images as the "Beauty of Medusa," the *femme fatale,* the different versions of Satan, the idea of Byzantium, and, in a special appendix, the cult of flagellation, *"le vice anglais,"* in Swinburne's writings. Praz's exposition, buttressed by ample quotations from French, Italian, and English literature (German is neglected and Dostoevsky is the only Russian mentioned), is studiously restrained and detached. One may assume that he was attracted by these topics but that he morally condemned much of what is exhibited in the book. We need only to have read his travelogue about Spain, *Penisola pentagonale* (1928, English translation by the author as *Unromantic Spain,* 1929), to know that he detested the cruelty of the Spanish bullfights and even more their glorification by French writers such as Gautier, Barrès, and especially Montherlant. Published in English by the highly respectable Oxford University Press, *The Romantic Agony* became something of a *succès de scandale* and remains Praz's most widely known book. In my review I voiced one wish—that Praz would attempt a psychological explanation of the phenomenon he had studied. To say that "sex is the main spring of works of imagination" (*Agony,* 5) seems not enough.

In 1935 I came to London as Lecturer of Czech Language and Literature at the School of Slavonic Studies of the University of London and became absorbed in Czech topics and soon in the vain struggle against the Goebbels propaganda preparing Munich. When Hitler invaded Prague on 15 March 1939, I decided to emigrate to America: at first I found refuge at the University of Iowa. Only after the war (1946), when I was settled as professor of comparative literature at Yale, did I resume contacts with Mario Praz. I sent him my paper "The Concept of the Baroque in Literary Scholarship" and my (and Austin Warren's) *Theory of Literature,* published in 1948. In 1950–51 one of his students, Agostino Lombardo, who became his successor, spent a term at Yale and attended my seminar. In May 1952 I returned for the first time since my youth to Rome: I visited Praz and saw at 147 Via Giulia his magnificent collection of Empire furniture, which was later, in his book *La Casa della vita* (1958; English translation by Angus Davidson as *The House of Life,* 1964), not only lovingly described but skillfully used as a frame for an autobiography. I then understood something of Mario's youth, his life in England, his marriage, and events during the war.

Since his book *Flesh, Death and the Devil in Romantic Literature* (as I would have preferred to call it), Praz had accomplished much: he had continued his studies of emblem literature with *Studi sul concettismo* (1934).

These were later developed and enlarged in English editions, particularly *Studies in Seventeenth Century Imagery* (2 vols., 1974), which contains an almost complete bibliography of emblem books. The labor that went into these studies is enormous. It concerns literature only marginally, though there is a learned chapter on the role of emblem books, mainly in English poetry. Simultaneously Praz gathered his studies of Italian influences on English literature. *Machiavelli in Inghilterra* (1942) reaches back to some of his earliest publications in England: the essay "Chaucer and the Great Italian Writers of the Trecento" was first published in 1927, the lecture on Machiavelli was given in 1928. Praz took up almost every conceivable topic in the literary relations of the two countries and surveyed them in "Rapporti tra la letteratura italiana e la letteratura inglese," a contribution to the volume *Letterature comparate* in the series *Problemi ed orientamenti critici di lingua e di letteratura italiana*, edited by Attilio Momigliano (1948). Though a professor of English, Praz had become a comparatist, a specialty for which in Italy there was no provision in academic organization, although Francesco De Sanctis had the title of Professor of Comparative Literature at the University of Naples from 1871 to 1876. All Praz's papers—Petrarch in England, Ariosto in England, Tasso in England, T. S. Eliot and Dante, and so on—are nourished by a scrupulous attention to detail and a sense of proportion which never succumbs to the temptation to claim for Italy more than its due. An English version, *The Flaming Heart* (1958), combines these studies of Italian influence in England with a translation of the early monograph on Crashaw.

As the new Professor of English at Rome, Praz felt strongly the obligation to furnish the Italian public, particularly students, with reliable information about English literature. His *Storia della letteratura inglese*, in different editions and updatings, has served since 1937 as an excellent manual—accurate, judicious, supplying biographies, plot summaries, extensive bibliographies, and capsule characterizations and judgments which rarely betray Praz's own predilections and prejudices. I am struck only by his low estimate of Hazlitt, which he had developed before in an article in *English Studies* (vol. 13, 1931). Praz preferred Lamb, whose *Essays on Elia* were in his Italian translation, in 1924, his first independent book. I also wonder about his coolness toward Blake and Gerard Manley Hopkins and do not share his assessment of Meredith as the first modern novelist. Praz supplied other pedagogical instruments for Italians: an anthology of English poetry, *Il Libro della poesia inglese* (1951, 2d ed., 1967), from the earliest medieval lyrics to Dylan Thomas, with elaborate notes in Italian and information on the authors, and an anthology of English criticism, *Prospettiva della letteratura inglese* (1947), which contains, in Italian translation by various authors, essays on English poets beginning with Chaucer and ending with Virginia Woolf. To all of this activity we must add Praz's many translations of English poetry, including several plays of Shakespeare, much of the poetry of Donne, a generous selection of nineteenth-century poetry (*Poeti inglesi dell'Ottocento*), and T. S. Eliot's *Waste Land*. Praz in these years succeeded in forming what should be called the Roman school of English studies: he attracted many gifted students who developed English studies (to which American studies later were added) on a scale totally unprecedented in Italy and hardly matched elsewhere. Besides his teaching he wrote weekly articles reviewing current English and American books—mainly novels and scholarly monographs—an astonishing feat of keeping abreast, particularly if one considers the deplorable state of the libraries in Rome, remedied only recently. Many of these articles are collected in the four-volume *Cronache letterarie anglosassoni* (1950–66). The sheer energy, the productivity, the devotion, and the competence displayed in every one of these undertakings is truly amazing. Praz's achievement as the founder of English studies in Italy will endure.

More and more Praz's interest expanded into the history of art and particularly to neoclassicism. *Gusto neo-classico* (1940; English translation as *On Neoclassicism*, 1969) is largely concerned with Georgian houses, the Empire style in furniture, the sculptor Canova, Piranesi, and the discovery of Herculaneum, but literature always provides background or parallel. The splendid essay on Winckelmann tells the story of his murder vividly but also describes his aesthetics. The essay on Foscolo focusing on the poems speaks well of *Le Grazie*, and the essay comparing Milton and Poussin, which goes back to 1939, is one of the first elaborate exercises in the parallelism of the arts and culminated in Praz's Mellon lectures in Washington, published as *Mnemosyne* (1967). The interest in neoclassical architecture brought Praz for the first time to the United States in 1952; he visited the cities which still preserve much of what in America is called colonial architecture and on that occasion visited New Haven also. He gave a lecture on Dante in England at Yale and had dinner at my house. After that we were in uninterrupted contact by letters and postcards and through my frequent visits to Rome. In 1959–60 I was Fulbright Research Professor in Florence and Rome, and in 1961 I received an honorary degree from the University of Rome. Praz came for a short time to New York in 1963 to speak at the Congress of the International Federation of Modern Languages and Literatures on historical and evaluative criticism, and I was appointed to discuss his paper.

Up until then I had considered Praz a strict historicist, judging by the assumptions behind his historical research and his very definite taste. This creed was most consciously formulated in Germany and more recently by the German-Jewish emigré Erich Auerbach. It requires us to enter the mind of an earlier age, and of all ages, with sympathy and thus to suppress our own present-day point of view and to avoid anachronism. Praz, to give some examples, chides Granville-Barker for considering Cleopatra's desire to present herself in all the splendor of her queenly pomp as "a flash of hypocritical vanity"; it seems to Praz only a case of the virtue of magnificence which the period, saturated in Aristotle's precepts, wanted from a sovereign (*CA*, 3:226). Elsewhere Praz rejects John Lawlor's attempt to defend the composition of *Piers Plowman:* its rambling manner is calculated "to communicate in wholly imaginative and poetic terms the central riddle of our experience." Lawlor then hints even at a likeness to Wordsworth's *Prelude* (*HEC*, 69). But in Praz's view, "a historical perspective is always required for understanding" (*Perseo*, 371). We thus can comprehend what at first sight does not please us. We may end up by liking a repellent picture (or, presumably, a literary work). Praz sees that this leads to universal tolerance, to eclecticism, to a "vertiginous carrousel of all possibilities and all impossibilities." He speaks of modern art, its rapid succession of disparate tendencies, and wonders whether on the whole mankind does not suffer from the "dizzy simultaneous re-evocations which precede drowning" (*Casa*, 99). Auerbach cites our understanding of the most diverse art forms—Neolithic cave paintings, Chinese landscapes, Negro masks, Gregorian chants, Homer, and T. S. Eliot—as the triumph of historicism and relativism and as a positive achievement of our civilization. Praz seems to fit this picture of the all-enjoying and all-understanding man who finds aesthetic pleasure in wax figures, conversation pieces, and the novels of Trollope, as well as in Empire furniture, Shakespeare and Donne, Dante and D'Annunzio.

It may be impossible to fix a date for Mario Praz's shift, when he came to see that historicism is not enough. He undoubtedly kept faith to the end of his life on many essential issues. But in the paper "Historical and Evaluative Criticism" Praz abandoned strict historicism and recognized that a work of art lives in history. Praz acknowledged, using the striking image of seeds provided with wings or parachutes, launched upon the wind, that art acquires what I call an "accrual of meaning," has to be seen as "undergoing that inevitable stratification of homages which every successive generation will render it." It "will become something different from the original, it will become a collective, choral work" (*HEC*, 73). In various rephrasings, Praz recognizes that "every century puts its patina of interpretation on its poets" (*CA*, 1:25), without any pejorative meaning to the word "patina." The whole history of criticism and the history of literature itself is seen as "a history of taste" (1:80), which cannot be more than a chronicle. There cannot be any laws of evolution. Praz expressly endorses the theory of taste he read in Lawrence Alloway, *The Venice Biennale 1895–1968: From Salon to Goldfish Bowl* (1969; see *Perseo*, 80). He rejects the fear that relativism would lead to the breakup of the canon, to a universal "entropy" in which we would not distinguish between geniuses and mere hacks. Still, a history of taste represents the only way of admitting that art is tied to its cultural environment, or to a determinate phase of taste. Our early reliance on the *grand goût* is gone: impressionism becomes the term of comparison according to which other currents are judged. History is falsified if it is reduced to an alternation of simple antitheses. One should not rush to condemn this or that manifestation of taste. What does not seem alive today could be so tomorrow, or the other way round. We must develop a feeling for the various climates of taste and their respective canons rather than codify our own preferences. Praz need not have appealed to Alloway: he constantly uses the idea of a *Zeitgeist* which somewhat mysteriously but perceptibly changes with every generation. The address in New York ends with a ringing pronouncement: "A history of criticism of art and literature is thus to be envisaged as a history of taste. Its final aim is not the discovery of absolute truth, but the survey of the manifold aspects the idea of beauty has taken through the ages. It was Shelley's idea that once the painted veil which lures and waylays mortal man should be torn, truth would shine before their eyes in all its splendor. Perhaps our conclusion should be that men ought to stick to the painted veil—because Truth *is* the painted veil" (*HEC*, 76–77). It is a kind of illusionism, I commented then, a denial of the possibility of objectivity, of universal truth. Actually Praz was not and could not be such an extreme relativist. Every critic must be convinced that his interpretations are correct and that his judgments are right, and not merely reflections of the taste of the time, impersonal and collective, as they could not have been for such a pronounced individualist as Mario Praz. He himself gives many examples of what he recognizes as wrong and even preposterous interpretations, for example, of *Hamlet*: Hamlet is obviously not a woman in disguise or in love with Horatio, nor is Miss Winstanley right when she argues that Hamlet is King James. Neither is Ophelia the Church, Polonius Absolutism, the Ghost the voice of Christianity, and so on. One can distinguish between correct or at least plausible readings and misreadings. I have shown, for instance, that one can convincingly refute the widely accepted misinterpretation of "The Legend of the Grand Inquisitor" in *The Brothers Karamazov* perpetuated by D. H. Lawrence.

In theory Praz seems to reject the view that judgment is necessary and that judgments make any claims to truth beyond the time-bound validity of a pronouncement of subjective taste. Praz's work is full of judgments which he presumably considered to be true. Some of those in *The Hero in Eclipse in Victorian Fiction* (1956) I listed in my comment on his FILLM address. The chapter on Walter Scott is a striking example. In an earlier essay in *Studi e svaghi inglesi* (1937) Praz tells us why he had to refuse an invitation to write an essay on Scott and Ariosto for a volume on Scott prepared by Sir Herbert Grierson, and how his argument with the highly respected editor of Donne only showed the depth of their disagreement. Grierson, like many Scotsmen, believed Scott to be the greatest writer in English next to Shakespeare and would have endorsed the view that "the test of a gentleman is his ability to enjoy Scott" (John Lucas quoting a senior Shakespeare editor in *TLS*, 13 January 1984, p. 29). Praz need not have read Croce's essay in *Poesia e non poesia* or even Emilio Cecchi's *Storia della letteratura inglese nel secolo XIX* to conclude that Scott's novels are "mechanically contrived" (*Hero*, 59), a "museum of waxworks" (62). Surely Praz wanted to express more than a subjective like or dislike when he called Dickens's plots "mechanical, artificial, melodramatic" (164), concluding that he must be classed with "the small rather than the great masters" (182–83). We must accept at face value his view that George Eliot is inferior to Hardy and that her "novels contain more dead portions than Trollope's" (354, 364). In Praz these judgments, which could be multiplied, are not merely apodictic obiter dicta but are embedded in characterizations that often start as simple descriptions. The whole series—description, analysis, characterization, interpretation, judgment—is continuous, flowing, fluid. With any good critic the characterization establishes the basis for the judgments and the judgments are linked to general theories. Thus Praz takes up the distinction between universal and local art from Baudelaire (a criterion familiar even to Samuel Johnson) and thus can justify his relegation of Dickens to the small masters: "Principally the minor and the least important artists hand on to posterity the flavor peculiar to a period, its manners, its feeling towards its surroundings, whereas the great artists seem to be outside any specific place or time, to be universal" (182). But it is hardly a paradox to say that Praz, in practice, prefers artists who strongly represent a particular *Zeitgeist*. Praz believes in the spirit of clearly defined periods and tries to buttress this belief by two rather questionable arguments.

He is greatly interested in fakes and shows that with time the "profile of fakes" emerges from beneath the disguise. He quotes Max Friedländer, a German art historian, to the effect that a Donatello faked in 1870 immediately gives itself away in 1930. The examples from literature are, however, far less convincing. The Ossianic poems seem to us fake at first glance but so they did to discerning contemporaries, Samuel Johnson and David Hume being only the most prominent. Chatterton's Rowley poems were immediately exposed. On the other hand, fakes in the arts and possibly also in literature have certainly gone undetected. Museums are full of them. The other argument used in *Mnemosyne*—that there is a parallelism between fashions in clothes and in the arts throughout history—can be true only in a long perspective. The pointed hats of women in the late Middle Ages hardly parallel Gothic spires, and the typography of Didot corresponds only vaguely to the architecture of Ledoux. Elsewhere Praz states it categorically: "The style of an epoch leaves its imprint on all the human manifestations, even those which by definition are considered the most capricious, fashion" (*Volti del tempo*, 145). Praz sometimes presses the parallelisms between the arts very hard and arrives at fanciful and often witty and illuminating juxtaposition, but surely the whole argument for a pervasive *Zeitgeist* cannot be so easily refuted as E. H. Gombrich did in his harsh review of *Mnemosyne* (*Burlington Magazine* 114 [1972]: 345), where he contrasts the black dresses of Venetian gentlemen with the riotous coloring of Venetian paintings. I myself have made skeptical observations on the parallelism between the arts. Praz quotes me and is well aware of the pitfalls. He objects, however, to my examples of the disparity, within the work of single artists, between their style in poetry and in painting, between Blake's "Tiger, tiger, burning bright" and his ridiculous illustration of a toy tiger, or between the subtle portrait of Becky Sharp in the novel and Thackeray's crude picture of a smirking minx. Praz does not refute these examples, but gives counterinstances of other people who exhibit a close unity of style and talent both as artist and as poet, for example, Dante Gabriel Rossetti. Although the parallelism of the arts is undeniable, as is the concept of a time-spirit, the methods of investigating them thus still involve purely intuitive guesswork. While steering away from some of the worst errors, like Helmut Hatzfeld's (whom Praz criticized; see *Bellezza*, 169–70), Praz falls into some traps himself. It seems to me an indefensible generalization to call the eighteenth century "feminine" (*Patto*, 28), apparently thinking only of the Rococo. It is a mere witticism to think of the succession of styles from the Renaissance to the Baroque and the Rococo as a "shifting of emphasis to the various parts of a woman's body in turn, from the head and shoulders to the

waist and flanks, and finally to the lower portion of it" (*Mnemosyne,* 146).
Praz considers the spiral lock of hair a symbol of the essence of the whole
century of Rococo, its curves suggesting the decorative shell whose "cozy
concavity" in turn suggests a woman's pudenda (144). Praz recognizes
that the Age of Reason is problematic, with men like Addison and Samuel
Johnson (and one may add such masculine figures as Immanuel Kant),
but he dismisses it as a simple contrast between reason and imagination.
Only Praz could have said to himself on looking at a pseudo-Gothic chair
in the Victoria and Albert Museum, "How very Keats!" (*House,* 296).

Praz in his later years became extremely hostile to abstract art and other
developments like *objets trouvés,* pop and op art. He denounced them as
symptoms of dehumanization (*CA,* 4:86–87), as the objective correlative
of anxiety, existential *Angst.* "Abstract painters," he says bluntly, "mostly
have no discipline and pass off as design or pattern any arbitrary scribble"
(*Perseo,* 89). Praz cannot conceive of art without any reference: one could
then speak of art only as Indian mystics do, saying: *Neti, neti, neti* (39).
More and more Praz feels that modern art reflects the end of civilization as we know it, but this once he seems to recognize that the situation
of modern art is very different from that of literature and other activities of mankind: "Modern painters and sculptors do not belong to the
same race, to the same culture, which otherwise continues in Europe, in
religion, institutions, laws, customs" (*House,* 46). He seems here to have
abandoned the strict parallelism.

One can best get at Praz's position in regard to literary criticism by examining his views of other critics and the history of criticism in general.
The anthology of English criticism compiled in 1943, but published only
in 1947 as *Prospettiva della letteratura inglese da Chaucer a Virginia Woolf,*
shows that even at that time Praz had abandoned the strict historicism
of his youth. He recognizes that "every literary history presupposes a
balance-sheet from a present point of view, that it sees the past in regard to present-day problems, or at least in regard to contemporary taste.
It judges according to categories and formulas which seem at the moment the best" (5). Praz defends his selection of critics, minimizing for his
present purpose the historical and political background, as well as the role
of the Bible and antiquity, and dismissing attempts to define the national
characteristics of English literature. He chooses what he considers the
best essays on the main English authors. The introduction justifies this
choice of authors and comments on them briefly without regard to the
selections that follow. Thus we hear about Chaucer and the Italians from
Praz while in the body of the book we read the chapter "The Greatness
of Chaucer" from Chesterton's little book *Chaucer* (1932). The selection

shifts disconcertingly from essays of purely historical importance, such as Macaulay's on Milton and Thackeray's on Swift, to modern discussions of historical figures, like T. S. Eliot's on Dryden and Geoffrey Tillotson's on Pope. Praz likes essays with a light touch. Lytton Strachey is represented by essays on Boswell, Macaulay, and Carlyle, Sir Walter Raleigh by essays on Burns and Blake, David Cecil by an essay on Thackeray, and J. B. Priestley by a piece on Dickens. Scholar-critics of serious import are not absent: C. S. Lewis writes on Spenser, George Williamson on Donne, W. P. Ker on Keats, and J. W. Beach on Joyce. The essay by J. Buchan seems intended as an *amende honorable* for Praz's own unfavorable view of Scott. The date of the book, which necessitates the limitation to criticism preceding the Second World War, and the pedagogical function must account for its deficiencies. It is not a selection of English criticism based on importance in a history of criticism.

Praz unreservedly admires one modern critic: T. S. Eliot. Pound seems to him eccentric, particularly in his narrow selection of literature in *How to Read* (*Casa*, 391; *Patto*, 488). Praz has little interest in I. A. Richards and refers to F. R. Leavis in the book on the Victorian novel only to disagree with him on Dickens and George Eliot, particularly on *Daniel Deronda* (*Hero*, 354, 363, 407n, 408). Among American critics Praz cared most for Edmund Wilson, who much later wrote a fine essay on Praz. Praz found *The Wound and the Bow* the one convincing book of psychoanalytical criticism, whereas he had early written a long sarcastic review of Marie Bonaparte's psychoanalytical book on Edgar Allan Poe (see *Studi e svaghi inglesi*, 165–88). He was also impressed by Leslie Fiedler's *Love and Death in the American Novel*, though he complained rightly that Fiedler, who knew Praz personally, never even referred to *La Carne, la Morte e il Diavolo* (*CA*, 4:263). Praz defends Edmund Wilson against the aspersions of Stanley Edgar Hyman in *The Armed Vision* (3:251), arguing that "translating" in the sense of paraphrasing or reproducing is a principal task of criticism. Praz, in discussing current American criticism, accepts Hyman's notion that the special characteristic of the New Criticism is the use of neighboring disciplines: sociology, philosophy, psychology, psychoanalysis, linguistics, anthropology, and so on. The result is that Kenneth Burke appears as the typical New Critic (4:249), in accordance with Hyman's last chapter, where Burke is the perfect critic "who has done almost everything in the repertoire of modern criticism." But there is little evidence that Praz was interested in Burke's writings. He knows that R. P. Blackmur belongs to the "best philological tradition" and is considered by some as "the perfect type of the 'New Critic'." But Praz paid little attention to him or to the other critics who practiced close reading. He quotes Allen Tate at some length from "Our Cousin, Mr. Poe," apparently agreeing with his impression of Poe's deadness, of his "glutinous style," though Praz would make an exception for the "admirable" style of the *Narrative of Arthur Gordon Pym* (4:229). He discusses Cleanth Brooks in the context of other "close readers" (William Empson and Leo Spitzer); he mentions Brooks's eulogy of metaphor but obviously disapproves of his, Middleton Murry's, and Earl Wasserman's attempts to burden Keats with metaphysical meaning, in order to update him in accordance with recent taste. Praz sides with E. C. Pettet's *On the Poetry of Keats* (1957), which argues that the analytical method is applicable to Donne but not to Keats. But Brooks's point in *The Well-Wrought Urn* was that it could be. Praz also reviewed *The Verbal Icon* of Brooks's close collaborator, William K. Wimsatt. He was struck by the portrait on the jacket, which seems to him to show "the head of a bull" and suggests "a Byzantine grammarian with intestines of bronze" (*CA*, 4:240–41), an impression totally belied by that gentle man. Praz sees that Wimsatt's theoretical position is diametrically opposed to Croce's. He briefly discusses "the intentional and the affective fallacy" without committing himself to approval or disapproval except to recognize "excellent observations" in the book (4:241).

Praz became more and more inimical to myth criticism, which was the great fashion in the fifties. In "Mythopoetic Criticism," the address Praz gave as president of the International Association of Professors of English at its meeting in Venice in 1965 (printed in *English Studies Today* 4 [1966]), he considers much of American criticism simply fiction. He singles out Geoffrey Hartman's *Unmediated Vision* (1954) and applies to it and others Eliot's term "etiolated criticism," which was originally aimed at Walter Pater and Arthur Symons: frustrated artists who tried to satisfy their creative urges in literary criticism. Praz turned out to be right in the case of Hartman, who later advocated the complete identity of criticism and creation. But Praz's criticism extends to all modern critical writings, which he sees as imitating the techniques of works of art fashionable in their time. Thus criticism of Shakespeare's characters, as in A. C. Bradley or Granville-Barker, follows the great vogue of the English nineteenth-century novel. The fashion of imagery studies, such as those of Caroline Spurgeon and Wolfgang Clemen, follows imagism in poetry and the novels of Virginia Woolf are organized on images, the studies of human time by Georges Poulet follow Proust, Empson's *Seven Types of Ambiguity* would not exist without Joyce, structuralism follows the *nouveau roman*, and the Polish literary scholar Jan Kott would not be possible without existentialism and Beckett. Praz is right in arguing for a "close connection between fashion in criticism and the techniques of creative artists" though the example of structuralism is refuted by chronology. Structuralism comes from Saussure, whose *Cours de linguistique générale* was published posthumously in 1916, and was developed early in 1934 under that name by Jan Mukařovský in the Prague Linguistic Circle, long before Robbe-Grillet. But Praz seems right to conclude that "hunters of paradoxes, symbols, ambiguities and myths will eventually lead to the death of criticism" (*English Studies*, 11). In my reply to his address I had a hard time refuting his pessimism. I tried to argue in favor of a general progress in literary studies, at least in the United States, in "the degree of sophistication, of involvement, in the finesse of sensibility, the acuteness of observation, the breadth of knowledge displayed" (28) compared with the situation fifty years before. But the events of the past decades have confirmed Praz's prediction. The newest developments, particularly the fashion of deconstruction, which has spread in the United States like an infection, are by their own admission profoundly nihilistic and lead to a wholesale destruction of all literary studies. One can only hope that this is a passing fashion. All over the world there are still scholars who acknowledge an ideal of truth, of right interpretation, who recognize the difference between scholarship and fiction and are working within the centuries-old tradition of literary studies. Praz belongs to these men: sane, enormously learned, many-sided, a student and scholar who loved literature, enjoyed it, and was able to communicate this joy and knowledge. Literary criticism was only one aspect of his activity: he was a personal essayist who conveyed his sense of life in hundreds of essays; he was an art historian and an antiquarian who knew more about Rome than any local historian; he was a collector; and he was a teacher. The devotion of his pupils belies his own confession that he cared most for things: he loved his students and his friends, and they reciprocated and will always cherish and honor his memory.

I remember my last visit with Praz, some months before his death. He had just returned from the Tyrol and seemed ailing. We talked about reputations, fame, and Nobel Prize winners. He contemptuously brushed aside all laureates from the Scandinavian countries as local favorites, but singled out Gabriel García Márquez's *One Hundred Years of Solitude* (1967) as a book without parallel. It deserved the Nobel Prize, which was often given to nonentities or to solemnly installed local idols. I shall never forget the man and the writer. His fertility and range are probably unique, not only in Italian literature but almost everywhere in Europe. His memory should not die.

EMILIO CECCHI (1884–1966)

Emilio Cecchi established his reputation as a specialist in English literature. He visited Great Britain several times in the 1920s, and in 1930–31
he spent a year at the University of California at Berkeley. In 1940 he
wrote *America amara*, a clever satire on the United States during the De-
pression, so gloomy and exaggerated that Cecchi never had it reprinted.
Cecchi had established a reputation as a reviewer long before. He was an
extremely successful professor of English at the University of Rome and
published a history of nineteenth-century English literature entitled *Storia della letteratura inglese nel secolo XIX* (1915; reissued as *I grandi romantici
inglesi*, 1961). In 1935 Cecchi collected his various articles on English and
American writers as the two-volume *Scritti inglesi e americani*. In 1947 he
added comments and a few new articles. Only after his death did his admirers collect his extensive writings on Italian literature of the nineteenth
century in two stout volumes with photographs and commentary.

The essays in *Scritti inglesi e americani* were originally published in different periodicals and newspapers between 1905 and 1945. They are
utterly miscellaneous and arranged not according to their dates of publication but according to the approximate chronology of the English writers
discussed. The collection begins with "The Shadow of Byron," a sketch
of the history of Byron's impact in Italy and elsewhere in Europe, thus
providing a bridge to the earlier book. Cecchi's attitude to Byron is hostile. He calls Byron a "moral ventriloquist" and therefore equivocal and
corrupt. Some of the other essays are little more than translations from
English, sometimes with minimal comment. "Poe and Manzoni" (1923)
simply describes Poe's review of *I promessi sposi*. "Dr. Burney's Evening
Party," an essay by Virginia Woolf, is translated with little comment other
than identifying Fanny Burney. Other essays are reviews, which make
only a hesitant attempt at criticism. An essay on the minor Melville (1931)
gives an elaborate description of the almost forgotten novel *Israel Potter*. A
piece on the love letters of Poe (1928) suggests only at the end that much
in his writing is contrived and invented and that Poe is "the prince of all
the decadents" (*SIA*, 1:149).

Another group of essays consist of interviews and conversations with
authors. Cecchi called on G. K. Chesterton and corresponded with him
several times between 1929 and 1934. Chesterton apparently considered
himself a true exile in America, as if he had arrived in a heathen land
before the coming of Christianity. An essay on Max Beerbohm, whom
Cecchi visited in Rapallo, gives a well-phrased account of Beerbohm's
physiognomy. Cecchi describes how Beerbohm used decadent preciosity

to achieve an anti-decadent art and combined his bitter jokes about aestheticism with decadence. After reporting Beerbohm's unfavorable opinions on Lytton Strachey, D. H. Lawrence, and Shaw, Cecchi stresses Beerbohm's isolation and serene classicism of taste; by 1934 Beerbohm knew that he belonged to the preceding century. Beerbohm appealed to Cecchi long before he visited him in 1945. Cecchi admires his essays and even the comic novel *Zuleika Dobson* and defends Beerbohm against the usual criticism, recognizing the basic romanticism behind his mask of levity. Cecchi uses the impression of Beerbohm as a personality who constructed a theoretical moral as an argument against the Crocean dismissal of the relevance of the writer's personality. For Cecchi, Beerbohm was the most exquisite prose writer among the English writers of the twentieth century. In an essay on Lytton Strachey (1934) Cecchi deftly sketches his surroundings in Bloomsbury and some of his opinions; for instance, Strachey found D. H. Lawrence repulsive, as he could not suffer prophets. Cecchi greatly admires Strachey for his *Eminent Victorians*. But he recognizes that Strachey loved those he persecuted, that the book *Queen Victoria* is really a celebration in spite of its satirical tone of irony. *Elizabeth and Essex,* which Cecchi also praises for its portraits of the figures of the queen, Cecil, Bacon, and Raleigh, seems to him nonetheless inferior to *Queen Victoria.*

Still another group of essays are largely descriptive accounts of books Cecchi had read, with some critical remarks. In a few cases these become brilliant essays with strongly voiced opinions and judgments, often supported by insights into the psychology of writers and an excellent grasp of the particulars of the situations and issues of the times.

In the earliest essay of the collection, dating from 1905, Cecchi makes the mistake of taking Frank Harris seriously. In his discussion of *The Women of Shakespeare* Cecchi completely ignores the obvious lack of any evidence for the role of Mary Fitton, the supposed Dark Lady. Cecchi complains only that Harris seeks explanations outside of Shakespeare rather than inside, but he is far too uncritically taken in by Harris, who, as later writings show, was a gross liar, charlatan, and con man. Cecchi also gives Harris's *Contemporary Portraits* too much attention, impressed by his skill in inventing or repeating anecdotes and calumnies. It is a deliberate exaggeration to say that Harris's interview with President Harding was "one of the important events of the century."

The best and most elaborate essays are devoted to Cecchi's favorite English writers, such as Robert Louis Stevenson, G. K. Chesterton, Joseph Conrad, H. G. Wells, Max Beerbohm, Katherine Mansfield, Virginia Woolf, Lytton Strachey, and D. H. Lawrence—which is not to say that he does not criticize them severely. He treats Stevenson (1920), whom he admired almost unreservedly, the most gently, comparing him favorably with Gauguin and Kipling. Cecchi reproduces and translates some excerpts from *In the South Seas;* Stevenson's last stages in Tahiti seem to Cecchi illuminated by "the blessed light that illuminated the first Mediterranean navigations." Chesterton appealed to Cecchi because of his unconventional Catholicism, his joyous optimism, his robust and "colossal" taste, his humor and inventiveness, and, finally, his almost filial reverence for Rome. Cecchi thinks highly of Chesterton's writings on literature, particularly *The Victorian Age in Literature,* which seems to him a masterpiece.

In an elaborate essay Cecchi surveys the life of Joseph Conrad (1924) and his individual books. Like others before him, Cecchi sees that Conrad is not simply a writer remembering his years at sea, but a profound psychologist whose analysis of the inner man finally consumes the story. But Cecchi had trouble with Conrad's sadness and monotony, his predilection for intricate indirect narration by a third or even a fourth person, and his extremely ornate writing. He did not believe that Conrad would ever become a popular author.

Cecchi was, however, much taken by Katherine Mansfield (1945), and he admired her short stories greatly, overrating her originality. He does not see, for instance, her dependence on Chekhov, and his judgment is strongly colored by his sympathy for Mansfield's fate and her early death. He believes in her search for truth, reality, order, and moral clarity, which in her last days induced her to exact cruelty upon herself. When she was in the final stages of tuberculosis, Mansfield was persuaded to visit the spa founded by the Russian Gurdjieff at Fontainebleau, where she had to take cold baths and swim in ice-cold water and thus hastened her early death.

To the Lighthouse particularly attracted Cecchi to Virginia Woolf, with its purity and modernity of tempo and tone. He gives an excellent account of the novel, of its picture of calm but desolate suffering, of its great lyrical tone. In a separate article, Cecchi comments on the Italian translation of the novel and on Woolf's essays, most notably "The Death of the Moth." With the exception of Joyce's *Ulysses, To the Lighthouse* seems to Cecchi the greatest book of recent English literature.

Cecchi comments on D. H. Lawrence's message, comparing him to Carlyle as a puritan and reformer but one who emphasizes sex and blood, elements that Cecchi despises. He gives a mainly satirical account of *Lady Chatterley's Lover,* which seems to him one of Lawrence's worst books. He is particularly offended by the scenes where the lovers decorate their nudity and dance among the trees, which he finds not immoral but decadent in a way that reminds him of the Pre-Raphaelites. Cecchi especially objects to Lawrence's lack of humor and to his prophetic pretensions. He couples Lawrence with the aesthetics of cruelty, which flourished at a certain time also in France, Germany, and America with Malraux, Jünger, and Hemingway, all deriving from Wilde and D'Annunzio and ultimately from Nietzsche.

All these essays were intended to introduce Italian readers to the major figures of modern English literature. The propagation of two American authors, Faulkner and Hemingway, is even more systematic and deliberately informative. Trying to explain the violence in their work, Cecchi quotes an Italian writer who described the American character as a puritan mind in a pagan body. He emphasizes *Light in August* and *Sanctuary* and, unfortunately to my mind, endorses D. H. Lawrence's melodramatic view of American literature as some kind of dark, almost demonic incubus. Cecchi describes Hemingway in some detail, complaining about the monotony of his depictions of hunting, war, and bullfighting and remarking on his nihilism, which he illustrates with a quotation from "A Clean, Well-Lighted Place": "Our Nada who art in Nada, Nada be thy name." *Death in the Afternoon* seems to Cecchi to be Hemingway's best book. He doubts Hemingway's democratic faith and thinks him dangerously unprogressive, but sees him as an artist who tortured himself with a sense of inferiority and a constant demand for supermasculinity, and who was only marginally interested in politics. Still, admits Cecchi, after Faulkner, Hemingway is the most potent voice of present-day American literature.

This account of Cecchi's publications on English and American literature should not obscure the fact that Cecchi wrote even more extensively on Italian literature of his time. He was an indefatigable book reviewer who produced hundreds of articles, reviews, and extended essays on practically every figure of twentieth-century Italian literature. Cecchi's particular interest was in the two Florentine periodicals to which he began to contribute as a young man, *La Voce* and *La Ronda*. He also reviewed at great length Giovanni Papini, and several essays show his tremendous early sympathy for the Catholic revival. But Cecchi's reviewing extended to all the literature of the time, from dozens of writers like Moravia, who seemed to him of little permanent importance, to novelists like Cesare Pavese and critics like Giuseppe De Robertis, Renato Serra, and Mario Praz. He praised Praz as an essayist, particularly for his book *La Casa della vita*. Cecchi also wrote a rather cautiously approving review of Gramsci's volume on literature, *Letteratura e vita nazionale*. One gets the impression that Cecchi did not care for Gramsci's irony and anticlerical invectives, but that he felt obliged to pay respect to a victim of the twenty black years of Mussolini's reign. Cecchi himself managed to escape persecution under the Fascist regime by staying out of direct political quarrels and by skirting the great issues of the time.

Some years after his death Cecchi's writings on Italian literature were collected by Piero Citati in two volumes under the title *Letteratura italiana del Novecento* (1972). Reprinted in these two large volumes are all the daily reviews, articles, and monographs that Cecchi had written over the years in an order that vaguely follows the history of Italian literature in the twentieth century. The first volume in fact begins with a number of reviews of the poetry of Giovanni Pascoli, who is actually a figure of the late nineteenth century. This is followed by a series of essays on the writers who interested Cecchi most—Croce and D'Annunzio, the two most prominent figures of his youth.

Cecchi greatly admires Croce and explains in considerable detail how he moved away from Croce's concept of poetry, particularly on the question of the classification of the arts. He rejected Croce's concept of the basic unity of the arts and, as a student of painting, became more interested in the changing historical relation among the arts. Cecchi himself wrote a number of books on figures of art history—some very much in the wake of Bernard Berenson's books on Italian painters of the sixteenth century—in a florid, ornate style reminiscent of Pater. Cecchi disagreed also with Croce's view of Dante and with his rejection of the unity of the *Divine Comedy* in favor of the distinction between structure and poetry, but he preserves considerable reverence both for Croce's liberalism and anti-Fascism and for his general command of the history of ideas. He sympathizes in practice with many of Croce's literary opinions, though he has trouble with some of them, including Croce's preference for *Madame Bovary* over *L'Education sentimentale* (*LIN*, 1:180).

In his articles on Croce and D'Annunzio, dating mainly from 1911, Cecchi discusses Croce's slowly changing attitude toward D'Annunzio. At first Croce admired him because D'Annunzio liked to think of poetry as an almost autonomous realm, and he proceeded in his usual way to review the criticism of D'Annunzio, admitting that what he wrote was really a criticism of criticism, a procedure he considered inevitable. Despite his admiration for the earlier D'Annunzio, Croce must still, Cecchi argues, be considered the genius of anti-rhetoric who propagates a "virile and affable classicism" (*LIN*, 1:181), where "classicism" is defined precisely as absolute clarity and logical coherence—all following in the great tradition of eighteenth-century philosophy, which for Croce began with Vico. Croce was anxious to distinguish the tradition of pure poetry—in the sense of poetry free from emotional excess and obscurity—from decadence. The term *decadence* for him implied a sick and pathological interest in the morbid and decayed. Defending Baudelaire against his own self-accusation of decadence, Croce argued that Baudelaire's greatest glory did not consist in his having anticipated Verlaine, Mallarmé, and Rimbaud, but in his having been the St. John the Baptist of symbolism (1:189).

Croce, Cecchi notes, considered symbolism's stress on childhood reminiscences as something old and not surprising. He ranked Proust with those who want to return to their childhood and identified this desire with the poet's yearning for childhood experiences and memories. In Croce's view, then, D'Annunzio is a great poet who wants to return to his childhood, to a time when poetry is to him something obvious, something natural, something that is simply part of his nature. Cecchi appeals to Croce, who, at least in his early years, considered poetry an elementary and possibly very early stage of human development. As D'Annunzio's writings began to reflect his growing participation in politics, he and Croce also became estranged, but Cecchi never ceased to admire "the primitive fleshiness and the insatiable joy which is, however, in D'Annunzio always colored by a sadness of solitude."

Cecchi is an almost uncritical admirer of the early D'Annunzio, particularly the songs of "Laus Vitae," which seem to him among the finest examples of Italian poetry. Cecchi does not mind the morbid grotesquery, even a certain sadism, that is especially prominent in D'Annunzio's French writings, and he even likes the heritage of graveyard poetry. Cecchi was not blind to D'Annunzio's histrionics, to his meretricious behavior toward Mussolini and his enthusiastic acceptance of the gifts and praise showered on him by an Italian government eager to exploit his fame. But although Cecchi disliked D'Annunzio's increasingly bellicose rhetoric against Austria during the crisis over Trieste and later during the First World War, he never completely broke with him. The editors reproduce D'Annunzio's signed dedication to Emilio Cecchi dated 1921; even then D'Annunzio thought of Cecchi as "a reader who knows how to read him." By that time, of course, D'Annunzio had become the hero of the propaganda flight over Vienna in 1918 and of the capture of Fiume in 1919. Cecchi is so taken by D'Annunzio that he accepts some of his theatrical uses of the Sermon on the Mount and even his view that war has a sacrificial meaning. Cecchi does not seem to mind what he rightly calls "the spiritual mask that [D'Annunzio] puts over the horrors of war."

In a short summarizing article written on the centenary of D'Annunzio's birth in 1963, Cecchi attempts to see D'Annunzio as a spiritual fire, which he constantly compares with Croce's spirituality. In a late article (1966)

Cecchi deplores Croce's inability to recover the unprejudiced and at the same time comprehensive and even affectionate tone of his first essay on D'Annunzio. Though Cecchi makes no attempt to hide the differences between Croce and D'Annunzio, he does envisage some kind of vague ultimate synthesis. Italy in the early twentieth century was dominated by these two luminaries, who in Cecchi's mind ultimately support each other. They achieved the rebirth of a poetic and intellectual life in Italy which, given Cecchi's low view of much nineteenth-century Italian literature, has meant a real rebirth of Italy as a new or, rather, renovated spiritual power. All Cecchi's writings on Croce and D'Annunzio show his central preoccupation with some reconciliation of the most extreme opposites. Cecchi always tries hard to formulate a position that he calls "synthesis," which seems to me not very different from "compromise."

Cecchi is the most prominent essayist in all of Italy's history. He understands the essay very much in the English tradition represented by Lamb and Hazlitt, both of whom he admired. He preserves a great deal of their sense of concrete life and interest in things, in art, in objects of art, and he has a real grasp of what beauty is—something which seems almost to have disappeared from modern criticism, in Italy and elsewhere. Everything he wrote was inspired by a clear common sense and a great, almost instinctive feeling for rational argument and clarity. Cecchi's commitment to a rationalistic ideal of reason in poetry and writing in no way contradicts, however, his basically romantic taste and his final gestures toward poetic mystery.

16 : ITALIAN MARXISM

ANTONIO GRAMSCI (1891–1937)

ANTONIO GRAMSCI IS GENERALLY CONSIDERED the father of Italian Marxist criticism. He certainly was the most important political figure in the early years of the Italian Communist party. Gramsci was born in 1891 in Sardinia and came to Rome, where he took part in the early Socialist movement. He edited *Avanti* and after the Russian Revolution helped to found the Italian Communist party, of which he became the chairman. In 1922 Gramsci went for the first time to Moscow as a member of the executive committee of the International. In Moscow he met Evgenia Schucht, who was a prominent member of the propaganda section of the Communist party. They married, and he visited her fairly regularly in his official capacity. In 1925 Gramsci was arrested by the Fascist government. Although he thought he was protected by a law that gave deputies of the Parliament immunity from prosecution, he was condemned to twenty years in prison and sent to a penitentiary in Turi in Calabria. He apparently had some access to books brought by friends, and he kept elaborate journals, diaries, and reflections, which were published only after his death shortly following his release from prison in 1937. He had suffered from tuberculosis all those years.

Gramsci's *Opere* were published between 1947 and 1966 in eleven volumes. The bulk of these writings are political, defending historical materialism and concerned with arguments about the philosophy of Croce. Only volume six, *Letteratura e vita nazionale* (1954), is of interest for a history of criticism. Gramsci presents few ideas, and all within the framework of Marxism, but they reveal an original and, at least for Italy, shocking concern for the broad masses of readers. Gramsci pursues these ideas with considerable force and acuteness and demonstrates a large acquaintance with Italian history and sociology. He begins with reflections on De Sanctis. Having retired from his professorship of comparative literature in Naples, De Sanctis gave public lectures, which, surprisingly, embraced the contemporary French novel, Zola included (cf. this *History*, 4:116).

Gramsci interprets these late lectures as a complete break with De Sanctis's past and as an appeal to the proletarian masses.

Gramsci is well informed and quite skeptical about the actual state of the readership among the proletariat, who, according to him, are simply swamped by bad romances, crime novels, and detective stories. While acknowledging the low taste of the proletariat, he believes that it is necessary to create a new "cultural basis for a new literature" (*LVN*, 14). The new cultural basis is, of course, the Communist revolution. But Gramsci also has some ideas about what this new literature will be like. He mentions Dostoevsky, and he seems to like Chesterton for his detective stories, and even Arthur Conan Doyle and Edgar Wallace. Gramsci is violently opposed to what he calls *brescianesimo*—clerical literature—which he considers anti-national and anti-state, "state" meaning the secular Italian monarchy of the time. Gramsci in many of these notes tries to ally himself with Croce, who certainly was resolutely secular—but Croce was also steeped in German idealistic philosophy, which Gramsci, as a Marxist historical materialist, completely rejects.

Gramsci is particularly interested in the language question. He is strongly conscious of the difficulty of the Italian literary language. Even Dante, he notes, can be understood only by a highly educated Italian, whereas "a statue by Michelangelo, a musical passage by Verdi, a Russian ballet, a painting by Raphael, etc., can, on the contrary, be understood almost immediately by anyone in the world" (*LVN*, 25). Gramsci reflects very sensibly on what he calls "functional literature," literature that would serve as social "coercion," that would help the masses to develop taste and finally elevate their taste, which he sees as becoming more and more corrupted by commercialism and sensationalism (28).

In these reflections Gramsci rarely distinguishes between artistic literature and simply informative or argumentative writing such as philosophy and sociology. Still, whatever the lacunae in Gramsci's reflections, we can agree with and in many ways admire his views on the pernicious effect of Renaissance humanism, which created a literature remote from the people and a criticism embellished by an artificial rhetoric that had survived in Italy for centuries. Gramsci is very much aware of the difficulty of converting the Italian intellectual to a real love for the people, the proletarian masses. He suspects the intellectuals of deliberate snobbery and of an often unconscious prejudice against the people, whom they flatter for political reasons but do not care for sincerely. Sincerity is one of Gramsci's constant criteria: Italy is corrupted by insincerity, by rhetoric, by bombast and pomposity. He is severe toward those who view the Greeks as "moderns" and condemns the Greeks as a slave society that is in no way a model for modern Italy. Though Gramsci is anticlerical, he admits a nostalgia for the Middle Ages and admires writers like Augustine and Thomas Aquinas for their sincerity and clarity.

Although Gramsci rarely discusses recent literature, many of his remarks show his distaste for what in Italy is called *ermetismo*, modern poetry that includes Ungaretti and Montale, who seem to him obscure and pretentious. But Gramsci likes some modern writers who have broken with the oratorical style. He condemns D'Annunzio and Marinetti, but the stories of Verga and the plays and stories of Pirandello appeal to him, if only for their spoken language. He sees promise for the future in these writers, who might create or forecast a new "spoken" literature. Gramsci is no defender of an absolutely unified written language. He welcomes the distinctions between regions and comments at some length on vocabulary and syntax, always insisting on an emphasis on content rather than form. Only occasionally does he show a grasp of the fusion of content and form. In this sense he belongs to an older period of criticism.

The volume also contains reprints of Gramsci's early theatrical reviews. He wrote daily reports on the theater in Turin, most of which are now totally out-of-date and meaningless to anyone who does not know the actors and actresses or all the plays, some of them French or imitating the French. He criticizes Sardou and the younger Dumas, often sarcastically, by retelling their plots and reducing them to grotesque farces. Still, one must admire the spirit of Gramsci's early reviews and the good sense of many of his reflections, for instance, a longer essay on a 1916 performance of *Macbeth*, which Gramsci discusses as a character study of an isolated individual. He comments that the play is "not a horror tragedy or a tragedy of ambition" (*LVN*, 242), but rather a tragedy solely of one individual, Macbeth. While characterizing him extensively, Gramsci dismisses the role of Lady Macbeth, but he always admires Shakespeare's sympathy with his characters, which is unaffected by "melodramatic sentimentality" and untouched by "decadence" (244).

Gramsci's reflections on popular literature and on the whole question of the gulf between the Italian classes are certainly admirable, as are his sensible proposals for a new literature of the masses. But one cannot help reflecting that these journal entries were not published until 1954 and thus were completely ineffective. Being in prison, Gramsci was necessarily cut off from any participation in the ongoing life of literature. His rival and successor as leader of the Italian Communist party, Palmiro Togliatti, at that time wisely stayed out of Italy and in 1964 was immortalized when the Soviet city of Stavropol was renamed Togliatti. Gramsci deserves particular attention because he understood that there was no hope of raising the corrupted taste of the masses with so-called proletarian literature, which is contrived and artificial and seemed to Gramsci ineffective, even though he approved of the ideal it represents. He believed that the taste of the laboring classes would be elevated when the victory of the revolution replaced present low-class literature with a new type of literature. Gramsci admits this to be, for now, a utopian belief.

GIACOMO DEBENEDETTI (1901–1967)

Giacomo Debenedetti was born in 1901 near Turin, where he studied law and literature. His first published book was *Saggi critici* in 1926, which was followed by two more in that series in 1927 and 1929. Because he was strongly anti-Fascist and Jewish on his mother's side, Debenedetti was unable to publish anything else for a long time. During the Second World War he published only a translation of George Eliot's *The Mill on the Floss* (1940). Under Mussolini's racial laws, Debenedetti had to go into hiding, and it was not until 1950 that he joined the University of Messina as a professor of Italian literature. Soon after he transferred to Rome, where he gave a successful series of lectures on the history of the novel, which were not published in book form until after his death.

Debenedetti grew up in Turin with such contemporaries as Mario Fubini and Piero Gobetti, the founder of the Marxist-oriented *Journal of Criticism*. He was deeply impressed by Benedetto Croce. Among Debenedetti's early essays is an elaborate article called "Sullo 'stile' di Benedetto Croce" (1922). It is extremely laudatory and sympathetic not only on Croce's style but also on his whole personality and life. Debenedetti considers Croce's philosophy a "cosmic romance" (*Saggi*, 110), a "philosophy of particular facts" which are restored by the poet "lyrically" (111), and he illustrates how Croce's "true morality" is revealed in typical episodes and characters (112). Debenedetti has a strong sense of the "disillusioned melancholy" underlying Croce's apparent enjoyment of quoting his poets, whom he treats often with a smiling affability (113). Debenedetti admires a kind of "evocative magic" in Croce's writings and reflects on his meditations on fame (114). Croce sees true fame to consist only in an effective survival of one's works among readers and not in names or slogans. Debenedetti shares Croce's strong contempt for pedants, for whom the scholar Wagner in Goethe's *Faust* and also Faust himself serve as models. Dante, however, is the great example of a "cordial and painful humanity" (116).

Debenedetti's admiration for Croce did not last, however, and an essay he wrote in 1949, "Probabile autobiografia di una generazione," is one

of the sharpest rejections of Croce's philosophy, criticism, and particularly aesthetics. First he criticizes Croce for dismissing Italian criticism as
lacking "the Spirit of the Earth." All of Croce's philosophy is the "doctrine, catechism and apologetics of liberty, an exhortation to use this
liberty" (*Saggi*, 35). Debenedetti refers to the aestheticians who have opposed Croce: Adriano Tilgher and Giuseppe Borgese, who criticized his
aesthetics, and Alfredo Gargiulo, who particularly attacked the "impas-
sive wisdom of the oracles of his 'style'" (35). Debenedetti then seems to
side again with Croce in his rejection of the so-called hermetic criticism
and praises Croce for having re-thought the centuries-old assumptions
of aesthetics. But he then alludes to the long conflict between Croce and
Gentile, and then to Gramsci, who like the others arrived at a moment
of "rupture" (*rottura*) with Croce (39). They must be and have been lis-
tened to.

Debenedetti then analyzes and criticizes Croce's philosophy for its four-
fold division and for its circular return to the starting point. He complains
that Croce discounts logical and religious motives and rejects his view
that all the arts are a totality. He dismisses particularly Croce's comments
on music. The *Filosofia dello Spirito* is an "aseptic and disinfectant": Croce
serves as a "hygienist" (41). Debenedetti also agrees with the view that
Croce is a romanticist who only pretends to be a classicist. He suspects
Croce of a "psychic and mental *pruderie*" (42). The Crocean system is a
"flawless code of manners which allows us to express ourselves on all problems of the universal and the particular without ever descending to the
shocking" (42). Debenedetti continually chides Croce for restricting himself to the field of history and to his own dialectic of distinctions, which
according to Debenedetti is "the most ferocious negation of the dialectic of opposites" (46). Croce erects a kind of "sanitary cordon" around
science in order to feel justified in knowing reality, which is nothing but
history. But this makes it impossible for him to understand science. He
cannot analyze the structures or the conditions of the scientists' existence.
Debenedetti quotes Gramsci: "Croce believes he is making philosophy,
but only makes ideology" (47). Croce, in conclusion, seems to Debenedetti
to be outmoded, out of touch with modern science, limited to history,
which he sees as a story of events and does not explain, as Debenedetti
would, by social and economic causes.

Debenedetti's lectures on the history of the novel were published a few
years after his death, based on his manuscripts and on the reports of his
students, as *Il Romanzo del Novecento* (1971), with a preface by Eugenio
Montale. The lecture course he gave in 1960–61 begins by meditating
on the notion of contemporaneity, as these lectures were apparently an-

nounced as lectures on the contemporary novel. Debenedetti tries to define contemporary art, which seems to him to begin with the very first Cubist pictures in the early years of the twentieth century—at the same time that Max Born formulated his quantum theory, and Einstein formulated the theory of relativity, and Freud made incisive steps to describe the unconscious. Debenedetti thinks that this first decade of the twentieth century changed the attitude of man, gave him a new perception of the world and a new sense of being in this world. He then alludes to the changes in the novel and singles out three names: Joyce, Kafka, and Proust. The changes in literature seem to Debenedetti slower than any in the other arts, and less visible. He thinks that Italian novels are far less radical, but that they will soon acquire a sense of what he calls the "continuous grasp of consciousness." The Italian novel came late, but it had definite novelties, like Moravia's *Gli Indifferenti* (1929). All of Svevo's writings seem to be the first clear pronouncements of the new attitude toward the world. Debenedetti, however, agrees with Michel Butor that there is little agreement between the reality they describe and the reality that surrounds them. Criticism, Debenedetti argues, should not simply propose a priori aims, but rather should examine works already accomplished and then discover what makes them most capable of determining the premises and forces and sentiments of our becoming. He finally settles for the view that the anthology *Poeti d'oggi* (1920) is the landmark in the history of Italian poetry, in which D'Annunzio is firmly relegated to the preceding age.

Debenedetti then reflects on literary periods in general, referring to Thibaudet's splendid book on the history of French literature and adopting his interest in the question of classification by generations. He describes how generations struggle against the preceding literature or reflect changes (Verga, for instance, who now is known for his Sicilian stories, began as a fashionable novelist in Milan). Vulgar realism was replaced by a new kind of realism, which Debenedetti finds most strikingly expressed in Italy in Carlo Emilio Gadda's *Quer brutto pasticciaccio in via Merulana*. Debenedetti refuses to accept the differences between generations in any literal sense. Starting in the period 1918–21, under the influence of the First World War, the Italian novel reinvented the novel, in a completely new atmosphere. Debenedetti then discusses the writers grouped around the periodicals *La Voce* and *La Ronda,* writers who were basically Croceans. Their novels often reflect a "sociology of the literal and medium bourgeoisie." Debenedetti sees that these so-called schools did not really represent coherent trends with unified philosophical tendencies, but rather were extremely vulnerable to all sorts of invasions and personal heresies.

Debenedetti singles out Giuseppe De Robertis in particular as the critic who defined the new novelists and credits him with teaching the public to read them. Theory often becomes a defense of "fragmentarism," which Renato Serra propagated. The new Italian novel is anti-narrative and its characters appear isolated. They are hardly ever described, but appear only in action and are comprehensible by their special voices. The new novelists are constantly apprehensive of the presence of the narrator. The "evaporation" of the characters is now almost complete. According to Debenedetti, the figure of Prince Myshkin in Dostoevsky's *The Idiot* remains vague and indeterminate. Debenedetti comments at length on Ardengo Soffici and seems puzzled in many ways by the new narrative devices, which are arbitrary and abandon firm characterization of the person as an individual. The Italian novel of Soffici seems to Debenedetti too static. He quotes Stendhal's famous definition of the novel as a mirror that is carried along a road, but asserts that in Soffici it remains an immobile mirror. Debenedetti reflects on the increased role of language and of myth, which he however considers a "disease of language"—language that is incapable of directly affirming the truth in its naked essence and thus condenses the truth into a fable or an allegory, which for the most part he finds too obvious and even simplistic. He favors a novel that is at least indirectly autobiographical, which leads to a digression about Balzac. This passage becomes crowded with names, and Debenedetti delves into an author like Federigo Tozzi, who writes about men as beasts. Pages are devoted to the Italians' relation with French literature and their eventual assimilation of French decadence, whereas Kafka did not appear until later in Italy, mainly with *The Metamorphosis*. The whole lecture course culminates in praise for Tozzi and Svevo.

The lecture series for 1961–62 begins by summarizing the preceding discussion, particularly the victory of *verismo*, for which Debenedetti credits the poetics of "impersonality." He finds this formulated also in Zola, who thought that the novelist should write an impersonal account of ordinary daily life, "une tranche de vie." Debenedetti doubts, however, that this impersonality can always be sustained. Stendhal, for instance, keeps the author out of the novel but still writes a disguised autobiography. After discussing the causal relationships in the nineteenth-century novel, Debenedetti then illustrates the new techniques by contrasting Pasternak's *Doctor Zhivago* (1957) with Moravia's *La Noia* (1960). He characterizes *Doctor Zhivago,* I think somewhat extremely, as completely destroying any causal relationship, ignoring any plausible motivated logic of events, and cutting up time into pieces almost independent of one another. Moravia, employing a totally opposite technique, starts from a generalization about sexual obsession, which he then illustrates with the old man's love for an insignificant and even evil young girl who is the central figure of *La Noia*. Reflecting on changes in the early twentieth century, Debenedetti assesses the impact of modern physics, of Einstein, quantum theory, and so on, without, to my mind, relating them convincingly to the modern novel. The rest of the lectures concentrate on novels by Borgese and Tozzi and the *Notebooks* of Pirandello, with some digressions on Kafka, whom Debenedetti interprets largely in psychoanalytical terms as exemplifying the conflict between generations, emphasizing Kafka's letter to his father.

The third series, 1962–63, begins with a discussion of the "epiphanies" in Joyce and Proust. Debenedetti gives a full account of Joyce's *Portrait of the Artist as a Young Man* (1916), reproducing long passages, and comments on the aesthetics that Stephen Daedalus develops very early based on the aesthetics of Thomas Aquinas. Debenedetti is particularly interested in the concept of radiation, which is Joyce's version of the Latin *claritas*. He thinks that Stephen is a Platonist in aesthetics and cultivates an archetype. Debenedetti also considers Proust's aesthetics a kind of Platonism, which he describes as based entirely on the concept of "intermittences of the heart," or more clearly, "the spots of time," "the involuntary memory." Calling *A la recherche* "the absolute masterpiece of our century and probably of all literature known to us" (*RN*, 295), Debenedetti comments in detail on the famous passages with the *madeleine* and the tea and the spires of Martinville. He sees the modern novel as an example of Joyce's *claritas*. The novelist is trying to find the essence of objects, which Debenedetti graphically illustrates with the story of Proust stopping in front of a rose bush and looking at it for a long time, completely ignoring the friends who were accompanying him on his walk. Debenedetti uses the concept of epiphany to explain what he considers the almost complete elimination of adventures and changes in the modern novel. The most typical manifestation of this concept is to immobilize things in order to express the *claritas* of objects, their obvious power. Debenedetti then quotes Husserl, as reproduced by Sartre, and sides with Sartre against Husserl's intentionality: "Proust and Joyce seem to support the intentionality also of objects which then explode against us." In the modern novel objects or things "explode" in our face. The actions and the plot completely disappear. The remainder of this lecture course is a long analysis of Pirandello's novel *Il fu Mattia Pascal* (1904).

In the lecture series for 1963–64, Debenedetti again explores the problem of dating the origins of the new novel. What is important to him is the rejection of naturalism: that is the beginning. Debenedetti repeats his assertion that the outstanding figures in the twentieth-century novel are those who broke completely with the earlier tradition: James Joyce and Marcel Proust. He admires E. M. Forster's *Aspects of the Novel* (1927) and thinks that Forster makes a good distinction between *homo sapiens,* the actual living man, and *homo fictus,* the fictional man. The fictitious man, according to Debenedetti, may be a person "whom we know better and grasp better than we grasp most of our acquaintances or fellow human beings" (*RN,* 437). He enumerates examples of this from Balzac, Flaubert, Tolstoy, and from *The Possessed.* This *homo fictus* is only a fragment of the real man. He consists entirely of the words the author puts into his mouth: a group of words makes him a person. If we are not told the color of his hair, for instance, we might be surprised or disappointed to see an illustration of, say, a man with red hair, a possibility that we had not imagined.

Alluding to many scenes in recent novels, Debenedetti makes the not surprising statement that fictitious people are different from real people. Forster has little to say about birth and death in the novel, and almost nothing about eating and elimination: love and courtship are its main topic. Debenedetti corrects this somewhat by going through the history of the novel, pointing out the meals in Cervantes and in Proust and, of course, the role of the kidney in *Ulysses* and the family dinners in Thomas Mann's *Buddenbrooks.* Debenedetti also questions Forster's statement that no one sleeps in the novel, again citing Proust and the famous passage on Albertine, *La regarder dormir.* He mentions the influence of Freud's *Interpretation of Dreams* and of Joyce's *Finnegans Wake,* the most famous account of dreaming. *Homo fictus* is always "present," while the real man, when we discuss him, is divided from us by a distance that is rarely overcome.

In the modern novel, according to Debenedetti, every trace of physical beauty has disappeared. The modern novel shows a "victorious invasion of ugly people" (*RN,* 440). There are exceptions, of course—for instance, the school that in Italy was called *i cavalieri dell'Ideale,* the "cavaliers of the Ideal," but which is now definitely out-of-date. Dostoevsky seems to him the first writer who objected to naturalistic narration, in spite of the fact that he frequently depicts an ugly and crude environment and his figures are often transformed physically into "grimacers." Examining Proust again, Debenedetti interestingly shows how many ugly traits are found even in his beautiful or handsome women, moral traits rather than strictly physical ones. Debenedetti goes so far as to say that brutishness or ugliness "has become the inevitable attribute of man as he is represented in the novel" (444). He tries to demonstrate that the new conception of man is obsessed with bad faith, with vanity and pride, and with the violence which is most clearly seen in German expressionism. In his appreciative review of Hermann Bahr's book on expressionism, Debenedetti especially notes *The Cry* (1893) by the Norwegian painter Edvard Munch, one of the pictures Bahr discusses.

Debenedetti contrasts the scandals and quarrels and conflicts that typify the modern novel with the figures in Victor Hugo's novels, who may be repellent physically but always have "hidden beauties of the soul and mind" (*RN*, 449). He refers to a well-known book by Günther Anders, *Man Is Obsolete*. Emphasizing the division in modern man, the inner conflicts, Debenedetti also discusses the problem of "doubles" prominent in German romanticism and in Dostoevsky. Man in the modern novel is often afflicted by a deforming, distorting illness, his face a mask that hides any expression of sorrow or suffering. Man struggles with an "other," who is beyond himself and lives with him in a sometimes dangerous symbiosis. The "other" lives within the "I," within us. Referring to Raskolnikov, Debenedetti asserts that the "other" within us can be a demon. To escape this division, man has tried to return to the primitive ages of humanity or to take refuge within himself: Debenedetti refers to Picasso and to the fashion for Negro art. A renewed interest in the early stages of mankind goes along with a revolt against the machine, which is contradicted by Marinetti, who glorified the machine. Debenedetti alludes only briefly to the concept of alienation, which he gets from Marxism. Expressionistic art seems to him to reflect only despair and horror of death: "Never before has such a sepulchral silence reigned in the world" (457). Man becomes smaller and smaller, and the concept of liberty has disappeared. We seem to be incapable of defending ourselves. All that remains is a "cry of anguish" (457). Debenedetti is greatly interested in expressionistic art, particularly in a pamphlet by the German painter Franz Marc, who constructed ideas of modern painting that reject expressionism as purely passive and bourgeois. Noting that the new art can aim at the abstract, Debenedetti refers to the Russian painter Kandinsky. Debenedetti conceives of modern art as a compensation for the unease of man, an instrument which he adopts in order to find himself again. He talks of Schoenberg in music, Picasso and the German expressionists, and draws a sharp line at the aestheticism of D'Annunzio, which seems to him a false theatrical pose.

Debenedetti then makes much of Freud, whom he sees as the discoverer of the unconscious, and he picks Nietzsche's *Die Geburt der Tragödie*, with its isolation of the "Dionysiac" element in the Greek mind, as a confirmation of Freud's psychoanalysis. He points out that as a physician who looks for causes Freud still belongs very much to the nineteenth century, but that he also believes in determinism, whereas Jung has a view of man striving to attain an aim in the future, to reconcile the Self and the Other. Debenedetti praises Freud for opening a new epoch in the exploration and understanding of man, but he sides with Jung. He continues to believe in progress, at least as a future aim of humanity, and disapproves of the book *Les Illusions du progrès* (1908) by Georges Sorel. The Freudian revolution, Debenedetti says, can quite rightly be compared to the Copernican revolution, which changed the picture of the universe. He seems to disapprove of the decay of religion, however, and considers Freud's book *The Future of an Illusion* (1927) as his most contested work. He sees that Freud believes in the deterministic model and, as a physician, wants to heal us. Debenedetti distinguishes between two antithetical conceptions of disease: the physician sees it as an interference from outside by microbes, something that must be healed; Jung sees disease as a positive factor in human life, something that reveals its meaning. The sense of life remains immersed in an obscured sense of the finality of life. Modern art moves in this realm. Debenedetti sees anticipations in antiquity: in Eurydice, in Orpheus, and in other myths. He appeals even to Lukács's description of realism as a phenomenon of the decaying bourgeoisie, whereas in the Jungian concept of illness one can rise to archetypical metaphorical schemes: with Jung we have entered the realm of the "irrational" (*RN*, 470). Debenedetti disapproves of this term, however, because it seems to depreciate irrationalism. The unconscious life is also susceptible to a rational approach. He speaks of the psychiatrist Jozef Babinski, who studied with Charcot and later was Proust's physician. Debenedetti emphasizes the rejection of imitation and mimesis, of Aristotle and the attempt to create a "non-objective" art, an art without object. Recalling Proust's reflections on Renoir, whose fat women, red and green, became models of beauty, Debenedetti asserts that artists have ceased to look for beauty and look instead for moralistic and finally metaphysical art. Naturalism was, he quotes, "carried to the grave in a little bier: the camera" (473).

Debenedetti then gives examples of the new art by briefly discussing Kafka. Again there is a conflict between the Self and the Other, and man is transformed into an insect. Debenedetti quotes Kafka: "Our art is blinded by truth. Only the grimace that shows on the face is true, and nothing else" (*RN*, 474). Debenedetti finds the calendar time in *Ulysses* significant: the fact that Leopold Bloom lives through all these events on this particular date—the sixteenth of June in 1904—seems to Debenedetti to illustrate how protagonists, like Bloom, are fixed in a certain time. Debenedetti appeals to Jung's psychological types, particularly his interest in somnambulism and in multiple personalities in the same individual. Jung described man as divided between the outer and the inner world: a man may be an angel with strangers but a devil within his own family. This division can be completely normal, but frequently people are disappointed in themselves, ignoring their real personality. Debenedetti accepts Jungian terminology, which speaks of a *persona*, a name derived ultimately from the mask of ancient actors, while he calls *individual* what identifies him with that mask. But of course the real individuality may differ from both the public and the private person, from both masks. This persona begins to express itself theoretically with philosophies of existence and with anxieties, and in practice through the great wars, the extermination camps, and genocide. There is a preoccupation with the end of the world, with the atomic bomb, and with the contemplation of a sort of "apocalyptic beauty" in this final catastrophe (482).

Suddenly Debenedetti picks up the work of C. Wright Mills, an American sociologist whose book *Sociological Imagination* (1959) seems to him a striking formulation of man's division, of the antithesis between object and subject: the modern disease is described as the feeling that one is only an object rather than a subject in this world. Debenedetti quite rightly sees in Wright Mills a Marxist, even if he does not appeal to Marx by name, and likes him for the psychology he brings into sociology: "Psychology chased out by the door re-enters by the window." Wright Mills argues that human nature is terribly vast. Man lives in a definite society and construes his own biography, but within a determined historical period, which he may not be aware of in detail. Wright Mills gives interesting examples of how we live in a certain broad epoch that generates feelings and ideas.

Debenedetti appeals then to a short book by Albert Thibaudet, *Le Liseur des romans* (1912), in which he argues that before Balzac the great novels were biographies of single individuals or pictures of the world seen from the perspective of the individual. With Balzac appears the idea that the creative drive of the novel must coincide not only with an individual, but also with a whole world, with a superior mentality that manifests itself in all its affinities and contradictions. Next appears the domestic novel, the novel of the family. Debenedetti cites *The Brothers Karamazov* and then turns to the domestic novels of the English, particularly George Eliot. *The Mill on the Floss* seems to him a masterpiece, which incorporates many autobiographical elements. He dwells at length on Eliot's irregular, informal marriage. Debenedetti considers *The Way of All Flesh,* by Samuel

Butler, to be the sharpest satire of the conflict between generations, at least in English.

Debenedetti's constant running argument is that literature does not simply reflect contemporary society, but also anticipates something or attempts to solve the problems of the time. He makes a distinction between scenes and content that are not dictated simply by the social situation and problems that are expressed or raised within the society. He again appeals to Sartre and finds examples also in Russian: the first scene of Mayakovsky's *Bedbug* and the descriptions in Pasternak's *Doctor Zhivago*. Finally he cites *Escape from Freedom* (1941), by Erich Fromm, who thinks that man's destructive capacity is his way of evading a sense of frustration and impotence. Debenedetti apparently foresees an imminent end to the world as we know it. These lectures on the novel exude gloom.

The lectures of 1964–65 contain a long summary of the preceding lectures and a discussion of Italo Svevo, with sections on Svevo and Proust and on Svevo and Joyce. The series for 1965–66 is devoted to a study of Renato Serra, the young critic who was killed in the First World War (see this volume, p. 293). There are chapters on Serra in connection with Carducci, De Sanctis, and Croce, on Serra and Cecchi, and on Serra and Borgese, as well as sections on Serra's relation to Romain Rolland.

Debenedetti apparently was the first translator and admirer of Proust in Italy. His 1925 essay on Proust ("Proust 1925") comments sarcastically on the attacks on and disparagements of Proust, who was either dismissed as a satirist of the Parisian upper crust or dismembered in anthologies as *morceaux choisis*. In this essay Debenedetti protests against the view that Proust can be cut up into little scenes of poetic charm. He also considers the emphasis on the scenes of involuntary memory mistaken. Proust is not, as he was often criticized for being, a poet of idiosyncrasies. He wanted to distill the essence of objects, which he sought not in an ordinary series of observations but in an essentially mystical grasp of essences. A second essay, "Commemorazione di Proust," written in 1928 in memory of Proust, reflects on the break in his life and work. The early Proust lived like a *flâneur*, an idler, only occasionally writing little imitations and parodies, published as *Les Plaisirs et les jours* (1896). The great series actually treats this time as a lost time. But *la recherche* seems to Debenedetti a misnomer, as Proust did not search for that particular lost time and is misunderstood if his great series is considered as a cypher, as a *roman à clef*, a "cyphered autobiography" (*PD*, 25). The tone of Proust is not that of a finding or rediscovery of the past, but one of retreat, of penance. At most, it is that of an elegy. But what Debenedetti considers Proust's most important contribution to the so-called crisis of the novel is what he calls the "strike [in the sense of work stoppage] of the personalities" (26). Debenedetti is most emphatic in his assertion that the person who says *je* in the novel is not Proust and must not be identified with him: only at the end of the series is the name Marcel used, and suddenly the *je* becomes identified with the author. What unifies the series is the leading motive of the "intermittences of the heart," and the tone in which characters forget is always that of sorrow, even pain. What troubles Proust particularly is the question of the validity of art, the difference between, say, Venice seen and observed and Venice written. One cannot say that there is a search for lost time; the protagonist actually is completely passive, subject to the caprice of the "intermittences of the heart," and these intermittences mean a complete suspension of any judgment or will. It is an involuntary gesture. The protagonist is in a pure state of passivity and is a completely amoral individual. Proust the author, however, becomes a moral individual when he wants these intermittences, and the prosy observation becomes poetry, which is always moral, always constructive. For a long time, Proust posed what he calls *disponibilité*, waiting for the revelation. He is a victim of his temperament. Only late in the final volume of the series does he genuinely try to find the time lost. Debenedetti admires particularly Proust's account of the cathedrals of France and of the whole Paris of the early twentieth century. He concludes that, whatever one thinks of Proust, he will remain the great recorder of the Paris of Napoleon III, just as Balzac was of that of Napoleon I.

In "Personaggi e destino" (1947) Debenedetti reflects on how the new attitude differs from Thibaudet's charming *Le Liseur de romans*, which strikes him as belonging to the past. One can read it only "with nostalgia" (*PD*, 110). The new novel has accomplished a "divorce . . . between the protagonist and whatever happens to him" (111). Debenedetti thinks that this new emphasis on the isolated modern man as described in existentialist terms does influence, however, the epic of reality, the old kind of novel as formulated by Zola. He quotes Bourget deploring the "systematic diminution of plot, the almost complete suppression of dramatic facts, the multiplicity of quite insignificant details" (115). Debenedetti speaks constantly of a "revolt of characters," a "strike among the characters." He again appeals to Proust, and calls the last volume of *Le Temps retrouvé*, somewhat strangely, "one of the highest religious experiences of our century" (118). Debenedetti then comments at length on the change of generations and describes Kafka as an example of revolt against the father. He brings in Freud and the unconscious, along with Kafka's *Metamorphosis* and Joyce's *Ulysses*, as a "descent into the inferno" (128). The rediscovery of, or return to, ancient myths and oracles seems to Debenedetti a main characteristic of the new time and the new novel.

Proust figures again in an article called "Confronto col diavolo," which begins by referring to *La Psychographie de Marcel Proust,* by Charles Blondel, and then compares him with Leopardi. Proust appears to Debenedetti as an example of the introduction of the Devil into the modern novel. He quotes Baudelaire saying that "the finest trick of the devil is persuading us that he does not exist" (142). In Mann's *Doktor Faustus* the Devil raises the same question as Proust: can people today save themselves through art? Debenedetti appeals also to Jung, who speaks of the special "power of evil," of a "particular divine will" (148). Somewhat oddly, to my mind, Debenedetti considers aestheticism to be a temptation where the "too spiritualized man is most exposed to the demonic" (149). Mann and Jung are the "callboys" (*buttafuori*) of the Devil, and Mann is a person who expounds the "positivity of evil" and believes in some kind of dualism between good and evil (149). Both Mann and Proust go back to what Jung calls the "archaic layers" of the mind; both have found the "legendary dread of the Devil" (150). Debenedetti calls Proust's great novel a "novel of inhibition" (150). He repeats his interpretation of *A la recherche:* Proust knows that he cannot heal himself; he actually has a somber doctrine of grace which is like that of St. Augustine or the Jansenists. The enormous paradox of Proust is that a writer so marvelously talented does not succeed in sitting down to work because he cannot write what he should write. Proust defends in bad faith his right to leisure, then his right to punish himself, and then his right to make up for all these new pretenses with remorse. Debenedetti, rightly to my mind, considers Proust a Platonist for whom platonic love is the symbol of his whole search. At this moment Proust does something "really diabolic": he brings in a system which "only the Devil could have suggested to him" (154). As the Devil puts souls into the different circles of hell, so the protagonist of the novel sequesters Albertine, making her *La Prisonnière.* Debenedetti quotes a passage where Albertine first appears as an "objectivation réelle et *diabolique*" (155). Like Mann in *Doktor Faustus,* Proust has made his pact with the Devil, has enchained life in order to follow art. He is, like Mann and many others, "a writer in crisis" (155). Surprisingly, the essay ends with a reference to Goethe's horoscope, which is borne out by his masterworks, whereas Proust sacrifices himself to his masterwork. Proust embraces, says Debenedetti, "a 'tragic destiny' to which successive artists could only add the smell of sulfur" (156).

The introduction of the Devil and the smell of sulfur surely grates on a sober reader. Debenedetti's indulgence in old superstitions is perhaps farfetched and not particularly illuminating. But the body of his work is solid and reasonable, well informed, and unpolemical.

17 : THE CATHOLIC RENAISSANCE

LIKE FRANCE, ITALY HAD its Catholic literary renaissance. The man whose critical writings apparently supported it most strongly was Giovanni Boine. In the preface to Boine's collected essays, *Plausi e botte* (1918; reprinted, 1978), Geno Pampaloni fervently advocates the return to spirituality, in practice to Catholicism. The "religion of poetry" is the "expression of the divine in man." Poetry, the lyric, is "a life above life" (*Plausi e botte* [1978], x). The poet overcomes what we call alienation, or what Pampaloni calls "aimless wandering in the absence of God" (xi). True criticism confronts the souls of authors and shows the difference between one soul and another. He admits that such criticism cannot avoid a return to moralism. A religious man will give of himself from "the superabundance of his soul" and will spend himself "without ever reaching exhaustion" (xi). Boine, Pampaloni concludes, ultimately identifies the religion of poetry with the religion of life. In the text Boine alludes to Gianfranco Contini as a great critic who fulfills these hopes. I have had to ignore Contini, however, as all his books belong to the sixties and seventies and are outside of my scheme.

CARLO BO (1911–   )

One of the most productive and influential critics in Italy, Carlo Bo was born in 1911 near Genoa. He was an extremely prolific journalist, particularly interested in promoting the Italian avant-garde, for example, *ermetismo*. In 1939 he began teaching French literature at the University of Urbino, where he also became the rector. His writings are so miscellaneous and range so widely over French and Italian literature and criticism that it is difficult to make any valid generalizations. The books vary widely in method. *Il Surrealismo* (1953), for instance, is little more than a collection of extracts, ranging from Apollinaire and Jarry to long quotations from André Breton in French; only the discussion of Dadaism and the Rumanian Tristan Tzara is of interest, as it demanded some narration and required Bo to speak of the 1915 founding meeting of Dada in Zurich.

Bo's early writings are largely essays on French literature. His first book was a monograph on Jacques Rivière (1935). It is a personal book, obviously written with deep sympathy for the man and for his struggles with religion and God. Yet it is hardly a work of literary criticism, even though Bo often refers to essays on literary figures and draws quotations from them. All the emphasis is on Rivière's religious feelings and ideas. The book contains a subtle analysis of Rivière's psychology, occasionally using concepts from Freud or from Proust's *A la recherche*. Bo assumes that all Rivière's writings, including those not directly concerned with religion, parallel his religious conflicts. Bo even interprets Rivière's essay on the "adventure novel" as a religious document. He focuses on the differences between Rivière's early writings, which are Catholic (*cattolicesimo*), and the writings composed during his imprisonment in Germany, which are filled with doubts, misgivings, and reservations and show an obvious acquaintance with the positivism of the late nineteenth century. Bo knows how to describe the style of Rivière's writings, which are often attempts to evoke his subject in metaphors and poetic developments.

In the collection of essays entitled *Saggi per una letteratura* (2d ed., 1946) Bo ranges more widely over French literature. He begins with a short note on Gide and has much to say on Claudel, Valéry, Bernanos, and others. In a later volume of writings on various French subjects, *Della lettura e altri saggi* (1953), Bo engages in often long-winded reflections on reading, stressing well before the present fashion the role of the reader and the importance of a second reading. Bo pays a great deal of attention to French poetry of the Resistance and to French religious poetry, also of the past. He worships Claudel. An essay on Proust is extremely well informed and makes much of Proust's concern with metaphysics and transcendence. There is an essay on Sartre and his early writings as well as one on Camus, whom Bo prefers to Sartre as a writer, though not as a philosopher. He also discusses Colette. An essay on French criticism between 1910 and 1914 emphasizes the Catholic renaissance. Rivière and Du Bos are Bo's heroes, whereas he is ambivalent about Thibaudet and Valéry. A shorter essay explains the conflict that arose after Rivière's death when his friends published writings that his widow did not consider orthodox enough. A piece on Supervielle dated 1951 concludes this extremely miscellaneous volume.

The collection *Reflessioni critiche* (1953) has the subtitle *I Pericoli della letteratura,* but after introductory reflections on the modern commercialization of literature we get essays on Spanish lyric poets, on Ungaretti and

Svevo, and, surprisingly, two essays about Walt Whitman, whom Bo treats as a prophet. The volume is filled with comments on current Italian literature: for instance, polite complaints about Moravia, who "puts water in his wine" (312). Bo was among those who praised the then little-known Svevo. While in general he wrote only on Italian and French literature, Bo nonetheless reflects at some length on Kafka in surprisingly positive terms; he knows, of course, of Kafka's despair, but he argues that Kafka penetrates into the "closed layer of divinity," because in Kafka "love is a perilous pause on our road to death" (158). But the Kafka essay is an exception that will hardly persuade those who see him as a man deeply tinged with melancholy and suicidal yearnings.

Among Bo's other works is *L'Eredità di Leopardi e altri saggi* (1964), a collection of miscellaneous essays headed by the title piece on Leopardi, whom Bo interprets in terms of his descent from the tradition of classical studies. Other essays in the volume are devoted to D'Annunzio and what he called *le parole del silenzio,* "the words of silence"; to the French Catholic regional writer Bernanos; and to Sartre. One section of the book, "Una Recensione parlata," purports to be improvised ("spoken") reviews of various contemporaries. Another large section is called "Letteratura e società," in which Bo distinguishes his concept of a sociology of literature from anything that would resemble Marxism. There is a great deal about Italo Svevo, whom Bo admires and considers neglected, as he was at that time. Another volume is entitled *La Religione di Serra: Saggi e note di lettura* (1967), which opens with the title essay on the religion of Renato Serra and then touches on a wide variety of writers and topics, including a discussion of surrealism and Breton.

Bo, who is credited with some forty books, is an extremely eclectic writer, mostly appreciative of what he selects to review and strongly committed to a revival of Italian literature in the spirit of the Catholic religion and church. The French Catholic renaissance is obviously the model for the Italian, for reasons that are easy to explain. After the foundation in 1870 of the new secular realm of Italy, with its strong anticlerical policy, Catholic writers were practically limited to the priesthood, and only recently were some of them able to engage or take part in the general literary life of Italy.

18 : THE CLOSE READERS

RENATO SERRA (1884–1915)

RENATO SERRA was an astonishingly precocious young man. The son of a doctor in Cesena, a town not far from Bologna, Serra became a librarian in 1900, when he was just sixteen, at Cesena's Biblioteca Malatestiana, which housed an important collection of books saved in part from the library of the Knights of Malta. Nine years later he was appointed director of the library. Serra began writing mainly on editorial techniques and composed a pamphlet something like a publisher's style sheet. He also wrote articles, particularly on Carducci and Croce. He appeared to be a completely bookish young man, who opposed, for instance, Italy's invasion of Tripoli in 1911. But the impression of complete bookishness is belied by an affair the same year in which he was seriously wounded by a jealous husband. Serra increasingly took part in public demonstrations over Italian foreign policy and became deeply involved in nationalistic proclamations and demands. He supported the whole movement for the liberation of the southern Tyrol and in January 1915 presided at a violently anti-Austrian demonstration in which the journalist and patriot Cesare Battisti (1875–1916) was the main speaker. His journals show, however, that Serra was constantly torn between his original pacifism and the wave of nationalism that swept Italy into the First World War. He himself joined the army as a lieutenant in April 1915. In May he was seriously injured in a car accident and spent two weeks in the hospital and another month recuperating at home in Cesena. But in July, still not completely recovered, Serra rejoined his regiment at the front. Two weeks later he fell in battle, killed by a shot to the head.

Serra has become a hero of Italian nationalism. After his death his writings and journals were published in various editions, often augmented or annotated, as well as many of his letters, all of which show Serra's complicated spiritual development. The letters and journals made a great impression, and his literary criticism has been edited and highly praised.

It is certainly extremely well informed and well written, even passionate on occasion, and, considering the author's youth, constitutes a quite
unusual achievement, unfortunately broken off by his sudden death.

Serra began by constructing a parallel between Carducci and Croce,
and he tried to persuade others and probably himself that they could
be reconciled. Carducci was a figure of the past, but Croce encouraged
Serra, praised him lavishly, and thought of him as a disciple. Serra in
fact moved away from Croce in the last years of his short life and wrote
in a quite different tone and attitude about recent Italian literature. His
1914 essay on Croce is far from uncritical. Serra sees the continuity with
European irrationalism and Bergson and condemns Croce's new concept
of *liricità*, which seems to him an attempt to escape the purely ethical
preoccupation of most of his essays. Croce, he writes, has the "face of
a myopic Neapolitan" who hides his "unknown thought" behind a "stiff
mask" (*SLMP*, 456). Serra is harsh in his opinions of contemporary critics.
Actually only Borgese appeals to him, and even there he holds back and
doubts that the "revision of values" promised by Borgese has been successful: "The formulation of the problem is just, but the solution is almost
always erroneous" (464). Finally he even says that Borgese "is not a critic
in the true sense," but rather "a rough reader, with no delight in precise
impressions." There is always something "mechanical" in him (467).

Among newer contemporaries Serra singles out Cecchi as promising.
Cecchi manages to "transform artistic impressions into corpulent and
pathetic abstractions." He has taken his criticism "from the hands of Borgese" (471). Serra praises him, but always with strong reservations. Cecchi
tries to reproduce "the impression of a poet in his totality, and then all
the emotion and the feeling and the love of poetry in general, and, on
top of that, every sensation of nature and of life: all of it. A chaos" (472).
Serra also criticizes De Robertis, who "has the defect of young people who
better understand large theoretical questions . . . than the small problems of living people" (475). In his theoretical reflections Serra always
emphasizes the art of reading. Criticism is reading—sincere and honest
reading. He strongly disapproves of modern irrationalism and a leveling democracy. In a 1911 essay on Kipling, Serra writes admiringly of
Kipling's passion, of the almost sensual delight with which he describes
Mowgli and also implicitly defends British imperialism.

One must, I think, conclude by lamenting that such a gifted young man
perished before he could fulfill his great promise.

GIUSEPPE DE ROBERTIS (1888–1963)

Giuseppe De Robertis was born in Matera and studied in Florence. He originally prepared for a musical career at a conservatory, but began writing for the main Florentine periodicals, *Marzocco* and *Leonardo,* as a freelance journalist. In 1938 he was given a chair of Italian literature at the University of Florence, where he lived until his death in 1963. De Robertis was a great admirer of Renato Serra, whom he considered "the only genius of his generation," a critic who had a "visionary intelligence" (*Saggi,* 169). But De Robertis deemed his own work much more modest— very close reading—an achievement that he considered simply a conse- quence of studying to pass Latin exams. He thought of all his writings as close reading deriving from the tradition of humanism. Identifying with Poliziano, the fifteenth-century humanist, De Robertis considers his own reading, which covers the whole of Italian literature from the fifteenth century to the end of the nineteenth century, justified by the tradition of classical philology. Responding to a disparaging account of older stylistics by Gianfranco Contini, where he is apparently classified as "rustic" and "primitive"—quite wrongly, I think—De Robertis defends himself elabo- rately, going through his writings and showing that he is uninterested in stylistic criticism in the sense of Spitzer, Vossler, Bally, and Curtius. He discusses his writings one by one, showing not only his great erudi- tion but also his method, which is concentrated often on the parallelism between literature and music, particularly emphasizing the "tone" of spo- ken prose, which he tries to define as "rising" or "falling," "louder" or "softer," and so on.

From the beginning De Robertis wrote elaborately on such problems as the harmony of Ariosto, the rhymes of Alfieri, the structure of *I promessi sposi,* and the learning of De Sanctis and Carducci. He never, in print at least, seems to go outside Italian literature, unless it is some reference to Latin poetry—no French or German writer is ever discussed or, I think, even alluded to. De Robertis is a solid, erudite, straightforward, honest student who has nothing to do with the methods introduced from linguis- tics and semiotics by Contini, or with the stylistics of Spitzer and other cultivators of historical linguistics. We have to conclude that he belongs largely to the past as an excellent specialist on nineteenth-century Italian literature. He does, however, always recognize that valuative criticism, in the sense of telling what is good and what is inferior, is required of a proper reader. He praises Cecchi in passing (*Studi II,* 345). He himself rarely says in so many words what is good and what is bad, but we can sense from his articles that he has a low opinion of Giovanni Berchet and that he appreciates other sides of De Sanctis than those displayed in Contini's anthology (*Scelta di scritti critici*, 1949). In his article "Contini e il mito di De Sanctis" (1950) De Robertis strongly disagrees with Contini's selection, which must have provoked Contini's unfavorable classification of him. De Robertis remains a solid investigator of the art of poetry and narration in nineteenth-century Italy.

CESARE DE LOLLIS (1863–1928)

Cesare De Lollis is admired in Italy as the initiator of a modern sophisticated scholarship which drew mainly on German conceptions of the writing of literary history, but did not surrender the older interest in literary scholarship misleadingly called "positivistic." Italian scholarship, as it actually descends from humanism, is nourished mainly by the tradition of classical philology. The editing of and commenting on classical texts was the main preoccupation of humanist scholarship, and it survived with little change into the nineteenth century. De Lollis is particularly admired for his enormous erudition in what can be described as Old Italian, Old French, and Spanish. De Lollis's first book of criticism was *Cervantes reazionario* (Spanish edition, 1913; Italian edition, 1924), for which De Lollis read all the works of Cervantes and the sources behind them. Cervantes wrote, he shows, lengthy chivalric and pastoral romances, often in the style of the most fantastic fairy tales. Cervantes handled all the material that went into Ariosto's *Orlando furioso* with great skill and often at enormous length. He is, then, "reactionary" in the sense that, with the exception of *Don Quixote*, he wrote in a style that would have been acceptable in France in the fourteenth and fifteenth centuries. Cervantes spent his youth producing this highly fantastic literature and shared the most imperialistic ideas of the time of Philip II. He volunteered for the navy and took part in the battle of Lepanto (1571), where he lost the use of an arm and became an invalid for the rest of his life. His writings were all in the style of the later Middle Ages until *Don Quixote* (1605). De Lollis argues that *Don Quixote* is mainly a satire of chivalric romances, and that Cervantes characterizes Don Quixote as a ridiculous knight errant who tries to live by the models in the romances he reads. De Lollis approves of the scenes in which the priest examines Don Quixote's library and condemns it to flames. De Lollis sees no sympathy on Cervantes's part for the ambitions and dreams of Don Quixote. The book appears to him an integral part of Cervantes's campaign against the fantastic chivalrous romantic literature which he himself produced for so many years. The whole of *Cervantes reazionario* consists of a description of Cervantes's writings, which go back to 1564. De Lollis not only describes these books but also studies them in the context of the times and with regard to their sources and analogues in earlier literature. De Lollis of course knows Pio Rajna's famous book on the sources of *Orlando furioso* and shows how Cervantes was simply saturated with this chivalric literature. To my mind, De Lollis's enormously learned book ignores what to modern readers is the most appealing feature of Cervantes's work, his sympathy and even love for Don Quixote. He is not simply the fool that the people around him make of him. In the end, De Lollis both minimizes Cervantes's sympathy for Don Quixote and exaggerates Sancho Panza's skepticism. While Sancho sometimes implicitly rejects Don Quixote's delusions or imaginings, at other times he seems to accept them; for example, when Sancho invents a special word for the supposed helmet that is actually a barber's basin: *baciyelmo*. De Lollis does not see the enormous difference between Cervantes's earlier writings and *Don Quixote*, which is a unique masterpiece completely removed from the thin and flimsy romances of the early years.

De Lollis's later writings are all extremely learned contributions to early medieval philology. He held a chair that was expressly limited to the early Middle Ages, and his writings mostly concern periods for which my own knowledge is completely inadequate to give anything like a critical account. The collection of essays by De Lollis called *Scrittori d'Italia* was assembled in 1948 by Gianfranco Contini and Vittorio Santoli. This large volume (more than six hundred pages) begins with a section devoted to early writers in the *dolce stil novo* and to the Provençal poet Sordello. The section contains also an elaborate discussion of Dante's faith in art and an attack on Giuseppe Toffanin's *La Fine dell'Umanesimo*. De Lollis convincingly destroys Toffanin's thesis, which tries to defend what we would call "Baroque," meaning the whole of Italian literature of the seventeenth and early eighteenth centuries. A chapter only remotely related to the main subject is devoted to a close study of Leopardi's Petrarchism. In the next large part of the book De Lollis shows how Manzoni's historical conception is rooted in the tradition of the French liberal historians of the Restoration, particularly Thierry. Manzoni is represented as believing in a complete determinism derived from the French. In the third section De Lollis studies the Italian poetic form of the late nineteenth century, including all the main Italian poets up to Carducci. There is a special chapter on the contacts of the Italian romanticists with German poetry, mainly Heine.

The appendix of *Scrittori d'Italia* reproduces an autobiographical article called "La Confessione di un figlio del secolo passato," which was originally printed in *Reisebilder e altri scritti* (1929). It tells of De Lollis's teachers, for instance, Domenico Comparetti, whose book *Virgilio nel medio evo* (1872) enjoyed great critical success in Germany. Theodor Mommsen praised it, and De Lollis notes parenthetically that "this was a time when one had to go to Germany in order to study Italian literature thoroughly" (*Reisebilder,* 132). De Lollis deplores, however, the extreme specialization of recent literary studies, not only in Italy: "Everybody has now a specialty, as they would have had one in medieval corporations" (136). De Lollis, himself a specialist of great erudition, deplores specialization and the current dislike of philosophy in literary studies. He is disturbed by the influx of women into literary studies because he believes that most of them are interested only in pedagogy and will lower the prestige of scholarship. De Lollis also deplores the spread of the requirement of a written thesis and ridicules an unidentified American who defended such trivial doctoral theses by saying that they "have ground out some peppercorn of truth" (144).

In a collection of articles on French subjects, first published in 1920 as *Saggi di letteratura francese,* De Lollis discusses the French sixteenth century and four of Corneille's plays, and then expends a great deal of effort to show that Manzoni drew on Chateaubriand's *Les Martyrs* (1809) for *I promessi sposi.* There are two further chapters on Lamartine and an essay identifying Musset as a classicist, which coming from De Lollis is no praise at all. He considers Musset a second-rate imitator, passive and lazy, and inferior even to Hugo, whom De Lollis does not value highly either, calling him "a bombastic orator" and "a childish sentimentalist."

As his students Contini and Santoli indicate, though De Lollis was partly influenced by Croce and De Sanctis, he was much more closely interested in the whole theory of relativism and historicism which he knew from German expositions. De Lollis was one of the first, at least in Italy, to worry about such problems as the second reading and how it differs from the first, or the influence of oral recitation on the reader or listener. He was also among the first to adapt the ideas of Heinrich Wölfflin to a study of literature, devising such contrasts as precision/imprecision, measure/dismeasure, equality/inequality, distinction/familiarity, and so on. De Lollis made an elaborate attempt to adapt Wölfflin's *Kunstgeschichtliche Grundbegriffe,* which he translated into Italian, to a study of literary stylistics. Finally, however, I have the impression that De Lollis did not really apply these oppositions he construed, that his ideal of stylistics, while critical of Spitzer, remained an unfulfilled, unrealized, distant aim. Still, De Lollis is rightly revered as a great, immensely learned scholar who had a clear commitment to historicism and, ultimately, to historical relativism.

EUGENIO MONTALE (1896–1981)

Eugenio Montale is generally considered the most eminent Italian poet of the twentieth century. Oddly enough, in earlier years his reputation was overshadowed by that of Quasimodo, who received the Nobel Prize for literature in 1959. Montale was apparently passed over because of his pronounced pro-Communism and possibly because of his general cultural pessimism, which at that time was listed as a prohibition against receiving the prize. Montale received the prize in 1975.

Montale came from Genoa and established his reputation as a poet in 1925 with the oddly titled collection *Ossa di seppia* (Cuttlefish bones). Montale was librarian of the Gabinetto Vieusseux in Florence for many years but was dismissed under the Mussolini regime and moved to Milan, where he became a prominent journalist. Beginning in 1948 he wrote the literary page for the daily *Corriere della Sera*, the most influential Italian newspaper. He thus produced a bulky body of criticism that has only partly been collected, mainly in a volume called *Sulla poesia* (1978). Montale reviewed and discussed almost every Italian book of any value for years, and his opinion carried considerable weight for other papers and other reviewers. It would be inappropriate in this context to examine what he wrote on every current Italian author. At best we can single out some of his excursions into English poetry or writings that might be of particular interest to an English-speaking audience.

Montale was interested in Ezra Pound and wrote about him over the years, both expounding his writings and criticizing his behavior during the war. His 1953 article seems the fullest account of five he wrote on Pound, whom Montale describes as a writer pretending or wanting to be a "primitive." With some irony, he treats Pound's message as if he thought of himself as the prophet of a new barbarism, even as a child, which to Pound was the necessary condition of poetry. Montale gives a reasonable account of Pound's literary background, particularly his reading in a truncated edition of Whitman. He describes the *Pisan Cantos* as a "flashing recapitulation of world history (one world's history) without any link or relationship of time or space" (*SLA*, 207). These comments are supplemented by a brief obituary in 1972 which praises Pound's early imagistic writings, particularly the volume *Personae*. Montale reflects reasonably that Pound's so-called insanity was "a happy invention of those who wished to save him from the electric chair" (284). Montale generously explains Pound's sympathies for the Fascist regime as deriving from his hatred of what he called "usury," the whole economics of capitalism. His personal impression was that Pound was a profoundly good man who succumbed to the game with words, the reduction of the facts of history to mere fireworks.

But Pound was not Montale's only discovery. He met Ettore Schmitz, from Trieste, who later, partly because of Montale's propaganda, became famous as the author Italo Svevo. Montale induced him to publish, or rather republish, the books known as *Senilità* and *La Coscienza di Zeno*. To my mind, Montale grossly overrates Svevo if he is evaluated in a European context. But as an Italian novelist he has permanent appeal as a psycho-analytical psychologist and as a portrayer of the inhabitants of Austrian and later Italian Trieste and their often uncertain national allegiance.

Montale's interest in Pound apparently stimulated him to get ac-quainted with modern English poetry, and he became one of the first promoters of T. S. Eliot. In 1950 Montale was in London and attended a reading of Eliot's poetry. He then called on Eliot in the London office of the publishing firm Faber and Faber. Strangely, Montale notes that Eliot's "reserve which he also imposes on others . . . prevents me from revealing the nature of our conversation" (*SLA*, 179). Montale was deeply impressed by Eliot's public reading of the *Four Quartets*. Recognizing the deficiency of Eliot's elocution, Montale still considers it a miracle, "an inner read-ing performed aloud" (179). He comments on the concept of "objective correlative" and compares Eliot to Cubist painters who "attempt to con-trast objects that will admit feeling without declaring it." Montale has his doubts about Eliot's classicism, remarking that "to say 'I am a classic' is already to admit that you are not one." Surprisingly, Montale likes Eliot's dramas and reviewed a performance of *The Cocktail Party*. Montale con-siders the English theater a cultural institution, whereas the theater in Italy is a "practical joke" (184).

W. H. Auden also attracted Montale's interest. Auden wrote the libretto for Stravinsky's opera *The Rake's Progress*, which was performed in Venice in 1952 and reviewed by Montale. He does not pay attention to the music at all. While admitting Auden's "true gift for the musical impromptu," Montale treats him as a "cosmopolitan poet in every sense of the word." Auden's poetry is "gnomic, satirical, discursive, eloquent and very often (why not say it?) prosaic." Montale likes his *Age of Anxiety* and the poem "In the Time of War" and asks, "Can a too elegant poet also be a man in despair?" But he qualifies this, saying, "In him the comic muse came forth from the tragic muse and overcame her."

In Montale's further excursions into English and American poetry he comments at some length on Emily Dickinson, in whom he sees "a vir-ile soul" (*SP*, 440), and on an unknown poet, Henry Furst, who lived in Rome and published his poetry in elegant private editions with designs by Leonetta Cecchi. Montale acknowledges Edgar Lee Masters, whose *Spoon River Anthology*, oddly enough, was translated in toto into Italian. He also discusses D. H. Lawrence favorably as a poet, with reference to the criticism of F. R. Leavis.

Montale's comments on English and American poetry contrast with his clearly distant and even reluctant interest in French poetry. He analyzes in detail St. John Perse's *Anabase*, but his comments on Valéry, René Char, and other French poets are almost always unfavorable. Montale is repelled by Valéry, whom he describes as "a prodigious recapitulator" in the "tradition of preciosity and obscurity" (*SLA*, 158), though he does in passing praise Valéry's notes on the painter Corot.

On occasion Montale reaches even further, writing on Chinese poems (in the English translation of Arthur Waley) and on the Greek poet Constantine Cafavy. He wrote extensively on Italian poetry, of course, discussing dozens of poets whose names are now unfamiliar or totally obscure, but also the Italian classics. "Dante Yesterday and Today" (1962) is a long, well-informed report on Dante scholarship, which Montale disparages as dilettantish. The essay quickly surveys the history of Dante's reputation since the Middle Ages and then discusses the question of relativism and absolutism. Montale sees both as extremes. We cannot transform ourselves into men of the thirteenth century, and yet we cannot read Dante simply "as a modern poet, selecting the most vivid parts and leaving aside the rest" (*SLA*, 138). Montale considers this view most persuasively expounded by Croce in *La Poesia di Dante* (1914). Montale comments perceptively on the different styles that entered into the making of the *Divine Comedy*. He states that "no other poem has actual history and the atemporal history of myth or theology so closely fused" (*SLA*, 147). Montale disapproves of what he considers the excesses of the philosophical commentators, always rather emphasizing Dante's concreteness and his stretches of narrative. He recognizes Dante's didactic aim, drawing also on modern poets, the romantics, who knew Dante. Dante, according to Montale, was not a true mystic. Montale seems to accept the view that Dante invented himself as a "holy poet" and "at a certain moment with the help of forces greater than himself saw his invention become reality." A resolutely secular man, Montale says he has no evidence with which to contest the miraculous nature of the poem, as true poetry is always in the nature of a gift and presupposes the worthiness of its recipient (154).

Montale also writes well on Leopardi and, with many reservations, on D'Annunzio. He disliked the application of the term *decadence* to late-nineteenth-century Italian literature and would prefer to restrict it to certain French authors, like Huysmans. *Decadence* is a pejorative word, whereas *naturalism* and *modernism* are acceptable descriptions of trends in modern literature.

The bewildering variety and enormous scope of Montale's writings, particularly on poetry, should not obscure the essential center of his convictions, the firmness of his opinions, and the general sanity of his theoretical outlook. Montale is an ardent defender of simplicity and clarity and an enemy of irrationalist methodologies. He thinks of criticism largely as "reading," *lettura*—I would say "close reading"—though this close reading must be supplemented by what he calls "framing," meaning an interest in history and in the social milieu, which Montale conceives in the widest terms as the whole of Western civilization. This criticism demands from the critic a personal engagement and even justifies a serious participation in contemporary life. Montale for a time professed to be a Communist and after the war was appointed a Communist senator. This demand for clarity, for rooting criticism in the eighteenth-century Enlightenment, is oddly emphasized by Montale's insistence that modern poetry be "intense and obscure" and that it be looked at as an almost physical object. While looked at from the outside as a text, the work, however paradoxically, is still capable of expressing values that Montale describes in terms of "the exaltation of the virtue not only of the people but also of the search for and the discovery of the integral soul of man which is a fact of culture and civilization no less than of nature." Finally it is man that counts, not the beautiful, the imminent end, the sense of a crisis that is coming. Its gloom and terror are compensated by a "hope that burns more slowly than a hard log on the hearth" (Carpi, 2:3445). Montale, so morose on the whole, maintains this faith in the value of poetry, philosophy, and all the higher endeavors of man. The gloomy Montale continued to hope that despite ages of destruction and darkness the *bouteille à la mer* will reach the shore and be found again.

PART III   SPANISH CRITICISM
1900–1950

IN DEVISING THE SCHEME OF THESE VOLUMES, I have postponed and possibly minimized the Spanish share in criticism. I have taken too seriously Azorín's statement in "El Artista y el estilo" (*Obras completas,* 8:835): "We Spaniards have many scholars but not a critic. What is a critic? A man who is equipped with literary experience, who can above all conceive a central idea and system which permits him to articulate a total organic concept of the work of an author and the literature of a period. This criticism will have to serve, moreover, internal interpretation and psychological use." In Ortega, a generation later, we find similar expressions of admiration for scholars like Menéndez y Pelayo and Menéndez Pidal and a low opinion of literary criticism in Spain and of literary criticism in general. With this in mind, I thought it wise to discuss in detail three critics—Azorín, Ortega y Gasset, and Dámaso Alonso—and to glance more briefly at others who are predominantly historians of literature or even of politics and society. Américo Castro stands out among the historians with literary interests.

19 : AMÉRICO CASTRO (1885–1972)

AMÉRICO CASTRO'S REPUTATION is largely based on his book *España en su historia* (1948), an enormously learned history of Spain in the Middle Ages. Castro argues that the Spanish nation was deeply influenced by the long Moorish occupation in the south and by the role of the intellectual Jews who produced so much of the written work until their expulsion in 1492. He asserts that the extreme anti-intellectualism of the Spaniards is due to the loss of the Jewish element. Primarily a detailed history of Spain in the Middle Ages, the book has only small episodes of literary criticism. Castro interprets the *Poema del Cid* more or less in the manner of Menéndez Pidal, but goes much further, radically rejecting any attempt to make the poem something like a collective labor. He believes it was the work of a single author, which was then adopted by the public. In his discussion of *La Celestina* Castro emphasizes the fact that the author, Fernando de Rojas, was a Jew who was expelled in 1492 and went to Genoa.

Castro was also a literary critic of great range and learning, mainly on topics suggested by his theories about the coming together of Spain in the late Middle Ages. One of the essays collected in *An Idea of History* (1977) is clearly a contribution to comparative literature. "The Presence of the Sultan Saladin in the Romance Literatures" (1954) is an investigation of the image of Sultan Saladin in French, Italian, and Spanish literature. The long essay reflects Castro's extensive reading in the most obscure corners of medieval literature, in chronicles, ballads, and pamphlets, and argues convincingly that whereas the Spanish discussions of Saladin are tolerant and understanding, those of the French are dogmatic and rationalistic. This essay seems an exception in Castro's miscellaneous writings. He also wrote elaborately on Cervantes, both in the large book *El Pensamiento de Cervantes* (1925) and in minor pieces. "Cervantes y Pirandello" (1924) argues surprisingly that Cervantes was what the Germans describe as a writer who constantly breaks the illusion of writing and tells you that he is the author of a fiction. He can, for instance, make a figure simply disappear or die, or change his behavior completely in opposition to what he had done before, or even change the color of his eyes and hair. In referring to Pirandello, Castro must have been aware that he knew the Germans and for a time studied in Germany, as did Castro himself. Castro comments at length on the scene in which Don Quixote and Sancho are surprised and puzzled to find a book written by someone named Avellaneda that purports to be the continuation of their adventures.

Castro also wrote an ambitious essay called "The Baroque as Literary Style," which was, of course, stimulated by the many German attempts to discuss the term at that time. In Castro's unusually wide and undefined terms, the style becomes a description of all Spanish writings from the Renaissance up to the Enlightenment. Castro is very sympathetic to the new attempts to revive the Baroque style, which he often understands simply as rhetorical, ornamental, and highly argumentative. This essay on the Baroque is somewhat unusual for Castro in the interest shown in language and in words. Words and phrases are, however, among Castro's main preoccupations in his late writings, in particular the study of what he called the "vital dwelling place of history," a term which should not be confused with ordinary historical consciousness. According to Castro, this "vital dwelling place" is not a specific time. It is a historical concept which is finally a value concept, a demand for feeling a collectivity that is not turned to the past but directed toward the future. Castro wants to distinguish this attitude from the "spirit of a nation." He rejects the German concept violently, as it leads, he argues, to acceptance of any and all events and values, to complete relativism. Castro recommends something we might call "philosophy of life," existentialism in the sense of Kierkegaard. The emphasis is entirely on man's experience, sympathetic understanding, and penetration of life. Castro rejects all relativism, which does not recognize a hierarchy of values. A history, he asserts, can be written only with such a hierarchy in mind.

All of Castro's main works reflect this feeling of hierarchy. His many books cover a wide range of subjects, beginning with a life of Lope de Vega in 1919, which was followed by the large, detailed *El Pensamiento de Cervantes* and such thematic studies as his monograph on the drama of honor in Spain (1961) and one on spiritualism, messianism, and personal activity from the fourteenth through the sixteenth century in Spain (1949), as well as his book *Iberoamérica* (1941). Though not primarily a literary scholar, Américo Castro must be admired for the breadth of his interest in many literary subjects, mainly in Spain. He is one of the most impressive Spanish scholars after Menéndez y Pelayo and Menéndez Pidal.

THE 1898 WAR between Spain and the United States, which the Spanish sometimes call the Cuban War and in which they lost their empire, is generally considered a turning point in Spanish history and intellectual development. The so-called generation of 1898, which includes the poet Antonio Machado, did not produce any real literary critic, though a slightly younger contemporary, Miguel de Unamuno, became famous with his book *Vida de Don Quijote y Sancho Panza* (1905).

Miguel de Unamuno y Jugo was born in Bilbao in the Basque country, of a Basque father and a Spanish mother. Early on he went to Madrid, where he studied at the university and became an excellent Greek scholar. He was appointed professor of Greek at the University of Salamanca and advanced quickly to become its rector in 1900. In his scattered publications before the *Don Quixote* book, Unamuno caused a great stir with his attacks on *casticismo*, the dominance of the Castilian center over other regions such as the Basque. He became a deputy in the Cortes and played a considerable role in the opposition to the dictator General Primo de Rivera. I will not enter into this complicated history of Spanish politics, except to say that in 1924 Unamuno was banished to one of the Canary Islands, from which he was rescued by political friends and brought to France. He lived for a time in Hendaye, the French Basque town nearest the Spanish frontier. In 1931, when Spain was declared a republic, Unamuno was reappointed rector of the University of Salamanca, where he taught until the outbreak of the civil war. Unamuno sided in the beginning with the Franco faction, but soon reversed himself and died a few months later on 31 December 1936. His fame at that time was mainly due to his philosophical work, especially his book *Del sentimiento trágico de la vida* (1913). His point of view has often been considered an early version of existentialism.

I am not sure that the *Don Quixote* book can be called literary criticism in any strict sense, but it has been so influential in the history of *Quixote* criticism that it cannot be ignored. It is hardly criticism if that is defined as an attempt to find the real meaning of a work of art. It is almost a novel about a novel, apparently in the tradition of German romantic irony, which Unamuno may have known mainly through his friend Luigi Pirandello, who had studied in Germany. *Vida de Don Quijote y Sancho Panza* is deliberately contradictory. On the one hand, it is preoccupied with the myth of Don Quixote, which Unamuno expounds in an introductory essay called "The Sepulchre of Don Quixote," wherein the Spaniards are asked to find Don Quixote's tomb. After many wanderings, they have to conclude that there is no tomb, that they must think of Don Quixote only as the incarnation of the Spanish mind. Unamuno belongs to those writers and scholars who are keenly aware of the role of the author, who can decide to let a fictional character die or suddenly reverse his behavior completely. Yet Unamuno attempts to reconstruct Don Quixote's life as if he were a real person, called in his time Quiñana. Unamuno expresses mock annoyance at the dearth of any information about Quixote's youth before he set off on his first foray with Sancho Panza. These two contradictory conceptions—Don Quixote as a national myth and Don Quixote as a historical personality—are further complicated by Unamuno's insistence on drawing parallels between Don Quixote's life and the life of the founder of the Jesuit order, Ignatius of Loyola. In these often forced parallels, Unamuno gives vent to his own strong anticlericalism and to his own religious beliefs, which were grounded in a belief in God but were vigorously antidogmatic and occasionally blasphemous.

Unamuno retells the whole story of *Don Quixote*, constantly referring to the text, which at that time must have been familiar to all university and even high school students in Spain. He distorts the events and sometimes develops or parodies them. He inserts long meditations of his own, suddenly referring to a chapter in the book or to a saying by Sancho or Don Quixote. Only with great difficulty could one distinguish between Unamuno's correct and his deliberately incorrect interpretations of individual chapters. Unamuno can be seen as a forerunner of some of the newest trends in American criticism, which advocate "creative misunderstanding." But while it sometimes completely departs from the book we know, it can also suddenly address the author (Unamuno) or the reader. Unamuno is aware of such problems as reader response, the difference between first and second readings, and the whole question of our preconceptions when sitting before a book called a "novel" or a "poem" or a "play." Unamuno thus occasionally anticipates several recently debated questions, particularly by German students of novelistic technique.

The book contains perceptive discussions of the relationship between Don Quixote and Sancho Panza, as when Unamuno reflects on the episode in which Don Quixote pretends or rather believes that a barber's basin is a helmet. Sancho, who is a man of common sense, recognizes it as a barber's basin but keeps faith with his master by taking refuge in the verbal coinage that it is a basin-helmet. Unamuno likes and admires this synthesis of empirical truth and fantasy. He interprets the scene as Don Quixote's savoring of defeat and attempt to turn disaster into victory. Unamuno alludes here to Spain's apparent attempt to turn defeat into an occasion for reform and even rebirth. He strongly supported the effort to restore Spain to its former greatness. He sees that this cannot be achieved without modern technology. Unamuno distrusts the new technology deeply but admits that Spain cannot return to a preindustrial age, that it needs roads and railways, cars and buses. Still, he is often horrified by the devastation he sees imposed by the modern age on the genuine Spanish peasant, who in Unamuno's view may be ignorant but has a deep ethical commitment to his nation and to his property. This is why Unamuno rejects socialism, as it aims to deprive men of their independence and individual quality. Unamuno is very concerned with religion, which for him is centered on the question of man's survival after death, his immortality. All Unamuno's writings are permeated by the question of immortality, and every writer he discusses is judged according to whether he is preoccupied with the same question. Unamuno must be viewed largely as a religious figure, possibly—at least in ambition—as a prophet who wants to determine the path his nation will take. While warning against a rash Europeanization and preaching a return to old values, he recognizes the need for change and acknowledges that, in many ways, the past is obsolete and cannot be restored. *Vida de Don Quijote* is a tract of the times, a call to an examination of Spanish feelings and ideals.

21 : MARCELINO MENÉNDEZ Y PELAYO (1856–1912) AND RAMÓN MENÉNDEZ PIDAL (1869–1968)

TWO GREAT SCHOLARS HAVE DOMINATED Spain's literary scene. Though literary historians rather than critics, they both indulged in criticism, if by that we mean judgments on contemporary writers and books. Marcelino Menéndez y Pelayo ruled the literary scene at the end of the nineteenth century and during the first decade of the twentieth century. He can be described as a one-man importer of European ideas into Spain. The *Historia de las ideas estéticas* (1883–91), for instance, provides literal translations of writers like Schiller, Kant, and Hegel without any kind of comment or clearly stated point of view. From what I have seen of Menéndez y Pelayo, I would class him as an importer and cultural mediator in his time, but he also wrote essays on current writers which I'm afraid I cannot judge.

Ramón Menéndez Pidal, who died three months before his hundredth birthday, was one of the most eminent medievalists not only in Spain but in the world. His edition of the *Poema del Cid* and studies of the *romancero* were the foundation for his large book on medieval Spain. Menéndez Pidal belongs to the school of anthropologists who derive all early epic poetry from oral poetry, from popular legends and traditions. Throughout his life Menéndez Pidal collected ballads and songs from all over Spain. On his wedding trip he heard by chance an old woman in Asturias singing a ballad that reflected events dating as far back as the eleventh century. Menéndez Pidal devoted a great deal of effort to proving that there was a long folk tradition in Spain that led finally to the *Poema del Cid*. His critical edition of the poem, *Cantar de mio Cid* (1908–12), is based on the unique manuscript of the *Cid*, which was then in the possession of his uncle, the marqués de Pidal. In the edition Menéndez Pidal seeks to reconstruct a hypothetical tradition of folk poetry in Spain by arguing at length for the survival of grammatical forms and syntactical configurations dating from the eleventh century, which he believed was when Spanish was established as a literary language and began to be used in the courts and law offices. Much of Menéndez Pidal's work is philological. In his history of the Spanish language, *Los Orígenes del español* (1926), he tries to trace it back as far as the Visigoths. On the whole he ignores or minimizes Spanish contacts with the French and the Italians, even in later periods. One of his last books is a history of references to the *Cid* throughout Spanish literature up to the late nineteenth century. Here Menéndez Pidal examines in detail José Zorilla's nineteen thousand-line epic poem on the Cid, *Leyenda del Cid* (1882), tracking down the sources of all the allusions and events that Zorilla took either from the poem itself or from medieval and later sources. This is a history of a theme, with little interest in questions of criticism in the sense of judgment. Menéndez Pidal must have known that Zorilla was an inferior poet; he is merely interested in the survival of the name and the events of the *Cid*.

Menéndez Pidal's most important work was, of course, his critical edition of the *Cid*. The poem has been interpreted as the labor of a singer of that time, a theory Menéndez Pidal would not have disputed. His main interest is in reconstructing the Spanish epic tradition, which implicitly rejects the theories espoused largely by the followers of the French scholar Joseph Bédier (1864–1938). Bédier's book *Légendes épiques* (1908–13) sees the epic tradition as the work of individual poets and the *Chanson de Roland* as the work of a genius, totally inexplicable by any study of sources and backgrounds. When I was a student at the University of Prague, the Professor of Comparative Literature there, Václav Tille, went even further in endorsing the individualistic tradition of Bédier. He brushed aside all folk traditions as irrelevant to the production of poems like the *Cid* or the *Chanson de Roland*. Scholars like Bédier and Tille reacted strongly against the German glorification of the folk and its creativity. More recent English studies—Colin Smith's is the best-known—have argued that the *Poema del Cid* cannot be reduced to folk conventions, as it contains allusions to legal terms and seals. The defenders of Menéndez Pidal, however, interpret these as later additions by clerical scribes which do not refute the general folk origins of the Spanish epic. Menéndez Pidal's edition brings together a large body of linguistic and factual evidence to support his theory of an indigenous Spanish epic tradition. He must be honored as the protagonist of this view, which has also greatly influenced Spaniards' pride in their distant past.

22 : AZORÍN (JOSÉ MARTÍNEZ RUIZ) (1873–1967)

THE MOST EMINENT SPANISH CRITIC of the late nineteenth and early twentieth centuries was Azorín, the pseudonym of José Martínez Ruiz. (*Azorín* seems to combine a reference to *azor,* meaning "hawk," with a reference to *azorar,* "to confound, to excite.") Martínez Ruiz began as a journalist and even edited a humorous magazine called *Charivari,* which was suppressed by the government in 1897. When his publishing career was interrupted, Martínez Ruiz turned to what could be called philosophy, in practice a popularization of Schopenhauer's pessimism. Azorín eventually turned to serious philosophizing and became known as *pequeño filósofo,* or "little philosopher," both because he was small in size and because he treated his philosophy with irony. His philosophizing was mainly expressed in novels that only slightly concealed their autobiographical content. These novels established a solid reputation for Azorín.

Only comparatively late in his career did Azorín start to write literary criticism. His most widely publicized series of articles were devoted to the generation of 1898, which he apparently delimited decisively. His article "The Two Generations" (1910) defined the 1898 generation and listed Valle-Inclán, Benavente, Baroja, Maeztu, Unamuno, and Rubén Darío as its members. Azorín saw these new writers as the beginning of a revival of Spanish literature in the wake of the Spanish-American War. Azorín fits Spain's defeat into a philosophy of history, where he distinguishes between great periods of expansion and periods of constriction. After the defeat, Spanish culture turned inward and built up unconsciously a newly conceived spirit of Spain. This "spirit of Spain" must not be confused with the German *Volksgeist.* In Azorín's conception it is an ideal which Spain hopes to reach and fulfill. Much of his writing is concerned with defining the Spanish spirit, which he always prefers to the spirit of France or Italy. Azorín could be a target of Leo Spitzer's frequent attacks on what he called "national tautology": If you are great, you are Spanish, and if you are Spanish, you are great.

Azorín, however, has a concrete knowledge of the history of Spanish literature, particularly of the period 1850–1950. He has a low opinion

of the Enlightenment, which he considers shallow, and attacks its representatives, Voltaire and Rousseau. He also detests romanticism, especially
in Spain. He criticizes the extravagant figure Larra as empty, vainglori-
ous, and bombastic—adjectives Azorín uses also for foreigners like Victor
Hugo, whom he detests as "a pompous and impious rhetorician." The
new Spanish literature is, for him, personified mainly in the novelist Pío
Baroja, whom Azorín knew intimately and admired as the greatest Spanish author since the Golden Age. Azorín also appreciates writers who
change their outlook over time. He invented a whole theory which makes
a distinction between writers who are stable and possibly monotonous
and those who change with the times in a wavelike evolution. Those who
change are sometimes simply thrown about by external events and circumstances. Azorín is insistent on the impact of external events, both
political and social. His early writings especially often reflect the influence of Marxism and a general view that literature is a mirror of society,
although it is not completely mirrorlike—that is, the mirror can be distorting or convex and the author and the audience may see completely
different aspects of reality.

Azorín, like many critics, makes sharp distinctions among genres. Spanish literature has a thin but brilliant tradition of lyricism, which differs
completely from the quite separate tradition of the novel. Azorín picked
up evolutionary theories from French critics like Brunetière and Hennequin which he applies to Spanish literature with great freedom. In
his seventy disparate books, we can find almost every kind of reflection
on history and literature. He would argue, for instance, that Spanish
literature is mainly "ocular": "We have seen and not been able to rise
above visible reality," a tragedy he finds peculiar to Spain (Obras completas, 2:900–02). But in other contexts he admires Spain precisely for its
transcendental ambitions and tastes. Azorín studied psychology and philosophy, particularly the whole tradition of positivism and the peculiar
Spanish version of German Herbartism known as Krausismo. But he has
not worked out a truly systematic philosophical point of view. Azorín's
main importance lies rather in his formulation of the concept of generations and particularly of the 1898 generation. This generation is conceived not in exact chronological terms but as having been inspired by
the ideal of the "new Spain"—ready to emerge from the defeat as a new
force in literature—with the poet almost prophesying the resurgence of
Spain. As a practical critic Azorín has surveyed the whole body of Spanish
literature with a specific taste and a sharply defined hierarchy of values,
not only aesthetic but also social and political. He remains one of the two
or three most impressive Spanish critics.

23 : *SALVADOR DE MADARIAGA Y ROJO*
(1886–1978)

SALVADOR DE MADARIAGA WAS MARRIED to an English woman and lived for many years in England, where he stayed after the toppling of the royal regime in Spain. The remarkable title essay from his book *Shelley and Calderón* (1920) demonstrates convincingly that in *The Cenci* Shelley used a passage from one of Calderón's *autos,* closely following several lines and ending with a literal translation of Calderón's conclusion: "The melancholy mountain yawns" (El monte melancólico bosteza; 35). Madariaga astutely develops the relation between Shelley and Calderón, often on what seems very slight evidence. The volume also contains an essay called "The Case of Wordsworth," in which Madariaga trounces Wordsworth ruthlessly. He cannot convince, as he did not know the early versions of much of Wordsworth's poetry and, on the whole, has only a feeble grasp of Wordsworth's development and setting.

Madariaga's *Englishmen, Frenchmen, Spaniards* (1928; 2d ed., 1969) is a bold attempt at generalization based in most cases on ordinary folklore: the French are reasonable, the English are utilitarian and interested in money and power, and the Spaniards are people of passion. There is a chapter on art with the usual stereotypes, always *ad majorem gloriam* of Spain and the Spaniards. Art in Spain is "more a gift of nature than a conquest of man. It is genius rather than talent. . . . The contrast between the strength of its creative genius and the weakness of its critical talent is the key-note of Spanish artistic development" (196). Madariaga emphasizes the preoccupation with color among Spanish painters and writers. We hear, for instance, that there is no landscape in Spanish art; it always concentrates on man: "Every man is wholly himself" (199). Spanish art is extremely individualistic. The main point of this chapter is to attack French art and literature as rationalistic, while noting that the work of art in England supposedly "must tell a story," the artist "must hand over something tangible, substantial" (206). In England, writers like Wordsworth, positive in his morality, and Oscar Wilde, defiant amoralist, are exceptions, they stand out. The French have no single great writer, no giants; they have no geniuses but simply talents. The book is, again, a display of Madariaga's wit and eloquence, but primarily indulges in stereotyping and hardly deserves mention in a history of criticism.

Madariaga's book *On Hamlet* (1948; 2d ed., 1964) has, I believe, hardly been noticed in the literature on Shakespeare. This neglect is probably due to the fact that the small book was first published in 1948 with a little-known publisher, Hollis and Carter, and later by Frank Cass, neither of whom did much to publicize the book. It is, however, an impressive performance, extremely well written and clearly argued. Madariaga knows the literature on *Hamlet*. He refers to A. C. Bradley and Dover Wilson, as well as to Elmer Edgar Stoll and Levin Schücking. He argues, I think clearly and effectively, for a concept of Hamlet as a decisive and even aggressive young man, considering his relationships with Rosencrantz and Guildenstern, with Polonius, and with Ophelia. Without entering the thicket of conflicting interpretations, Madariaga has convincingly refuted the traditional, though by no means only, view of Hamlet as a melancholy weakling. He also recognizes, however, that Hamlet is unhappy and that he procrastinates. Madariaga sees the other side, but does not succeed in reconciling these two views of Hamlet. His rejection of the "idealization of Hamlet's moral sensibility" (98) makes sense, but then he admits that Hamlet's ambition is frustrated and that melancholy "lends a somber background to the play." Hamlet "is ever wandering in that zone of disenchanted boredom, yet of attraction and tension towards others, to be expected of his inner contradiction—refusal to give himself to the world of men—need of the world of men" (106). Madariaga thus assures us that there is "no mystery about Hamlet" (107). He leaves us simply with contradictions, which are not illuminated by farfetched speculations about Shakespeare's supposed disappointment and frustrations (129).

Madariaga's main Spanish collection of critical essays is called *De Galdós a Lorca* (1960). The first section of the volume begins with two chapters on the general character of Spanish literature. They repeat what had been argued before, mainly by Américo Castro—that Spain is a country with a few great geniuses such as Cervantes, Velázquez, and Calderón, whose followers are of less interest. The main point of the two articles, however, is to set apart Spanish literature from French literature. Madariaga constantly describes French literature in stereotypical terms as extremely rationalistic and unimaginative, whereas Spanish literature is the greatest of all literatures with its geniuses and peaks. Madariaga sees a severe imbalance between the creative faculty and the critical faculty of the Spanish people. He ridicules a taste that cannot distinguish between Ibsen and Lehár. Spanish literature is also in general extremely impartial and often deeply religious, its greatest works having been inspired by religious enthusiasm. These two essays are followed by a long piece on the popular poetry of Spain, which Madariaga values highly as genuinely reaching down to the depths of popular feeling.

The second section of the volume consists of smaller essays on the main Spanish authors. Madariaga emphasizes Spain's preeminence as the country of the drama and the novel. The novel's greatest representative is Benito Pérez Galdós, who is a wonderful depicter, without prejudices, of Spain in the nineteenth century. Madariaga's sketches of individual authors display considerable acuteness of observation and psychological penetration: for example, he admires Unamuno as a popular philosopher, "popular" meaning a philosopher who is not a professional and manages to express the deepest feelings of the country's soul in the language of the people. Madariaga's essay on Azorín and Gabriel Miró portrays them as extremely similar. He refers to these two writers as Spanish "impressionists." Azorín is a "genuine miniature painter." The volume concludes with an essay on Federico García Lorca, whom Madariaga greatly admires. He tells of Lorca's appearance at his home when Madariaga was apparently absent; Lorca simply made himself at home with Madariaga's wife in the house and the next day suddenly set sail for New York, the beginning of his strange experience in America.

Madariaga has acquired a reputation as a Spanish eccentric, due partly to his discussion and edition of *Hamlet* but also to his deeply personal comments and meditations. But he is a serious writer and, as the essays in *De Galdós a Lorca* testify, a genuine critic, who because of his distance from the Spanish metropolis and the whole literary milieu has received much less attention than he deserves. *De Galdós a Lorca* was in fact published in Buenos Aires, which he visited in the course of his world travels. Madariaga has dropped out of the mainstream of Spanish criticism. Perhaps he requires some restitution.

24 : JORGE GUILLÉN (1893–1984)

JORGE GUILLÉN WAS ONE OF THE MOST EMINENT Spanish poets of the twentieth century. He belonged to the group loosely called the generation of 1927, but he was really quite an independent entity. His poems were collected under the title *Cántico*. When the Spanish civil war broke out, Guillén fled first to France and then to the United States, where he was Mellon Professor at the University of Pittsburgh and later taught at Wellesley College. In 1957–58 he was invited to be the Charles Eliot Norton Lecturer on Poetry at Harvard University. The lectures were published in English in 1961 as *Language and Poetry: Some Poets of Spain* and in Spanish the following year. They are well-argued discussions of the main figures in the tradition of verse poetry in Spain. The first lecture is devoted to Gonzalo de Berceo, a verse chronicler of the first half of the thirteenth century. Guillén illustrates Berceo's use of prosaic language in verse with many persuasive examples. Berceo's precise language is totally free of any aspiration to be embellished poetry. Guillén shows convincingly how Berceo—a clerk, not a monk, attached to the monastery of San Millán de la Cogolla—lived in a completely isolated world. He treated the figures of Christ and the Virgin Mary as if they were his neighbors, with no pretense of devotion to a supernatural God or saint. One might think they were people one meets in daily life. Berceo fulfills his duty as a believer by telling his story about God and the Virgin in quite simple early Spanish. Guillén contrasts this simple prosaic language with that of Rimbaud, who called himself "a magician or an angel."

The second lecture presents a comparative contrast by discussing the poetic language of Luis de Góngora. The most difficult and elaborate of all the Spanish poets of the late sixteenth and early seventeenth centuries, Góngora constructed a language like "an enigmatic object" (*Language and Poetry*, 29). In his interpretation of often difficult passages, Guillén shows how Góngora quite deliberately not only invented words but constructed his poems as if they were "edifices of words" (34). He is, in Guillén's view, the greatest verbal genius in the Spanish language. He planned his poems within the mythological tradition of antiquity, often basing them on complex allusions to stories like those of Ulysses and of Polyphemus, which he used as a starting point for his greatest work, the *Soledades* (1613). Guillén gives examples from other poems to illustrate Góngora's method of continuous and persistent metaphors, allusions, and symmetries. He argues that Góngora's manner is far removed from anything like modern "hermetic" techniques. He compares Góngora with Mallarmé, who said that he created his work "only by elimination," whereas Góngora created his work by constant embellishment. Góngora begins by offering us "an enigma," but this enigma often "dissolves our reading into separate moments that progress too slowly." We have to struggle with his language, which is different from our ordinary language. Góngora aims at what Guillén calls "purity," but his purity is cruel: "The poet wishes to create a poem wrought of genuine elements, only the most genuine, and this intransigent severity must operate during the whole course of the poem, always on the same high level of poetry that is poetry" (74).

The third lecture, "The Ineffable Language of Mysticism," is a study of the great Spanish mystical poet St. John of the Cross. Guillén first produces three poems by St. John which he considers the culmination of Spanish poetry, and he presents them without saying that they are anything other than ecstatic love poems. The most famous, *Noche oscura del alma,* as it was later entitled, does not allude to anything spiritual. This is even more true of the second poem, *Cántico espiritual,* which is simply an ecstatic love poem, in which the lovers are shepherds, and "the eagerness of the Bride takes her by sheep-folds and river banks, through woods and meadows," until at last the lovers are united (84). We are told that they consummate their love, and the Bridegroom "adores [the Bride] and watches over her sleep" (85). The third poem, *Llama de amor viva,* which is only a short postscript, is "all astounded exclamation and fire, fire that illumines love while it burns in it" (86). Only after expounding the poems does Guillén refer to St. John's commentary in which he allegorizes the love scenes, making them a mystical experience of the union between the soul and God. Guillén is impatient with any attempts to interpret these poems in terms of "an all-important subconscious" (99). He thinks that even the undeniable allegorical meaning that the author wanted us to find is an inadequate description of a profound experience, in which the religious sense is not hidden or veiled but provides a sort of spiritual accompaniment that is nonetheless not conceptual: "An air is insinuated into the verses that gives them a significance at once human and divine" (116). Guillén closes by relating how St. John, shortly before he died in 1591, remembered the lines of his *Cántico espiritual,* saying:

"Rejoice, my love, with me / And in your beauty see us both reflected" (120). Guillén's admiration sometimes seems extravagant, for example, when he describes the line "Let us enter deeper into the thicket" (Entremos más adentro en la espesura) as "among the best, perhaps the best, in the Spanish language" (121).

The fourth lecture, devoted to the romantic Spanish poet Gustavo Adolfo Bécquer (1836–70), describes him much from the point of view of German romantic poetry. Guillén has obviously read and refers to Béguin's book *L'Ame romantique et le rêve*. He sees the German romantics' meditations on dreams and dreaming as the background to Bécquer's poems. Bécquer seems much more sentimental, however, saying, for instance, that "love is poetry, and religion is love" (131). "Woman, emotion, poetry" form the "essential trinity" (132). Guillén, expounding Bécquer with great sympathy for his devotion to the ineffable, describes him as a "visionary," noting that the "world of visions—profane ecstasies—still holds its magic for us" (156). Guillén regards Bécquer as a precursor of the most recent Spanish poets.

In the fifth lecture, "Adequate Language," Guillén selects Gabriel Miró as the most representative of these recent poets, a poet who created a strange concrete language which he considered to somehow precede the poem: "'Awareness of things,' Miró believes, is given us 'under the influence of the word'" (162). Language comes first; the names of things achieve full value as images. Guillén finds Miró's obsession with place-names significant: "Ibi, Tibi, Famorca, Benisa, Jávea—these names of villages in Alicante would intoxicate Miró as if they were solid substances that nourish and fortify him" (164). Not only a writer but a strange sportsman, Miró tells us: "I walk, tramp, climb mountains, scramble over the rocks and sands of the seashore, cross the fields, hear the roar of my blood like a torrent inside me; and when I cannot go any further, I lie on the ground looking up at the sky" (166). His writings are full of concrete landscapes, plants and animals, birds, lizards, gardens. He always acts by submerging himself in the exact recollection of sensation, one's own genuine sensation. He could be labeled an extreme impressionist and also a lover of nature, particularly animals. The cruelty of nature, man's cruelty to animals, man's cruelty to man—all these things incited Miró's resentment, in an odd kind of semimystical pantheism, or better, panentheism. Guillén knew Miró and admired him as "a man without peer: handsome, blond, blue-eyed, tender, mocking." Miró, he says, was a "Concrete Man," representing "with extraordinary intensity the type of man destined to the concrete world" (196). Guillén quotes a passage from Miró: "What I ask is man without a Guardian Angel on his right hand nor a Devil on his left. Man face to face with himself; let sin grieve him because he has offended himself; let all nature resound within his inmost being; astonished and complex; more a man than a person" (197).

The series of lectures concludes with Guillén's reflections on the generation that was active, in its prime, in the twenties and thirties. Guillén emphasizes that although they knew one another and the European periodicals and were interested in what could be called the Europeanization of Spain, the members of this generation were individually very different. The one thing they had in common was their antisentimentalism and antirealism. Guillén reflects that the break with the past precipitated by the First World War and its aftermath was much more gentle in Spain than it was in the rest of Europe. He quotes a Russian émigré writer, Wladimir Weidlé: "In Spain, poets are not obliged to distrust everyday language unduly, since that language has been divested of its poetic qualities much less than in France or in England" (214). Guillén closes with these lines from his own *Cántico:* "Let the dead bury their dead, / Never their hope" (216). With this apparent rejection of the past the book ends, on an optimistic note.

25 : DÁMASO ALONSO (1892–1990)

DÁMASO ALONSO wrote on almost every figure in Spanish literature, often in considerable detail and with great learning. I shall comment on some of his most striking essays.

Like every student of Spanish literature, Alonso comments on *Don Quixote,* in a piece published in 1950 called "Sancho-Quixote, Sancho-Sancho." There, very convincingly, he shows that Unamuno and Papini simplify the relationship of the two protagonists when they argue that Sancho was taken by the ideal of knighthood and thus became a second Quixote. After all, they say, he left his home and family and became Quixote's squire, accompanying him on all his adventures and sharing in his troubles. They argue that like Quixote, he himself becomes some kind of madman. Alonso argues that this is simplified and exaggerated. Sancho, he shows clearly, is by no means simply a madman or a fool. He enters into Don Quixote's service out of greed: he hopes to become rich and perhaps, as Quixote promises him, the ruler of an island. Alonso points out, however, that Sancho often recognizes that these are Don Quixote's fantasies and only rarely is convinced by his master's explanations. For instance, when Sancho is thrown by the windmill he seems to believe, as his master does, that the windmills are giants. At times he is caught up in the Quixotic dreamworld of knighthood himself. But sometimes Sancho revolts; when he is thrown out of the inn he shouts quite brusquely: "You have again forgotten that I am no knight!" At times he is simply disenchanted. Sancho at first has no belief in the world of his master, but he becomes more and more enticed by it and increasingly deceives himself. Alonso makes a good argument to show that Sancho constantly shifts from delusion to disenchantment. In some cases he understands clearly that Don Quixote is hallucinating and lives in an unreal world, for instance, when he believes that he has received a letter from Dulcinea del Toboso, who Sancho knows is really a simple illiterate peasant girl. Especially in the second part of *Don Quixote* Sancho recognizes that all these ideas of palaces and fortresses are Don Quixote's fancies or hallucinations.

According to Alonso, Unamuno and Papini's concept of Sancho is too simple. Sancho does not belong to the world of ordinary reality: he would then be a deliberate liar who pretends to his master. Yet neither is he a foolish illusionist. He has become a knight in Don Quixote's imagination. This constant changing from one point of view to another is characteristic of the whole work, which is dramatized that way. Cervantes, Dámaso Alonso concludes, praises a double world, the world of both dream and reality.

"Sancho-Quixote, Sancho-Sancho" is exceptional for its brevity and its concentration on one point, the character of Sancho. Alonso's other essays are much more detailed explorations of great works of Spanish literature. In his striking essay on style and creation in the *Poema del Cid,* Alonso argues that the work has been greatly underrated. It seems to him one of the eternal miracles of poetry, and of Spanish poetry especially. The style of the *Poema del Cid* is still in part definitely oral. It was recited by minstrels, whose art falls between narration and drama. The author had constantly to have in mind the recital of the minstrel, who often performed not alone but in dramatic form with several participants.

Alonso argues persuasively that the *Cid* is quite different from the *Chanson de Roland,* to which it is not only often compared but considered a successor. Stylistic examination shows how the Spanish text avoids connectives like *then, therefore,* and *while.* Alonso comments on individual scenes and figures, particularly the meeting between the Cid and King Alfonso. In the French *Chanson de Roland* there is a feudal relationship between Charlemagne and Roland, the king and his liege, whereas the Spanish poem has many humorous nuances, for instance, in the scenes where the Cid's sons-in-law flee from the conflict with the king of Morocco. Alonso tries to show that the *Poema del Cid* is quite independent of the heroic epic of the French, for instance, in its sometimes brutal naturalism, which he finds elsewhere in Spanish literature. Quevedo, for example, does not flinch from referring to the smell of corpses or to the necessity of physical elimination. The Spanish heroes appear much more earthbound and realistic as presented in frank combinations of the chivalric and the picaresque. Alonso finds in the twelfth century a constant abundance of contrasts and characterizations clearly formulated and set off from each other. The article ends with an unusually lyrical gesture: "Thus we part from the Cid and his warriors. They ride in a stormy gallop, losing themselves in the profound medieval night. But the miracle of a work of art is that a motion of our heart accompanies them, a soft resonance, a veiled emotion of the astonished and disturbed heart of the Spaniards" (*Ensayos sobre poesía española,* 110).

In an essay on the psychological realism of *Lazarillo de Tormes* Alonso comments on the passage in which Lázaro is hired by the hidalgo but immediately begins begging on the streets of Toledo. Alonso sees the hidalgo's shame when Lázaro goes out begging and then boasts of getting a leg of beef as a triumph of realism. It takes the picaro quite a while to discover that the impoverished hidalgo is at his wits' end and then to feel compassion for him. They try to deceive each other. A scene that Alonso finds quite astonishing, worthy of being called "magical realism," is where Lázaro follows his master through the streets of Toledo. We sense the smells of the market, the bad smell of the church with its stale incense, and the steep narrow lanes suddenly turning shady. Things here are in intimate contact with the human beings moving through them. Alonso argues that this is a particular feature of Spanish realism.

Alonso's 1927 lecture "Scylla and Charybdis in Spanish Literature" develops the idea that Spanish literature is constantly alternating between realism and some supernaturalism. Alonso argues that Spanish literary criticism was flattered by what other Western criticism labeled its indulgence in primitive and cruel realism. Spanish literature was called primitive, cruel, and even vulgar, and the picaresque novel described as the most typically Spanish form. Alonso protests against this false isolation of Spanish literature and against the French and German hispanists who often completely ignore or dismiss the other tradition of Spanish literature, which Alonso finds central to the work of Luis de Góngora.

Alonso's earliest scholarly work was devoted to a study of Góngora. More than just learned research, this work, in particular his essay "Clarity and Beauty in the *Soledades* of Góngora," shows in detail that the story of the *Solitudes* can be told very clearly and that it exploits the possibilities of metaphors, not only in boldness and clarity but in original power and beauty. Alonso tries to refute those hispanists who deny that Spain had a Renaissance. He defends the astonishing ingenuity and power of Góngora's comparisons and metaphors and explains his underlying formal scheme. He calls Góngora "Baroque," drawing on the German discussions of Baroque that had been ignored in Spain and France. Góngora lives up to Alonso's ideal of plenitude and beauty. He paints a scene flooded with light, glowing with beauty, in spite of his underlying gloomy view of man's mortality and inconsequence in the immense universe. Alonso pursues the tradition of Góngora throughout the history of Spanish literature and finds it renewed in the poetry of his own time, particularly in

García Lorca. Alonso admires him as a poet in spite of his, at that time, small record of publications. He obviously loved the man. Alonso thinks of Lorca as an artist and tells the story of Lorca's asserting that although he is a revolutionary, he will never be a politician. Lorca's last words to Alonso were "I shall never be a politician, never." But this did not save him from execution by Franco adherents a few days later.

Alonso's most important scholarly work is *Poesía española: Ensayo de métodos y límites estilísticos* (1950). I shall pay attention mainly to the topics of the subtitle, as I cannot reproduce and judge his detailed examinations of the six main Spanish poets to whom the book is devoted: Garcilaso, Fray Luis de León, St. John of the Cross, Góngora, Lope de Vega, and Quevedo. The principal thesis of the book is that literary scholarship should attempt to define the uniqueness of a specific work of art by rational means of analysis, but always appealing finally to an intuitive insight which allows the scholar to define the center of the work's individuality. Alonso repeatedly declares that we cannot solve the problem of uniqueness and individuality. I am occasionally puzzled by his gestures toward the ineffable and toward some kind of mystical insight which he admits we can never actually reach. He uses *stylistics* in such a broad sense that all examinations of the individuality of a work of poetry are considered to fall under this rubric. Alonso says many times that stylistics is the only admissible method of scholarship, and he is violently and often unjustly critical of conventional literary history and particularly of the concern with the biography of an author. Alonso belongs to the whole group of scholars who reject the preoccupation with biography and argue that a poet may even be a scoundrel, like Rimbaud. Life and work are totally separate— an argument made most strikingly by Proust in *Contre Sainte-Beuve* (see this volume, p. 64ff). In practice, Alonso cannot completely observe this creed. He makes frequent concessions to biography, as he cannot very well ignore the adventurous life of Lope de Vega or the politics of Quevedo. I have also noticed instances where Alonso seems inadvertently to confuse life and work; he at one point apparently confuses a fictional nymph with a real-life love of Garcilaso named Isabel Freire (*PE*, 105).

Alonso makes much of the Saussurean distinction between *signifiant* and *signifié*—though he appears to reduce *signifiant* to what is usually called "form" and *signifié* to what is usually called "content." Alonso, like almost all scholars of the twentieth century, is concerned with this distinction between content and form, which he wants to abolish or reconcile. *Poesía española* is in many respects an elaborate attempt to overcome this gulf and to achieve a union of content and form, which Alonso finally admits to be beyond his or any other scholar's grasp. The linguistic terminology should not, however, obscure the fact that Alonso actually rejects any behavioristic or simply pragmatic conceptions of language. Language is, for him, an almost mystical entity which the poet in some way enters and uses, or which even uses him. There are passages where Alonso says "we are spoken," "we are poeticized." The poet is seen almost as a passive recipient of the inspiration of language. But Alonso always hesitates to draw consequences from this. Actually, he recognizes the role of chance or of sudden inspiration, which to him remains inexplicable. He is quite reasonably concerned with the position of a work of art within a tradition and within a historical situation—the sort of problems that the Saussurean terminology obscures or ignores.

The study of the six Spanish poets in *Poesía española* is not primarily historical at all. Alonso's emphasis is on the actual texts, even to the extent of seeing them in complete isolation from ordinary life. Rather than making the poetry depend on the past, Alonso starts from scratch, so to speak, to achieve from it a unique feeling or intuition. In spite of his linguistic terminology, I think that Alonso was much more deeply impressed by Croce than is generally recognized. He quotes Croce frequently and obviously admires him greatly. But Croce, of course, had no use for technical linguistics, or even stylistics, and he endorsed only Leo Spitzer's work on stylistics, without properly facing the issues. Alonso is correct to dismiss Spitzer as concerned mainly with individual words and syntax and not with what he himself considers central—a kind of "general intuition," as he calls it—an insight into the motivation and meaning of a work of poetry.

There is little in the book about the antecedents and sources of Spanish poetry, though Alonso quotes Dante and a sonnet on a dream by Giovanni della Casa in Italian and occasionally refers to Latin poets such as Horace and Ovid. Alonso treats the poems one by one, in great detail and with an acute sensitivity and power of observation. He selects the poems so skillfully that they illustrate a progress in the method applied. Thus the first chapter on Garcilaso de la Vega simply takes a fine descriptive poem and tries to show such parallels as that between the timbre of vowels and the statement being made in the poem. Alonso even indulges in graphic representations of the rhythmic waves of a poem or of sudden changes in the position of an accent. He always wants to go further, trying to find—even when the text itself leaves hardly anything to find—the "star of melancholy" underlying every one of Garcilaso's poems. Alonso is particularly interested in such old problems as the effect of vowels and vowel repetitions and synesthesia—something as simple as Góngora's "infame turba de nocturnas aves," which Alonso quotes several times as an example of the effect of dark vowels (*turba, nocturnas*). He demonstrates convincingly that the words *turba* and *nocturnas* in isolation would have no deeper effect, and that the impression of dark and gloom is achieved by the stress put on the syllables with the dark vowels (the fourth and eighth syllables) and by the content—the "infamous crowd of nocturnal birds." A feeling of gruesome darkness is evoked. Alonso calls this effect a "black light" (*PE,* 348) and reflects on the impact of the word order, which is usually neglected in stylistic investigations of poetry.

Alonso notes the parallelism between Garcilaso's simple sketch of an idyllic scene along the River Tajo and the sweet running of his verse. Describing the monster Polifemo in Góngora's poem *Fábula de Polifemo y Galatea,* Alonso starts with the content and studies the implied philosophy or, more accurately, the attitude toward reality that he derives from a study of the poet's background, of his models, even in antiquity. He is mainly interested in showing the final harmony, the final coming together of *significans* and *significatum,* form and content. Alonso tries always to bring these two sides of the poetic transaction together and to demonstrate that they form a unity. He has to admit, however, that although this is the ultimate goal of stylistics, he cannot achieve a perfect unity. It is only an ideal which cannot be reached, or has not been reached by him. Alonso defines the term "baroque" as the "coincidence of opposites," *coincidentia oppositorum.* The monstrous Polifemo contrasts with the charming little Galatea in what Alonso describes as "the *chiaroscuro* of the baroque."

In between these detailed stylistic analyses, Alonso reflects that literary scholarship aims at providing scientific knowledge about a unique subject, a unique poem which is specific, a cosmos, a world in itself. Alonso harshly condemns a stylistics that limits itself to the study of affective words and phrases, in speech, the kind of linguistic stylistics that André Bally founded. For Alonso, only a synthesis of all possible aspects of intellect and feeling is legitimate, and he always locates this problem of stylistics at the point where the physical and the ideal come together in a poem. He believes that by his method he can try to penetrate the inner structure of a poetic texture. At the same time, however, he emphasizes that what is needed is an original intuition, a grasp, possibly quite irrational, of the center of a work. The center is not, of course, anything measurable: it must be grasped by intuition.

Alonso emphasizes the life of mystical experience in the work of St. John of the Cross, which has its models and sources in the whole tradition of mysticism, unlike Lope de Vega, a multifaceted author whose personal experience is embodied in his lyrical work. Alonso recognizes that such confessions may often be just artistic tricks. He says strangely, "We cannot trust Lope as we cannot trust a woman; his very name was unreliability." Alonso claims that Lope de Vega is the first author before the nineteenth century who translated life so immediately into art. But then he himself gives such examples as that of Lope addressing a love poem to a specific woman and then using it in a play written later, where the lines are even delivered by two speakers. Alonso is well aware of these problems and sees that the truth is often obscure or not supported by evidence. But in the case of Lope, he feels that his person draws us into a poem in a way that no other European author can match. He ends the chapter on Lope by calling him "the link of Spain, the knot of Spain, the symbol of Spain" (*PE*, 510).

Alonso pays special attention throughout the book to the imaginative in the sense of actual imaging, of seeing or being shown something visual, or even something of taste or hearing or smell. Alonso always argues that signs have a threefold character: conceptual, affective, and imaginative—the three aspects of a work of art that can be examined by stylistics. Alonso is so enthusiastic about his concept of stylistics that he asserts that it is the only way of studying literature scientifically, although he admits that even his type of stylistics cannot quite achieve the synthesis that he demands. "The problems of scientific methods for the knowing of a literary work remain," he concludes, "and the fortress has not yet fallen. We have examined its walls, its battlements, the exterior of the fortress, but only the arrows of intuition fly over the walls and penetrate into the inhabited interior, and there reigns the light" (*PE*, 634).

When I read Alonso's assertion in the *Times Literary Supplement* that stylistics is the only way to study literature, I doubted this sweeping claim. After Alonso pointed out that I had not properly seen the all-embracing character of what he calls "stylistics," I had to recant, admitting that I had not understood his concept. I still think that there are concepts of stylistics, like that of Spitzer, which differ in approach and focus instead on individual words and phrases or etymologies and derivations of the poetic language, attempting to define different periods by characteristics derived from such stylistic observations. But while praising Spitzer, Alonso would, of course, reject this approach as a kind of atomism or positivism that has failed to achieve a total unity of form and content, the final sense of *significans* and *significatum*, which he believes he has almost reached. Whatever we may think about his individual interpretations, Dámaso Alonso remains one of the finest critics of the twentieth century—one of the few to face resolutely the question of the nature of literature as an aesthetic phenomenon. However, many of the foremost critics of this century, writers like Poulet and the critics of consciousness, have all but abandoned the idea of the *art* of poetry and are far more interested in problems of time and space or in the philosophy implied in a work of art.

26 : JOSÉ ORTEGA Y GASSET (1883–1955)

JOSÉ ORTEGA Y GASSET WAS BY FAR THE MOST FAMOUS general critic in Spain. He cannot be described as a literary critic only, but rather as a critic of civilization and of Spanish civilization in particular. He was extreme in his condemnation of contemporary Spain, quoting the historian Joaquín Costa (1846–1911): "Spain is a country which seen from the outside was unstructured, without real and living institutions, without schools and universities, without administration, without a parliament, without deputations, without councils or courts of law, without an army or diplomacy, though it had the appearance of all this." In many writings, particularly *España invertebrada* (1922), Ortega develops this theme at great length, blasting Spanish conditions, contrasting them, always to Spain's discredit, with the rest of Europe, and recommending the Europeanization of Spain. Spain, he argued, must open its doors particularly to German thought. Ortega spent four years, 1904 to 1908, in Germany as a student: one year in Leipzig learning German, the second year in Berlin, where he knew Georg Simmel (1858–1918) and attended his lectures on history, and the third year at Marburg, where he came under the spell of Hermann Cohen (1842–1918). He admired Cohen greatly as a person, but never really adopted his abstract Kantianism. He seems, however, to have talked a great deal with Cohen's two very prominent students, Hans-Georg Gadamer and Heinz Heinsoeth. Ortega only began to publish in 1914. His early writings are deeply marked by such Teutonic speculations as those of Houston Stewart Chamberlain in *Die Grundlagen des neunzehnten Jahrhunderts* (1899). Ortega is, surprisingly, quite taken in by the view that Spain owes its greatness to the Germanic inheritance. He obviously accepted without question that not only Germans and Englishmen are of Germanic descent, but even figures like Michelangelo and Descartes— on what basis seems to me totally obscure, apart from the mere assertions of Chamberlain, who made Jesus Christ to be an Aryan.

Ortega's first book, *Meditaciones del Quijote* (1914), belongs to the large Spanish literature in which *Don Quixote* is treated as a personification of the Spanish national soul. He hopes to define the world of Cervantes and claims that a profile of Cervantes's style would bring about new philosophical, moral, scientific, and political conceptions and would even "awake us to a new life." Ortega strongly disapproves of earlier interpretations, particularly that of Menéndez Pidal, who praised Cervantes for his good sense (*MQ*, 107). In Ortega's view, *Don Quixote* represents the new European genre, the novel, which was in complete contrast to the epic. The novel, according to Ortega, is born with a comic sting and will preserve this nature forever. The criticism, the banter of *Don Quixote* is not an unessential ornament, but rather the very texture of the genre and perhaps of all realists (147). Ortega is a strong defender of the independence of genres. In a later context (*Ideas sobre la novela*, 1925) he asserts that every work of art belongs to a genre, as an animal belongs to a species. According to him, Croce's attack on genres failed and left no trace. Cervantes's hero is not an epic figure, not a hero in the classical sense, but still a hero. Don Quixote is a hero whose desire for his tragic destiny stems from free choice. Ortega strongly disapproves of determinism. Everything is left to the free decision of a single man. This is also the basis of his political creed, which stridently approves of an almost anarchic individualism—what Ortega calls liberalism—and at the same time condemns modern democracy. Democracy and liberalism are to Ortega incompatible. His most famous book, *La Rebelión de las masas* (1929), is a gloomy philosophy ascribing the decay of civilization to this revolt of the common man.

Ortega is a lively and witty writer, often indulging in metaphors, digressions, and anecdotes that show his original training in journalism, but he can also move into abstract philosophy, particularly the philosophy of history, which he sees as constantly changing with the times. Ortega is an enemy of relativism and skepticism, which he tries to combat with a theory he calls "perspectivism." I have used this term in my own writings, but obviously misunderstood it. Perspective in Ortega is *in* the things themselves. It has nothing to do with Nietzsche's usage. Perspectivism, Ortega says expressly, is "one of the components of reality" (*OC*, 2:137) and thus has nothing to do with point of view, which is personal, though Ortega strongly approves personal points of view and attitudes toward metaphysical problems. An author who ignores them is of no interest.

Ortega's concept of literature lies in the view that literature is disguised philosophy, though at other times he seems to defend an extreme aestheticism that ultimately relegates art to an irrelevant imaginary island within civilization. The function of art, he sometimes says, is to divest the outer world of reality. In his rather rare pronouncements on poetry in the sense of verse, he takes the striking view that the mentally retarded often display poetic talent, Rimbaud being his doubtful example. The whole point of Ortega's famous book *La Deshumanización del arte* (1925) is that man has disappeared, has been suppressed in modern art. Ortega is quite shocked by writers like Pirandello and particularly by modern artists like Stravinsky and Picasso. He depicts the whole history of modern art in terms (one must not forget the date of the book) of the disappearance of human characters of the kind we find in Dickens and Galdós or even of the personal feelings displayed in Wagner's music. Ortega goes to extremes in condemning both older nineteenth-century, or romantic, art, which displays personal prejudices and emotional responses, and more recent art like that of Baudelaire and Mallarmé, who by their negations prevent emotional resonance and fly from personality. Poetry becomes a higher algebra of metaphor. Metaphors in this new art are the real heroes of the action—in Proust and in Joyce. Ortega also sees the aversion to the human form as a reaction against the classicism of an earlier time, for example, Baudelaire's "Black Venus." Under the mask of pure art, which these modernists defend, there may really be a hatred of art. The artist himself now considers art as unimportant: it saves him from real life and awakens his basic childishness. The pure-art claim is not arrogance but modesty. Ortega condemns the new art as a flight from reality and from humanity. Commenting on Picasso, however, Ortega says that Cubism still cannot avoid having recourse to reality in its distortion of human figures. Actual literary criticism is only incidental in this book on dehumanization, the title of which should be translated in English as "the expulsion of man from art."

Ortega's main literary criticism is in his book *Ideas sobre la novela*. It begins with a strong defense of the necessity of genre criticism and then enters into a discussion of the nineteenth-century novel. According to Ortega, Balzac is insufferable trash, an illustration of how later perfect works (those of Stendhal and Flaubert) destroy earlier forerunners. Ortega admires Stendhal for his complete presentation. Stendhal does not merely talk about Julien Sorel falling in love with Madame de Rénal, he presents it. Balzac merely tells about it. Ortega strongly emphasizes the visualization of a character, a narration that is a direct showing and telling. We must not be merely told about the characters, for a report suggests absence. Ortega wants complete vision, not a system of signs: "A novelist, for instance, who tells me that a character is morose makes me work to imagine a morose person, but he should show me and make me discover that so-and-so is morose without telling me."

Ortega claims that adventure today has no interest: it can be used only as a pretense, as a red thread, though he admits that *Don Quixote,* together with the whole tradition of the picaresque novel, is very much a story of actions. But the novel moves then from action to character. Ortega contrasts the Spanish theater, which is a series of popular actions, with the French drama of the seventeenth century, which is an analysis of passions. The new novel is interested in character and not in actions, as art draws its life from form rather than from action or narration. The philistine thinks that action is the main thing. Ortega agrees that a work of art without some action is impossible, but its aesthetic appeal is nonetheless due to its formal structure. He is correct to say that Dostoevsky is wrongly considered a demonic writer, when in actuality he was a professional, careful craftsman and master of technique, often keeping to the structure of tragedy, even to the three unities. But Ortega criticizes Dostoevsky for having his characters oscillate and for handling them too openly. The novel demands that in reading it we do not feel it as a novel. Balzac makes us work by drawing attention to his poetic scaffolding. Ortega finds Proust too extreme in the way in which he ignores action and concentrates everything on character. In Proust the atmosphere is the hero. The reader is in a contemplative position: contemplation and interest are the two poles of the novel. In Proust we are forced to look at things. Proust is anticipated particularly by Stendhal, whose unfinished novel *Lucien Leuwen* is a work in which nothing happens, and when the intrigue begins the fragment breaks off. Ortega thinks that Stendahl, however, is extreme: the novelist should see to it that we are drawn into his world. Oddly enough, Ortega considers the historical novel a complete failure. The clash of two horizons seems to him fatal. Ortega thinks that artists should be content to be artists and not make a pretense of leading the masses or being prophets. These writers should write political pamphlets or sociological investigations or moral sermons. Dostoevsky's religious and political opinions have their power only within the novel; they have their status as fictions, just as do the passion and feeling of his characters. A novelist should be a "divine somnambulist." The novel, because it is a realistic genre, cannot get along without reality. The novelist should cover the real world with his imaginary world, and he can do so only with a dense net of clearly seen details. He must inevitably draw on his experience. The quality of detail decides the rank of the novel. The main subject is a creative psychology of possible souls: the novels of Dostoevsky may contain some sociology, for instance, but they must not be sociological. Construction of an imaginary family of spirits, a community of remarkable souls, seems to be the future of the novel, according to Ortega.

There are a few essays on specific authors among Ortega's extremely

diverse writings. Some seem to me rather conventional, though he is skillful, for example, in contrasting the authors Azorín and Pío Baroja, characterizing them as two different minds, one wandering all over Spain
and history, the other completely retired, absorbed in the observation of
minute details of Spanish life. The most interesting of the essays is on
Goethe, "Pidiendo un Goethe desde dentro" (1932), written on the centenary of Goethe's death. Ortega is skeptical about Goethe's standing as a
classic, arguing that he can only be a classic of second rank. The Germans,
according to Ortega, indulge in sterile idolatry. He believes that Simmel
has written the best book on Goethe, but for him Goethe the man is not a
problem. One should avoid monumental optics and try to enter into the
interior of his life. Ortega, as in his other writings, thinks that man must
decide his calling (*Berufung*), and in this he thinks that Goethe failed. The
faithfulness to his fate should be examined and the genuineness of his
life determined. Goethe struggled with his calling all his life, but he was
shipwrecked and lost. Goethe reflects on his life, but he has a biological
and botanical view of life and thus surrenders to some kind of natural necessity. But this destiny should not be confused with spiritual and voluntary choice. Goethe saw his life as a development, as a biological growth.
He looked at it with Spinozistic optimism, ignoring the reality that life
is a drama, that man must decide each moment what he will be. A great
many of Goethe's characters search for their destiny and try to escape
it. Goethe thought he had found himself at age thirty-seven in Rome in
1788, but this was an error, and he continued to wander. The conclusion
to *Wilhelm Meister* is completely artificial and false. Actually it was the conflict between a benevolent world-order and his own dissatisfaction which
resulted in Goethe's stiffness and bitterness and sense of constant desertion from his inner destiny. Ortega considers the flight from his poetical
vocation to Weimar the biggest misunderstanding in German literary history. The variety of Goethe's talents misled him. In his early Strassburg
years he had a strong feeling for reality: Ortega quotes him as saying "wie
wahr, wie seiend," and notes that this praise was evoked by the sight of
a donkey sunning itself. Thus Goethe put himself under the sterile protection of Weimar. Weimar cut him off from Germany, turned him into
a statue. He engaged in completely unreal activities: he was a minister
who actually was no minister, he was a theater director who detested the
theater, he descended into the mines, and he drafted soldiers.

Ortega sees Goethe as a horrifying example demonstrating that a man
can have only one genuine life to which he is called. In Goethe everything
that he touched later evaporated into a symbol, his relations with women,
for example. His relationship with Charlotte von Stein is, in Ortega's view,

ambiguous, and his relationship with Marianne von Wilemmer equally unreal. Ortega harps on the theme of flight—to Olympus, to the Orient. Even a German theme like *Hermann und Dorothea* (1798) is distanced by the hexameter, by the forced solemnity and long monologues. Weimar became a cocoon, and Ortega is quite shocked that Goethe had no interest in German idealist philosophy, though he lived only a few miles from Jena and Fichte. The same is true of his attitude to the French Revolution, which he saw only from the outside, and also to the German war of liberation. It is paradoxical that a man who constantly escaped his calling, who was unfaithful to his ego, persistently admonishes us to be ourselves. His biological ideas about life and his personal conduct of life as the path to one's own self and fate are of no value, but luckily Goethe is also the great admonisher, constantly telling us, "Befreie dich von dem anderen zu dir selbst" (Free yourself from the other to yourself). Ortega ends by defending his essay with a quotation from an unnamed pupil of Theodor Mommsen, the famous historian of Rome, at the University of Berlin, who wrote a dissertation on the thesis that history should be written *cum ira* and *cum studio*.

The essay is obviously a penetrating psychological study of Goethe's flight from reality, a theme since taken up by Erich Heller, the author of a widely known book on Thomas Mann, *The Ironic German* (1958). But Ortega cannot solve, even if all the allegations and observations were true, the real problem: how could this man who congealed into a statue and became a stiff *Geheimrat* produce such wonderful works of poetry as are found in much of the second part of *Faust,* or in *Der West-östliche Divan,* which is not simply a flight to the Orient, or in a novel like *Die Wahlverwandtschaften,* which Ortega does not even mention? The problem of Goethe's greatness as a poet is really glossed over or not addressed.

Ortega's other essays on individual writers seem to me less distinguished. The one on Góngora contains little that had not already been said by Dámaso Alonso. Ortega calls Góngora a polypheme, a one-eyed giant. He refers to the contrast between his popular realism and the Baroque extravagances of some of his cultist poetry. The essay on Anna de Noailles (1923) is a rather obvious hymn of praise, declaring her the best modern poetess, but pointing out only her concern for feminism and her love of what Ortega calls "vegetable sensibility." The essay on Mallarmé (1923) also is hardly striking. Ortega sees his poetry as a flight, a strenuous avoidance of the real. Mallarmé conceives of poetry as "vocal silence," the hiding of the immediate names of things, which to Ortega seems to be the essence of poetry. The essay on Proust (1934), while sensitive and well phrased, belabors the term "impressionism." In discussing the recovery of the past, Ortega says rather that Proust "picks up the ruins of the past" (*OC*, 1:524). The essay came too late to say anything really new.

Ortega has a low opinion of literary criticism—or, rather, he says that it should not rank, but only characterize. He rejects attempts to make criticism literature and thinks that its function is to "induce the heart to dwell on a page just as a bee on a tulip collects pollen" (*OC*, 1:120). On the whole, Ortega is not truly a literary critic, but a critic of civilization who indulges in speculations on the decay of modern civilization that are strongly influenced by his reading of Houston Stewart Chamberlain and Oswald Spengler. Still, he always stands opposed to determinism and frees himself in a direction that could be called existential. Ortega emphasizes man's freedom and his right and power to make decisions.

BIBLIOGRAPHIES AND NOTES

The bibliography is highly selective; only books actually referred to are listed. A few items of the secondary literature were included if they seemed important.

SELECT BIBLIOGRAPHY: FRENCH CRITICISM, 1900–1950

FRENCH "CLASSICAL" CRITICISM IN THE TWENTIETH CENTURY

Charles Maurras. *Les Amants de Venise* (1905).
———. *L'Allée des philosophes* (1924).
———. *Un Débat sur le Romantisme* (with Raymond de la Tailhède) (1928).
———. *Dictionnaire politique et critique,* comp. Pierre Chardon, 5 vols. (1933). Cited as *DPC*.
———. *Poésie et vérité* (1944). Cited as *PV*.
———. *Maîtres et témoins de ma vie d'esprit* (1954).
———. *Oeuvres capitales,* 4 vols. (1954). Cited as *OC*.
Léon Daudet. *Le stupide dix-neuvième siècle* (1922).
———. *Ecrivains et artistes,* 8 vols. (1927–29).
———. *Goethe et la synthèse* (1932).
———. *Mes Idées esthétiques* (1939).
Pierre Lasserre. *Maurras et la Renaissance classique* (1902).
———. *La Morale de Nietzsche* (1902).
———. *Le Romantisme français* (1907). New ed. (1919), cited as *RF*.
———. *La Doctrine officielle de l'université* (1912).
———. *Mistral* (1919).
———. *Les Chapelles littéraires* (1921).
———. *Mes Routes* (1924).
———. *Mise au point* (1931).
Pierre Gilbert. *La Forêt des Cippes,* 2 vols. (1918). Cited as *FC*.
Jean-Marc Bernard. *Oeuvres,* 2 vols. (1923).

Eugène Marsan. *Instances* (1930).

Pierre Lièvre. *Esquisses critiques.* 2d ser. (1924); 3d ser. (1929).

Henri Massis. *Comment Zola composait ses romans* (1906).

——. *L'Esprit de la Nouvelle Sorbonne* (1910–11).

——. *Jugements,* 2 vols. (1923–24).

——. *Défense de l'Occident* (1927).

——. *Réflexions sur l'art du roman* (1927).

——. *Evocations: Souvenirs 1905–1911* (1931).

——. *Les Idées restent* (1941).

——. *Maurras et notre temps,* 2 vols. (1951; definitive ed. 1961).

Robert Brasillach. *Présence de Virgile* (1931).

——. *Portraits* (1935).

——. *Pierre Corneille* (1938).

——. *Les Quatres Jeudis* (1943).

——. *Chénier* (1947).

Thierry Maulnier. *Nietzsche* (1925).

——. *Racine* (1936).

——. *Introduction à la poésie française* (1939).

——. *Langages* (1946).

Julien Benda. *Le Bergsonisme* (1912).

——. *Belphégor* (1919).

——. *La Trahison des clercs* (1927).

——. *Exercice d'un enterré vif* (1944).

——. *La France byzantine* (1945).

W. M. Frohock. *Pierre Lasserre* (1937).

Léon S. Roudiez. *Maurras jusqu'à l'Action française* (1957).

Ivan P. Barko. *L'Esthéthique littéraire de Charles Maurras* (1961).

NOTES TO PAGES 4–21

1. The term "Ecole romane" was invented by Maurice du Plessys. Charles Maurras, then twenty-two (Moréas was thirty-four), was not the moving spirit of the "Ecole romane." See *DPC,* 3:118.

2. Largely in a long series of articles in *La Revue Encyclopédique Larousse* between 1894 and 1900. The exact chronology of the adoption of the term and slogan is obscure. Neither Roudiez nor Barko pays attention to this problem.

3. The lecture on *Phèdre* in *Epoques du théâtre français* (1891); and *Evolution de la poésie lyrique* (1894), e.g., 1:71.

RETROSPECT

ALAIN

Les Propos d'Alain, 2 vols. (1920).
Système des beaux arts (1920).
Propos de littérature (1933).
En lisant Dickens (1945).
Les Dieux (1947).
Propos, 2 vols. (1956–70).
Les Arts et les dieux (1958). Cited as *AD.*
Les Passions et la sagesse (1960).

RÉMY DE GOURMONT
Le Latin mystique (1892).
Le Problème du style (1902; 6th ed., 1907). Cited as *PS.*
Physique de l'amour (1903).
Un Coeur virginal (1907).

Karl-D. Uitti. *La Passion littéraire de Rémy de Gourmont* (1962).

THE NOUVELLE REVUE FRANÇAISE

Justin O'Brien, ed. *From the N.R.F.* (1958).

ANDRÉ GIDE
Prétextes (1903). In English as *Pretexts,* trans. Justin O'Brien (1959), cited as *P.*
Nouveaux prétextes (1911).
Dostoïevski (1923). In English as *Dostoevsky,* trans. Arnold Bennett (1925); New Directions ed. (1949), cited as *D.*
Journal, 1889–1939 (1939).
Pages de journal, 1939–1942 (1946).
Journal, 1942–1949 (1950).
The Journals of André Gide, trans. Justin O'Brien, 4 vols. (1947–51).

Justin O'Brien. *Portrait of André Gide: A Critical Biography* (1953).
————. *The French Literary Horizon* (1967).

JACQUES RIVIÈRE
Etudes (1911). Cited as *E.*

L'Allemande (1918).
Nouvelles études (1947). Cited as *NE*.

Carlo Bo. *Jacques Rivière* (1935).

RAMON FERNANDEZ
Messages (1926). Revised and enlarged ed. (1981). English translation of 1926 ed. by Montgomery Belgion (1927), cited as *M*.
Balzac (1943).
Proust (1943).

BENJAMIN CRÉMIEUX
Vingtième siècle (1924).
Essai sur l'évolution littéraire de l'Italie de 1870 à nos jours (1928).
Panorama de la littérature italienne contemporaine (1928).
Inquiétude et reconstruction: Essai sur la littérature d'après querre (1931).

L. Parrot. *L'Intelligence en guerre: Ecrivains en prison* (1945).
A. Eustis. *Marcel Arlaud, Benjamin Crémieux, Ramon Fernandez: Trois critiques de la Nouvelle Revue Française* (1961).

ALBERT THIBAUDET
La Poésie de Stéphane Mallarmé: Etude critique (1912). New final ed. (1926), cited as *PSM*.
Trente ans de vie française. Vol. 1: *Les Idées de Charles Maurras* (1920).
Trente ans de vie française. Vol. 2: *La Vie de Maurice Barrès* (1921).
Gustave Flaubert, 1821–1880: Sa Vie, ses romans, son style (1922). New final ed. (1935), cited as *GF*. ("Madame Bovary," trans. Paul de Man, in *Madame Bovary,* ed. Paul de Man [1965], 371–83.)
La Campagne avec Thucydide (1922).
Trent ans de vie française. Vol. 3: *Le Bergsonisme,* 2 vols. (1923).
Intérieurs: Baudelaire, Fromentin, Amiel (1924).
Paul Valéry (1924). Cited as *PV*.
Les Princes lorrains (1924).
Etranger, ou Etudes de littérature anglaise (1925).
Le Liseur de romans (1925).
Cluny (1928).
Amiel, ou La Part du rêve (1929).
Mistral, ou La République du soleil (1930).
Physiologie de la critique (1930). Cited as *PC*.
Stendhal (1931).

Histoire de la littérature française de 1789 à nos jours (1936). New ed. (1947), cited as *HLF*. In English as *French Literature from 1795 to Our Era*, trans. Charles Lam Markmann (1967), cited as *FL*.

Réflexions sur la littérature (1938). Cited as *RL*. ("Marcel Proust and the French Tradition," trans. Angelo P. Bertocci, in *From the N.R.F.*, ed. Justin O'Brien [1958], 108–17; reprinted as "Faces of Proust," in *Proust: A Collection of Critical Essays*, ed. René Girard [1962], 47–52.)

Réflexions sur le roman (1938). Cited as *RR*.

Réflexions sur la critique (1939). Cited as *RC*.

Réflexions sur la littérature II (1941). Cited as *RL2*.

Montaigne. Text established by Floyd Gray based on manuscript notes (1963).

Thibaudet also edited the Pléiade editions of Montaigne's *Essais* (1933; new ed. 1950 and, jointly with Maurice Rat, 1963) and Flaubert's *Oeuvres*, 2 vols. (1936; new ed. 1946).

Hommage à Albert Thibaudet. *Nouvelle Revue Française* 46 (1936): 5–176. Contains tributes and articles by Paul Valéry, Henri Bergson, Alain, Jean Wahl, Ramon Fernandez, E. R. Curtius, Benjamin Crémieux, and others. (Bergson's contribution, "Remarks on Thibaudet as Critic and Philosopher," trans. J. Robert Loy, is in *From the N.R.F.*, ed. Justin O'Brien [1958], 261–67.)

Maurice Blanchot. "La Critique d'Albert Thibaudet," in *Faux pas* (1943), 334–38.

Leo Spitzer. "Patterns of Thought in the Style of Albert Thibaudet," *Modern Language Quarterly* 9 (1948): 259–72, 478–91. Reprinted in *Romanische Literaturstudien* (1959), 294–328.

D.Z.H. "Thibaudet, or, The Critic as Mediator," *Yale French Studies* 2, no. 1 (Spring-Summer 1949): 74–78.

Alfred Glauser. *Albert Thibaudet et la critique créatrice* (1952).

John C. Davies. *L'Oeuvre critique d'Albert Thibaudet* (1955).

Gérard Genette. "Thibaudet chez Montaigne," *Critique* 20 (1964): 66–70. Reprinted as "Montaigne bergsonien," in *Figures* (1966), 139–43.

Marcel Devaud. *Albert Thibaudet: Critique de la poésie et des poètes* (1967).

MARCEL PROUST

A la recherche du temps perdu (1913–27). Pléiade ed., 3 vols. (1954), cited as *ARTP*. In English as *Remembrance of Things Past*, trans. C. K. Scott Moncrieff, 2 vols. (1934). Revised translation by C. K. Scott Moncrieff and Terence Kilmartin, 3 vols. (1981), cited as *RTP*.

Pastiches et mélanges (1919). Cited as *PM*.

Chroniques (1927).

Correspondance inédite, 1903–14 (1948).

Contre Sainte-Beuve (1954). Expanded Pléiade ed. (1971), cited as *CSB*.

Choix des lettres, ed. Philip Kolb (1965).

Textes retrouvés, ed. Philip Kolb (1968).

Pleasures and Days, ed. F. W. Dupee (1957).

On Art and Literature, 1896–1919, trans. S. T. Warner (1958). Cited as
    OAL.

Also: *La Bible d'Amiens* (1904), translation of John Ruskin's *The Bible of
    Amiens.* Cited as *Bible*.

Robert Dreyfus. *Souvenirs sur Marcel Proust* (1926).

Emeric Fiser. *L'Estétique de Marcel Proust* (1933).

Marcel Proust: Reviews and Estimates in English, comp. Gladys D. Lind-
    ner (1942).

Ramon Fernandez. *Proust* (1944).

J. M. Cocking. *Proust* (1956).

Walter A. Strauss. *Proust and Literature: The Novelist as Critic* (1957).

George D. Painter. *Proust,* 2 vols. (1959).

Richard H. Barker. *Marcel Proust: A Biography* (1962).

Milton Hindus. *A Reader's Guide to Marcel Proust* (1962).

Howard Moss. *The Magic Lantern of Marcel Proust* (1962).

Germaine Brée. *The World of Marcel Proust* (1966).

René de Chantal. *Marcel Proust: Critique littéraire,* 2 vols. (1967).

Milton Hindus. *The Proustian Vision* (1967).

Erich Köhler. *Marcel Proust* (1967).

Henri Peyre. *Marcel Proust* (1970).

Joyce M. Megay. *Bergson et Proust* (1976).

David R. Ellison. *The Reading of Proust* (1984).

THE CATHOLIC RENAISSANCE

CHARLES DU BOS

Approximations, 7 vols. (1922–37), cited as *A.* Reprinted, without the
    Goethe essays, in a single volume (1965), cited as *Ap.*

Extraits d'un journal (1928).

Byron ou le besoin de la fatalité (1929).

Le Dialogue avec André Gide (1929).

What Is Literature? (1940).

Journal, 9 vols. (1946–61). Cited as *J.*

Goethe (1949). (As I have no access to this edition, I quote the original essays in *A*, vols. 5 [1932], 6 [1934], and 7 [1937].)

Angelo P. Bertocci. *Du Bos and English Literature* (1949).
Charles Dédéyan. *Le Cosmopolitisme littéraire de Charles Du Bos*, 5 vols. (1967).
Cornelius Joseph Martens. *Emotion et critique chez Charles Du Bos* (1967).
Angelo P. Bertocci. "Composing Literatures: The Experience of Charles Du Bos," *Comparative Literature* 24 (1972): 1–31.

JACQUES MARITAIN AND HENRI BREMOND
Jacques Maritain. *Art et scolastique* (1920).
———. *Frontières de la poésie* (1935).
———. *Situation de la poésie* (1938). Cited as *SP*.
———. *Creative Intuition in Art and Poetry* (1953). Cited as *CI*.
———. *Art and Scholasticism and The Frontiers of Poetry*, trans. Joseph W. Evans (1962).
Henri Bremond. *Histoire littéraire du sentiment religieux en France depuis la fin des guerres de religion jusqu'à nos jours*, 6 vols. (1916–33).
———. *La Poésie pure* (1926).

PAUL CLAUDEL
Oeuvres en prose, ed. Jacques Petit and Charles Galpérine (1965).

DADA AND SURREALISM

Tristan Tzara. *Sept manifestes Dada, lampisteries* (1963). In English as *Seven Dada Manifestos and Lampisteries*, trans. Barbara Wright (1977).
André Breton. *Manifestes du Surréalisme* (1962). In English as *Manifestoes of Surrealism*, trans. Richard Seaver and Helen R. Lane (1969).

Anna Balakian. *Surrealism: The Road to the Absolute* (1959; rev. ed., 1970).
———. *André Breton: Magus of Surrealism* (1971).
Elmer Peterson. *Tristan Tzara: Dada and Surrational Theory* (1971).

THE GENEVA SCHOOL

Sarah N. Lawall. *Critics of Consciousness: The Existential Structures of Literature* (1968).
Albert Béguin et Marcel Raymond: Colloque de Cartigny, ed. Georges Poulet et al. (1979). Contains bibliographies.

MARCEL RAYMOND

L'Influence de Ronsard sur la poésie française (1550–1585), 2 vols. (1927).
  New ed., 1 vol. (1965).
De Baudelaire au surréalisme (1930).
Génies de France (1942).
Etre et dire (1970).
Le Sel et la cendre (1970).

ALBERT BÉGUIN

L'Ame romantique et le rêve, 2 vols. (1937). Revised ed. (1946), cited as *ARR*.
  In German as *Traumwelt und Romantik*, trans. Peter Grotzer (1972).
Balzac visionnaire (1946). Revised ed., *Balzac lu et relu* (1965).
Poésie de la présence de Chrétien de Troyes à Pierre Emmanuel (1957).
Création et destinée, 2 vols. (1973). Cited as *CD*.

GEORGES POULET

Etudes sur le temps humain (1949). In English as *Studies in Human Time*,
  trans. Eliott Coleman (1956), cited as *SHT*.
La Distance intérieure (1952). In English as *The Interior Distance*, trans. Eliott
  Coleman (1959), cited as *ID*.
Les Métamorphoses du cercle (1961). In English as *The Metamorphoses of the
  Circle*, trans. Eliott Coleman (1966), cited as *MC*.
L'Espace Proustien (1963). In English as *Proustian Space*, trans. Eliott Cole-
  man (1977), cited as *PS*.
La Pensée indéterminée, 3 vols. (1985–90). Cited as *PI*.

ALBERT CAMUS

L'Envers et l'endroit (1937; reissued in 1958).
L'Etranger (1942).
La Peste (1947).
La Chute (1956).
Selected Essays and Notebooks, ed. and trans. Philip Thody (1970). Cited
  as *SEN*.

JEAN-PAUL SARTRE

Baudelaire (1946). In English as *Baudelaire*, trans. Martin Turnell (1950),
  cited as *B*.
Qu'est ce que la littérature? (1947). In English as *What Is Literature?* (1949),
  cited as *WIL*.
Situations, 10 vols. (1947–76). Cited as *S*.

Literary and Philosophical Essays, trans. Annette Michelson (1955).

Les Mots (1963). In English as *Words* (1964).

L'Idiot de la famille: Gustave Flaubert, 1821–1857, 3 vols. (1971).

Mallarmé: La Lucidité et sa face d'ombre (1986). In English as *Mallarmé, or the Poet of Nothingness*, trans. Ernest Sturm (1988).

Simone de Beauvoir. *La Cérémonie des adieux* (1974). In English as *Adieux: A Farewell to Sartre*, trans. Patrick O'Brian (1984).

Annie Cohen-Solal. *Sartre* (1985).

PAUL VALÉRY

Variété, 5 vols. (1924–44).

Poësie (1928).

Pièces sur l'art (1931).

"Réflexions sur l'art," *Bulletin de la Société française de Philosophie* 35 (1935).

Mélanges (1941).

Tel quel, 2 vols. (1941–42).

Oeuvres, ed. Jean Hytier, 2 vols. (1957–60). Cited as *O*.

Cahiers, 29 vols. (1957–61).

The Collected Works of Paul Valéry, ed. Jackson Mathews, 15 vols. (1956–75). Cited as *CW*.

Frédéric Lefèvre. *Entretiens avec Paul Valéry* (1926).

Jean Hytier. *La Poétique de Valéry* (1953). In English as *The Poetics of Paul Valéry*, trans. Richard Howard (1966).

Ralph Freedman. "Valéry: Protean Critic," in *Modern French Criticism*, ed. John K. Simon (1972), 1–40.

NOTES TO PAGES 161–83

1. A facsimile edition of the *Cahiers* covering the years 1894–1945 appeared in 1957–61 in 29 volumes. It fills 26,600 pages. Two volumes of a printed transcript, edited by Judith Robinson, were published in 1973–74 in the Pléiade series.

2. Valéry uses the term in *Cahiers* in 1911 (4:488). He claims to have "started the expression going" (*Cahiers*, 11:877; 1926 or early 1927). The term "pure poetry" is, however, quite common in English, e.g., Joseph Warton, Leigh Hunt, and others.

3. Letter to Jean Prévost, 16 May 1943, *O*, 1:1814. First published in *Confluences*, nos. 21–24 (July–August 1943); not in *CW*.

4. *Amphion* and *Sémiramis*, in *O*, 2:166–96; *CW*, 3:223–309.

SELECT BIBLIOGRAPHY: ITALIAN CRITICISM, 1900–1950

BENEDETTO CROCE

La Critica letteraria (1894).

Lirici marinisti (1911).

Estetica (1902). 8th ed. (1946), cited as *E.*

Brevario di estetica (1912).

Goethe (1917). 4th ed., 2 vols. (1946), cited as *G.*

La Poesia di Dante (1921). 6th ed. (1948), cited as *D.*

Conversazioni critiche, 5 vols. (1924–39). Cited as *CC.*

Primi saggi, 2d ed. (1927).

Pagine sulla guerra, 2d ed. (1928).

Ultimi saggi (1928). 2d ed. (1948), cited as *US.*

Filosofia della practica, 4th ed. (1932). Cited as *FiPrac.*

La Poesia (1936). 4th ed. (1946), cited as *P.*

La Storia come pensiero e come Azione, 2d ed. (1938), cited as *Storia* 1938. 4th
    ed. (1943), cited as *Storia* 1943.

Pagine sparse, 3 vols. (1941). Cited as *PS.*

Ariosto, Shakespeare e Corneille, 3d ed. (1944). Cited as *ASC.*

Discorsi di varia filosofia, 2 vols. (1945). Cited as *Discorsi.*

Poeti e scrittori del pieno e del tardo Rinascimento, 3 vols. (1945). Cited as *PoSc.*

Poesia e non poesia, 4th ed. (1946). Cited as *PNP.*

Poesia popolare e poesia d'arte, 2d ed. (1946). Cited as *Ppo.*

Storia dell'età barocca in Italia, 2d ed. (1946). Cited as *Età.*

Nuove pagine sparse, 2 vols. (1948). Cited as *NPS.*

Nuovi saggi di estetica, 3d ed. (1948). Cited as *NSE.*

Filosofia e storiografia (1949). Cited as *FiSto.*

Problemi di estetica, 4th ed. (1949). Cited as *PE.*

Letture di poeti (1950). Cited as *Letture.*

Poesia antica e moderna, 3d ed. (1950). Cited as *PoAMo.*

Indagini su Hegel e schiarimenti filosofici (1952). Cited as *Indagini.*

Terze pagine sparse, 2 vols. (1955). Cited as *TPS.*

La Letteratura della nuova Italia, 5th ed., 6 vols. Cited as *LNI.*

Luigi Russo. *La Critica letteraria contemporanea,* 3 vols. (1942–43), passim,
    especially 1:110–286.

Lienhard Bergel. "Croce as Critic of Goethe," *Comparative Literature* 1
    (1949): 349–59.

René Wellek. "Benedetto Croce: Literary Critic and Historian," *Comparative Literature* 5 (1953): 75–82.

William K. Wimsatt. "Expressionism: Benedetto Croce," in William K. Wimsatt, Jr., and Cleanth Brooks, *Literary Criticism: A Short History* (1957), 499–521.

Calvin G. Seerveld. *Benedetto Croce's Earlier Aesthetic Theories and Literary Criticism* (1958).

Aldo Scaglione. "Croce's Definition of Literary Criticism," *Journal of Aesthetics and Art Criticism* 17 (1959): 437–56.

Adelchi Attisani. "Introduzione all'Estetica di Benedetto Croce," *Letterature moderne* 11 (1961): 440–60, 569–85.

———. "L'Estetica di Francesco De Sanctis e dell'idealismo italiano," in *Momenti e problemi di storia dell'estetica*, pt. 4 (1961), 1465–1507.

Gian N. G. Orsini. *Benedetto Croce: Philosopher of Art and Literary Critic* (1961). In Italian as G. N. Giordano Orsini, *L'Estetica e la critica di Benedetto Croce*, trans. Anita Piemonti and Remo Ceserani (1976).

Vittorio Santoli. "Croce e le letterature boreali," in *Fra Germania e Italia* (1962), 132–57.

Mario Puppo. *Il Metodo e la critica di Benedetto Croce* (1964).

Gianfranco Contini. *L'Influenza culturale di Benedetto Croce* (1967).

Mario Fubini. "Croce critico," in *Benedetto Croce (1866–1966)* (1967), 11–19.

Mario Sansone. "Croce critico," in *Letteratura italiana: I Critici* (1969), 2:1465–1524.

Ernesto G. Caserta. *Croce, critico letterario (1882–1921)* (1972).

NOTES TO PAGES 187–223

1. On Borchardt, see this *History*, 7:57–61; his assessment of Croce is in Vol. 1 of his *Prosa* (1957), first published in *Reden und Abhandlungen* (1928).

2. *Letteratura e critica: Studi in onore di Natalino Sapegno* (1979), 5:620.

3. Ibid., 623.

4. Croce comments on Dewey in *Discorsi*, 2:112–19, *NPS*, 1:248–49, and *TPS*, 2:29.

5. Spingarn reviewed Croce's *Tesi fondamentali di un'Estetica* and *Estetica* in *The Nation*, 15 November 1900, 386, and 25 September 1902, 252–53, respectively. Cf. Marshall Van Deusen, *J. E. Spingarn* (1971), an excellent monograph.

6. John Crowe Ransom, *Poems and Essays* (1955), 92. R. P. Blackmur read a paper on Croce at the meeting of the Modern Language Association of America on 27 December 1954, which I do not believe has been reprinted. A good discussion of the relation of Croce to the New Criti-

cism is Edward Wasiolek, "Croce and Contextualist Criticism," in *Modern Philology* 57 (1959): 44–52.

7. *Carteggio Croce-Vossler* (1951).

8. Spitzer's disagreement with Croce is stated most strongly in his last lecture, "Les Etudes de style et les différents pays," in *Langue et littérature. Actes du Huitième Congrès de la Fédération internationale des langues et littératures modernes* (1961), 23–38. Cf. my *Discriminations* (1970), 196.

9. See Johannes Volkelt, *System der Ästhetik*, 3 vols. (1925), 3:378n: "In Croce's volume there is hardly a page which does not contain things not properly thought through. He works all the time with approximate, ambiguous, unanalyzed concepts." See also pp. 390, 278.

10. Cf. Graziella Pagliano Ungari, *Croce in Francia* (1967).

11. Cf. *Poesia española* (1950), 34ff., on "intuición toda lizadora."

12. On Engelhardt, see Aage A. Hansen-Löwe, *Der russische Formalismus* (1978), 184n; on Vinogradov, see Wolf-Dieter Stempel's preface to *Texte der russischen Formalisten* (1972), 2:xvi and n; on Potebnya, see this *History*, 4:278.

13. See the discussion in Carlo Antoni, *Commento a Croce* (1955), especially 152–55.

THE FOLLOWERS OF CROCE

LUIGI RUSSO

Metastasio (1915).

Giovanni Verga (1919; new ed., 1933).

Salvatore di Giacomo (1921).

I Narratori (1923). Cited as *N.*

Francesco De Sanctis e la cultura napoletana (1860–1885) (1928; new ed., 1943).

Elogio della polemica (1933).

D'Annunzio (1939).

La Critica letteraria contemporanea, 3 vols. (1942–43). 2d ed., 3 vols. (1946–47), cited as *CLC.*

Machiavelli (1945; new ed., 1966).

Personaggi dei Promessi sposi (1945). New ed. (1974), cited as *PPS.*

Ritratti critici di contemporanei (1945).

Ritratti e disegni storici, 4 vols. (1946–53), cited as *RD* 1946. New ed., 4 vols. (1960–65), cited as *RD* 1960.

Problemi di metodo critico. 2d ed. (1950). Cited as *PMC.*

Il Dialogo dei popoli. 2d ed. (1955).

Letture del Decameron (1956).

Carducci senza retorica (1957).

Storia della letteratura italiana. Vol. 1 (1957).

Il Tramonto del letterato (1960). Cited as *TL*.

Prose polemiche, ed. Giovanni Falaschi (1979). Cited as *PP*.

"Scritti su Luigi Russo" (Writings on Russo), *Belfagor* 16 (November 1961).

Riccardo Scrivano and Walter Bini. "Luigi Russo," in *I Critici*, ed. G. Grana (1969), 3:2123–72.

Giovanni Da Pozzi. *La Prosa di Luigi Russo* (1975).

Sergio Antonelli. "Luigi Russo e i suo storicismo," *Belfagor* 35 (January 1980): 29–46.

FRANCESCO FLORA

Dal romanticismo al futurismo (1921). New ed. (1925), cited as *RF*.

Croce (1927).

I Miti della parola (1931). New ed. (1958), cited as *MP*.

Poesia ermetica (1936; 3d ed., 1947).

Storia della letteratura italiana, 3 vols. (1940–42), Rev. ed., 5 vols. (1947–49), cited as *SLI*.

Cività del novecento, 3d ed. (1949). Cited as *CN*.

Saggi di poetica moderna (1949).

Scrittori italiani contemporanei (1952).

Orfismo della parola (1953). Cited as *OP*.

La Poesia della Bibbia, 2 vols. (1960).

La Poesia dell'Egitto e della Mesopotamia (1960).

Poesia e impoesia nell'Ulisse di Joyce (1962). Cited as *PIU*.

Carlo Calcaterra. *Con Guido Gozzano e altri poeti* (1944).

Luciano Nicastro. *Con Francesco Flora: Avvenimenti ed uomini del nostro secolo* (1964).

Ettore Mazzale and Giuseppe Ravegnani. "Francesco Flora," in *I Critici*, ed. G. Grana (1969), 3:2173–2208.

MARIO FUBINI

Alfred de Vigny (1922).

Jean Racine e la critica delle sue tragedie (1925).

Ugo Foscolo (1928; 3d ed., 1962).

"L'Estetica e la critica letteraria nei Pensieri di Giacomo Leopardi," *Giornale storico della letteratura italiana* 97 (1931): 241–81.

Alfieri (1937).

Stile e umanità di Giambattista Vico (1946).

Dal Muratori al Baretti (1947; 2d ed., 1954).

"Ufficio e forme della critica" and "Genesi e storia dei generi letterari,"
   in *Tecnica e teoria letteraria,* ed. A. Momigliano (1948).
"Arcadia e illuminismo," in *Questioni e corranti di storia letteraria,* ed.
   A. Momigliano (1949).
Metrica e poesia. Vol. 1, *Dal Duecento al Petrarca* (1962).
Romanticismo italiano (1965).
Critica e poesia, 2d ed. (1966). Cited as *CP.*
Il Peccato di Ulisse e altri scritti danteschi (1966).
Saggi e ricordi (1971).

Gianni Grana. "Mario Fubini," in *I Critici,* ed. Grana (1969), 5:3503–32.
Ettore Bonora. In *Critica e storia letteraria: Scritti offerti a Mario Fubini*
   (1970), 602–25.

ATTILIO MOMIGLIANO
Storia della letteratura italiana (1932).

THE AESTHETICIANS

GIUSEPPE ANTONIO BORGESE
Storia della critica romantica in Italia (1905).
Poetica dell'unità (1934)

Antonio Rufino. *La Critica letteraria di G. A. Borgese* (1969).

ALFREDO GARGIULO
Letteratura italiana del Novecento (1940).
Scritti di estetica (1952).

CRITICS CONCERNED WITH ENGLISH AND AMERICAN LITERATURE

CESARE PAVESE
La Letteratura americana e altri saggi (1951). In English as *American Literature: Essays and Opinions,* trans. Edwin Fussell (1970), cited as *AL.*
Il Mestiere di vivere (1952). In English as *This Business of Living: Diary,
   1935–1950,* ed. and trans. A. E. Murch (1961), cited as *BL.*

MARIO PRAZ
Secentismo e Marinismo in Inghilterra (1925).
Penisola pentagonale (1928). In English as *Unromantic Spain,* trans. Praz
   (1929).

La Carne, la Morte e il Diavolo nella letteratura romantica (1932). In English as *The Romantic Agony,* trans. Angus Davidson (1933). 2d ed. (1951), cited as *Agony.*

Studi sul concettismo (1934; 2d ed., 1956).

Storia della letteratura inglese (1937).

Studi e svaghi inglesi (1937).

Gusto neo-classico (1940; 2d ed., 1959). In English as *On Neoclassicism* (1969).

Machiavelli in Inghilterra (1942).

Prospettiva della letteratura inglese da Chaucer a Virginia Woolf (1947).

Cronache letterarie anglosassoni, 4 vols. (1950–66). Cited as *CA.*

The Hero in Eclipse in Victorian Fiction (1956). Cited as *Hero.*

La Casa della vita (1958), cited as *Casa.* In English as *The House of Life,* trans. Angus Davidson (1964), cited as *House.*

The Flaming Heart (1958; 2d ed., 1973).

Bellezza e Bizzarria (1960). Cited as *Bellezza.*

Volti del tempo (1964).

"Historical and Evaluative Criticism," in *Literary History and Literary Criticism: Acta of the Ninth Congress, International Federation for Modern Languages and Literatures,* ed. Leon Edel (1965), 65–77. Cited as *HEC.*

Mnemosyne (1967).

Il Patto col serpento (1972). Cited as *Patto.*

Studies in Seventeenth Century Imagery, 2 vols. (1974).

I Giardino dei sensi (1975).

Perseo e la Medusa: Dal Romanticismo all'avanguardia (1978). Cited as *Perseo.*

Vittorio and Mariuma Gabrieli, eds. *Bibliografia degli scritti di Mario Praz* (1967).

EMILIO CECCHI

Storia della letteratura inglese nel secolo XIX (1915). Rev. ed., *I grandi romantici inglesi* (1961).

Scritti inglesi e americani, 2 vols. (1935). Cited as *SIA.*

America amara (1940).

Letteratura italiana del Novecento, 2 vols. (1972). Cited as *LIN.*

ITALIAN MARXISM

ANTONIO GRAMSCI

Opere, 11 vols. (1947–66). Vol. 6, *Letteratura e vita nazionale* (1954), cited as *LVN.*

GIACOMO DEBENEDETTI

Saggi critici (1926).

Il Romanzo del Novecento (1971). Cited as *RN*.

Personaggio e destino (1977). Cited as *PD*.

Saggi, 1922–1966, ed. Franco Contorbia (1982). Cited as *Saggi*.

THE CATHOLIC RENAISSANCE

Boine, Giovanni. *Plausi e botte* (1918). Reprinted (1978).

CARLO BO

Jacques Rivière (1935).

Diario aperto e chiuso, 1932–1944 (1945).

Saggi per una letteratura, 2d ed. (1946).

Della lettura e altri saggi (1953).

Reflessioni critiche (1953).

Il Surrealismo (1953).

L'Eredità di Leopardi e altri saggi (1964).

La Religione di Serra: Saggi e note di lettura (1967).

THE CLOSE READERS

RENATO SERRA

Scritti, ed. G. De Robertis and A. Grilli, 2 vols. (1938; 2d ed., 1958).

Scritti letterari, morali e politici: Saggi e articoli dal 1900 al 1915, ed. Mario Isnenghi (1974). Cited as *SLMP*.

GIUSEPPE DE ROBERTIS

Saggio sul Leopardi (1944).

Studi (1944).

Saggi con una noterella (1939; 2d ed., 1953). Cited as *Saggi*.

Studi II (1971).

CESARE DE LOLLIS

Cervantes reazionario (Spanish ed., 1913; Italian ed., 1924). Reprinted with other essays as *Cervantes reazionario e altri scritti d'ispanistica* (1947).

Saggi di letteratura francese (1920).

Reisebilder e altri scritti (1929).

Scrittori d'Italia, ed. Gianfranco Contini and Vittorio Santoli (1948).

Cristoforo Colombo nella leggenda e nella storia. Definitive ed. (1969).

EUGENIO MONTALE

Sulla poesia (1978). Cited as *SP*.

The Second Language of Art: Selected Essays of Eugenio Montale, ed. and trans. Jonathan Galassi (1982). Cited as *SLA*.

Umberto Carpi. "Montale critico," in *I Critici*, ed. G. Grana (1969), 1:3419–48.

SELECT BIBLIOGRAPHY: SPANISH CRITICISM, 1900–1950

Emilia de Zuleta. *Historia de la crítica española contemporánea*, 2d ed. (1974).

AMÉRICO CASTRO

El Pensamiento de Cervantes (1925). New, enlarged ed. (1972).

España en su historia (1948). In English as *Spain in History*. Revised as *The Spaniards* (1971).

An Idea of History: Selected Essays of Américo Castro, trans. and ed. Stephen Gilman and Edmund L. King; introduction by Roy Harvey Pearce (1977).

MIGUEL DE UNAMUNO

Vida de Don Quijote y Sancho Panza (1905).

Ensayos, 2 vols. (1951).

Martin Nozick. *Miguel de Unamuno* (1971).

MARCELINO MENÉNDEZ Y PELAYO AND RAMÓN MENÉNDEZ PIDAL

Marcelino Menéndez y Pelayo. *Obras completas* (1940).

Ramón Menéndez Pidal. *Cantar de mio Cid: Texto, gramática y vocabulario*, 3 vols. (1908–12).

——— . *La España del Cid*, 2 vols. (1947).

——— . *Romancero hispánico*, 2 vols. (1953).

——— . *La Chanson de Roland y el neotradicionalismo* (1959).

Manuel Olguín. "Marcelino Menéndez Pelayo's Theory of Art, Aesthetics, and Criticism," *University of California Publications in Modern Philology* 28, no. 6 (1950): 333–58.

Steven Hess. *Ramón Menéndez Pidal* (1982).

AZORÍN

Obras completas, 9 vols. (1947–54).

Anna Krause. "Azorín, the Little Philosopher: Inquiry into the Birth of a Literary Personality," *University of California Publications in Modern Philology* 28, no. 4 (1948): 159–280.
Edward Inman Fox. *Azorín as a Literary Critic* (1962).

SALVADOR DE MADARIAGA Y ROJO

Shelley and Calderón (1920).
The Genius of Spain and Other Essays on Spanish Contemporary Literature (1923).
Englishmen, Frenchmen, Spaniards (1928; 2d ed., 1969).
Don Quixote: An Introductory Essay in Psychology (1934; rev. ed., 1961).
On Hamlet (1948; 2d ed., 1964).
El Hamlet de Shakespeare (1949).
Essays with a Purpose (1954).
De Galdós a Lorca (1960).

JORGE GUILLÉN

Cántico (1928).
Language and Poetry: Some Poets of Spain (1961). In Spanish as *Lenguaje y poesia* (1962).

DÁMASO ALONSO

La Lengua poética de Góngora (1935).
Ensayos sobre poesía española (1944).
Poesía española: Ensayo de métodos i límites estilísticos (1950). Cited as *PE*.

JOSÉ ORTEGA Y GASSET

Meditaciones del Quijote (1914). 8th ed., with *Ideas sobre la novela* (1950), cited as *MQ*.
España invertebrata (1922).
Deshumanización del arte (1925).

Ideas sobre la novela (1925).
La Rebelión de las masas (1929).
Obras completas, 8 vols. (1957–62). Cited as *OC*.

Julián Marías. *Ortega. I. Circunstancia y vocación* (1960).

INDEX OF NAMES

INDEX OF TOPICS AND TERMS